5.25.99

For Tom,

    Its been my great fortune to study software applications and quality assurance under your guidance. I hope that this study provides you with an equally exciting and sure-handed guide towards understanding what made the Soviet Union tick.

FACTORY AND COMMUNITY
IN STALIN'S RUSSIA

CO
IN

The Making of an
Industrial Working Class

KENNETH M. STRAUS

FACTORY
AND
MMUNITY
STALIN'S
RUSSIA

University of Pittsburgh Press

Published by the University of Pittsburgh Press, Pittsburgh, Pa. 15261
Copyright © 1997, University of Pittsburgh Press
Manufactured in the United States of America
Printed on acid-free paper
10 9 8 7 6 5 4 3 2 1

Straus, Kenneth M., 1952–
     Factory and community in Stalin's Russia: the making of an
industrial working class / Kenneth M. Straus.
          p.   cm.—(Pitt series in Russian and East European studies)
     Includes bibliographicas references and index.
     ISBN 0-8229-4048-5 (cloth: acid-free pager)
     1. Working class—Soviet Union—History.   2. Working class—
Soviet Union—Political activity.   3. Soviet Union—Social
conditions—1917–1945.   4. Communism—Soviet Union.   I. Title. II.
Series: Series in Russian and East European studies.
HD8526.S87   1997   97-21046
305.5'62'0947—dc21   CIP

A CIP catalog record for this book is available from the British Library.

For my parents

Doris Olender Straus

Lawrence Straus

CONTENTS

PREFACE

This project began to take shape in my mind as a student at Oberlin College in the early 1970s as an investigation into the social sources or bases of Stalinism. Also at Oberlin, I began to conceive of a second project: reconceptualizing working-class formation in Russia and the Soviet Union as a process that could be understood methodologically as paralleling E. P. Thompson's narrative in *The Making of the English Working Class*. These projects were conceived under the influence of Ronald Grigor Suny, and then they began to combine in my thinking. Even though I could not yet articulate this idea, it was in Ron's lectures, seminars, and in our frequent conversations outside the classroom, that this book was born. I was also deeply influenced at Oberlin by Marcia Colish, whose seminars on British constitutional law and Renaissance and Reformation history taught me how to read primary sources.

My second "university" was the Quincy Shipyard, where I worked as a welder from 1976 to 1979. In the four years that I spent there building Liquefied Natural Gas tankers, I learned a thing or two firsthand about crash (thirty-day) mass apprenticeships and about how the unskilled, semiskilled, and skilled workers were defined by a modern corporation. Seeing chaos and improvisation as the daily reality, I came to understand how a work crew actually functioned on the docks as opposed to on a manager's chart. I also came to see how this allowed for work crews to take on strong solidarity, in some cases, or sharp antagonisms, in others. In this setting, sometimes a dynamic foreman or worker could begin to control and shape the process of production in important ways. With prefabricated units and with automated welding guns, in this putatively modern, rational, hierarchical complex industrial organization of over five thousand men and almost five hundred women, it turned out, work was not much like a modern assembly line but more like a craft-dominated construction site. Yet, in terms of the skill categories and shop-floor status that the corporation and industrial union had worked out, semiskilled and fairly homogeneous work crews predominated, and pay differentials, while real, were relatively slight. This combination of production processes (that are never as modern as "through-put" would suggest) and a modern classification of workers in skill and pay hierarchy, has come back to me time and time again in my thinking about the USSR and the process of "combined development" in its industrialization.

The University of Pennsylvania was my third university. I was fortunate to find there both faculty and fellow graduate students who shared my interests in the working class and Stalinism. My advisor, Alfred Rieber, challenged my long-standing assumptions about class, and I began to grapple with his ideas on Russian "entrepreneurial groups" and on Late Imperial Russian society. Much to my surprise, his approach has found an echo in this book in the form of a powerful professional group, the factory technical and managerial personnel, personified in the Red Director. Al's tireless work on the many drafts of my dissertation, and his many insights in helping me to revise it, will not be forgotten.

I would like to thank my fellow graduate students and colleagues at Penn who heard my ideas and responded to them over and over again. Wendy Goldman, Gyan Prakash, Karl Ittmann, Marcus Rediker, Steve Zdatny, Barry Bergen, Rob Gregg, and Leslie Rimmel all made what was often a difficult passage a highly worthwhile experience, by making me feel that I was a part of an intellectual community. Wendy Goldman, in particular, had a great deal to do with the shaping of this project at every step of the way.

I was also influenced in seminars and discussions by Alexander Vucinich, Thomas Childers, Moshe Lewin, Walter Licht, Jack Reece, and Alexander Riasanovsky. To Professor Vucinich I owe special thanks: his consistently sound advice on how to keep my dissertation manageable, and his encouragement, were deeply appreciated.

In Champaign-Urbana and then in Moscow, on the IREX program from June 1986 through July 1987, Stephen Kotkin and I began a dialogue which has not yet ended. If my study of the Moscow industrial community resembles his study of Magnitogorsk in many respects, it is a reflection, both of the centralizing tendencies of Stalinism and also of our nearly constant interaction in 1986 and 1987. If I have, in this study, presented a convincing picture of a working class in formation and of a class undergoing a parallel integration, then it is largely because of Stephen's persistence in challenging me to clarify my ideas.

Mark Saroyan deeply influenced my thinking on how to make use of sociological theory in this project through his own work and his comments. We exchanged and discussed our work frequently until his most untimely death in 1995.

In Moscow, I met frequently for formal consultations with the late Professor Vladimir Z. Drobizhev, of Moscow State University and then of the Academy of Sciences. His unparalleled knowledge of the archives and memoir source materials and of work process was highly useful. He called a number of important sources to my attention, loaned me a copy of his manuscript to be published later that year as *Sovetskoe Obshchestvo v Vospominaniiakh i Dnevnikakh, 1917–1941,* and gave me a 1937 dictionary of occupations drawn up for the 1937 All-Union Census. The influence of his fine, co-authored study, *Rost Rabochego Klassa SSSR, 1917–1940 gg* and of my discussions with him has been most important in my attempt to reconceptualize the process of Soviet working-class formation.

The Soviet historian-sociologist who has most influenced my thinking in this attempt at reconceptualization is Academician O. I. Shkaratan. We met several times in 1987, and he commented on a grant proposal which was, in effect, an early prospectus for this book. We discussed my critique of his outstanding study, *Problemy Sotsial'noi Struktury Rabochego Klassa SSSR,* and he urged me to continue to work along the lines of reconciling the homogenizing and differentiating tendencies that I argued he had left in contradiction in his study. The reader will see that I have.

Dr. Igor L'vovich Kornakovskii, of the Institute of Soviet History in the Soviet Academy of Sciences, provided me with the single most important source for this study: *Martenovka,* the factory newspaper at SiM. In the spring of 1987, when it was still impossible to obtain access to the factory archives or to the factory newspapers at the Lenin Library, Kornakovskii arranged to bring ten years of *Martenovka* to me, two volumes at a time. I doubt that Kornakovskii was taking much risk to get this material to me in 1987, as by then, *glasnost'* was already in full swing. However, he certainly spent a great deal of time and went to considerable inconvenience on my behalf. Why, I wondered, this generosity on behalf of an American *stazher* whom he hardly knew? I still can only find one answer: he hoped I would convey to an American audience some of the pathos and drama of the 1930s, of industrialization and of the workers' lives, and of their crucial importance in the ultimate Soviet victory in the Great Fatherland War. I can only hope that I have, in my own way, conveyed some of that sense of pathos and drama.

I would also thank A. K. Sokolov, now of the Russian Academy of Sciences, at the time a professor at Moscow State University, with whom I met frequently and who generously loaned me a copy of his dissertation to read and then later gave me a copy of his book, *Rabochii Klass i Revoliutsionnye Izmeneniia v Sotsial'noi Strukture Obshchestva* (M, 1987). I also consulted with the Academicians L. I. Rogachevskaia and A. V. Mitrofanova, at the Soviet Academy of Sciences, and with my academic advisor, Professor Anastasia M. Panfilova, of Moscow State University.

In 1988 and 1989, I was frequently at the Kennan Institute, where Blair Ruble provided helpful commentary on chapter 6, as did Richard Stites at Georgetown University. David Hoffmann offered critical suggestions and called to my attention several important sources. John Barber, Vladimir Andrle, and R. W. Davies have also been very helpful.

Since 1990, while teaching at Binghamton University, I have been fortunate to have as my colleagues Melvyn Dubofsky and Mark Selden, both of whom offered fine insights on early drafts of the manuscript.

Stephen Kotkin and Lewis Siegelbaum read the manuscript in the fall of 1995 and, although I was revising aspects of their work, they suggested how I could sharpen my study by presenting its findings in relation to the many other studies in the field, including their own. Critical suggestions made by Ron Suny and Jonathan Harris caused me to write a new and broader introduction on the problem of class and Soviet society. Michael Lambert also urged me to write a new introduction elucidating class theory and clarifying how I have used it in this study. He was one of several graduate students in my seminars who read and commented on what became chapter 1 of this book. Michael then read the entire manuscript and offered many helpful suggestions.

The individuals mentioned above are, in large part, responsible for whatever contribution that this study makes. None of them is responsible for the remaining errors of fact or weaknesses in interpretation, which are entirely my own responsibility.

In preparing the manuscript for submission, Susan Thornton provided me with excellent assistance as editor and indexer. Since then, it has been a pleasure working with Jonathan Harris, editor of the Russian and Soviet Series at the University of Pittsburgh Press, with Catherine Marshall, editor-in-chief, and with Jane Flanders, senior editor. They have helped me in seeing this project through its final stages, as have Eileen Kiley, editorial assistant, and William Nelson, mapmaker. William Husband, with whom I frequently consulted at Champaign-Urbana in putting together my *nauchnyi plan* for research in Moscow, provided me with a great deal of useful advice on maps and on how to locate factories in Moscow, which was critical in devising these maps. The photos from the Stalin Auto Plant were copies taken from the factory archives for an exhibit on the history of the plant in the spring of 1987 at the Palace of Culture. An exhibit worker, a young fellow named Victor, provided me with these copies.

Funding support for this project has included an IREX Developmental Grant in 1983, an IREX Exchange Grant for research in Moscow in 1986–87, an SSRC Dissertation Fellowship in 1988–89, and a Summer Research Grant in 1992 and Dean's Research Semester for fall 1994 provided by the dean's office at Binghamton University.

I have made extensive use of the following libraries and archives for this study: the library of the University of Pennsylvania; the Library of Congress;

the Lenin Library in Moscow and its filial at Khimki, which I was finally able to work at in 1992; the INION Library in Moscow; the BAN Library in Leningrad; the Central State Archives of the October Revolution and of the National Economy, formerly known as TsGAOR and TsGANKh and are now GARF and RGAE; and the Moscow City Archive now known as MGAOD, and which includes the former MPA or Moscow Party Archive (where I was able to gain access in 1992). I would like to thank all these institutions and the many fine librarians and archivists staffing them, for their very considerable help in locating and bringing source material to me.

My thanks to my parents are of a different sort. They taught me the meaning of persistence and perseverance by their example. My wife, Elizabeth Ross Straus, lived through this book with me, day by day for ten years. For that, and for much else besides, I am deeply grateful to her. Our children, Hannah and Aaron, have been highly curious about what I was doing for so many hours on a computer, which periodically printed out something that Hannah has come to know as "chapters" and that we have celebrated together whenever I finished one.

A NOTE ON TRANSLITERATION AND THE FIVE-YEAR PLANS

I have adopted the Library of Congress system of transliteration, with the exception of a few famous proper names, such as Trotsky, which have become well known in their English spelling.

Trotsky and every other historian of the Russian Revolution had the nuisance of dating events according to the Julian calendar, which lagged thirteen days behind the Gregorian or New Style calendar in 1917. The historian of the 1920s and 1930s has another nuisance: the Soviet "economic year" began on 1 October and ended on 30 September until 1931. Thus, the First Five-Year Plan (FYP), which began on 1 October 1928, was scheduled to end on 30 September 1933. Even more confusing, the final, "maximum" plan was adopted at a contentious Party Plenum held in July 1929, nine months after the plan putatively began. Furthermore, the First FYP was revised even before the ink was dry, as annual and quarterly plan targets in 1929 and 1930 were upgraded. Then, a Special Quarter was tacked onto the economic year 1929/30, spanning the months October–December 1930; thus, starting in 1931, the economic year coincided with the calendar year. Finally, at the end of 1932, after four years and three months, the First FYP came to an end by decree, in which it was declared to have been "fulfilled and overfulfilled."

The Second FYP began on 1 January 1933, although it was not ratified until a Party Plenum a year later, in January 1934. It ended on 31 December 1937, as originally planned. The Third FYP began on 1 January 1938 and ended, by decree, some three years and six months later, on 22 June 1941 when the Nazi invasion began. The first three FYPs, known as the prewar FYPs, marked the beginning of the era of sixty years of planned economy, which lasted through the Twelfth FYP, concluding in 1990.

During the 1930s the FYPs were ratified by both the leading party and state organs, generally about one year after they had already begun. Actual output almost never corresponded to the initial plan targets. A detailed discussion of FYP variants, how the FYPs were adopted, and how performance did or usually did not correspond to planned targets, is presented by Alec Nove in *An Economic History of the USSR.*

FACTORY AND COMMUNITY
IN STALIN'S RUSSIA

INTRODUCTION:
STATE AND SOCIETY REVISITED

I n the current *fin-de-siècle* malaise, class analysis is no more popular than it was roughly a century ago among the intelligentsia and reading public in Freud's Vienna or in Verbitskaia's St. Petersburg.[1] It might now appear that all types of structuralism and class analysis have exhausted their potential for understanding modern European history in general and Soviet history in particular. With the turn toward "discourse," or the "linguistic turn," widely popular now among historians, both class analysis and structuralism are generally seen as archaic relics of nineteenth-century materialism if not of a crude positivism. For many historians today, *mentalité* offers much more promising avenues for inquiry, in approaches which can range from the full-blown idealism of the Hegelian zeitgeist, the "universal spirit of the era," to a Bergsonian neoidealism which is concerned with how an individual, through memory, constructs a sense of self-identity by means of ideational ordering of the stream of sensory perception.

This study is not about discourses, although I use the term concerning the Red Directors, who were "intermediaries" between the regime and the workers and who seemed to speak both their languages. This study is also not about *mentalité*, although in attempting to reconstruct the "social identity" of peasant-migrants, housewives, and students as they came into the factory, and in attempting to trace how and why they developed a working-class consciousness, I am not far from a type of *mentalité* study discussed below as "intermediate *mentalité*." A final disclaimer: this study does not attempt to offer a comprehensive rethinking of the party ideology of "class" under Stalinism, although I argue that there was a major shift away from "class struggle" ideology and toward an "ersatz social contract" following Stalin's "Six Conditions" speech of 23 June 1931. This study is focused, instead, on Soviet working-class formation, structure, and consciousness."[2]

The study of *mentalités* originated in France with the Annales school. Johan Huizinga, in *The Waning of the Middle Ages*, describes and brings to life a duality of chivalry and hierarchy in the late medieval zeitgeist. By now, a very different type of study of *mentalité* is widely popular in what is called "discourse studies," or the "linguistic turn," or in the "new historicism." These postmodernist approaches are all obsessed with the text itself, the author, and the audience, and they are all informed by a Bergsonian-type concern with individual consciousness or self-identity.[3] Perhaps the most prevalent current trend in the study of *mentalités* is at what might be called an "intermediate" level, situated somewhere between the "universal spirit," on the one hand, and the individual's ordering of reality, on the other. Such intermediate *mentalité* studies consider the ways in which identities are socially "constructed," typically an ethnic identity, gender identity, generational identity, religious identity, and less frequently, a class identity.

Those relatively few *mentalité* studies which look at class usually attempt to rethink the meaning of working-class identity or consciousness, either by coupling it with some or several of these other social identities, or by "decoupling" class identity from them, that is by "deconstructing" class.[4] The latter approach has been much more frequent, as many studies have focused on how a universal notion of the working class as articulated by intellectuals, union leaders, workers, or historians has excluded or subordinated women or ethnic or racial minorities. My study would clearly fall into the minoritarian "coupling" camp, as I am showing how the Soviet working class was historically "reconstructed" during the 1930s. A new working-class consciousness evolved, based on a new sense of inclusivity. This was the universalizing of the disparate cultures or *mentalités* of the new labor recruits.

In the field of twentieth-century Russian and Soviet history, the *malaise* with class analysis, however, runs deeper than the linguistic turn. It stems from three interrelated but distinct factors. First, in the field of French Revolution studies, the social history paradigm, long championed by Marxist historians, has been supplanted by "the rise of modern politics," a perspective pioneered by François Furet and adopted now by a large new cohort of historians. The social history paradigm in Russian Revolution studies, which I discuss in detail in chapter 1, thus appears to be quite out of step with the prevailing paradigm in French Revolution studies. Simply put, if the French Revolution was not a "bourgeois revolution," one wonders if the October Revolution was a "workers' revolution."[5] Second, the collapse of the USSR in 1991 and the opening of archives since that time would also point toward a fundamental rethinking of the history of the Russian Revolution as a workers' revolution. So far, however, nothing like the Furet school has emerged in Russian Revolution studies.[6]

Third, and most important for this study, the Bolsheviks, when they came to power, were quick to invent class categories or use existing ones as a convenient political shorthand justifying their ad hoc policies. This practice was adopted even before the Civil War. These class categories corresponded poorly to sociological realities, thus discrediting the use of class analysis among historians. For example, in their 1918 campaign against the kulaks, the Bolsheviks not only discredited "class politics" among the peasant population but also, and for posterity's sake, among historians of the peasantry.[7] The same could be said about the proletariat of 1919 or 1920. Putatively still the foundation for the "dictatorship of the proletariat," urban depopulation saw the working class, as the party leadership had acknowledged, literally disappearing. The Mensheviks and the Workers' Opposition openly taunted Lenin about this.[8]

The simplistic assertions of the regime that it was acting on behalf of the proletariat or that it constituted a "dictatorship of the proletariat" have led historians to shy away from class analysis.[9] The most important factor retarding class analysis of Soviet society, however, particularly during the long years of the Stalin dictatorship, has been the inability of historians to escape conceptually from the dichotomy between the Russian state and Russian society formulated by the Russian State school. This dichotomy makes it very difficult to conceptualize Russian or Soviet society as something more or other than the "nonstate."

Marxist historians and activists have thought that if they could define the class that ruled society through the Stalinist state (for historians working within the modernization and the totalitarian frameworks, the issue is to uncover the workings of the apparatus governing Soviet society), then the question of the nature of the "system" and therefore of "society" will be resolved. Society thus became a sort of residual category, in which the non-elite or non-ruling-class social groups, such as "peasants," "workers," and "technical intelligentsia," were descriptively and rather uncritically assimilated from the

Stalin-era sources themselves. In the dichotomous state-society approach, all modes of analysis or theories of the Soviet social structure under Stalinism begin and end with the state.

Furthermore, Marxist and class-based approaches to defining the new Soviet "ruling class" had so bungled class analysis that the wise historian simply avoided the fray of what had long been a highly "scholastic" debate.[10] E. H. Carr, for example, whose history of the first twelve years of Soviet power was organized institutionally-chronologically, and whose superb account of that era is unlikely to be surpassed, avoided discussing the nature of the Soviet state in terms of its class character or theories of the "ruling class." So did T. H. Rigby, whose analysis of the Soviet regime as a "mono-party" system provided an explanation of functional evolution and of the social composition of the elite that neatly dovetailed with Carr's account of structures and policies during the 1920s and fleshed out, for the 1930s, the ideas of Schapiro and Fainsod.[11]

It is my premise that the Stalinist regime, for which I will use the term *party-state,* was neither a class in itself, nor did it rule on behalf of any other dominant or ruling class, such as a "managerial class" or a "technocratic class," let alone on behalf of the working class.[12] It was, as has been suggested by sociologists and widely adopted by political scientists, the classic historical case of a new "power elite."[13] By "power elite," I mean something very similar to what C. Wright Mills had in mind in 1956 for America, and also similar to what Dwight Eisenhower meant a few years later, in coining the term *military-industrial complex.*[14] Of course, the power of the Soviet power elite during the 1930s relative to Soviet society was many times that of the American power elite during the 1950s relative to American society.

The Stalinist regime was not any kind of new ruling class, whether bourgeois or managerial, because it had no means of passing on any of its control (not to mention ownership) over state property (enterprises) to its children. Children of the elite might typically inherit some prime apartment space. They might even "inherit" admission into a college or university for their higher education. None of that, however, automatically or necessarily translated into an administrative position being passed on from one to the next generation. In fact, it seems that the sons of prominent officials under Stalin rarely followed in their father's footsteps.

Still more important, the Soviet power elite was not a ruling class because, far from reproducing itself in the next generation, it was, itself, decimated in 1936–38. It might be argued that any theory of a new power elite fails in the face of the bloodletting of 1937. The concept, however, is sufficiently flexible to allow for a virtually complete turnover in personnel, so long as the established structures and functions of power are replicated under the new personnel much as they had been under the old. That is precisely what happened after 1938, as has been argued by Merle Fainsod, Leonard Schapiro, T. H. Rigby, Sheila Fitzpatrick, and Seweryn Bialer.[15]

Almost all the newcomers of 1939, while they might or might not have come from a working-class background, had completed a Soviet-era narrow technical education and had some working experience in technically specialized occupations before moving up on the economic or party administrative ladder. This contrasted very sharply with the pre-1937 elite, who, if they had higher education, were usually members of the prerevolutionary Russian intelligentsia with its broad humanistic traditions and literary culture. Most of the others, working-class promotees without higher (or often even secondary) education, were already too old and highly placed in 1930 to begin a program of technical study.[16] The newcomers, however, virtually reconstituted the identical Stalinist power elite as it had existed in 1936: the structure and function of the apparatus, their positioning within the hierarchy, and above all, their relationship to the Soviet society and their methods of governing.

The crucial fact, in terms of party-state structures and functional rule, was not the events of 1937, when the NKVD under Yezhov, technically an organ of the state, was destroying the leading personnel of both the party and state and seemed to be beholden to Stalin alone.[17] Rather, the crucial fact was that the party-state apparatus resurfaced in 1938 and 1939 to govern once again, much as it had in 1934 and 1935, but with new personnel at every level. The only notable change was that state economic organs (commissariats, soon to become ministries) superseded the equivalent party organs (departments of the Central Committee Secretariat), perhaps during the terror, or perhaps during the Second World War, or perhaps after 1945.[18]

Members of this power elite, in its pre-1936 and especially in its post-1938 incarnation, shared a powerful ideology or even *mentalité* and discourse. They may or may not have believed that the dual process of industrialization and collectivization was the true path to socialism, to class justice, and to a classless society; but they certainly understood that it would lay the foundations for a "military-industrial complex" and was the basis for the "modernization" of Soviet society. This was the ideological cement of the new power elite. Along with personal status in the hierarchy and the functional position of the apparatus-men, the *apparatchiki*, it made them into the governing power elite rather than an amorphous collection of Stalin's sycophants and their clientele networks, which is roughly where the terror appeared to be headed at the height of the chaos in 1937.

Where does this leave us in thinking about Soviet society? Governing elite, or ruling class, we would appear to be resurrecting the Russian State school in the era of Stalinism. Whether it was totalitarianism or not, the party-state was the dynamic force, while Soviet society lagged passively behind it. Social science theory can define and describe the power elite and the party-state structures and functions, but it is at a loss to define or conceptualize the structure of Stalinist society and class consciousness and other social identities.

Here we find ourselves on the horns of "Presniakov's dilemma." A century ago, when A. E. Presniakov confronted the work of his teacher S. M. Soloviev, and of V. O. Kliuchevsky, the last two master historians of the Russian State school, he attempted to develop a "theory of the conscious" by studying law and philology, in order to revise their perspective on the state as the motor force in Russian history. His theory resembles what I have described as intermediate-level *mentalité*. Meanwhile, Presniakov's use of the legal codes and language as his primary sources, and his methodology of textual analysis, resembles the postmodern methods despite his naive search for a scientific history.

Contrary to his intentions, however, in *The Formation of the Great Russian State,* Presniakov only found himself reinventing the power of the autocracy on still more solid foundations. The "conscious" of Russian society were, it turned out, beholden to the state for the idea of Russian-ness.[19] With the study of Stalinist society we are, as it were, back at square one, at Presniakov's dilemma. The study of language, not to mention of the law, would appear to entrap us within the Russian State school, which reappears once again in the 1930s in the guise of either "Stalinism" or of "totalitarianism."[20]

Classes, occupational groups, interest groups, gender, and ethnicity all apparently bow before the overwhelming power of the state, or, worse still, are shaped and defined by the state. Thus, theorizing about Soviet society is stymied. Perhaps that is why the most perceptive modern sociologists, not having studied the Soviet Union, have argued (from their West European perspective) that it and other state socialist societies in Eastern Europe are not class societies at all.[21] While I think they are wrong, I must admit to feeling, at least in part, stuck on the horns of Presniakov's dilemma.

In attempting to rethink Stalinist society in terms of classes and social groups rather than in terms of either individual or universal *mentalités,* I have focused on how four social groups at the intermediate level of *mentalité* coalesced into a new Soviet working class and developed a new and relatively autonomous working-class consciousness. These four were the established workers, peasant-migrants, housewives, and student-youth. The new Soviet working-class, I argue in this study, defined itself *inclusively,* that is, as absorbing the three new social groups and redefining them as well as redefining the established workers in a new working-class culture.

This new working class defined its class interests neither in opposition to the regime *(negative integration),* nor in accordance with the regime's objectives *(positive integration),* but with an important degree of social autonomy. I am suggesting, here, something like "relative autonomy" of Soviet urban society and of the working class from the Soviet state.[22] There was, however, a powerful type of social integration in the process of class formation and inclusivity, which might best be called *parallel integration.*[23] It was parallel because the regime would have to begin to take into account the outlook of the working class and shift its ideology and policies in order to fulfill even a part of its objectives. The idea of a semiautonomous working class and parallel integration is developed in part 3 below.

Part 1 of this study examines the question of working-class formation in Russian and in Soviet history. Chapter 1 considers the paradox of a revolutionary Russian proletariat followed by a quiescent Soviet working class, reexamining the problem in the context of the "inversion" of the labor market and its impact on class composition. Chapter 2 presents a case study of Soviet working-class formation in the southeast quadrant of Moscow, the Proletarian District, and its steel plant, Hammer and Sickle.

Part 2 considers the labor market in terms of recruiting workers (chapter 3), attaching workers (chapter 4), and training workers (chapter 5). In all three chapters, and more directly in chapter 6 on shock work and socialist competition, I contrast the sound and fury of the state's labor policy in the industrialization drive with its more mundane underlying objective of forming an industrial work force by transforming peasant-migrants, urban housewives, and students into urban workers. These labor policies would eventually work, not because they were well-conceived or implemented. I argue that state policy vacillated between a type of populist workerism in the socialist competition and shock-work movement and a contradictory and crude paternalism with the draconian labor laws. State policies worked, I also argue, not because of the regime's use of the "class struggle" ideological weapon, but rather, they would work despite such bungled efforts because of the process of parallel integration.[24]

How that happened is explained in part 3, which examines working-class formation on the shop floor and in the community from four different angles.[25] The first angle, the work team, or in Soviet terminology, the work brigade, as I argue in chapter 6, would emerge in strengthened position from the routinization of the shock work and socialist competition movement, while in chapter 7, the work brigade is shown to be the building block for a stable factory work force. The second angle, the entire factory work force, is the central subject of chapter 7, where I argue that even pay differentiation and job specialization fostered homogenizing tendencies in the factory social melting pot. The third angle, addressed in chapter 8, continues this discussion of working-class formation and social integration by considering an emerging urban protocommunity in which the factory became the community organizer.[26] The ninth chapter examines the fourth and the final angle, that is, the articulation of the interests of the new working class. Here, I argue, we see yet another striking paradox in the Stalinist system, in that the clearest articulation of workers' interests came from the Red Directors. Chapter 10 examines the sociological metatheories of Marx, Durkheim, and Weber and reconsiders the problem of Thompsonian class formation in the Soviet context.

Part 1

1

Working-class Formation and a Moscow Case Study

1

FROM REVOLUTIONARY RUSSIAN PROLETARIAT TO QUIESCENT SOVIET WORKING CLASS

erhaps the greatest paradox in modern European history was the rise of a militant working-class movement and the triumph of a type of socialist revolution in 1917 in the Russian Empire, one of the least developed regions on the European periphery. This paradox was debated furiously at the time by the Bolsheviks and Mensheviks and remains a fertile source of historical analysis and debate even now. A second striking paradox, although one that has received far less attention from historians, was the sixty-year quiescence of Soviet workers dating roughly from 1929 and the introduction of the First Five-Year Plan (FYP), until 1989.[1] If Imperial Russia, from 1905 through 1917, seemed to be following a script for a socialist revolution as drafted by Karl Marx, then Soviet Russia, from 1929 through 1989, seemed to be following a script for a modern industrial society as drafted by Emile Durkheim.

An original attempt to explain the first paradox in terms of the "peculiarities" of Russian history was developed by Trotsky with his "law of combined development" and his theory of "permanent revolution." Trotsky, however, never spelled out the implications of his theory as it concerns the prerevolutionary peasantry, the working class, the intelligentsia or the bourgeoisie, and the bureaucracy. Furthermore, he never applied this law or theory to the Soviet paradox of the 1930s, when his insights in analyzing Soviet society from abroad were limited.[2]

Decades later, Leopold Haimson would recall some aspects of Trotsky's theory in his "dual polarization" article, which seemed to assume a "combined development" in politics and the economy under both autocratic and bourgeois auspices, and which suggested a dual or a type of "permanent revolution" that was likely to end either with the triumph of the Bolsheviks or anarchism if the Bolsheviks could not contain the *nizy*, that is the lower classes.[3]

Haimson's article and his earlier work on the revolutionary intelligentsia sparked a new wave of research on workers, peasants, and intelligentsia, and also on the Russian autocracy and its bureaucracy. His initial explanation for proletarian militancy and rising Bolshevik influence after 1912 was founded on the *buntarstvo*, or spontaneous militancy of the peasant-workers and particularly the Stolypin victims who migrated to the cities. Twenty years later, in his preliminary analysis of strikes in the Central Industrial Region (CIR), Haimson shifted his emphasis, focusing instead on the leading role of skilled, "hereditary" urban workers in the revolutionary movement. Now, after another decade of research, he and others analyzing strike waves have confirmed that reassessment.[4] So has research over the past three decades on soviets, factory committees, trade unions, on labor-management relations, the Red Guards, and the Bolshevik Party.[5] However, these accounts have not, by any means, discarded the element of rural and urban *buntarstvo*, and some recent studies have shifted the emphasis back in this direction.[6] This entire body of research allows us to state with certainty that the degree, intensity, and depth of Russian working-class militancy was unique in Europe and was decisive in the outcome in 1905 and again in 1917.[7] However, why that was so has still not been adequately explained.

The competing theories originate, as with Haimson's shift, in the alternative explanations of Mensheviks and Bolsheviks themselves. Mensheviks attributed Bolshevik influence over the working class to primitive peasant rebelliousness, which they and the Bolsheviks both called "spontaneity." Bolsheviks attributed their own success to the working-class "avant-garde," the "hereditary," skilled, urban workers, the *metallisty* and *tekstil'shchiki* who dominated the politics of St. Petersburg and Moscow working-class movements. I would suggest that both are right, if we discard their shared hierarchy of class consciousness.

Both Mensheviks and Bolsheviks separated "cadre" workers, at the top, from recent arrivals, or peasant-workers, at the bottom of the proletarian hierarchy. The distinction was the Social Democratic ideological reproduction of power relations on the shop floor. The Russian workers experienced factory work and urban life through the prism of a very sharply bifurcated "dual" labor market.[8] A privileged "labor aristocracy" was separated by a very wide gap from "subaltern" workers, in ways that made the income gap or the cultural gap between "respectable" British artisan-mechanics and unskilled factory laborers seem almost trivial.[9] The dual labor market shaped a Russian proletariat that was polarized between city and village in a way that was unique in European, and perhaps in world history, prior to 1917.

What distinguished the Russian labor aristocracy and made it more castelike than any comparable group of workers in Western Europe was their status as "hereditary" urban workers. Social Democrats could call them "cadre," but in the cities of the Russian Empire, they were the only wage earners who were able to reproduce themselves and establish an intergenerational continuity as urban artisans and factory mechanics. They were only able to do this by maintaining control over the labor market and the work process, dominating key occupations in the factories and artisan shops, making themselves indispensable in the production process and able to command much higher wages. This meant that they were able to find and afford housing in the city for their families. Raising children in the city, they would then pass on their occupation, through apprenticeships, to sons or nephews.

By 1900 in Vienna, Berlin, Paris, or London the vast majority of workers could manage self-reproduction in the cities, whereas in Imperial Russia only the labor aristocrats could. Thus, the term *hereditary urban proletariat,* if it ever had been used, would have been almost meaningless in Western Europe by 1900, but it meant everything in European Russia, since it was the first factor by which such a worker defined himself. Some artisan shops were owned by such hereditary aristocrats, while in metals and textiles, in large-scale industry, the hereditary workers may have comprised about half the total work force in 1900. Still, they were only a tiny fraction of the total number of wage earners, perhaps 10 percent.[10]

The shift from peasant in-migration to a self-reproducing urban working class did not occur until the mid-1930s, as the seminal study by M. Ia. Sonin showed.[11] This was the fundamental break in Russian and Soviet social history and in the history of working-class formation, since it marked, in Sonin's demographic terms, the end of the dual labor market and the first stage in the integration of the castelike grouping of urban labor aristocrats. The demarcation point was the First FYP and the industrialization-collectivization drive.

The subaltern work force consisted of three large and overlapping subgroups: peasant-workers, female workers, and employed youth.[12] These workers should be defined as the counterparts to the aristocrats by their inability to reproduce themselves in the city. Married males typically lived in households split between village and city, with wife and children remaining in the village. Married females who worked in textile factories often walked from village to mill each day. Single workers, male and female, typically lived in barracks or in crowded communal apartments in the city, where they were lucky to have their own beds. In all these arrangements, the subaltern workers differed from their Western European counterparts, the unskilled and the industrial reserve army or underclass, in that they were defined not only as distinct subcultures and by low wages, but also by their inability to maintain a family life in the city. Seasonal or year-round factory workers, these peasant-proletarians lived with one foot in the village and one in the city. The two other large subaltern groups, women and youth, were again distinguished from their Western European counterparts primarily by their family life and only secondarily by their low wages and lack of bargaining rights and market capacities or skilled occupations.[13]

The subaltern workers were numerically predominant in agricultural wage labor, loading and unloading work, construction, mining, and unskilled and semiskilled factory labor. Those who worked in factories typically continued with their seasonal patterns of migration and lacked job security. Some peasant-migrants might have preferred this arrangement, which gave them maximum flexibility and did not tie them down to their factory jobs. However, they could not even be sure of their own job security from day to day, let alone passing on their "job" to a son. Most of them had no defined occupation to pass on, in any case. During strike actions, they were prone to return to the village. Thus, Social Democrats and subsequently historians assumed that these factors made them passive, an assumption which should now be modified if not entirely discarded.

Social Democrats and historians have also assumed that these workers were sporadically prone to spontaneous uprisings, derived from rural cultures. Recent historical research has confirmed that assumption.[14] However, recent work has not reconfirmed the term *spontaneity* as counterposed to *consciousness* of the *kadrovye* (cadre workers) by the Mensheviks and Bolsheviks alike. This was meant to disparage the organizational capabilities of peasants, women, or youth. The problem with both *passivity* and *spontaneity* is that they fail to take into account the intermediary social position and the broad influence of the subaltern workers on rural and urban households and communities. Furthermore, both terms fail to take into account what ideas or visions motivated these subalterns.

The migrant peasant-workers had one foot in the village and the other in the urban factory, as has long been stressed in the literature. While social historians have convincingly shown that this was a highly functional eco-nomic symbiosis, with clear benefits for the household of the migrant-worker, we should not assume that these adaptable peasant-workers were well integrated socially, culturally, or politically. Instead, I would suggest, they de-veloped a "combined" sense of injustice, originating in both urban and rural grievances, and they were very poorly integrated in the cities, where their legal status as peasants reflected their real status as outsiders. This was the first factor pushing them toward revolutionary parties or movements in a consistent pattern, in a conscious and persistent way, rather than sponta-neously. The second factor was their ability to adapt the revolutionary vision of the aristocrats and to infuse it with new meaning.[15]

The revolutionary vision of the aristocrats has been described well in a number of volumes on the workers' movement.[16] That vision took concrete form in the struggle for "workers' control," which in 1917 was driven by the factory committees, and which fed into the broader movement for "Soviet power." The labor aristocrats and the subaltern workers were normally sharply divided by the shop-floor hierarchy, in which the aristocrats super-vised the subalterns in a quasi-managerial capacity. This sharp division al-lowed even a weak autocracy to maintain control in the cities after 1905. In 1917, however, the aristocrats' vision of workers' control was adopted by the subaltern workers, who interpreted it to mean job security and basic job rights (the eight-hour day, minimum wage standards, and so on). The fusion of grievances and visions of a just future that occurred in 1917 would sweep away not only autocracy, but also the parties and institutions of the gentry, bourgeoisie, and middle classes. That, indeed, was "permanent revolution" through "combined (social) development."

That explains events in Petrograd, Moscow, and other industrial cities. The radical outcome in 1917, however, depended on another factor, namely the passive or active support of rural and small-town Russia, and the active support of soldiers and of nonworkers in the cities. In this respect, it was pre-cisely the subaltern workers, with their links to the vast rural population, who would prove to be decisive as intermediaries.

The subaltern workers were the most numerous intermediaries between urban and village society, and they could fluently communicate to kin and friends in the village in ways that the intelligentsia and revolutionaries (or labor aristocrats), coming from the city to the village, could not. The social links between the working class and peasant society, family life both rural and urban, and the youth in school and army, were all forged by the inter-mediates, that is, by the subaltern workers. Thus, they were not an "urban mob," an "underclass," or a "lumpen proletariat," nor did they lack organiza-tional ability even if they left behind few or no records of their activity in archives of trade unions. These intermediaries spread a common revolutionary vision from factory to field, from factory to urban or rural household, from factory to army, and then back again. Or, was it from field to factory and back again?[17]

Although 1917 seemed to obliterate the dual labor market and the bifurcated working-class culture in a single, chiliastic, revolutionary movement, and although the First World War, the 1917 revolutions, and the Civil War wreaked havoc with the labor market from 1914 to 1921, the legacy of the dual labor market was felt once again in 1921 with the New Economic Policy (NEP). Under NEP, industry and industrial employment were restored to their 1913 levels by 1926.[18] With restoration, a modified dual labor market reappeared, but in this case, under the auspices of the Commissariat of Labor (NKT) and the trade unions (VTsSPS).

NKT and VTsSPS worked out formal rules that governed hiring and firing and replaced the informal kinship and personal connections that had determined so much of hiring practice before 1914. As industry was restored, those with prior industrial work tenure and with Red Army service were given priority in job placement by the labor exchanges, the *birzhi truda,* which were modeled after the French syndicalist *bourses de travail.*[19] The result was, once again, a polarized working class, although not so sharply divided as under the tsarist regime. The labor aristocrats could no longer guarantee the hiring of their offspring, and so they were losing an important element of their hereditary status. At the same time, the splitting up of the housing of the urban upper classes into communal apartments afforded new opportunities for subalterns to establish an urban family life.[20] Perhaps the distinction for the 1920s should be drawn in terms of skilled workers, rather than aristocrats, and unskilled or semiskilled workers as well as unemployed or semiemployed subalterns.

Soviet data from the 1926 All-Union Census indicate that skilled workers constituted about half the work force in large-scale industry (roughly comparable to Rashin's "cadre" at the turn of the century), and that unemployment was disproportionately high among urban youth and women.[21] Unemployment among peasant-migrants could not be measured, and economists assumed that a staggering figure of anywhere from 5 to 30 million peasants were, in effect, superfluous on the land. They would migrate permanently from the overcrowded village to the city if there were permanent jobs in the city for them.[22] The same applied to millions of urban women and youth, who were not even counted as unemployed because, having no prior industrial experience, they could not qualify to register at the labor exchange.[23] Thus, when embarking on the industrialization drive, the regime was counting on tapping these three great labor reserves.

The gap between skilled and subaltern workers during NEP remained a deep structural and social problem for Soviet power. It reflected the still broader gap between rural and urban society and the limitations or even the failure of the *smychka*, or worker-peasant alliance, which Lenin had called the regime's social foundation.[24] Rather than understanding this failure merely in terms of the party's difficulties in "saturating" rural Russia, as historians of the party have emphasized, it would make sense to turn to the broader problem of this social gap, of two societies and two cultures under NEP.[25]

I am not suggesting that NEP was doomed because it was a mixed market economy with high unemployment. NEP's deep social problems were not caused by markets but rather by the legacy of the poorly developed markets of the prerevolutionary past, first among them the dual labor market that reflected the age-old division between rural and urban Russia. This was a serious problem, far more important than convincing skilled workers to endorse Taylorism, which the regime and particularly Trotsky were fixated on, and far more important than peasant "class stratification" which also inordinately concerned the regime and the Left Opposition. Whether this problem could have been resolved within the NEP framework remains an open question.[26]

This deeply ingrained historical pattern of Russia's bifurcated working-class formation changed dramatically in less than two years with the onset of the First FYP under what I call the "inversion" of the Soviet labor market. The inverted labor market was one in which the demand for labor power in industry always exceeded the supply, thus obliterating the dualism in which only the aristocrats (skilled workers) had secure access through the factory gate. The factory gate was no longer any obstacle to the subalterns, and, as the labor reserves that the regime counted on, they could not come quickly enough into the factories.

Mistakenly called a "full employment economy," this inverted labor market had its own disequilibrium which was as characteristic of the Soviet economy as was the chronic unemployment that plagued capitalist economies. This disequilibrium spanned the six decades of planned economy, from 1930 until 1990, and it was historically unprecedented, having no counterpart in capitalist economy or society nor in other socialist societies after the Second World War. The Chinese and Indian efforts at socialist construction after 1949 would never suffer this type of imbalance.[27] Part 2 of this study explains how that inversion dramatically ended the deeply ensconced dual labor market, establishing the preconditions for obliterating the distinction between aristocrats and subalterns and for creating a newly integrated urban community via the process of working-class formation. The "year of the great breakthrough," as Stalin called it on Revolution Day, 1929, was indeed the decisive year.[28]

Robert Tucker is surely right that the slogan "revolution from above" encapsulated Stalin's own outlook, his self-image as Lenin's heir and perpetuator of the revolutionary ideals and agenda of October 1917. However, the slogan is self-contradictory (as was Stalin) and poses an obstacle to our understanding of what happened. Nor do the phrases "revolution from below" or "Stalin Revolution," as used by non-Soviet historians, or "Cultural Revolution" or "great breakthrough," coined by the Stalinists, help to clarify the events in that chaotic period.[29]

I would suggest that there was neither "permanent revolution" extending from 1917 to 1937, nor "Thermidor" in 1921, or 1931, or 1937, and that the "continuity question" ultimately cannot be resolved historically, but is philosophical-political.[30] To avoid confusion, I will not use the term *revolution* at all for the 1930s, but only the terms *First FYP* and *industrialization-collectivization drive.* As my discussion of labor markets and the working class already makes clear, however, it is my assumption that what happened in the four years and three months of the First FYP marked the most radical and fundamental of historical discontinuities.

In this respect, I am consciously adopting Moshe Lewin's methodological breakthrough on collectivization and the peasantry. The argument that Stalinist economics were improvised and centrally administered rather than a planned economy had already been part of the literature on Soviet economics for a long time before Lewin applied it in his study of collectivization that was initially published in 1966.[31] Furthermore, while something similar to this historical approach had been developed by Isaac Deutscher and E. H. Carr, their studies focused on the first ten years of Soviet power and demonstrated the regime's constantly evolving concept of socialist construction, a concept that was quite fluid as it moved from War Communism to the New Economic Policy during that ten year period. Both Deutscher and Carr assumed that subsequently Soviet history moved into the era of "planned economy." Lewin rejected that premise and adopted the approach of economic historians who found an improvised and extremely voluntarist type of planning under Stalinism, while extending the findings of Deutscher and Carr on the fluidity of the regime's conception of socialist construction into the 1930s. Thus, he found that, with forced collectivization, the era of the so-called planned economy was inaugurated with a totally unplanned, spontaneous, and improvised military-style offensive in which Russian peasant society's response was neither considered nor factored into the equation. When the peasant response was not overwhelmingly positive, the regime then quickly improvised the draconian policy known as "dekulakization."

The methodological breakthrough consisted of reintroducing Russian society, or at least Russian peasant society into the political equation. This allowed Lewin to construct the most convincing narrative of the Stalinist policy of forced collectivization as it evolved both through conflicts at the top and also through a series of regime assaults and retreats in handling the "peasant problem" and the so-called grain crisis. Forced collectivization evolved out of these regime initiatives and peasant reactions and was justified by the regime as a response to the largely manufactured crisis. Lewin's conclusion that the Stalinist collectivization policy was improvised in the conflict with Russian peasants over grain has held up under scholarly scrutiny.[32]

A recent study of NEP labor in the textile industry extends Lewin's approach from the peasant and the village to the workers and cities. These studies have shown that the attempt to raise labor productivity in 1926–1928 under the campaign headings "rationalization" and "regime of economy," were as disruptive in industrial relations as were the Ural-Siberian and other strong-armed methods of cheap state grain collections adopted in agriculture in those same years. The most disruptive shift in industry was the introduction of the "continuous production" workweek and the seven-hour workday.[33] While the latter act reduced the workweek by almost five hours, the continuous workweek obliterated the weekend and constantly rotated the worker's shift schedule, provoking universal dissatisfaction and early exhaustion of factory machinery and equipment, which could not be properly repaired and maintained.

Furthermore, Lewin's breakthrough has also been reconfirmed during the First FYP, in the microstudies on industrialization, urban life, and factory work at Dneprostroi, Magnitogorsk, and in my own study of Moscow's Proletarian District during the 1930s. Starting in 1926 and 1927, project designs for Dneprostroi and Magnitostroi, and for the Hammer and Sickle steel plant and the Moscow auto plant, were drafted, then discarded, and then redesigned each year until the initial project design and its scale in the FYP had become entirely irrelevant. As chapter 2 explains, reconstruction of such "shock project" factories in 1929 or 1930 negated all the project designs, as the actual levels of investment became a function of political decisions and of political patronage, more than doubling the original First FYP targets.[34]

Thus, coherent economic planning had nothing to do with the decisions for the "shock projects," as the key new industrial enterprises under construction came to be called. They would reshape the outlines of the entire economy and the scale of the First FYP in unpredictable ways, except that one could predict that heavy industry would be favored.[35] The breakthrough that Lewin made by applying the idea of improvised rather than planned economy to social policy, showing rural society in flux under the assault of collectivization and how this flux was disrupting the regime's "plans," has now been applied in the microstudies to urban society in flux under the impact of the industrialization drive, also disrupting the regime's "program."[36]

The result, according to Lewin, was an urban "quicksand society," which would provoke the regime to adopt draconian labor and passport-residency laws that, according to Lewin, would play an important role in shaping a more stable urban society.[37] While none of the microstudies has adopted the term "quicksand society," and while none has found much evidence for the draconian laws or passports bringing about urban social stability, all have followed Lewin in emphasizing the sudden and very deep urban social flux caused by the regime's crash industrialization and collectivization and for which the regime was not at all prepared at the outset of the First FYP. Furthermore, all of the microstudies have adopted Lewin's methodological breakthrough with the shared assumption that the passage of ever more draconian labor laws in 1930–1932 was ineffective improvisation, even as they seemed to smack of the "totalitarian" ambitions of attempting to replace the labor market with a system of compulsory labor.

This was the mirror image of the series of ever more stringent *kolkhoz* laws, which regulated grain procurement and farm work, culminating in the infamous "five stalks of grain" law of 7 August 1932. The regime's "totalitarian intentions," as Lewin has shown in agriculture, were not born in 1917, but evolved in 1928–30, shaped in response to a rural society that it did not understand and that seemed, from Moscow's perspective, to be out of control, and thus obstructing its economic program. In industry, the artificially induced crisis of an inadequate labor force was a consequence of the inversion of the labor market, and it evoked the same seemingly totalitarian regime response in the form of the draconian labor laws.

Lewin's methodological breakthrough revised a long tradition in the historical literature as I suggested in the introduction, since the ideas that had originated during the nineteenth century in the Russian State School were repackaged during the 1950s in a modern guise with new emphasis on technologies of power and party ideology in the historiography of Bolshevism as "totalitarianism." Much of the work of the totalitarian school was an attempt to guess at power struggles and conflicts within the Kremlin and was devoted to finding Stalin's motivation for the "permanent purge," sparked first by the regime's own secrecy and second by sensational emigre accounts.

This was mostly a dead end for historians, except for those working on Stalin's psyche. Still, the first serious academic research on Soviet society was conducted in the Harvard Refugee Project, by researchers working within the totalitarian framework, who interviewed the World War II Soviet refugees who were able to settle abroad, and by Merle Fainsod, who conducted his own interrogation of the Smolensk Party Archives, also a sort of "refugee" which settled permanently abroad at Harvard. In the work of Inkeles, Bauer,

Fainsod, Brzezinski, and others who were involved in these projects, their theoretical assumptions that the Soviet Union was a totalitarian system were elaborated both analytically and in terms of a narrative chronology.[38]

E. H. Carr and Isaac Deutscher were the first to to introduce an element of contingency and suggestions of possible alternatives into this state school-totalitarian picture, particularly for the 1920s and NEP, but ultimately both historians continued to think of the 1930s as the triumph of planned economy or socialist economy superseding NEP along the lines originally suggested by the Left Opposition. And with this triumph, the power of the state administration expanded very broadly. As I have noted, Moshe Lewin's breakthrough on the peasantry adopted their findings of improvisation under War Communism and then NEP, and then applied them to the 1930s, showing how improvisation became the normal mode of operation in Stalinist politics and policymaking, and that forced collectivization served as its testing grounds.

A very different revisionist project was advanced by Sheila Fitzpatrick, who argued that the policies adopted by the regime during the Cultural Revolution had strong social support from below.[39] Her work opened a new debate between revisionists and orthodox, in which the revisionists were soon moving away from Lewin and Fitzpatrick, and mostly away from social history, and back to the turf of the totalitarian school and the Smolensk Party Archives and the protocols of the party plenums, conferences, and congresses.

The new revisionists began with Lewin's premise that the Stalin regime was unable to effectively implement its decreed policy, and also with Fitzpatrick's premise that the regime's policies reflected social pressures coming from below. They concluded that the Stalin regime was torn, through the 1930s, by policy debate at the center and that it could not even control party members, let alone the society, in Smolensk, a province just west of Moscow Province and the metropolis.[40] As the normal methods of the party purge proved to be insufficient in improving this situation, repression was used to shore up those weaknesses, and the great terror of 1937 was the unplanned and largely uncontrolled result. This was contingency, improvisation, and pressure from below carried to its ultimate extreme. A weak regime, in this approach, apparently reflected a fragmented society and would generate chaos through terror.[41]

This was far removed from Lewin's conclusions on the building of a powerful Stalinist state. Fitzpatrick, too, would eventually reject these conclusions of the new revisionism.[42] The problem is with the dichotomy of repression and resistance, which shapes the entire orthodox-revisionist debate and has produced ever diminishing returns on research in the primary sources.

This dichotomy has proved to be a dead end for Soviet history, I would argue, because the shared premise of both the dichotomous perspectives in this paradigm is that isolated individuals confronted the state and that society was incapable of preserving old or generating new social solidarities. The most it could do was disrupt state plans.

In labor history the dichotomies of the totalitarian-revisionist debate were replicated in the dichotomies of what I would call the *repression-resistance paradigm,* within which Solomon Schwarz (in 1951) and then Donald Filtzer (in 1986) produced important studies. In 1988, three new studies appeared by Vladimir Andrle, Hiroaki Kuromiya, and Lewis Siegelbaum which were based on new sources, methods, and ideas, and which yielded what I would call a new *contingent identities paradigm* that went beyond the repression-resistance paradigm. Also in 1988, Anne Rassweiler published the first micro-study of Dneprostroi; in 1994 David Hoffmann published the second on peasant-migration into Moscow; in 1995 Stephen Kotkin published the third on Magnitogorsk; and my study of Moscow's Proletarian District and its factories is the fourth. In the following survey of these three paradigms, I will consider only what each work and paradigm potentially indicates about Soviet working-class formation, even though mine is the only one to focus on this issue or to raise this "problematic" in the Soviet case, where it was long assumed to have no place.

Schwarz's early and pathbreaking work, explicitly adopting the totalitarian framework, argued unambiguously that the Soviet work force in the 1930s was an unskilled urban mass and not a working class. Starting with the Menshevik premise that peasant-recruits do not a working class make, he argued that the new Soviet workers had no notion of trade unionism or of working-class institutions or traditions. In this context, he claimed, the regime's draconian labor laws provided an effective means to isolate workers from each other and instill discipline through fear. He argued that pay differentials and "socialist competitions" constituted the party's divide-and-conquer schemes which aimed, particularly with Stakhanovism, at establishing a new labor aristocracy on the one hand, and a compliant mass of worker-consumers on the other. Schwarz presented a convincing picture of a cowed, unproductive, disorganized, and fragmented urban working mass.[43]

Filtzer shifted the emphasis from repression to resistance some thirty-five years later. For Filtzer, as for Schwarz, there could not be organized working-class resistance under Stalinism, but he saw the sum total of the individual acts of resistance amounting to workers "voting 'no' with their feet." Workers negated the regime's disciplinary laws and productivity schemes by moving from job to job, leaving the curse of labor turnover in their wake, a curse that would define and plague Soviet industrial relations until the Gorbachev era. For Filtzer, following Trotsky's analysis and also Schwarz, this turnover meant retarded class formation and class consciousness.[44] Thus, Schwarz's totalitarian approach in 1951 was revised but essentially recapitulated, I would argue, in Filtzer's revisionist approach. The two accounts were locked into a repression-resistance paradigm.

The monographs by Kuromiya, Andrle, and Siegelbaum all presented sharply different interpretations from the repression-resistance paradigm. While by no means cut from a single cloth, all clearly rejected the old paradigm's assumptions of fragmentation and individualist responses of fear or resistance, showing, instead, limited or contingent social identities emerging among Soviet workers at various key moments during the 1930s. For Kuromiya, the shock-work movement in the First FYP was just such a moment; it mobilized workers, or at least certain groups of workers, around the class struggle in favor of a program of superindustrialization. For Andrle, the work brigade that evolved by the mid-1930s was the key to new solidarities and identities and to a new, more modern, work culture shaped by the factory clock. For Siegelbaum, it was the Stakhanovite moment in late 1935 and 1936 that constituted an important new shift in workers' identities.[45]

Neither a fragmented mass of isolated individuals, nor, to be sure, the triumphant march of the working class in the Soviet historians' accounts, the three studies showed rapidly changing, shifting, and contingent new identities among Soviet workers, in patterns shaped both from below and from above. The three also cover the regime's sequentially shifting slogans for raising labor productivity and for social policy and industrial relations strategies during each of the three prewar FYPs. First came shock work and socialist competition, second came assimilation, and third came Stakhanovism. The three studies, focusing on three different moments, these showed shifting identities and thus temporally limited or contingent identities or social solidarities. I will discuss each at greater length in chapters 6 and 7. In chapter 7, I also reexamine the largely forgotten findings of what might be called the Soviet triumphalist school of working-class history, in which the revolutionary spirit of the working class of 1917 was somehow preserved intact and passed on through the 1920s and 1930s in the form of an expanding working class clamoring for rapid new socialist construction at all costs. Embedded in this work, despite its crude teleological assumptions, are the empirical foundations for a different theory of Soviet working-class formation during the 1930s.[46]

The microstudies by Rassweiler, Hoffman, and Kotkin, and the present study, find more lasting new solidarities, which will likely be further explored in forthcoming publications.[47] They reaffirm that Soviet society was not fragmented into a lowest common denominator of isolated individuals, as in the repression-resistance paradigm. Whereas the contingent identity studies by Kuromiya, Andrle, and Siegelbaum traced shifting identities that were limited by time or place, the microstudies all find more permanent types of urban social solidarity. Unlike most previous studies on the USSR, the microstudies resemble the scale and some aspects of the approach of the German *alltagsgeschichte* school. Perhaps its finding of more permanent solidarities than in the contingent identities paradigm could be explained, at least in part, by the relatively circumscribed geographic place under consideration. Obviously the widening availability of archival sources was critical to such work, and Rassweiler's study shows the opening began in the late Brezhnev years, while the subsequent studies show a wider opening under Gorbachev and after.

All four microstudies, as I have suggested, start from the Lewin premise, that Stalinist industrial and labor policies were improvised and not planned, that the First FYP industrialization-collectivization drive caused deep social chaos, and that the regime would then scramble to contain and control that chaos with rapidly improvised policies that would look quite totalitarian in intention. However, none of these studies affirms Lewin's argument that this chaotic situation was then overcome through state policy, that is by combining repressive and modernizing elements with a social conservatism taken from the tsarist regime.[48]

The microstudies diverge from Lewin on this point, emphasizing that if, indeed, there was a "quicksand society" during the First FYP, then it was very shortlived, and it was supplanted by new urban social solidarities that had little if anything to do with state policies of repression or modernization or the social conservatism of the "Great Retreat."[49] The microstudies also diverge from each other at this point, each finding rather distinct factors causing solidarity, and each of them also describing urban social solidarities differently. Part of the difference could be explained by regional variation, but more fundamentally, these differences reflect differing interpretations.

Rassweiler argued that at Dneprostroi solidarities were shaped by enthusiasm among the new recruits, mostly peasant-migrants, including many young and married women who were new to construction work. She also emphasized the role of state vocational training programs in forming a cohesive work force at the construction site. Her account assumed a near identity of interests of new workers and of the party-state, based either on their enthusiasm for the project of electrification or on the individual desire for upward mobility, as channeled by vocational training and educational opportunities provided by the state. Her study did not go beyond 1931, with the construction of the dam project, and therefore the solidarities she described were rather fleeting, as workers drifted off to other construction projects or other factories.[50] One might surmise from her study that the new enthusiasm and social solidarities did not, by themselves, amount to class formation. Perhaps her study is closer to the contingent identities school in this respect.

For Hoffmann, the underlying factor in the success of labor recruitment in Moscow was the peasants' desire to earn wages and their ability effectively to replicate village networks in the city. By preserving their village culture under difficult and oppressive conditions in Moscow, and largely in opposition to the regime, the peasants were able to adapt and thus became permanent Muscovites, turning the capital into a "peasant metropolis." Rather than assimilating industrial work habits, urban lifestyle, or working-class consciousness as promoted by the regime, they would transform the city according to their village work habits and lifestyle in the *artel'*.

Hoffmann thus presents an ironic twist on the Menshevik argument that the peasant-migrants negated working-class consciousness, arguing that they did so not because they were a fragmented mass suffering from Durkheimian *anomie,* but because they became well-adjusted urban dwellers by transforming city culture into village culture. A second irony is that, by negating regime ideology, the peasant-workers in Hoffmann's study were building the regime's new "socialist" capital, supplying it with the recruits it needed for construction crews and for staffing its factories, even as the regime was cursing them for lack of industrial discipline. My study, which looks at some of the same factories as Hoffmann's, reinforces his findings on the village-based pattern of migration and labor recruiting. However, whereas his approach assumes that there was no possibility of working-class formation because of the preservation of peasant values in the urban village networks, my study draws very different conclusions.

Kotkin's study of Magnitogorsk started with the regime's use of the stick and the carrot in "peopling" Magnitostroi, the construction site, before the plans for designing the factory had been agreed on. However, as the initial construction work was completed, unlike the electric power plant in Ukraine and much more like Moscow, a large number of the construction workers stayed on to work in the steel combine, becoming the vast majority of its production workers. Kotkin explains why they stayed by going far beyond the stick and the carrot to a careful reconsideration of the means of adaptation and the "positive integration" of the new workers in the new "Stalinist civilization."[51]

Anticipating many aspects of my own argument, Kotkin argues that the Magnitogorsk migrant-workers broke decisively from their past life as peasants, or artisans, or Moscow cadre on assignment, and adapted to the new work environment and to the new city quite rapidly. He argues that the new workers willingly became part of official society, but that this was not a hegemonic process, as they also learned to reconfigure the "grand strategies of the state" in terms of their "little tactics of the habitat" to their "minimum disadvantage" even as they learned to "speak Bolshevik."[52]

My study differs from Kotkin's primarily in reconsidering the meaning of "working class" for the workers. Kotkin argued that in the process of positive integration the workers in Magnitogorsk learned to "speak Bolshevik," and that "class analysis served [the regime] as a sophisticated technique of rule, and armed with this class-based view of the world, the Soviet leadership pursued as one of its chief goals the creation of a specifically Soviet working class."[53] I am suggesting a parallel integration, that is, a social integration of the workers that was the reason for adaptation of ideology, program, and policy by the Stalin regime. I would certainly agree that workers learned to "speak Bolshevik," but I would place equal if not greater emphasis on the process by which the Stalin regime haltingly began to discard its class struggle discourse after 1931, shifting instead to a discourse and policies of a new working-class inclusiveness.

In my account, that meant that the regime had to tone down its class struggle rhetoric against "class aliens,"[54] most importantly, against the former peasants and kulaks, in order to accommodate the new workers and adjust to the realities of Soviet working-class formation. The first step toward legitimating these new workers, came with Stalin's "Six Conditions" speech of 23 June 1931, which stridently denounced egalitarianism as "petty-bourgeois leveling" and as a non-Marxist deviation, but which simultaneously offered workers a new pay system based on equity, wherein the social origins of the worker, the worker's length of work tenure, or status as a cadre worker or as a newcomer would no longer play any discernable role in determining the worker's wages. I would suggest that couched here in Stalin's language of antiegalitarianism, ironically, was also the discourse of class inclusion, a discourse that aimed to fully integrate peasants, women, and youth. These themes were reiterated when Stalin legitimized all the new workers as full-fledged members of the Soviet working class and even legitimized the *kolkhoz* peasantry and the technical intelligentsia in his article discussing the 1936 Stalin Constitution. Here he proclaimed that Soviet society consisted of two nonantagonistic classes, peasants and workers, and a stratum of a loyal Soviet technical intelligentsia (see chap. 4 below).

That narrows, somewhat, Kotkin's parameters of positive integration, focusing more pointedly on the process of Soviet working-class formation and excluding considerations of party and state recruiting, bread and circuses, and other aspects of Stalinist civilization that loomed so large in Kotkin's study. The two approaches may, in fact, be compatible, but I am unconvinced that Stalinist ideology and "civilization" had a great deal of influence, except when it fell within the parameters of evolving social trends, in particular, working-class formation. Thus, we differ on the extent to which Soviet workers were politically integrated.

In my account, such political integration of the Soviet working class as was achieved was derived mainly through parallel social-class integration and consolidated when the regime was able to adapt to the new social realities. In my account of this, the Red Directors were important intermediaries in reshaping the party-state ideology, pushing it away from class struggle and from the dichotomy of "cadre workers" and the so-called class aliens, and moving the regime instead toward a new and all-inclusive conception of the working class. Despite these differences in interpretation, my findings concerning factory work and community life in Moscow, indeed, strikingly resemble the trends that Kotkin had also found in Magnitogorsk.[55] Chapter 2 suggests why that might be so, specifically in the newly industrialized outlying districts of the city, as my discussion of the industrial reconstruction in Moscow is situated in the industrialization of the USSR as a whole.

In tracing a trajectory from social chaos to social stabilization across the decade of the 1930s, this study argues that the "quicksand society" was beginning rapidly to solidify into firm, urban Soviet soil, to continue with Lewin's geological metaphor. Working-class formation in the 1930s saw an emerging social cohesion which was both anticipated and reflected in the shift from the class struggle ideology of the Cultural Revolution, to the ersatz social contract ideology of Stalin's "Six Conditions" speech. This shift, thus, was not a return to the cultures or practices of the former regime. In this respect, my findings mark a sharp departure from Trotsky, Berdyaev, Timasheff, and from Lewin, Fitzpatrick, and Tucker, all of whom had suggested, in very different ways, the triumph of social conservatism under Stalin after 1931 or 1933.[56]

Instead, I am suggesting that the Soviet Union experienced a unique pattern of working-class formation under Stalinism which did not resemble Russian working-class formation prior to 1917. With the parallel social integration of the subaltern social groups in the factories and the urban protocommunities, came a deep and far reaching social proletarianization that shaped the thinking and captured the minds of the entire generation of the 1930s.

MOSCOW'S PROLETARIAN DISTRICT AND THE HAMMER AND SICKLE STEEL PLANT

Why Moscow?

The reconstruction of Moscow during the 1930s was both unique and at the same time broadly representative of trends in other cities and regions of the USSR during the First FYP industrialization drive. It was unique because Moscow was the administrative center of the vast union, and because "inner Moscow," comprising the territory within the Garden Ring, was reconstructed in the 1930s and 1940s to showcase the paramount significance of the all-union administration, in what might be called a new Stalinist power architecture. The process was completed with the seven Stalin skyscrapers built after the Second World War.[1]

The most notable fact about Stalinist reconstruction of inner Moscow was that, contrary to all plans, including the 1935 "Plan for Reconstruction of Moscow," the center of the city was redesigned in such a way that it left the domination of the Kremlin visually intact, if not enhanced. All the design projects for massive skyscrapers to house the Commissariat of Heavy Industry, and the Palace of Soviets, which would have dwarfed the Kremlin and completely reconfigured central Moscow, were discarded. Instead, much more modest new buildings constructed across from the Kremlin, including the ten-story STO building (later Gosplan), the Lenin Library, and the Moscow Hotel, enhanced the existing architectural ensemble.[2]

Boris Mikhailovich Iofan's unimplemented, prize-winning design in 1933 for the Palace of Soviets, to be built at the site of the demolished Christ the Savior Church, would instead serve as a basis for seven derivative, "wedding-cake" skyscrapers, which were built after the Second World War. Six were along the Garden Ring; the seventh was the Moscow State University's new campus, located slightly beyond the Garden Ring at the bend in the river, where it towered over the city from the Lenin Hills. (The Garden Ring is shown in map 1 below.) These seven Stalin skyscrapers, rather than dwarfing the Kremlin, did the opposite. They visually demarcated inner, administrative Moscow from outer or industrial Moscow, from virtually every part of the city.[3] The writer Yuri Trifonov brilliantly evoked the oppressive, overwhelming, and yet imposing shadow that the Stalinist architecture of power cast over the inhabitants of the city in his novella *House on the Embankment,* which described events in the most prestigious of the new neoclassical apartment dwellings lining Gor'kii Street and the newly built embankments along the Moscow River in the vicinity of the Kremlin.

If inner Moscow was rebuilt to display administrative power and prestige, then outer Moscow, the territory beyond the Garden Ring, was rebuilt to showcase Soviet industrialization. The new Palace of Culture and the adjacent Stalin auto plant (ZiS) became a showcase for foreign trade-union delegations.[4] In the official slogan of the day, "calico Moscow" was to become "metal Moscow," and at the center of this transformation would be the Proletarian District (Proletarskii Raion, PR), which the Hammer and Sickle steel plant (Serp i Molot, SiM), and the ZiS auto plant and its Palace of Culture symbolized.

By the end of the First FYP, Moscow industry was indeed changing from textiles to metals, which made it typical of the industrialization process in the 1930s. Of course, "administrative Moscow," with think tanks and a large and expanding educational and scientific research establishment, would later dominate an entire academic district beyond the Garden Ring in the city's southwest. Still, the new metal-based industry made Moscow, during the 1930s, the most representative of major Soviet cities in the industrial reconstruction. The size and the technologies of its factories, the composition of its work force, and the evolving patterns of labor organization and industrial relations were indicative of changes that would soon spread throughout the Union. An emerging working-class "protocommunity," that took shape in the outlying industrial districts of the city, of which the PR was the most outstanding example, would also reflect the patterns of urban community formation throughout the USSR. Moscow, geographically intermediate, would also remain an industrial "intermediate" during the 1930s.

The leading industrial region of the empire and then the USSR, until the 1930s, was the northwest, with St. Petersburg or Leningrad as its hub. The imperial capital had been the center for machine construction, metalworking, shipbuilding, and military-based industries, and it boasted plants such as the Putilov, Izhorsk, and the Baltic and Nevskii Shipbuilding and Engineering Works, which were the largest in Russia and among the largest in the world at the beginning of this century. The *metallisty*, or metalworkers, were the predominant group, while the *tekstil'shchiki*, the textile workers, were secondary.[5] The leading workers in this region were male, middle-aged, and more than in any other part of the empire, they had severed their ties to the land and become a strictly hereditary proletariat, or what I call the Russian labor aristocracy.[6] Having played the leading role during the revolutions of 1917, the St. Petersburg *metallisty* continued to enjoy the Soviet title of "cadre proletariat" and "working-class avant-garde" during the 1920s.[7] In Petersburg and other cities in the west of the empire, the gender ratio was the most nearly equal, and one might assume, therefore, that the urban proletarian family unit was emerging most rapidly in this region.[8]

At the opposite extreme was what I would call the industrial periphery. It constituted a vast arc running from northeast to southwest, which included iron and coal mining and processing in the Urals, manufacturing based in the largest cities of the southern Volga, coal mining and steel in the Donbass, machine construction in Kharkhov, and oil refining in Baku. Predominant in this zone was the extraction of raw materials. In this peripheral arc, migrant-peasant labor was the more significant component of the work force and the hereditary proletariat hardly existed. The skilled workers and managers were brought in by entrepreneurs from the cities of western Russia, or in cases such as the Hughes Mines in the Donbass, from Western Europe.[9]

For the migrant-peasant laborer, work was typically seasonal (on *otkhod*), and many of these workers remained as unskilled day laborers all their lives. In mining or manufacturing they were performing the most arduous tasks, which provided nominally higher wages than they otherwise could have earned. They were young, male, and expendable, and in the grim factory towns of the region, many lived in *zemlianki* (earthen dugouts), or in the mine itself, and many others lived in company barracks. There was virtually no possibility of family life in the city for the majority of such workers.[10] These grim mining and mill towns were male-dominated factory towns, and married migrant men who worked in the mines and mills of the Donbass had to leave their wives and children behind in the villages.

The Central Industrial Region (CIR), which included Moscow and the surrounding seven provinces, was geographically intermediate, but more important, it was socially an intermediate case in the industrialization of Russia before 1917, and it remained so during the industrialization drive of the 1930s and afterward. Historically it was predominantly a center of light industry, and especially textiles, which meant an unusually high number of female workers in large mills, especially in small factory towns.[11]

In Moscow itself, peasant-migrant labor was widespread in construction and in the metallurgical industry, and was based on constant in-migration from the CIR. This meant that the gender imbalance was greater than in St. Petersburg, although much less than on the periphery. Moscow was also known as an artisinal center of scattered and small shops, and its artisans, together with its skilled factory mechanics, constituted a labor aristocracy second only to St. Petersburg's.[12]

Moscow's industry was the most diversified in the empire, with its small artisan shops and its giant textile mills starkly illustrating Trotsky's theory of "combined development."[13] More importantly, it was a socially "combined" case in ways that Trotsky never considered, because it was a composite work force, including the peasant-proletarian employed in all kinds of unskilled labor, the female semiskilled machine operative in textiles and other light industries, and the labor aristocrats and their apprenticing sons, industrial mechanics and artisans.

In the Soviet industrialization drive of the 1930s, the same industrial geography can be distinguished, albeit with a changing mix of industries in each region and greater uniformity over the entire USSR. The 1930s also saw a shift away from peasant-migrant labor and toward an urban gender balance and the urban proletarian family in cities in all three regions. Leningrad and the industrial northwest changed the least, since new investment in industry was limited in the 1930s and 1940s in that region. The periphery changed the most, because in these new cities the peasant-proletarian was becoming a permanent city-dweller, and urban family life was becoming the norm. As the Urals became a steel center with a proliferating machine-construction industry, and as the Kuzbass in Western Siberia became a second coal-iron-steel triangle that would surpass the original triangle in the Donbass, a settled urban population emerged roughly at the rate of construction of communal apartment dwellings. The CIR was again an intermediate case, shifting from calico-metal to metal-calico, and this made it the most widely representative pattern, combining elements from Leningrad and the periphery.[14]

What was new in Moscow, and in Moscow it was concentrated in a unique way in the USSR, were the new mass-production industries geared to transportation and communications: auto, truck and bus, train, plane, and bicycle, as well as electrical engineering. All these branches of the economy required a much enlarged machine-tool industry to support them, which was also established in Moscow during the 1930s, making it the rival of Leningrad in machine construction. The social impact of this industrialization process was striking, as a new culture of industrial relations evolved fusing peasants and women in a Moscow melting pot.

Moscow was at the cutting edge of social transition throughout the Soviet Union, due not only to its dramatic peasant in-migration, but also to the influx of both urban and rural women into its new metalworking industries. The social wedge opening the way for both the peasant-proletarian and women, was youth, that is, mostly unmarried young men and women. Young people, peasants and/or women, were more readily accepted by the established workers than the peasant *muzhik* or the urban married woman. They were also more adaptable by virtue of their primary and secondary education, which gave them literacy and numeracy, their lack of other commitments and family obligations, and their limited life experience and the energy and enthusiasm of youth. The latter factors made them especially tolerant of harsh working conditions.

Virtually all of them would marry in the city, and quite possibly the majority of them would marry partners whom they first met at work, or schoolmates or village mates with whom they entered the factory, in the "class" of 1930, or 1931, or 1932. This cohort of young adults was pivotal in the social transformation of the industrialization-collectivization drive throughout the USSR and was the key to its qualified success by 1941. In Moscow, these new workers would adapt most rapidly, establishing unionwide patterns, as the process of adaptation on the shop floor was shaped in critical new ways by the new mass production industries.

In these new industries, apprenticeships were unnecessary and even unwieldy, while short training and retraining sessions were a constant necessity. The new jobs resembled the existing work culture of the female textile workers of the CIR more closely than that of either the peasant-proletarian (of the periphery) or the labor aristocrat (of Leningrad). Like weavers and spinners in a textile mill, the new assembly-line jobs were semiskilled and were the most highly specialized occupations in Soviet industry, requiring very close coordination and cooperation within the work teams and between them, and requiring individuals who were punctual and responsible. Such was the new work culture that was developing in Moscow's industrial showcase, the Proletarian District, which came to be symbolized by the ZiS auto plant and "Fordism," which in the Soviet context simply meant the assembly line.

Why the Proletarian District?

Even before the First FYP, the party had adopted the slogan of transforming the city from "calico Moscow" (*Moskva sitsevaia*) into "metal
Moscow" (*Moskva metallicheskaia*).[15] That slogan was appropriate, not only because Moscow industry had been dominated by textiles, but also because its
large factories and small shops were scattered in patchwork fashion throughout the city. Historically, Moscow had never developed distinctly industrial
districts with working-class communities like Vyborg and Narva in St. Petersburg.[16] Instead, its largest textile factories and metalworking plants were distributed around the city, interspersed among thousands of artisan shops and
small manufactories. The one major exception was the Presnaia District, a
Moscow working-class community and factory district that became famous
for its role during the December 1905 uprising.

In October 1917, Moscow's major industrial establishments, were distributed around the city, almost all of them located beyond the Garden Ring
(see map 1).

On the western side of Moscow, in Red Presnaia District (Krasno-Presnenskii Raion), were the giant Prokhorovskaia textile plant (also known as
the Trekhgornaia Manufaktura), the Shmit and Mamontov textile mills, and
the Grachev and the Sakharnyi factories. On the city's northern side were the
Dukes, Dukat, and Kramer factories, Shelkovaia Manufaktura, the Krasnyi
Bogatyr plant, the Sokolniki Tram Park, and the five major railway stations,
which all employed considerable numbers of repairmen as well as transport
workers. These five railway stations, the Aleksandrovskii, Vindavskii, Niko-
laevskii, Iaroslavskii, and Kazan, were within the third zone of Moscow, just
beyond the Garden Ring. Together with the Kursk, Kiev, and Saratov stations
on the east, south, and west, and also just beyond the Garden Ring, these stations were all linked by subway in 1954. (See maps 1 and 2.)

The least populated and least developed districts, in terms of urban in-
frastructure, lay on the eastern edge of the city. In the Baumanskii (formerly
Basmanyi) and Rogozhsko-Simonovskii Districts (in April 1929 renamed the
Proletarskii or Proletarian District), were the Kursk railway station, the Zolo-
torozhskii Tram Park, the Mars factory, and three important factories, the
Guzhon plant (renamed Serp i Molot or Hammer and Sickle in 1922); the
Westinghouse plant, nationalized and renamed Dinamo during the First
World War; and the Moscow Auto Association plant, or AMO, renamed ZiS,
or the Stalin plant on 1 October 1931 (after 1956, called ZiL, the Likhachev
plant). In 1917, as in 1905, these city districts were still considered semiur-
ban factory suburbs.

On the southern edge of the city, just beyond the Garden Ring, were the

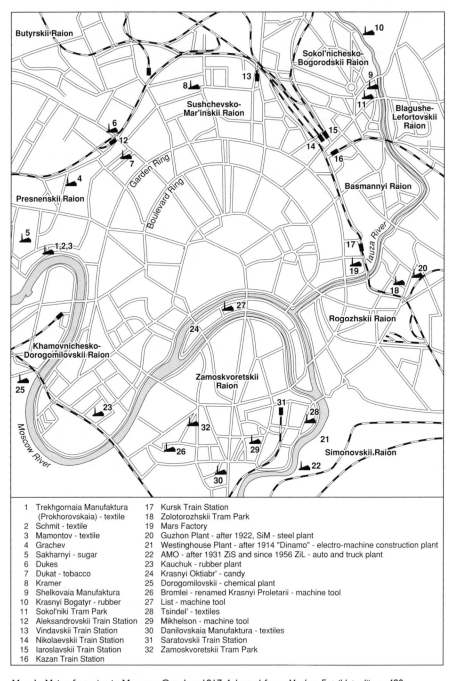

Butyrskii Raion

Sokol'nichesko-
Bogorodskii Raion

10

9

8

13

Sushchevsko-
Mar'inskii Raion

11

Blagushe-
Lefortovskii
Raion

6

12

15

7

14

16

4

Presnenskii Raion

Basmannyi Raion

5

Garden Ring

Boulevard Ring

17

Iauza River

1,2,3

19

20

18

27

Rogozhskii Raion

24

Khamovnichesko-
Dorogomilovskii Raion

25

Zamoskvoretskii
Raion

31

23

28

32

21

Moscow River

26

29

Simonovskii Raion

22

30

1 Trekhgornaia Manufaktura (Prokhorovskaia) - textile	17 Kursk Train Station
2 Schmit - textile	18 Zolotorozhskii Tram Park
3 Mamontov - textile	19 Mars Factory
4 Grachev	20 Guzhon Plant - after 1922, SiM - steel plant
5 Sakharnyi - sugar	21 Westinghouse Plant - after 1914 "Dinamo" - electro-machine construction plant
6 Dukes	22 AMO - after 1931 ZiS and since 1956 ZiL - auto and truck plant
7 Dukat - tobacco	23 Kauchuk - rubber plant
8 Kramer	24 Krasnyi Oktiabr' - candy
9 Shelkovaia Manufaktura	25 Dorogomilovskii - chemical plant
10 Krasnyi Bogatyr - rubber	26 Bromlei - renamed Krasnyi Proletarii - machine tool
11 Sokol'niki Tram Park	27 List - machine tool
12 Aleksandrovskii Train Station	28 Tsindel' - textiles
13 Vindavskii Train Station	29 Mikhelson - machine tool
14 Nikolaevskii Train Station	30 Danilovskaia Manufaktura - textiles
15 Iaroslavskii Train Station	31 Saratovskii Train Station
16 Kazan Train Station	32 Zamoskvoretskii Tram Park

Map 1. Major factories in Moscow, October 1917. Adapted from *Moskva Entsiklopediia*, p. 480.

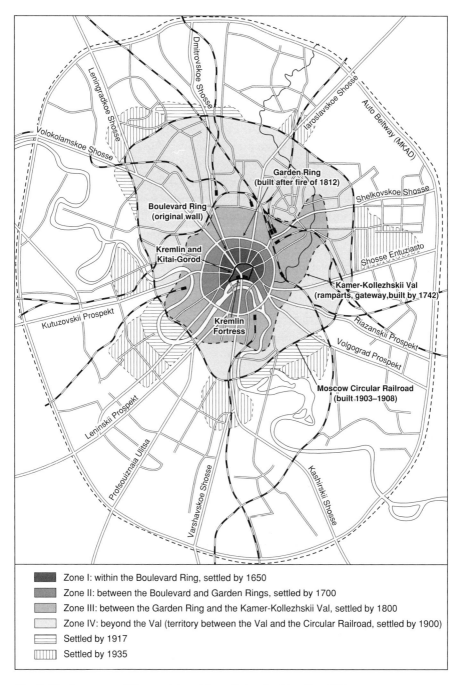

Map 2. The four zones of Moscow. Adapted from *Moskva Entsiklopediia*, p. 218.

Zone I: within the Boulevard Ring, settled by 1650

Zone II: between the Boulevard and Garden Rings, settled by 1700

Zone III: between the Garden Ring and the Kamer-Kollezhskii Val, settled by 1800

Zone IV: beyond the Val (territory between the Val and the Circular Railroad, settled by 1900)

Settled by 1917

Settled by 1935

Kauchuk rubber plant, the confectioners' factory (renamed Krasnaia Oktiabr'), and the Dorogomilovskii chemical plant. Further south, in the Zamoskvoretskii and Danilovskii Districts, were the Bromlei (later Krasnyi Proletarii), List, Tsindel', and Mikhel'son machine-building plants, and also the giant Danilovskaia Manufaktura textile works.[17]

The three large plants located in the PR already dominated many aspects of community life by 1917, when it was a sparsely settled, isolated district notable for its dirt roads, shanty dwellings, and semirural outlying districts. A French-born industrialist whose father, Peter Guzhon, had built a textile plant in Moscow, Iulii Guzhon moved to Russia in 1870 and opened the Guzhon plant in 1883. At the outset, it produced iron and manufactured nails, wire, and other iron products, monopolizing the Moscow market for iron products. By 1905, the Guzhon plant was known as a center both of the Zubatov police unions and of considerable strike activity. In 1917, a Guzhon worker, Astakhov, perished in a skirmish in the February Revolution leading a crowd across the bridge connecting Rogozhskii-Simonovskii to the central districts of Moscow. The plant began producing steel after 1905.[18]

The Westinghouse plant, built at the turn of the century, specialized in manufacturing electrical motors. AMO, founded by the Riabushinskii family and other industrialists and bankers, was designed and partially constructed during the First World War. It performed some repair work on Latvian-built cars after the Revolution, but only in 1924 did it produce the first Soviet-made car, the AMO-F-15.[19]

The outer districts were a social mixing ground, home to artisans, factory workers, and a large and annually fluctuating population of peasant-migrants who were legally distinguished as peasants, that is as members of the fourth estate. They were required to hold passports to work in the city until 1906, whereas many artisans and a few workers were legally more privileged as members of the third estate, that is, as "city dwellers." The symbiosis of peasant and proletarian shaped a distinct culture in these districts by 1900, which was architecturally reflected in the winding and narrow streets and the cupolas of thousands of churches, establishing Moscow's reputation as an over-enlarged village.[20] During NEP, the peasant-proletarians of the city's outer districts may already have been yielding to a more stable industrial proletarian. A key indicator of this was the shift in gender balance, from a heavily male to a slightly female majority by 1926. Also important was the proliferation of the urban proletarian family. It is possible that a decline in *otkhod,* or seasonal migration, accounts for these shifts, but it is more likely that the subdivision of middle-class and upper-class housing into tiny communal apartment units, the construction of some new housing in the city after 1921, and the demographic consequences of the First World War and the Civil War

(1914–21), with the disproportionate number of male deaths and with the temporary depopulation of Moscow, were equal if not more important factors.[21]

Another shift was from *kustar* and *remeslo* to large-scale factories. Artisan and cottage industry, with four or fewer hired workers, comprised over half the Moscow work force in 1912, but by 1926, it accounted for less than 10 percent of Moscow manufacturing workers.[22] By 1929, according to the standard Soviet account, large-scale industry employed 220,000 of almost 300,000 total industrial workers in Moscow.[23] Regardless of these claims, it seems likely that artisan and small-scale manufacturing were not disappearing in Moscow prior to 1928, but were growing less rapidly than large industry. It is obvious, however, that a decisive transformation took place during the industrialization drive of the First FYP. Occupational data for 1933 show, for small-scale manufacturing, only 76,200 *kustary* (of which 70,000 were employed in coops) as compared to 823,400 factory workers, an additional 437,600 white-collar employees (some employed in factories), and a further 214,600 MOP, or junior service personnel. The data also show a sharp increase in the ratio of employed to dependents.[24]

The changes came most dramatically in zones 3 and 4, with the SiM, Dinamo, and AMO factories just on the border between the two (see map 2). As population figures in table 2.1 show, zone 4, the city's outermost zone, saw the greatest absolute and relative increase in population from 1926 through 1933. Zone 3, between the Garden Ring and the Val, came second.

Furthermore, population in the sparsely settled eastern and southern districts of the city grew extremely rapidly, especially in the new industrial districts, created in December 1930 (see map 3).[25] The two eastern industrializing districts, the Stalinskii and the Proletarskii, doubled in population from 1928 to 1934, and density in the Proletarskii approached the Moscow-wide figure at the end of the First FYP (see table 2.2).

Table 2.1. Moscow Population and Density, 1912–33

	1912		1926		1931		1933	
	Pop.	Dens.	Pop.	Dens.	Pop.	Dens.	Pop.	Dens.
All Moscow	1616.4	92	2025.9	87	2781.3	109	3416.5	120
Zone One	148.4	244	210.4	347	295.1	486	318.1	524
Zone Two	345.4	262	486.1	369	590.7	448	659.2	50
Zone Three	789.1	153	932.0	180	1162.1	225	1340.3	259
Zone Four	333.5	32	397.4	24	733.4	40	1098.9	51

Source: Moskva v Tsifrakh (1934), p. 9.
Note: Population figures are in 1,000s; density in persons per hectare.

The population of the PR was already disproportionately working class in 1928, when it was one of the city's six *raiony* (consolidated from ten by 1922), but this discrepancy became much more pronounced during the First FYP, when it became one of the city's ten *raiony*. (See map 3.)

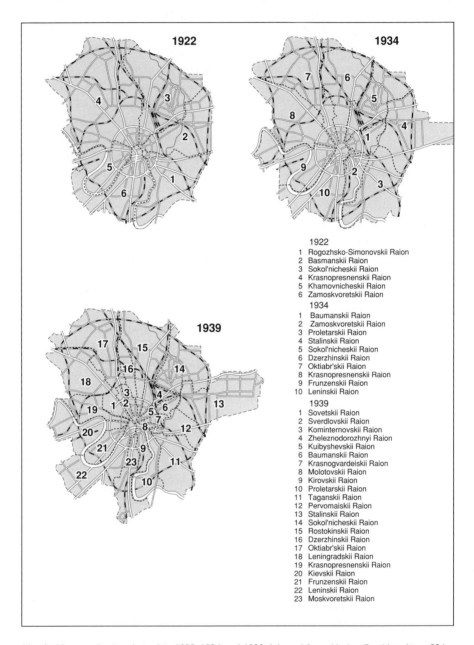

1922
1 Rogozhsko-Simonovskii Raion
2 Basmanskii Raion
3 Sokol'nicheskii Raion
4 Krasnopresnenskii Raion
5 Khamovnicheskii Raion
6 Zamoskvoretskii Raion

1934
1 Baumanskii Raion
2 Zamoskvoretskii Raion
3 Proletarskii Raion
4 Stalinskii Raion
5 Sokol'nicheskii Raion
6 Dzerzhinskii Raion
7 Oktiabr'skii Raion
8 Krasnopresnenskii Raion
9 Frunzenskii Raion
10 Leninskii Raion

1939
1 Sovetskii Raion
2 Sverdlovskii Raion
3 Kominternovskii Raion
4 Zheleznodorozhnyi Raion
5 Kuibyshevskii Raion
6 Baumanskii Raion
7 Krasnogvardeiskii Raion
8 Molotovskii Raion
9 Kirovskii Raion
10 Proletarskii Raion
11 Taganskii Raion
12 Pervomaiskii Raion
13 Stalinskii Raion
14 Sokol'nicheskii Raion
15 Rostokinskii Raion
16 Dzerzhinskii Raion
17 Oktiabr'skii Raion
18 Leningradskii Raion
19 Krasnopresnenskii Raion
20 Kievskii Raion
21 Frunzenskii Raion
22 Leninskii Raion
23 Moskvoretskii Raion

Map 3. Moscow districts (*raiony*) in 1922, 1934, and 1939. Adapted from *Moskva Entsiklopediia*, p. 536.

Table 2.2. Moscow Population and Density, 1 January 1928–34

District	Population		Density	
	1928	1933	1934	1934
All Moscow	2,167.3	3,663.3	3,613.6	126.7
Leninskii	256.1	436.4	419.9	105.8
Frunzenskii	295.1	497.3	492.6	175.2
Krasno-Presnenskii	276.2	466.6	449.9	130.9
Oktiabr'skii	203.1	379.2	387.2	94.6
Dzerzhinskii	260.9	403.6	397.1	109.2
Sokol'nicheskii	234.3	365.7	360.8	144.2
Baumanskii	248.9	360.4	359.1	391.6
Stalinskii	112.7	259.8	257.1	69.2
Zamoskvoretskii	138.4	197.7	205.3	253.0
Proletarskii	141.6	296.6	284.6	108.3

Source: Moskva v Tsifrakh (1934), p. 12.
Note: Population figures are in 1,000s; density in persons per hectare.

In Moscow as a whole, the percentage of workers increased in the First FYP from 31.6 percent to 39 percent, while in the PR it increased from 37.9 percent to 58 percent.[26] In the PR, metalworking was the dominant employer, accounting for 36 percent of the district's total industrial output in 1929/30. Of the metalworking output, 24.7 percent was in machine construction. By 1932, this had increased dramatically to 59.6 percent and 41.3 percent respectively.[27] No other district had a comparable base in metal industries in 1929, and none expanded as rapidly by 1932. The closest was the Krasno-Presnenskii District, which had 23.8 percent of its industrial output in metalworking in 1929/30 (18.8 percent in machine construction), and expanded to 39.1 percent in 1932 (26.1 percent in machine construction).[28]

Moscow remained a city of scattered factories from all branches of industry even in 1933, but the PR was unique. During the First FYP, its old and new plants were integrated into a new type of industrial network, making it the leading center of heavy industry in Moscow. Building around the original triangle of SiM, AMO-ZiS, and Dinamo, which all underwent fundamental reconstruction, more than a dozen new plants were constructed, and several other new factories built outside the city or in other districts of the city were vertically integrated with these three and the other new factories of the PR.

All three plants had pioneered the application of western technology in Imperial Russia, and in the First FYP they were, once again, expected to play the role of technological innovators in the USSR. SiM was fundamentally reconstructed so as to become the leading producer of special, high-quality steel alloys and was primarily a supplier for the auto and machine construction plants of the PR and for the Moscow Railroad Administration and the Moscow Metro construction.[29] Dinamo was substantially enlarged, to become the major producer of motors for trams and trolleybuses. The AMO plant, which still resembled a large artisan shop when it produced the AMO-F-15 in 1924, went on to become the first Soviet plant to adopt Fordism. It served as a prototype for assembly-line work in other auto plants and in other industries in the USSR, manufacturing 1,100 vehicles by 1930, 15,052 large cars and 97 buses in 1932, and over 65,000 trucks and 4,000 cars in 1938.[30] The expansion of AMO-ZiS was the most dramatic of the three plants, but SiM and Dinamo also more than doubled in size and in output. SiM expanded from twelve to eighty-two hectares during the First FYP.[31] The capital fund of AMO-ZiS grew from 10 to 87 million, of SiM from 20 to 41 million, and of Dinamo from 7.5 to 27 million between 1 October 1928 and 1 January 1934.[32] Their output as measured in the ruble-inflated figures in table 2.3 gives a rough measure of the scale of the enlargement.

These three plants were linked to each other and to more than a dozen new plants through classical, vertical, cartel-type arrangements. Thus, for example, new, high-quality steel and steel alloys needed for making ball bearings, motor vehicles, and calibrated steel were to be supplied by SiM. ZiS alone needed 133,000 tons of specialty steels, including 48,000 tons of steel sections, 20,000 tons of calibrated steel, and 65,000 tons of steel sheet.[33] The airplane motor factory and the Kaganovich ball bearing plant, newly built in the PR, needed even more steel.[34] So did the Moscow metro, the Moscow railroads, Elektrozavod, Velozavod, and factories in other cities.[35] The Kaganovich ball bearing plant, in turn, would supply the AMO-ZiS auto plant with ball bearings for its vehicles. Dinamo would supply motors and parts for trolleys and trams that were assembled in plants outside Moscow and would

Table 2.3. Three PR Factories: Net Value of Output
(in 1,000s of rubles)

	1927/28	1933	1932 % of 1927	1933 % of 1932
AMO-ZiS	10,154	265,557	1,929.4	135.5
SiM	22,654	82,630	330.9	108.2
Dinamo	8,735	58,831	570.5	118.1

Source: Moskva v Tsifrakh (1934), pp. 56–57.
Note: Even though inflation had reduced the value of the ruble by roughly one-half between 1927 and 1933 these figures still show a substantial increase in output.

supply some motors for the machines and assembly lines of neighboring plants. AMO-ZiS relied on its own machine shops to produce many of its tools, equipment, and workbenches, as well as components for its vehicles. A considerable number of its machines were supplied by neighboring plants, however, and some parts came from its filial plant in the PR.

New plants under construction or completed in the First FYP in the PR included the Aviamotornyi Zavod, which manufactured airplane engines; the Velozavod, manufacturing bicycles; and the Kaganovich First State Ball Bearing Plant (GPZ-1). Work began at the construction site at the swampy waste near the Peasant Gateway in 1929 for the latter. In September 1931, the first of the plant's shops went into operation, and on 29 March 1932, construction of the plant was completed.[36] The net output of the Kaganovich plant by 1933 was 81,892 thousand rubles, or just less than the net output for SiM that year.[37] In addition, the Parastroi plant, the Moskabel', the Elektro-provod, the Kompressor plant, and the Voitovich plant all employed more than one thousand workers by 1936 and were all either newly constructed or substantially enlarged during the First FYP.[38] Also located in the PR were the Bauman Kombinat, with its laboratory for scientific research in iron casting and blacksmith forging, and KIM, the Komsomol auto plant, which began manufacturing "light" vehicles in Moscow in the later 1930s, the prototype for the postwar "Moskvich," or small passenger car.[39] (See map 4.)

Situated outside the PR, but directly involved in the production process of many of its plants, were two large new factories that would cut and calibrate metal. The metal-cutting plant Frezer stood farther out along the southeast corridor, on a commuter line, in the new industrial suburb of Liubertsy, where an agricultural machine-construction factory was also located; the Kalibr plant was constructed in the Stalinskii District, in the city's northeastern quadrant.[40] These two plants went into operation on the first of May 1932 and July 1932, respectively.[41] The net output of the Frezcr plant was 14,987 thousand rubles and of the Kalibr plant was 5,153 thousand rubles. In the First FYP, investment in six plants exceeded 20,000 rubles in this network.[42]

The PR was apparently slated to become Moscow's new "high-tech" zone, manufacturing cars, planes, bikes, buses, and other mass-production, assembly-line products. These products were primarily for use in public civilian transportation, although the factories all had military departments as well. Not only were the products new in the USSR, but so were the production techniques, in particular the assembly line. Such techniques would be replicated in new plants, often larger ones, on the periphery. I suggest that the PR was "apparently" slated to be Moscow's new high-tech zone, because the available records from the discussions on planning for the "socialist recon-

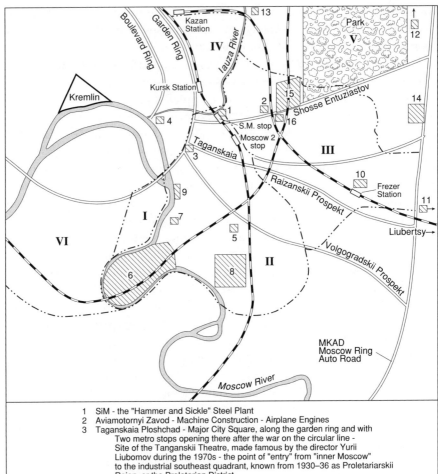

1   SiM - the "Hammer and Sickle" Steel Plant
2   Aviamotornyi Zavod - Machine Construction - Airplane Engines
3   Taganskaia Ploshchad - Major City Square, along the garden ring and with
        Two metro stops opening there after the war on the circular line -
        Site of the Tanganskii Theatre, made famous by the director Yurii
        Liubomov during the 1970s - the point of "entry" from "inner Moscow"
        to the industrial southeast quadrant, known from 1930–36 as Proletariarskii
        Raion, or the Proletarian District
4   One of the Seven Stalin "Tall Buildings" or Skyscrapers, known as the
        Kotelnicheskaia Building from its Location at the Kotelnicheskaia
        Embankement, at the juncture of the Iauza and Moskva Rivers
        - The Building was completed by 1952, and would serve as an office
        Building with hotel rooms
5   GPZ-1 The Kaganovich First State Ballbearing Plant - Sharikopodshipnik Zavod
6   ZiS The Stalin Auto Plant (formerly AMO, now ZiL)
7   Torpedo Stadium, Simonov Monastery, ZiS Palace of Culture
8   KIM (Kommunist Youth Plant), today Moskvich Auto Plant
9   Dinamo Factory
10 Frezer Factory
11 Agricultural Machine Construction Factory in Liubertsy
12 Kalibr Factory
13 Elektrozavod im. Kuibsheva - manufactured transformers
14 Novogireevo Housing Settlement of SiM workers
15 Sokolinaia Gora Housing Settlement of SiM workers
16 Dangauerovka Housing Settlement of SiM and other workers

Map 4. The PR factory network. Adapted from *Moskva Organizatsiia Dvizheniia Transporta na Osnovnykh Magistraliakh i Ulitsakh Goroda (v Predelakh MKAD)* (Moscow, 1987).

KEY TO MAP 4   I = Zamoskvoretskii Raion (renamed Kirovskii in 1934)   IV = Baumanskii Raion

II = Proletarskii Raion   V = Sokolnicheskii Raion

III = Stalinskii Raion   VI = Leninskii Raion struction of Moscow" from 1931 to 1935 indicate nothing about this at all.

The evolution of the "Plan for Reconstruction of Moscow" over these four years is recounted in the official *History of Moscow* which describes the institutions involved in the Plan and discusses the three plan variants that were abandoned.[43] These variants were Le Corbusier's "new city," to be located somewhere beyond the Moscow city limits in the Moscow Province hinterlands (which would have left old Moscow intact, as a "city-museum"); the "urban-giant" variant, in which Moscow would be completely rebuilt where it was and would be distinguished by surpassing all the capitalist capitals in population and size; and the "disurbanist" variant, in which the city of Moscow would expand over 200 square kilometers, with most of the city's inhabitants living in new two-story cottages, spread out at enormous distances.[44] As we will see below, three similar options for reconstruction had already been debated at SiM in 1929–30, and the option of reconstructing the existing factory *in situ*, while tripling its capacity, was the one chosen. Ironically, this was what happened to Moscow also, over the next forty years, although it was not supposed to according to the plan.

The "Plan for Reconstruction," as finally adopted by a resolution of the Council of People's Commissars (Sovnarkom, SNK) and the Central Committee of the Communist Party (TsK VKP[b]), dated 10 July 1935 stated: "It is essential that Moscow preserve its basic historical formation as a city, but with fundamental replanning of its transportation and decisive setting in order of its network of city streets and squares."[45] The city was to preserve its radial-ring layout, new construction was to expand the city toward the southwest (Lenin Hills) and the south (from Kuntsevo toward Lenino, formerly Tsaritsyno), but for housing only, and the size of the city was to increase from 28.5 thousand hectares to 60,000. Over the ten years in which the plan envisioned reconstruction of Moscow, no new industrial enterprises were to be constructed within the already overcrowded city, and a 5 million person limit was established.[46] Most of the new territory was to serve as a green zone surrounding the city. In fact, however, this green zone began to disappear even during the later 1930s, as both housing and enterprise construction encroached on it, and it disappeared altogether between the 1950s and 1980s, when the city grew out to the limits of the MKAD, the beltway constructed in 1960. All that was left of the green zone was the Izmailogo Park, formerly the Stalin Park. The population of the city would, by the 1980s, reach 10 million.

While the plan envisioned widening the central boulevards, doubling the expanse of Red Square, tearing down small-scale older buildings to make room for the Palace of Soviets, the greatest monument of all was never built, and instead, after the Second World War, the seven skyscrapers went up along the Garden Ring. Thus, as with Magnitogorsk, the plan had a strange life, both shaping and yet not really corresponding to the structure of the new "socialist city."[47]

More important for this study, neither the 1935 plan nor any published discussion of plan variants that I have been able to locate, envisaged an integrated network of factories in the PR. It appears to have happened haphazardly, after the political interventions of the Red Directors in 1929 and 1930, Stepanov at SiM and Likhachev at ZiS, resulted in the decisions to undertake major reconstruction of these two factories. It is my impression that, at least initially, individual decisions were taken on the original factory triangle, SiM, Dinamo, and AMO, but that, at some point during the First FYP, the decision to build a network of complementary and vertically integrated factories in the PR must have been taken by Moscow planners in conjunction with the Commissariat of Economics (VSNKh) and other commissariats.

Likewise, attempting to apply experience from Moscow's pilot plants to new satellite plants on the Soviet periphery was at least initially adopted as an ad hoc or improvised measure. It resembled the classical pattern of capitalist horizontal cartels, by which a few giants swallowed up competitors and then used the newly purchased factories to produce, for example, new car models. Soviet horizontal integration, as improvised during the First FYP, was the basis for the much more massive satellite system adopted during the Great Fatherland War, when the contents of entire factories were evacuated from the industrial northwest, the CIR, and the Donbass, to the Urals and Western Siberia, where satellite factory shells were being built. This closely resembled patterns of cartelization associated with the second Industrial Revolution, in particular the German and American patterns in the last decades of the nineteenth century.[48] Whether there was an initial plan, or as seems more likely, such a plan took shape only after the decisions were made to massively reconstruct SiM, ZiS, and Dinamo, the factories of the PR became Moscow's most advanced and newly integrated industrial high-tech zone.[49]

SiM: "To Be or Not to Be a Factory?"[50]

In 1928/29 there was a furiously contested debate over whether or not to reconstruct SiM at its Moscow location. Some important officials in the higher administration and engineers at SiM were against that option, arguing on technological and economic grounds that the plant was obsolete and should be shut down. The Red Director, Petr Fedorovich Stepanov, led the charge in favor of massive reconstruction *in situ*. A similar and equally acrimonious debate was raging at the neighboring AMO auto plant, where the Red Director, Ivan Alekseevich Likhachev, took the same position as Stepanov.

Such conflicts directly pressed on all the raw nerves of the Stalinist regime, since they involved making large decisions on investments when funds were very scarce, all the while depending on the recommendations of old regime or foreign specialists who were considered to be politically unreliable. Suspected of attempting to hide their anti-Soviet politics behind technical imperatives or economic expertise, such specialists were frequently scapegoated for industrial catastrophes not of their making, and their sound advice was often disregarded.[51]

According to the Stalinist regime, the reconstruction of plants such as SiM and AMO-ZiS depended, first and foremost, on victory over the "class enemies" who would have supposedly sabotaged these efforts. In other words, reconstruction was dependent on the class struggle, which meant mobilizing the working class for a revolutionary assault. Once reconstructed, these plants were held up as unionwide symbols of autonomous socialist industrialization. This scenario was played out at SiM and AMO in 1929 and 1930, when the priorities of the regime and of the Red Directors and the factory work collectives were aligned.

The conflict over investment resources at SiM began from the day Stepanov arrived there as Red Director, on 15 April 1925. By October 1925, Stepanov had asked Mashtrest (the Machine Construction Trust), Glavmetal (the Glavk or branch administration, responsible for metal industries), and VSNKh, the agencies above the factory in the chain of economic command, to allocate investment funds and materials to rebuild the antiquated rolling mill shop at SiM. He was bitterly disappointed in 1925 and 1926, when no funds were released for this reconstruction. In fact, prior to 1928/29, investment at SiM was inconsequential, and was limited to making relatively minor improvements in working conditions. There was no overall reconstruction, nor was there a plan for it.[52]

A factory census taken in 1927 showed that the plant was badly in need of new machinery in most shops. As of 1 October 1927, on the average for all the plant's shops, 36.7 percent of the capital stock was worn out. The situation was worse in the three most important shops for smelting and processing steel for autos, planes, and the new high-tech industries. In the open hearth shop, 45.1 percent of the equipment was exhausted, in the rolling steel shop 41.5 percent, and in the press shop 41.6 percent.[53]

Furthermore, figures for 1927/28 showed that steel accounted for only 4.5 percent of the plant's total output, and in 1928/29 for 7.9 percent.[54] Thus, SiM was still mainly producing nails, wire, and other iron products, in which the Guzhon plant had specialized. This plant, like so many Soviet plants by the later 1920s, was at a crossroads. Its capital stock was exhausted and had to be replaced. Either it would be reconstructed to meet the demands of modern machine-tool and mass-production industries for steel, or it would be shut down and replaced.

The administrative infighting over the reconstruction of SiM turned political in 1928 and especially in 1929, just as the conflict within the Politburo between the Stalin group and the Right Opposition spilled out into the open. Stepanov, facing stiff opposition from Mashtrest and Gipromez (the State Institute for Design of Metallurgy Plants), and also from many of his specialist subordinates in the plant, would make his case for the total reconstruction of SiM *in situ*, working with two rising young party stars in the plant, Sergei Filatov and E. I. Gaidul.' They would seize the upper hand against his opponents, labeling them the "liquidators." This was effective, not only in aligning his group with the Stalin faction, but also in mobilizing popular support within the plant.

The liquidator label was pinned on List and Sattel' in Mashtrest and also on Mattis and Babadzhan, two leading engineers at SiM. Most important, it was pinned on Veitsman, the technical director of Gipromez. They were allegedly connected to Bukharin and the Right Oppositionist leadership of the Moscow Party Committee (Gorkom), under the first secretary, Uglanov, in 1929. In the Rogozhsko-Simonovskii *raikom* (district party committee), the party secretary, Pen'kov, along with the secretary of the SiM *partkom* (party committee at the factory), Bogatyrev, were considered to be Uglanov's men and were alleged to have opposed the reconstruction of the SiM plant, joined with these so-called "liquidator" specialists and administrators.[55] Actually, these so-called Right Oppositionists and liquidator specialists who favored closing the plant and building a new one were closer to what we would usually think of as the Stalinist strategy rather than the Bukharinist.

By the summer of 1929, the conflict came to a head around three alternative designs for SiM that were presented for a type of public debate in the factory. The first proposal, and the one supported by Stepanov, was to reconstruct SiM at its existing location, converting it into a producer of high-quality steels for the machine-tool and metalworking industries. The second was to shut SiM and replace it as quickly as possible with a modern steel plant somewhere in Moscow Province but well outside the city. The third variant was also to build the new plant outside Moscow, but to keep the old SiM open until the new plant went on-line.[56] This debate foreshadowed the debate over reconstructing Moscow, and the resolution would be the same.

The "liquidators" were so labeled because they supported the second or the third variants, which would lead to shutting down the plant in the city. They argued that SiM was obsolete and worn out, and that building a new plant would be more economical because it would allow for a rational layout between shops; mechanized and continuous flow operations would replace the haphazard arrangement of shops that had grown up in the old Guzhon plant. Rational work flow between shops could never be achieved by reconstructing the old plant, they argued. They also argued that transporting the iron ore and coke that SiM needed was already a burden on the Moscow rail network and would become a still greater burden if the factory were expanded. Furthermore, the plant would need a new water supply in order to increase its output.

These latter objections were part of the more general concern about the SiM plant and the ecology and infrastructure of Moscow. The factory was located too close to the center of the city and would become an obstacle to residential development as the city population increased and strain the infrastructure as the city expanded. At the time, they emphasized the immediate problem that there was no way, without canalization, to get enough water from the Iauza River to supply an enlarged steel plant.[57] However, their long-term concern was that reconstruction *in situ* would damage the quality of air in PR, using valuable space near the city center in ways that were both uneconomical and antiecological. Building outside the city would avoid these problems and at the same time permit rational layout of the plant.

Today, these objections seem so reasonable that it is hard to understand how public opinion could have been swayed to believe that the opponents were "liquidators" and, indeed, "wreckers," as they were soon to be labeled by the Stalinists. Not only did these objections anticipate environmental concerns about SiM in the late 1980s, when the population, and especially the workers who lived nearby, had already suffered the ill effects of sixty years of air pollution, but they anticipated that the plant would eventually be an obstacle to neighborhood development, occupying scarce land and using scarce energy and water resources in what would be prime real estate in Moscow. Environmentalists, in 1989, described the plant as "Magnitka on the Garden Ring," invoking Magnitogorsk and its Metallurgical Combine as the symbol of ecological destruction and highlighting the irrationality of reconstructing a giant steel plant so near to the center of the sprawling metropolis.[58]

Furthermore, and what is most remarkable, the "liquidators" were actually much closer to the Stalin line than to the Bukharin line in at least one important respect. Stalin, Ordzhonikidze, Kaganovich, and other leading figures of the industrialization drive advocated building new plants on the largest scale in the world and with the most modern technology rather than utilizing the old plant more extensively or with partial reconstruction of the old plant. Bukharin and his supporters, on the other hand, argued in favor of squeezing the maximum use out of the existing plant and, where possible, adding new shops onto the existing plants.[59] In the case of Moscow's SiM, however, it would seem that these positions were reversed. The Stalinists rallied behind Stepanov, whose reconstruction *in situ* strategy was justified in terms of transforming "calico Moscow" into "metal Moscow," while the "liquidators" were linked to the "calico committee."

The same resolution was adopted in the plans to reconstruct Moscow. By 1935, the Stalin team, led by Kaganovich and Khrushchev, adopted the "Plan for Reconstruction of Moscow" that halted new factory construction and called for a park zone surrounding the entire city. One might have expected that, instead, from the "calico committee," except that by 1935, there was no such party committee left in Moscow. The 1935 plan's moratorium on new enterprise construction seems to have reflected the hiatus in the aftermath of the chaos of the First FYP, and it was soon violated. Thus, Moscow would be expanded simply by adding on to the original city, (geographic expansion) which was precisely the solution adopted at the SiM plant.

In 1929, for the Stalinists, the environment was not an issue and neither were urban land values. The fact that the plant would damage the health of the factory workers and the population of the PR was simply not considered. To convince the party leadership of the validity of his reconstruction program, Stepanov and his supporters had only to resolve the immediate supply and technical problems of obtaining the necessary iron ore, coke, and water, and of freeing up the city space necessary for reconstruction. Water supply was the most significant problem.

Stepanov's team proposed substituting scrap metal for iron ore, which would prove to be a practical solution in the First FYP; SiM used 277,500 tons of scrap metal in 1930/31 and over 450,000 tons in 1931/32, and the metal came primarily from Moscow and Leningrad. Some iron ore and fuel had to be shipped from the south to SiM, but transporting these supplies into the city did not prove to be an insurmountable problem for the transportation network. Supplying the plant with water was accomplished by building a new pipe directly from the Moscow River to SiM, at a distance of almost one kilometer, thus circumventing the Iauza tributary with its irregular flow and volume of water.[60]

If the plant was to be reconstructed at its existing location, it would need space for expansion. Already it was encroaching on the Kursk Railroad on its western edge and against the Andronnikov Monastery on its eastern edge. On 23 August 1929, the Moscow Soviet allocated lots numbered 1–7 to SiM, blocking any construction by another institution in the area bounded by Shosse Entuziastov, Prolomnyi Proezd, and First Prolomnyi Pereulok.[61] Thus, the issue of space was resolved, and a large modern steel plant would belch smoke into the Moscow sky for the next sixty years. The factory would also dominate the city's horizon around the "Il'ich Square," the public square in the center of this community, where finally in 1979 the metro stop of that name was opened. This connected the SiM factory and community around it on the Kalinskaia Line and made "Il'ich Square" the hub of that part of the city.[62] (See map 5.)

According to the "to be or not to be" document, in the summer of 1929, at several mass meetings at the plant, most of the work collective of 6,000 people demonstrated their support for the first variant and demanded that funds be allocated immediately for the reconstruction of SiM where it stood.[63] On 29 August the secretary of the *partkom* at SiM, Gaidul', spoke at an open meeting for the factory work force, stating that since the capital stock of SiM was worth 16 million rubles, only a "wrecker" could argue for closing down the factory.[64]

However, according to another document, Gaidul' gave this speech on 21 August, with over fifteen hundred workers attending. He attacked the "liquidators," using something like the Miliukov "stupidity or treason" formula: "It could only be either conscious wrecking or stupidity that, under conditions of [establishing a] rapid tempo of industrialization of the country, when the USSR is preparing against an imperialist attack, they pose the question of liquidating and closing the factory, the basic output of which equals 17 million rubles. The party committee of SiM considers this *proekt* [design] to be wrecking."[65] Stepanov spoke in a similar vein, stating: "Four

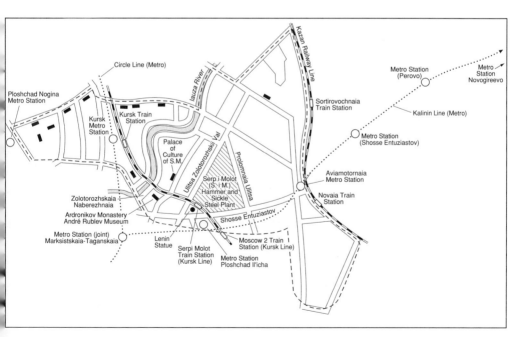

Map 5. The SiM factory and surroundings. Adapted from V. Trofimov, *Moskva: Putevoditel'po Raionam* (Moscow, 1981), pp. 216–17.

years ago we raised the question of retooling the basic shop of the factory—the rolling steel shop—and four years ago they raised the question of closing the plant. At that time, we had an output worth 4 million rubles, but now we have an output worth 19 million." He added that 2.5 million rubles had been invested in the reconstruction of the plant since that time.[66]

Shortly after that meeting Stepanov traveled to Leningrad to argue for reconstructing the plant *in situ*. He met in person with Veitsman, the former director of the Bromlei plant where Stepanov had worked as a machinist and now the technical director of Gipromez, Krutskii, List, and Miliukov (not the Kadet-historian), who had been director of the Podol'skii plant before Stepanov took over as the first Red Director.[67] Thus, a Red Director promoted from proletarian roots was confronting his old bosses and old regime specialists. Stepanov did not win that confrontation in Leningrad, but he would soon win it in a different setting in Moscow.

The archival sources report that the workers who attended the meeting at SiM in August 1929, when Stepanov and Gaidul' made these accusations, gave their unanimous support for the reconstruction of SiM *in situ*. Unanimous or not, some workers wrote an angry letter against the "liquidators" and sent it to the Moscow Party Committee, to the Moscow Soviet, and to VSNKh. The letter, translated here from the archives, was published in *Pravda* at that time.

HALT WRECKING

Of the three proekty [designs], the so-called second, worked out by the Moscow division of Gipromez, foresaw the liquidation of the existing SiM plant. We consider this proekt wrecking. Only counterrevolutionary wreckers or idiots could propose the liquidation of the factory, the basic capital of which is worth 16 million rubles, when the SSSR is preparing for imperialist assault. . . . We welcome the decision of the Moscow Soviet to reject this proekt. . . .

The American engineer and expert, Brandt, who is in charge of the reconstruction of AMO [who would soon be accused of sabotaging its reconstruction like the SiM "liquidators"] toured our plant not long ago and found that the SiM plant is entirely satisfactory, technologically average (not worse than many German and American plants), with the capacity to supply our machine construction and auto construction industries with qualitatively medium- and high-grade metal. Curiously (but facts remain facts!), this American engineer must [now] convince a group of our own [Soviet] engineers that the SiM plant is satisfactory. How do we understand this? How do we interpret the . . . [argument of the] Secretary of the Metalworkers' Union in the Tariff-Economic Sector [who suggested that we let] . . . the factory continue operating until it falls apart? What is going on here? We demand explanations![68]

The secretary of the Moscow Party Committee, V. Polonskii; the president of the Moscow Soviet, K. Ukhanov; and the president of the Moscow branch of VSNKh, Volkov, answered the workers' letter in a conciliatory vein. They established an OKS (Division of Capital Construction) for SiM in September 1929.[69] This would indicate that Stepanov, Gaidul', Filatov, and their supporters were winning the battle, and that the plant would remain in Moscow.

The decisive intervention from above came on 26 November 1929, when Mezhlauk, heading an evaluation committee, announced that SiM would be reconstructed, so that its yearly output of steel would grow to 250,000 tons. The plan that this committee announced included a new open hearth shop, a new model-forging shop, a new smithy, a new calibrating shop, a new repair and mechanic shop, a new laboratory, a materials warehouse, water pipes, compressor, fuel storage tank, and fire department. In December 1929, the president of Mashtrest issued decree no. 2341, stating that "SiM will become the metallurgical basis providing metal for auto and machine construction factories." The OKS was finally set up at SiM in April 1930, with ten bureaus.[70] The battle had been won. The plant would be fundamentally reconstructed at its existing location. While there would be haggling in 1930 and 1931 over funds, the future of the plant was no longer in doubt.

The dénouement for the "liquidators" came early in 1930, when an OGPU investigation described List, Sattel', Mattis, and Babadzhan as "wreckers, who had orders from abroad to conduct counterrevolutionary work in the trust, and at the plant . . . [where] a series of disasters and accidents . . . were the result of wrecking."[71] On 4 March 1930, at a meeting of SiM workers, a resolution was adopted: "Hearing the report of Comrade Krylenko on wrecking in our country, and the joint speech of Comrade Gaidul' on wrecking in our factory, the 7,000 workers of SiM together with engineers and technicians, with feelings of great disgust, condemn the shameful wrecking of Mattis and of his whole counterrevolutionary gang of helpers."[72] That same day, *Martenovka,* the SiM newspaper, ran an article by Gaidul' entitled "We Were Right," attributing the fires of 1925, 1926, and 1927, as well as the explosions at the wire mill of the rolling steel shop in the spring of 1929, to "wrecking."[73]

How the SiM workers and white-collar employees really felt about the issue of rebuilding the plant is impossible to discern from the documents. Common sense would dictate that Soviet workers, like their counterparts under capitalism, would have been unhappy if the plant were shut down, forcing them to relocate outside Moscow in order to work in the new steel plant or to find other jobs in a different factory in the city.[74] In 1929, that was not always so easily done. The work collective may or may not have believed that the specialists were responsible for fires and explosions in this crude but typical instance of specialist baiting. What the documents do clearly show is that Stepanov used this issue and worker discontent over the threat of shutting down the plant to establish his control and to increase his power against superiors and subordinates.

Stepanov and his staff repeatedly justified their case with the alleged economic advantages of preserving existing capital stock at SiM, and they deemphasized the problems of making it modern. A capital stock valued at 16 million rubles was not negligible, and the new investment of more than 36 million rubles during the First FYP only roughly doubled the existing capital stock.[75] However, the fact that the plant was to be converted into a producer of special steel alloys requiring new machinery might suggest that a more economical decision would have been to operate two plants—the older SiM *in situ* and a new plant outside the city. The archives and the plant newspaper, in any case, show how a new circle of young Stalinist party officials and managers at the plant and in the PR coalesced around the issue of reconstruction of SiM, politicized it, and brought about the triumph of the Red Director.

Writing in 1931 as secretary of the *partkom*, Sergei Filatov argued that SiM had to be immediately reconstructed on a large scale, both because it would liberate the Soviet Union from expensive foreign imports and because it would supply VATO (All-Union Auto and Tractor Combine) and its plants with the sheet metal and shaped metal parts that they needed. AMO, for example, was supposed to get 50 percent of its sheet and shaped steel from SiM in 1931. The Iaroslavl' auto plant and the VATO No. 2 plant were supposed to receive about 1,500 tons of very fine sheet metal and about 2,000 tons of magnesium and carbide steel castings. For 1932, AMO and the Nizhni Novgorod auto plant (GAZ) were supposed to receive a total of 25,000 tons of high-quality calibrated metals.[76]

Thus, the large-scale reconstruction that Filatov had in mind was only to be completed in 1931 and 1932, because not much had been accomplished in 1929/30 and the special quarter declared for the final three months of 1930, despite the victory over the "right" on the issue of plant reconstruction in 1929. Thus, in 1931, Filatov still would note the lack of progress, and he proclaimed that the final two years of the plan would be decisive. Investment in new capital construction at SiM had increased to 1,663,000 rubles in 1927/28, then to 2,449,000 in 1928/29, and finally to 7,558,000 in 1930, but this still was far short of the 40 million rubles that the plant needed to carry out the eight major reconstruction projects agreed on by the Mezhlauk Committee in November 1929, with the objective of transforming SiM into a producer of high-quality and specialty steels.[77]

Thus it is clear that the failure to reconstruct the plant in 1930 had causes other than "wrecking" since the "wreckers" had already been removed. The report of SiM workers in June 1930, at the Second Moscow Province Party Conference, concluded that "the factory has yearly plans for production and reconstruction, but it has no general plan for reconstruction or for the First FYP."[78] That provides us with a better clue. In January 1931, at the Eleventh Party Raion Conference, Filatov lamented the slow pace of reconstruction: "We have not fulfilled the program of reconstruction for the open hearth shop, the model-forge shop, and for a whole series of other shops."[79] Once again, on 18 April 1931, at the Second Moscow Province Congress of Soviets, SiM workers complained about the slow pace of reconstruction of their plant. The plant *partkom* called on the Central Committee of the Metallurgy Trade Union and the new steel combine, Stal', to approve the construction of a new model-forge shop, and a general plan for reconstruction.[80]

Finally on 21 June 1931, VSNKh passed a decree placing SiM and many other plants under the special and direct observation of the commissariat. It stated that by 1 January 1932, the calibrating shop had to go into operation and the reconstruction of the sheet metal shop had to be completed. By 1 July 1932, the rolling steel shop had to be completely rebuilt.[81] At the end of July 1931, at the Fifth Plant Party Conference, it was announced that some progress had been made in reconstruction. The "to be or not to be" document concluded on a positive note, but it stated that the task was made more difficult by "a series of changes widening the reconstruction [program] . . . during 1932."[82]

Precisely so. Throughout the USSR during the First FYP, the annual ritual of discarding existing plans and writing new plans, so-called counter-planning, not only destroyed the overall equilibrium of the First FYP, but also negated realistic efforts to improve the efficiency and quality of production by perpetually subordinating these tasks to expansion and new construction. In other words, in what would soon become official Soviet jargon, "extensive" rather than "intensive" growth remained the order of the day.

We can gather from the continuing difficulties with reconstructing SiM in 1930 and 1931, problems that persisted long after the removal of the "wreckers," that wrecking actually had nothing to do with it. The reasons for the delays had to do with obtaining the funds needed to meet the ever-expanding program of reconstruction in the network of integrated factories in the PR, requiring more steel and more specialized types of new steel products. Furthermore, the SiM shops were poorly designed for new internal rail transport and automated flow mechanisms, indicating that the arguments for building a new plant were not mere technical obfuscation.[83] Needless to say, failures and setbacks in reconstructing the plant in 1930 and 1931 were also directly caused by labor problems—recruiting, attaching, and training construction workers, discussed in chapters 3–5.

As Filatov's brochure and the other documents indicated, the decision to reconstruct SiM *in situ* was dictated principally by symbolic factors and by the general objective of converting "calico Moscow" into "metal Moscow." It was also dictated, as events unfolded, by the decision to reconstruct the nearby AMO plant on a massive scale, meaning that it would need sheet metal in vast quantities. Once these two plants were actually undergoing such massive reconstruction, an integrated high-technology zone in the new PR would begin to emerge in vertically integrated ball bearing plants, machine construction plants, and others. Of course, this would have been equally well served or better served by building a new steel plant (or several) outside the city and transporting the finished steel tubes, sheets, and rolled products into the PR factories. But in the political symbolism typical of the First FYP, in which steel itself meant heavy industry, the Stalinists mobilized support for the first variant for SiM.

Likhachev at AMO-ZiS: "Sewing the Coat Around the Button"[84]

The conflict over reconstruction at AMO followed a path very similar to the conflict at SiM, except that the dispute was even more dramatic, involving American specialists as well as Soviet. It culminated with Likhachev, the Red Director, presenting his case before the Politburo in January 1930. Until that moment, his opponents appeared to have had the upper hand, ensconced as they were in the trusts and also in the plant reconstruction agency.

Work on the design for reconstruction of AMO began in 1928. The government passed a decree at the end of that year calling for AMO, with a single shift, to produce (presumably by 1933) 25,000 two-and-a-half-ton vehicles per year.[85] In 1929, however, AMO's annual output was still only 1,303 vehicles.[86] To speed the plant's reconstruction, the government set up URRA (Administration to Expand and Reconstruct AMO) under the direction of M. L. Sorokin, from Avtotrest, the superordinate trust for AMO. URRA contracted with Brandt, an American firm that was supposed to draw up a design for plant reconstruction. When Brandt and a group of American engineers came to AMO in 1929, they developed a design for a factory with an annual production of 25,000 two-and-a-half-ton vehicles, the model to be called *avtokar*, on a single shift.[87] The Brandt design was sharply criticized.

A. V. Kuznetsov, in his excellent memoir-essay on Likhachev, argued that Brandt's design was submitted late, would have installed outdated American machines because of the particular contractual obligations that Brandt had with firms in the United States, and would have underutilized the expensive imported machines by limiting work to one shift. Kuznetsov, a machinist at AMO, was sent to the United States as part of an AMO commission to negotiate directly with American firms to import equipment and machinery; he later become director of the KIM auto plant.[88] Likhachev faulted Brandt for failing to design a whole series of departments (the mill shops, the forge shops, the machine design shop) and for failing to design any subsidiaries to AMO, which were needed for manufacturing such equipment as stamping machines.[89] Brandt's assumption that equipment and machinery would all have to be imported from abroad was anathema to a Soviet leadership determined to establish technological self-sufficiency, as Kuznetsov's memoir makes clear.

Sorokin supported Brandt's proposal, bringing him directly into conflict with Likhachev by the end of 1929. On 1 December, Likhachev and Sorokin presented their opposing points of view to the Moscow party bureau. The bureau supported Sorokin, and so on 10 January 1930, Likhachev took the issue directly to Ordzhonikidze, head of the party's Central Control Commission, commissar of Rabkrin (the Workers' and Peasants' Inspectorate, a "watchdog" Commissariat), soon to replace Kuibyshev as commissar of VSNKh, and already a key figure in the industrialization drive. On 25 January 1930, the Politburo met, and the entire bureau of the Moscow Committee was present, together with Likhachev; Ignatov, the AMO plant party secretary; and the head of the trade-union committee at AMO, F. Labutin. Likhachev apparently gave an impressive speech that convinced the leaders of the need for a much more thoroughgoing reconstruction than Sorokin or Brandt envisioned. Stalin spoke after Likhachev and accused Sorokin of failing to complete projects.[90]

Likhachev argued that the funds assigned by Sorokin to drawing up the reconstruction project were grossly inadequate, and so the Politburo instructed VSNKh to calculate the total funds required for the purchase of foreign equipment for AMO and for the complete reconstruction of the plant. It stipulated that the plant was to be equipped with state-of-the-art technology and was to become a model socialist enterprise, with the best working conditions and safety for workers. On 11 February 1930, the plant was removed from Avtotrest's authority and put under the direction of VATO.[91]

According to Soviet accounts, the Soviet side continued to honor the contract with Brandt despite their dissatisfaction, and it was Brandt who broke the contract. He allegedly left the Soviet Union and then recalled his engineers without ever completing the work contracted for. Sorokin was demoted and Likhachev was put in charge of URRA; Likhachev then sent Sorokin to the United States to wrap up remaining details with Brandt. The standard Soviet account praised several American engineers who came to the plant with Brandt.[92]

In March 1930, Likhachev also sent V. A. Zubkov and a team of engineers from the plant to the United States. Zubkov was the technical director of AMO-ZiS, and according to his memoirs, the Soviet engineers met with representatives from 800 firms in the United States, ordering the equipment and machinery that they needed for AMO-ZiS at the best prices.[93] Kuznetsov, who was part of this team, claimed to have signed contracts with different firms, saving thousands of rubles (in hard currency) by bargaining for the best terms, whereas Brandt had merely dealt with firms with which he was under contract, regardless of price.[94]

Several members of this team of Soviet specialists also worked at the Ford plant in Detroit for part of that year, and Ford and Likhachev toasted each other at a special dinner held before the specialists departed. According to the Soviet account, Ford managed to offend Likhachev by praising him for coming to learn from Ford, and Likhachev responded that the Americans would soon be the ones coming to learn from the Soviets.[95] Still, Ford and Likhachev were willing to sign a contract in which Ford would send technicians to Nizhni Novgorod and would also train Soviet technicians in Detroit. In 1931, Ford sent 40 technicians from its River Rouge plant to Nizhni Novgorod in exchange for 150 Soviet workers. Two of the Reuther brothers, Walter and Victor, went to the Nizhni Novgorod under this agreement in 1933, to help train the new Soviet auto workers.[96]

Soviet historians, in tracing these business dealings, have emphasized the condescending attitude of American firms and their attempts to swindle their Soviet partners. They have faulted the old Russian technical intelligentsia, which still played a significant role in Soviet economic and technical decision making, for slavishly adopting American proposals and technologies and for assuming that these had to be better than the Soviet equivalents. Soviet historians also generally accepted the claims of the Stalin regime, that many of the foreign firms and the old Russian elite were consciously working together to hinder Soviet industrialization and that they were often involved in outright sabotage or "wrecking."

Most Americans, on the other hand, have argued the opposite case in their memoirs. They claimed that Soviet firms signed contracts merely to gain access to new technologies and designs and then severed the contracts once their own people had mastered the technology. For example, a production manager at Ford who was sent to the Soviet Union to work under the joint contract claimed that tractors modeled after Ford's were already being built at the Putilov plant in Leningrad without any contract for the design.[97]

An American historian, Anthony C. Sutton, has analyzed both the scattered memoirs of foreign engineers who worked in the Soviet Union and State Department documents, trying to determine the extent and methods of technology transfer. In his three volumes, he tries to prove that American (and West European) technology provided the foundation for almost every Soviet industry and that the Soviet firms managed to accomplish technology transfer by industrial spying or by violating contracts. Thus, for example, on the Soviet agreement with Ford:

> The automobile industry is, then, an excellent example of a planned step-by-step transfer of Western technology at minimal cost. Ford was happy to sell $30 million worth of parts and throw in invaluable technical assistance for nothing. Technical assistance in production of axles, tires, bearings, and other items required payment but . . . the Soviets reaped a gigantic harvest of technological knowhow for almost no outlay. Although these plants [GAZ, AMO] were built completely by Western enterprise and equipped and initially operated by Western firms, the myth has been perpetuated that these were designed, built, and run by the Soviets.[98]

Sutton's strident assertions have been challenged, and we know now, after the Cold War, that the issue of technology transfer is quite complex.[99] The point here is not to attempt to evaluate the validity of Sutton's argument, but rather to understand the tense atmosphere in Soviet industry during the First FYP. In the Soviet industrialization drive, which was measured by the yardstick of "catching up" to America and under the assumption of foreign hostility, all Soviet engineers and managers were under extraordinary pressures and suspicion, and the mere introduction of the foreign element inevitably fueled class struggle rhetoric and paranoia.

Foreign experts and investment touched on every raw nerve in the Soviet body politic. The presence of foreigners was a daily reminder of how far they actually were from realizing their slogan of "catch up to and surpass the West." Administrators and engineers who went to the West, both there and back in Moscow, had to respond in public the way Likhachev responded to Ford at the banquet in Detroit. Serious conflicts with foreign firms and experts was inevitable. This conflict was at the very center of political debate in the Soviet Union over how to reconstruct the AMO-ZiS plant and over how to build an entirely new Soviet auto industry. Instead of dealing frankly with the complex problems of what we would now call technology transfer, the Stalinist regime reduced this conflict to "class struggle" and "wrecking." It was better for sloganeering and Soviet patriotism, but worse for smooth technology transfer and industrial results.

The disputes over reconstruction at SiM and AMO were but two cases in the widespread debate over industrialization. Stepanov and Likhachev were locked into virtually identical conflicts. Both succeeded because their immediate interests in enlarging their plants were aligned with the Stalin regime's determination to transform "calico" into "metal" Moscow. They both mobilized the support of their factory work collectives, smearing their opponents with the label of "wreckers." They also relied, most significantly, on new, loyal, appointed technical-management teams in their factories. Red Directors like Stepanov and Likhachev were already proving themselves to be consummate organization men by putting these teams of subordinates in place during the First FYP, just when their careers were apparently being established as hard-line proponents of Stalinist industrialization.[100]

The first reconstruction of AMO was declared to have been completed on 1 October 1931, the plant was renamed the Stalin plant or ZiS, and it was preparing to produce the first vehicles of the new design, the AMO-3 model light truck. The new shops were supposed to begin to go into operation on that date, but they would not actually work anywhere near projected capacity for almost another year. Still, on that evening, in honor of the *pusk* (putting shops on-line), a celebration was held at the plant, at which Ordzhonikidze praised the AMO-ZiS collective for blazing a new trail in Soviet industry and called on them to "master" the new technology, anticipating by more than a year the shift in the party line to "assimilation" of new technology. Likhachev proclaimed that they had "sewn the coat around the button." And, indeed, they had, if the criterion for success was to be measured in terms of the annual output of cars, which was continuing to increase rapidly despite the constant chaos of the first reconstruction of the factory.[101]

The regime measured success in terms of increasing annual output figures, regardless of cost overruns. In 1929, AMO produced 1,303 vehicles; in 1930, 3,227 vehicles; in 1931, only 2,891 vehicles; and then, in 1932, output jumped more than five times, to 15,149 vehicles; and in 1933, it increased to 20,916 vehicles. The party considered this a major success, awarding fourteen Orders of Lenin, and fifteen Orders of the Red Banner of Labor to workers and managers at the plant in 1933.[102] The fact that it employed 19,329 workers and personnel, and that productivity was very low by any measure, was of secondary significance.[103]

Six months before Likhachev's triumphant 1931 speech, two decrees of the Central Committee revealed that construction at AMO was not progressing very well and show why shops could not be completed on time. The resolutions, both dated 16 April 1931, show how cadre workers, managers, and ITR (engineers and technical workers), were transferred from ZiS "pilot" to GAZ "satellite." The two resolutions had almost identical titles: "On Party and Trade-Union Work and Preparing Cadre for the AMO Factory" and "On Party and Trade-Union Work and Preparing Cadre for the Nizhegorod Auto-Plant Construction Site."[104] Both were more concerned with construction work than output.

Reconstruction of the AMO plant, we read, in stark contrast with Likhachev's tone six months later, was still far behind schedule in April 1931. The construction plan for 1930 had only been fulfilled by 56.5 percent. Work had gone poorly, the resolution suggested, because the party layer *(part-prosloika)* in the construction division was only 5.3 percent, whereas, for the entire plant, 19 percent of the work force were party members. The decree also noted that the construction division had only 29 percent shock workers, as compared to 70–80 percent for the entire plant.[105] The resolutions contained eleven points, of which the most important concerned labor recruitment and training.

The first point instructed the officials at AMO to begin training programs for 2,500 new workers and for retraining 1,500 of the plant's existing work force. In addition, they were responsible for training 600 skilled workers, who were to be sent on a preliminary *stazherovka* (extended stay) to start up operation of the work benches at the Nizhni Novgorod auto plant. AMO was also supposed to transfer its production experience by initiating a mutual exchange of worker brigades and by sending fifty of its own ITR on *stazherovka* to Nizhni Novgorod.

The resolution on the Nizhni Novgorod plant also lamented the slow pace of factory construction and set specific quotas and responsibilities for recruiting personnel of every rank, from the top-level administrators to unskilled construction laborers. The resolution insisted that within twenty days, fifteen leading managerial personnel must be sent to the auto plant by VSNKh SSSR, Tsentrosoiuz, Soiuzstroi, and NKPS SSSR.[106] It gave the responsible trust, Avtostroi, only ten days to "conclude contracts with the factories which had prepared labor power for the auto plant" so as to "really guarantee 4,080 skilled workers." These workers were to come from the following sources. First, VSNKh and VATO were instructed to contract with Avtostroi, with VSNKh being responsible for 1,080 workers and VATO for 1,000. Additionally, VATO was instructed to prepare 2,000 skilled bench operators for the auto plant. They were to be commandeered from various factory vocational schools and from the mechanics shops of textile factories![107]

Thus, recruitment at GAZ was based on a strategy of establishing a skeleton work force, consisting of skilled and experienced workers, technicians, and engineers who would be transferred from AMO-ZiS and other large machine construction plants in Moscow and Leningrad. This defined its status as a "satellite" plant in relation to the metropolitan "pilots." A very similar type of relationship was established between SiM and the Putilov plant in Leningrad as pilots and the metallurgical combines in Magnitogorsk and at Kuznetskstroi as satellites. It was not merely personnel, but also the experience in the pilots that was supposed to serve as a guide for industrial organization and labor relations in the satellites.

These two decrees also revealed that the decision to establish a type of horizontal integration, linking older factories in Moscow or Leningrad with new factories built in the Urals, was apparently improvised out of the crying need for cadre familiar with the work processes. The improvisation was comparable to the vertical integration in the PR during the First FYP. Horizontal integration would be widely repeated, again with apparently minimal advance planning, during the Second World War, when the entire contents and the remaining personnel of plants were evacuated from the West to the Urals or Siberia.

As Likhachev's metaphor of "sewing the coat around the button" and the title "To Be or Not to Be a Factory" both indicate, the reconstruction of AMO and SiM were heatedly contested political decisions, and until they were resolved in principle in 1929 and in practice in 1930 and 1931, there could not have been any coherent idea, let alone a plan, for any vertically integrated production in the PR. Decisions to construct many other new factories, which were vertically integrated with these two plants and Dinamo, must have followed the resolution of the problems of where, when, and how to reconstruct these three plants, and on what scale. Likewise, the Central Committee decrees on AMO and the Nizhni Novgorod auto plant show that the paramount problems of recruiting an adequate labor force for construction and start-up of factories on the periphery drove the leadership to think in terms of pilot and satellite plants and of horizontal integration in producing autos or steel. Instances of the transfer of managers and worker "cadre" from ZiS to other factories, many in the PR vertical network or in satellite plants in the horizontal network, abound in the official history of ZiS, which provides short biographical sketches of, among others, N. A. Volkov, G. N. Korolov, Bronislava Moiseevna Lavler, Viktor Alekseevich Zubkov, Vasilii Aleksandrovich Chernushevich, and Kh. S. Lottershtein.[108]

Conclusion

This discussion leaves unanswered the fundamental questions of whether vertical integration in the PR, and the pilot and satellite model of horizontal integration, were economically efficient. On the face of it, such integration would seem to have been a benefit of planning; however, the problems of coordinating and allocating scarce resources, equipment, and personnel between factories was not resolved through either plan or markets under the Stalinist system.[109] Therefore, it is not clear that these enterprises were well integrated or that they avoided the problems of product duplication or of product incompatibility, both stemming from economic autarky or what could be called "socialism in one factory" or in one *kombinat* such as the MMK, or in one district such as the PR, or one city, or one region of the USSR.

Following Lewin's methodological breakthrough on collectivization, we can conclude that Soviet enterprise integration, both vertical and horizontal, was developed improvisationally rather than by plan. The FYP became a kind of summary, after the fact, of new enterprise construction and reconstruction across the USSR, which was determined on a plant-by-plant basis by political infighting. More significant, for our purposes, is applying Lewin's breakthrough to the workers, in tracing how they acted and responded in the midst of the improvised industrialization drive. As with forced collectivization, the regime would face unanticipated obstacles and would assume that its problems with recruiting, "attaching," and training a labor force were caused by peasant workers' resistance in the cities or by the resistance of other "class aliens." These problems and the regime's attempt to find solutions are the subject of the next three chapters.

Part 2

Stalinist Policy and Social Chaos

3

RECRUITING WORKERS:
THE LABOR MARKET TURNED
UPSIDE DOWN

uring the First FYP, a historically unprecedented situation developed in the USSR. Called the liquidation of unemployment by Soviet historians, it was actually a new and very serious economic disequilibrium of an opposite sort, a severe labor deficit.[1] This should be called an "inverted" labor market, since it was characterized by chronic labor shortage rather than chronic unemployment. The deficit was cropping up in various regions and branches of industry already in 1930, even while there was still registered unemployment. It became a widespread problem in 1931, and the gap widened further in 1932, until the deficit constituted a "labor famine" that disrupted the industrialization drive, just as the famine in the countryside disrupted the rural economy. The attempts to recruit workers, in particular from the so-called labor reserves, are analyzed in this chapter both in the microcosm of the PR and across the whole of the USSR.

Recruitment Plans for the Proletarian District

The reports of party and Komsomol meetings in *Martenovka* show that, by the end of 1930, the problems of finding enough workers to build and staff the new factories and the reconstructed plants of the PR were showing up everywhere, sparking an attempt to conceptualize recruitment needs and plan recruitment policies for the entire district. At the Third Party Conference at SiM, which opened on 10 May 1930, Comrade Davidson, the chair of the PR *raikom*, reported that 375 million rubles had been designated for investment in new industrial construction in the PR. This massive program could not be undertaken without a comparable labor recruitment drive. "For the First FYP, construction work in our *raion* requires [the recruitment of] about 30,000 workers. [Furthermore] despite the very sharp demand for skilled cadre for the growing industry, the enterprises still do not have precise plans to prepare skilled labor power. According to the data of the enterprises, they expect to get about 2,000 skilled workers [by transfer] from other enterprises, and no more than 8,000 workers from the labor exchange."[2] Davidson then suggested that the factories should train their own skilled cadre, and part of their middle-level technical personnel, at the factory itself.

At the Fourth Party Conference at SiM, six months later, on 23 December 1930, I. P. Gaidul' spoke on behalf of the *raikom* as its new party secretary.[3] On the one hand, he pointed out, recruitment policy would seem to have been successful in 1930, because the labor force at Dinamo was 11 percent above the planned level, while at SiM it was 17–20 percent above plan. On the other hand, he acknowledged that this was not a healthy indicator, but rather it was evidence of labor hoarding and poor organization of labor. The enterprises were compensating for their large deficit in skilled cadre by hiring new workers, yet the training of these workers was lagging far behind the demand for cadre.

Despite the substantial increase in enrollment in the FZUs (the factory vocational schools) at SiM, AMO, and Dinamo in 1929/30, these plants could only supply an anticipated 6 percent of the 20,000 trained cadre needed for 1931 in the PR. Furthermore, they could not hope to graduate more than a small fraction of the 60–70,000 additional skilled workers needed for the entire FYP. Gaidul' noted that shop-floor apprenticeship was expected to meet 45 percent of the demand for cadre for the PR in 1931. (In this context, he meant qualified workers, a designation that probably included semiskilled workers at ranks 3–4 on the wage scale, and certainly meant skilled workers at ranks 5–6 and highly skilled workers at ranks 7–8.) He concluded rhetorically, "and the remainder?" His solution was massive on-the-job training.[4] It was a conclusion that would be repeatedly drawn by enterprise directors and by party secretaries at all levels.

Obviously, there was no answer for 1931 and only one answer for the future: the recruits that brought the labor force above plan levels in 1930 at Dinamo and SiM, including those at levels 1–2, who were completely unskilled, would have to acquire experience on the shop floor *en masse* and gain promotion to the ranks of the semiskilled. Sometimes, this was glorified as "brigade apprenticeship" (see chapter 5). More often, such acquisition of experience was merely designated by promotion to the ranks of the semiskilled. Such promotion should be considered a broad status revolution rather than individual upward mobility, and it would prove to be the most important phenomenon in Soviet working-class formation in the 1930s. Workers, in the new conditions, would become qualified in two or three years, whether or not they had any formal shop-floor apprenticeship or classroom training. The 1930 and 1931 annual and FYP objectives for training qualified labor were, however, unrealizeable until 1933, at the very earliest.

It was also obvious, as Gaidul' noted in 1930, that hiring former workers who had lost their jobs and were registered on the labor exchange was no longer an option. Such officially defined unemployment in the PR had declined from 22,000, as registered at the beginning of 1930, to a total of 175 as registered on 23 December 1930.[5] This reflected unionwide trends, and in substantial part, it was the consequence of implementing the decree of the commissar of labor, Tsikhon, issued during the Special Quarter of 1930. Under this decree, all unemployment insurance payments were halted and the names of "labor deserters" were removed from the lists of the labor exchanges.[6]

The regime's harsh tactics to push the unemployed into the factories, however, were a minor part of the story. By the end of 1930, there already was a labor deficit in many regions, a reality that was obvious but hard to believe, given the high levels of unemployment until that year and the large "labor reserves," as the regime called them. These labor reserves were defined as excess peasant labor in the village, the unemployed urban housewives, and the youth graduating from secondary school. In other words, the subaltern workers, seasonally employed, underemployed, or unemployed, as I have defined them.

Part of the explanation for the sudden labor deficit in the PR was the shift to the seven-hour day and to the continuous workweek. Gaidul' could not make this connection, however, since the party line called for this shift, but his data showed that by late December 1930, half the enterprises of the *raion* were on the seven-hour workday and 80 percent were on the uninterrupted workweek. In 1931, these figures were supposed to increase to 94 percent and 100 percent respectively.[7] This scheduling, which kept the factories producing around the clock with insufficient downtime, was clearly exacerbating the already difficult problems of finding enough qualified workers and of training them.

At the same conference, both Gaidul' and Stepanov called attention to the problem of low labor productivity. In 1929/30, productivity was 8 percent below plan at SiM; throughout the PR, wages were at 105 percent of the planned level while productivity was only at 94 percent. Stepanov called for an increase of 28 percent in labor productivity at SiM in 1931, a 7.5 percent increase in wages, and an 11 percent reduction in production costs.[8] Obviously, low labor productivity was both a cause and a consequence of labor hoarding. Labor hoarding, just like the seven-hour workday and the uninterrupted workweek, was in itself a significant factor in spreading cadre too thin and was a basic cause of the labor deficit. While Gaidul' and Stepanov emphasized absenteeism and other indisciplines, to be consistent with the party line, their analysis exposed the more fundamental causes.

Meeting the deficit in skilled labor was also at issue during the Komsomol's Ninth District Conference in the PR, held at the very end of 1930. In 1929, there had been a total of six FZUs with 1,665 students in the PR, whereas in late 1930 there were fifteen FZUs with over 6,000 students. Furthermore, the number of *tekhnikumy* (schools for training technicians) had increased from three to nine, and these nine were training 3,000 technical workers.[9] While the numbers seemed impressive, and they more than doubled the FZU figures as given out by Gaidul' at the party conference, they still showed that more than two new workers were learning on-the-job for every new worker training in the FZU.

It was clear from these fragmentary reports, with their incomplete data on the need for labor power and their contradictory data on how many students would be enrolled, that even by the end of 1930, in the PR there were very large deficits of both unskilled construction laborers and of trained or experienced production workers, of "qualified cadre." Furthermore, it was clear that factory-based vocational schools could provide for only a small fraction of these needs. The rest would have to be met by on-the-job training.

It was well beyond the capacity of the *raion* organs—party, Komsomol and trade union—to plan or to organize labor recruitment. The best they could do was to muster a general estimate of the total labor deficit by summing the figures, after the fact, from each of the major *raion* enterprises, and they could only suggest how to meet the deficit by summing figures from each enterprise FZU and other schools and apprenticeship programs. The *raion* organs were not planning, in any real sense of the term; they were merely summarizing what was already happening at the factory or enterprise level.

Having exhausted the roles of the labor exchanges and hired virtually all unemployed workers, party leaders and economic administrators began to search for strategies to retain workers at the factories, that is, to reduce labor turnover and to provide training. They also looked to tap the so-called labor reserves from social groups with excess or underemployed labor power. Thus, they turned to the three large subaltern groups, most of whose members had been denied industrial jobs in the 1920s or, at best, had been marginalized into seasonal work: youth, women, and peasant-migrants.

Recruiting New Workers at SiM: Youth, Women, and Peasants

The documentary evidence on labor recruitment at SiM shows that plant officials paid far more attention to recruiting and training youth in the FZU than to any other form of organized recruitment. The evidence is silent about the *otdel kadrov*, the personnel department, which was formally responsible for hiring new workers. Rather, it was the factory triangle—the director and his administrative staff, the plant trade-union committee (*zavkom*), and the plant party committee (*partkom*)—that was actively involved in recruitment. They consistently devoted the most attention to planning enrollment in the FZU among youth; after that, they were periodically launching campaigns to hire workers' wives, the so-called social role call, and seemed to pay little attention to the *orgnabor* (organized recruitment) contracts for hiring peasants. Following the bias of the documentary evidence, therefore, I will begin with recruitment of youth, and then move on to the recruitment of women, and finally consider the recruitment of peasant-migrants. Keeping in mind that there was considerable overlap of the three subaltern groups, I would suggest that youth were also a wedge through which peasant-migrants and women broke longstanding barriers to industrial employment in various branches and occupations.

Youth

Throughout the USSR, about one million youth (twenty-two years old or younger) became industrial workers during the First FYP, comprising at least a third of the new recruits to industry. Whereas on 1 January 1930 there were 769,700 youth (under twenty-two years old) in large-scale industry, constituting 24.7 percent of the total number of workers and trainees, by 1 July 1935, they formed 34.1 percent of the total (or 2 million).[10] Of the new industrial recruits in 1931, over 50 percent were less than twenty-three years old, and 75 percent were less than thirty; in metallurgy, 64.7 percent of new recruits in 1931 were under twenty-three years old, and in machine construction, 64 percent were under twenty-three.[11]

At SiM, the average age of the work force declined from 31.8 years in 1929 to 27.4 years in 1932. In 1932–33, out of 9,151 workers and trainees at

SiM surveyed in the trade-union census, 11.7 percent were under seventeen, 16.2 percent were eighteen to nineteen, and 18.4 percent were twenty to twenty-three. Thus, defining youth as those twenty-three years old or less, slightly more than 46 percent of the SiM work force were youth by 1932–33. At AMO-ZiS, in 1929, 32 percent of the workers were under twenty-three, but by 1932, this figure rose to 49.4 percent. At Dinamo, the increase was from 22.3 percent to 47.6 percent over the same time period.[12] Thus, at the three most important plants in the PR by the end of the First FYP, almost half the work force was youth. Virtually all of them had been hired after 1 October 1928, the day the First FYP officially began.

At SiM, 62.4 percent of the new worker-recruits in the First FYP were twenty-two years old or younger, and if one includes trainees studying under the individual-brigade apprenticeship system, then 74 percent of the new recruits were twenty-two or younger.[13]

S. Filatov, who succeeded Gaidul' as *partkom* secretary at SiM on 6 October 1930, analyzed the "cadre problem" in 1931 in his booklet on party work at SiM. He claimed that the labor recruitment problem at SiM primarily consisted of finding or training skilled cadre, rather than in attracting new recruits. While the FZU at SiM had already trained 3,000 workers for SiM, many more were needed. Furthermore, the school was busy in 1931 with preparing 591 skilled cadre for Magnitostroi, Kuznetskstroi, and Uralmashstroi. Thus, the recruitment and training organs were saddled with the additional problems of providing skilled cadre for the giant new satellite plants in the Urals and Siberia.[14]

In the 1920s, teenagers had found it almost impossible to get jobs at SiM. The quota (*bronia*) for hiring teenagers was set at a minimum of 8 percent of new recruits, but because management preferred to hire older workers with experience, the quota was rarely met.[15] The collective contract for 1931 showed how that was to change. Clause 11 stipulated that teenagers were supposed to become the single most important social source for recruiting new workers at SiM. "The *bronia podrostkov* [quota of teenagers to be hired] is to cover for the natural loss of workers [due to retirement or death], plus a significant part of the growth connected with the expansion of the plant . . . [the *bronia*] should cover 60 percent of the general demand for worker cadre, that is a *bronia* of 1,083 people. The *bronia* must be fulfilled in one month, moreover, the children of shock workers and of workers with a long *stazh* [production tenure] at the plant, should be the first hired, and also, children raised in the children's homes must be hired." Clause 12 insisted that "the administration is obligated to guarantee a place in the FZU" for those teenagers hired under the *bronia* and that "the length of study, depending on the occupation, will be no less than two and no more than three years. Individual training in brigades also cannot exceed three years. If the trainee switches to another enterprise or shop, then the time spent in training in the original [shop or enterprise] still counts." Clause 14 of part 3 stipulated that the administration must guarantee an apprentice a job according to the occupation that he or she was trained for. These measures were all intended to protect the position of youth in the factories and thus to encourage youth to enroll in the factory vocational schools.[16]

Youth were not only expected to become the largest source of new worker-recruits, but, according to the Sixteenth Party Congress, held in June 1930, those trained in the FZUs were expected to become the basic source of qualified workers for Soviet industry. In addition, the FZU itself was expected to become a standard form of secondary education.[17] In a speech in April 1931, on the tenth anniversary of the founding of the FZUs, the commissar of VSNKh, Ordzhonikidze, noted that the schools must become "the basic channel of preparation of worker cadre."[18] The head of the All-Union Central Council of Trade Unions (VTsSPS), N. N. Shvernik, called on all factories to emulate SiM's example, to establish enterprise schools, the first of which was set up at SiM (see chapter 5) and, at the same time, to adopt the system of "technical training without interruption from production work" as the quickest way to train masses of qualified workers.[19] This argument is repeated in an archival document from SiM in 1932, which states that at SiM "the transition to a more organized recruitment of labor power is best characterized by the growth of the FZU to 3,000 trainees, with about 500 graduating each year."[20]

Thus, party leaders and SiM officials both emphasized that the FZU was the basic institution for recruiting young workers and for training them. In this, as in so many other respects, Soviet realities did not conform to expectations. In the overall picture of labor training for the masses of new factory workers, the FZU was actually rather insignificant, although its importance for a thin layer of young new workers should not be underestimated. For the purposes of recruitment, however, the impact of this institution was negligible. A few figures at the union level make this clear.

For the whole of the Soviet Union, the FZUs graduated 450,000 trainees during the First FYP, 1,400,000 during the Second FYP, and 500,000 during the Third FYP. During the First FYP alone, the so-called individual-brigade apprenticeship training (a glorified term for on-the-job training under the direction of the foreman) accounted for the training of over 6 million new workers or about half of all worker-recruits.[21] Thus, in slightly more than four years, more new recruits received this type of training than the FZUs trained in the entire twelve-year period from 1929 to 1941. The point here is not to compare types of training; rather it is to show how insignificant the FZU was as a recruiting mechanism. It was, however, the closest the regime ever came to devising an institutional form to organize and plan labor recruitment, with some preference given to the children of factory workers.

The vast majority of factory youth came to the factory spontaneously and individually and were trained on the job, in their assigned production brigades in a rapid and cursory fashion. The old patterns of apprenticeship tutelage could not cope with the demands of the situation during the First FYP and yielded to the individual-brigade apprenticeships. (See chap. 5 below.) On the other hand, neither could organized recruitment into the FZU cope with the situation, as the FZU program was shortened to six months in 1933. The situation changed somewhat in the Second and Third FYPs, when the slower and steadier patterns of recruitment and the restoration of a two-year FZU program resulted in some greater degree of success in FZU recruiting and training.

In October 1940, the State Labor Reserve System was established and the FZUs were replaced by FZOs, with the Commissariat of Education, in theory, replacing the factory as administrator of these vocational schools. The regime abolished voluntary quits with the law of 26 June 1940 and tried to strictly regulate hiring through the reserves after October. This was an attempt to replace the labor market with directed labor. The reserve system assigned children to the FZO and from there directly to a factory. That method of labor mobilization had success during the war, probably because patriotism motivated youth to comply; but it became increasingly irrelevant after the war, and efforts to distribute or mobilize labor atrophied. The FZO became obsolete, probably because it neither educated the children particularly well nor provided the factory director with the recruits he wanted. It was replaced by the voluntary PTU system of vocational education during the Khrushchev labor and educational reforms.[22] The labor market reasserted itself.

However they came into the factory, higher literacy rates and levels of schooling meant that youth tended to be more adaptable than other recruits, or even than established workers, to a variety of new jobs and especially to those in the more mechanized and automated plants. Furthermore, youth were not segregated as readily as women or peasants, because neither the young workers nor the factory management had strong prejudices about where they should or should not be employed. Youth, in particular young women and young peasant-recruits, were thus intermediaries with a dual self-identity among the subaltern groups on the shop floor. They opened up job categories that had been closed to older peasant-migrants and to older and married women by custom, managerial prejudice, and job market control by the labor aristocrats, before 1917, and then again by the established workers during the 1920s.

Women

According to trade-union statistics, on 1 October 1928 there were 2,394,500 working women, or 24.6 percent of the total work force. In 1929, these figures hardly changed, but from 1 October 1929 until 1 October 1930, the number of working women increased by one million. This still left the ratio of women almost unchanged, at 25.1 percent of the total work force. In the following year (1 October 1930 through 1 October 1931) the number of women increased by over 2 million, reaching 28.9 percent of the total. Then, from 1 October 1931 through 1 July 1933, there was a slowing of the absolute increase to just over 1 million, but the relative increase of women accelerated. Women accounted for 33.7 percent of the total work force by July 1933.[23] This reflected a slight reduction of the total size of the work force in 1933, while the number of women continued to increase, even if more slowly than in 1930 and 1931.

This increase began a trend which persisted through the Second and Third FYPs. The recruitment of peasants and youth was most intensive during the First FYP, their percentages peaking by the end of 1932. The increase in the percentage of women workers was most rapid during the Second and Third FYPs. During the Second FYP, one-half of the 10 million recruits (wage and salaried workers) were women.[24] The 1939 All-Union Census showed that women constituted 43 percent of the work force.[25] During the Second World War, this figure soared to well over 50 percent.[26]

Even though the most rapid relative increase in female employment came about after 1933, the First FYP marked a permanent break from the traditional pattern of recruitment of women workers, because more than half the female recruits in the First FYP went into heavy rather than light industry. In the auto-tractor branch, they constituted 40 percent of the new recruits for 1931 and 1932, while in heavy metallurgy, machine construction, and the electrotechnical industry they constituted between 46 and 53 percent of the new recruits for 1931 and 1932.[27]

At SiM, there were very few female workers until 1930. In the restoration period of NEP (1921–25), their numbers fluctuated between 4 and 6 percent of the work force.[28] After a slight increase in the reconstruction period (1926–29), there was a sudden explosion of female recruits from 1930 to 1932. Their numbers increased sevenfold in those three years, as table 3.1 indicates.

According to the 1932–33 trade-union census at SiM, out of a total of

Table 3.1. Women Workers at SiM, 1917–33 (as of 1 January)

	Absolute Number of Women	Percentage of Work Force
1917	375	13.5
1926	335	7.0
1927	312	6.2
1928	324	6.3
1929	356	6.3
1931	1,619	16.1
1933	1,951	24.2

Sources: Figures for 1917: Kornakovskii, "Zavod 'Serp i Molot,'" pp. 196–97, citing the GAMO archive; figures for 1926, 1927, 1928, and 1929: GARF f. 7952, op. 3, d. 337, l. 26; figures for 1931 and 1933: Lel'chuk, *Industrial'noe Razvitie,* p. 434.

9,151 workers and trainees who were surveyed, 2,184 or 23.9 percent were women. Of the workers, 21.7 percent were women, while 32.2 percent of the trainees were women. By way of comparison, at AMO-ZiS, out of a total of 12,671 workers and trainees who were surveyed, 3,197 were women, or 25.2 percent. Of the workers 24.1 percent were women, and of the trainees, 38 percent were women.[29]

According to another source, on 1 June 1931 at AMO-ZiS, there were 768 women out of a total of 6,734 workers, or 11.4 percent, while on 1 January 1933, there were 4,107 women out of a total of 15,197, or 27 percent.[30] While the percentages are roughly comparable, the absolute numbers show that women had significantly greater success in gaining employment at AMO-ZiS than at SiM. That was because it was a newer plant; it hired more new recruits; and more of the occupations were outside the traditional, male work culture and did not have male foremen who had been promoted from those occupations.

While women succeeded in using the industrialization drive to break down the barriers to employment in many industries, this does not mean that they swept aside all occupational barriers. At SiM, in fact, they had great difficulty breaking into the most highly skilled occupations or even lesser-skilled but highly paid "peasant" occupations in certain shops where jobs were denied to women due to health and safety regulations. The women at ZiS were less segregated by occupation and shop than the women at SiM because there were very few jobs that were regarded as too hot, heavy, or dangerous at the auto plant for women. Protective regulations at SiM may well have been motivated by reasonable considerations, but as was the case in the capitalist system, such regulations also reinforced patterns of occupational segregation. Women, coming to work at SiM during the First FYP, were segregated into the lower-skill and lower-paying shops and occupations because of traditional practices and prejudices in employment at a steel plant and also because of health and safety regulations.

The anecdotal evidence clearly indicates that there were serious obstacles to integration and promotion for women in the SiM plant. On 10 February 1932, *Martenovka* ran an article, "Women—To the Benches and Blast Furnaces." According to this article, a brigade from the Institute of Health and Organization of Labor had studied steel plants and listed fifty-three occupations that were safe for women. The article explained:

The basic obstacle to installing female workers at the plant is the low level of mechanization. . . . it is forbidden to allow women to work in . . . the shops for shaping molten metals. But study of female labor has shown that, with certain alterations in the technique of production, women could also work at these jobs. Thus, for example, a welder in the sheet metal shop does not need great physical strength, and this is the leading worker. In order to become a welder, a worker must undergo a difficult tenure as an apprentice. If this tenure was replaced by an equivalent program of theoretical training, then a [female] worker could [more easily and rapidly] become a welder.

Thus, installing female workers bumps up against the problem of mechanization of the plant. This requires special attention in 1932.[31]

The link between mechanization and the introduction of female workers was a prominent theme in the press during the First FYP. The official line blamed technological backwardness (and sometimes male chauvinism) for blocking women's progress. The second problem confronting women, according to this passage, was the obsolete and cumbersome apprenticeship system. This was felt to be a severe obstacle by most new recruits, but it was a particular obstacle for women. The foreman, *master* or *brigadir,* who trained the apprentices was invariably an older man with long work tenure. Traditionalists to the core, foremen were the least sympathetic to the idea of women coming to work in their factory.

The party made some attempt to plan the recruitment, training, and promotion of women at the regional and plant level. Such plans usually involved recruitment campaigns on International Women's Day. For example, on 8 March 1931, the Moscow Province newspaper, *Rabochaia Gazeta,* announced that every enterprise in the province was to be given a target for employing women. It projected that a total of 57,000 women were to be recruited in 1931. According to Meshchankanii, the head of the division of wages and output of the Moscow Province Council of Trade Unions, "In the first place, we must bring in the wives and daughters of the cadre workers. . . . Now a brigade of the [council] is investigating a series of occupations . . .

to clarify the possibility of replacing male labor with female."[32] This was typical of the official strategy. First, whenever possible, women were to be hired from the immediate family of a male worker. Second, while health and safety regulations were designed to protect women, they also limited women's options. This explained, in part, why women were segregated by occupation and by shop. They would "replace" men in certain occupations, which would be feminized, not integrate with men in all occupations.

Rabochaia Gazeta also noted that for the whole of Moscow Province, women already constituted 41 percent of the industrial work force in 1930. However, the majority of them were locked into the low-paying, low-skilled occupations of the textile industry, which remained the province's predominant industry until 1929. In 1929/30, 19,600 women had been hired, mostly in the metalworking industries. They were generally hired without any work skills or job specialization, and only a few had achieved the rank of skilled worker by March 1931.[33]

International Women's Day campaigns, it is clear, were no substitute for a year-round strategy to recruit women, to train them for new occupations, and to promote them. Official policy reserved half the vocational training positions in the FZUs for young women, and the party, given its desperate need for new recruits, was quite enthusiastic about recruiting and training women and about breaking institutional and individual instances of male chauvinism. However, this general enthusiasm was not accompanied by the establishment of any strong institutions that would have been able to implement a year-round strategy for the employment and training of women. In fact, dissolution of the Women's Section of the party, the *Zhenotdel,* at the Sixteenth Party Congress in June 1930 eliminated what was potentially the most effective advocate of women's objectives in the workplace. Plans for recruiting women in Moscow Province or the SiM factory were established on an *ad hoc* basis, and follow-up was very sporadic. As with the proposed figures at party conferences for labor recruitment in the PR, these were not really plans, but rather general objectives.

At SiM, the Women's Organization (*zhenorg*) was a strong advocate for hiring more women, training more women, and promoting more women. However, when the party dissolved its Women's Section, it left such factory-based women's organizations isolated and without a central lobby. The SiM Women's Organization had very little power, support, or control over hiring or training. It could only pressure the plant to live up to the professed party ideology of women's equality.

After 1930, the major problem facing women was no longer the lack of industrial jobs. Rather, the problem was job segregation and placement in jobs where skill and pay were comparatively low. From the standpoint of the regime, the problem was not recruitment but effective integration.

Most workers' wives had no choice but to become factory workers because of declining purchasing power during the First FYP and the lack of income-earning alternatives.[34] The major institutional problem was providing day care. Perhaps most significant, however, in explaining the rapid influx of women into factories, were the changing expectations of young unmarried and married women, who within a single generation came to anticipate working most of their adult lives. One might speculate that universal secondary schooling, established through grade seven in urban areas in 1931, was a significant factor in the rapidly changing life course expectations of these young women.[35]

Peasants

If approximately two-thirds of the new recruits to Soviet industry in the First FYP were youth (less than twenty-three years old), then many were also peasant-migrants. Likewise, if approximately 40 percent of the new recruits were women, then many of them were also peasant-migrants. This overlapping of social groups meant that peasant-recruits accounted for 8.5 million out of a total of 12.5 million new recruits during the First FYP, and even in the Second and Third FYPs, they constituted about 50 percent of the new recruits.[36]

Parents' occupation, or father's occupation, is generally the best indicator of social origins. In 1928/29, 46.6 percent of the workers in heavy metallurgy listed their parents' occupation as peasant. In 1930, this figure rose to 50.3 percent; in 1931, to 62.2 percent, and in 1932, it leveled off at 62.1 percent. In the airplane-auto-tractor industry, the corresponding annual figures were 41.6 percent, 47.2 percent, 58.1 percent, and 61.2 percent.[37] Thus, during the First FYP, the increase was quite dramatic: from about 40 percent to 60 percent of the total industrial workers were the children of peasants.

At SiM, according to the 1932–33 trade-union census, the sociooccupational status of the fathers of 48.8 percent of all workers was peasant. Among those workers recruited at SiM in 1928/29, this figure was 51.8 percent; in 1930, 54.7 percent; in 1931, 67 percent; in 1932, 70.2 percent.[38] Thus, there was a steady annual increase of recruits coming from peasant families.

In view of the fact that so many peasant-migrants were recruited at SiM, it is quite surprising that in workers' memoirs from the Gor'kii Archives and in *Martenovka,* there is very little mention of how peasants came to SiM or where they came from. Little is written about traditional forms of peasant migration—*zemliachestvo* (where a *zemliak,* or village leader, establishes a residence in the city and others gravitate to it), or *otkhodnichestvo,* (seasonal migration, in which the peasant-worker typically works part of the year on the communal land, and part in a city, on construction or in a factory)—or about the *artel'* (a peasant work-group, typically led by an elder or *starosta,* which acts as a type of subcontracting unit, often in construction but also in factories), or even about the new system of *orgnabor* (organized recruitment, in which the factory contracts with the collective farm for a certain number of laborers, usually for one year). Considerable historical controversy surrounds these types of recruitment and their effectiveness. Whereas for Soviet historians the debate was concerned primarily with the effectiveness of regime policy, the issue has considerably broader historical significance relating to the work patterns, family life, and community life of the peasant-worker.

M. Ia. Sonin provides a complete set of figures for *orgnabor* for the decade 1931–40. The figures for 1931, 5.45 million, and 1932, 3.64 million, include *otkhod.* The figure for 1933 fell to 1.88 million, but that did not include *otkhod.* Over 3 million were recruited annually from 1934 to 1936, 1.5 million in 1937, and over 2 million annually from 1938 to 1940.[39] Much of the confusion stems from the fact that in 1931, following the 30 June 1931 decree "Na Otkhodnichestvo," the first attempt at organized recruitment involved seasonal workers. This was the precursor to *orgnabor,* according to A. M. Panfilova.[40] Whereas Sonin and Panfilova consider *orgnabor* to have been a success, the maverick sociologist Iu. V. Arutiunian revised their approach in a short article published in 1964, which suggested that spontaneous peasant migration accounted for 70 percent of peasant recruitment in 1931 and about the same in 1932. He concluded that Stalin was wrong in his claim that peasants wanted to remain on the *kolkhoz* and that Sonin and Panfilova were wrong about the significance of organized recruitment.[41]

Panfilova herself showed the persistence of *zemliachestvo* and *artel'* networks under the guise of *orgnabor.*[42] Archival documents from as late as 1938 reaffirm this.[43] David Hoffmann emphasizes the persistence of these patterns. Arutiunian, however, emphasized spontaneity in migration, tending to lump peasant migration of all kinds except *orgnabor* in this category. Another unresolved issue is the persistence of seasonal migration or *otkhod.* Sonin believes it was dying out during the First FYP, and his *orgnabor* figures for 1933 and beyond do not include *otkhod.*[44] Panfilova believes that by the fall of 1931, most *otkhodniki* planned to stay permanently in the city, and thus that "the terms *otkhodnik, otkhodnichestvo,* one can only use conditionally."[45] A Gosplan document dated 20 May 1937 confirmed that the seasonal laborers employed in industry declined from 45 percent in 1932 to 28.5 percent in 1937. In absolute numbers, the decline was from 1,455,000 on 1 August 1932 to 999,000 on 1 August 1936. Based on this data, Gosplan's Sector on Labor and Cadre concluded that seasonal migration was being phased out.[46] While this was a substantial decline, the numbers of seasonal workers in construction, mining, logging, and other branches must have been much higher than the million in industry. (The importance of this confusion will become clearer in chapter 8, when I attempt to assess what it meant for urban community and family life.)

Most of the discussion of peasant migration at SiM focused on the housing question rather than on the migration itself. This was an appropriate emphasis, because information that peasant-migrants brought back to their fellow villagers, first and foremost about the availability of housing, was the single most important variable in the peasant's decision to migrate.[47]

Peasant-migrants had traditionally tried to find housing with members of their extended family or friends who were already living in Moscow, even if it meant nothing more than a bed in a corner of a room, partitioned by curtains or rags. Invariably, the apartment was already overcrowded. Usually a large family, or perhaps several families, shared a one- or two-room apartment, and the room was part of what was called a *kommunal'ka,* or communal apartment dwelling. The bathroom and kitchen were communal, with an entire floor of a building generally sharing the same facilities. Later, the *kommunalka* became a metaphor, in Soviet fiction and humor, for everything that was wrong and pathological in Soviet society.

Peasant-migrants working at SiM who hoped to remain permanently in the city would endure such conditions or even worse in barracks. If they became frustrated by the terrible living conditions, they usually returned to the village or left for another job. Frustration with factory work itself was the other major factor in the peasant-recruit's decision to return to the countryside or look for another factory job.

The success of peasant recruitment has to be measured, therefore, in terms of the housing situation. In late 1930, it was quite desperate at SiM. "About one thousand workers had no permanent place of living, sleeping anywhere, including in the *tsekh* itself! [In the shop of the steel plant where they worked.] The house for shock workers, which was under construction in 1930, was still not completed. The distribution of apartments by the Proletarskii Raisoviet for factory workers at Dangauerovka and at Dubrovka could not satisfy even one tenth of the total demand. In all, 200 rooms were distributed. . . . When the shock-workers' house was finished, about two hundred of the best *udarniki* [shock workers] settled there."[48] The overwhelming majority of the peasant-migrants at SiM were probably housed in the factory barracks. The dismal conditions of these barracks explains why they left SiM almost as quickly as they came. Getting peasants to come to Moscow was relatively easy; convincing them to stay was considerably more difficult. One worker who stayed despite the lack of housing was Naum Sirota, who was hired in the rolling mill shop at SiM in 1930, and for almost a year slept in the shop on top of a furnace. By the time he became an editor of the shop wall-newspaper, he had a bunk to sleep on in a barrack.[49]

Here, it is important to emphasize that the lack of discussion of *orgnabor* in the sources on SiM indicates that getting peasant-recruits to the plant was not a problem at all for the plant administration. Such recruits were coming in their traditional *zemliachestvo* and *artel'* networks, and the factory personnel department did not have to worry about sending pushers (*tolkachi*) out to the countryside to recruit them under *orgnabor* contracts.[50] Most peasants came to the SiM gate and personnel department individually, but based on a good knowledge of what their fellow villagers' experiences there had been—and with a bed in a barrack or room already reserved for them.

The most striking fact about the recruitment of peasants at SiM during the First FYP is that, like female recruits, they were concentrated in particular shops and occupations; that is, they were segregated. Whereas women were concentrated in the wire and cable finishing shops, the peasant-recruits were concentrated in the open hearth and blast furnace shops. This followed historical patterns in which the peasant-migrants had worked in the "hot" shops at the heaviest unskilled jobs at Guzhon, earning maximum wages for their unskilled labor in short stints. Segregation of peasant-workers on the shop floor followed from *artel'* and *zemliachestvo*.

Job segregation probably helped peasant-migrants to adapt to the factory environment during the 1930s, since it was usually fellow villagers, or at least fellow peasants, who explained to them a whole new vocabulary concerning the arcane details of the Soviet industrial system such as work norms, piece rates, shock-work, socialist competitions, obligatory state loans, draconian labor laws, and the role of factory trade-union committees as well as party committees. But, as with women, peasant-recruits faced the problem of occupational segregation, which potentially blocked their training and promotion.

Based on a careful study of the existing data on the social origins of workers at SiM, I. L. Kornakovskii concluded that urban recruits were disproportionately drawn into the "cold" (*metiznye*) shops and that peasants were disproportionately recruited into the "hot" (*metallurgicheskie*) shops. In interpreting this data, Kornakovskii points out that during the First FYP, the wire, cable, press, and casting shops, all *metiznyi* shops, were either entirely rebuilt or substantially enlarged, while the metallurgical shops—the open hearth, the rolling mill, and sheet metal shops—were much older both in terms of their capital stock and technology and in terms of the average age of their workers.[51] The data, however, are too crude to determine if peasant youth were less segregated than older peasant-migrants.

Old patterns of occupational segregation tended to persist longer in the steel industry, particularly in older plants like SiM, than in newer factories and in new branches of industry. SiM had a well-established work collective of over five thousand workers in 1928, and this core group of established workers still constituted between one-half and one-third of the work force when the dust settled from the First FYP, on 1 January 1933, when the size of the work force reached almost 15,000, according to some sources. Then, with layoffs in the first half of 1933, the size of the work force declined to under 10,000, and so the pre-1928 workers constituted roughly half of the SiM work force once the dust had settled from the First FYP reconstruction drive. (See table 3.2.) On the other hand, at an entirely new steel plant such as Magnitogorsk, the only established workers were those cadre sent from SiM or Putilov to help get the factory on-line. These were a tiny fraction of all the production workers at the MMK.

Likewise, at a new assembly-line auto plant, like Nizhni Novgorod, the only established workers were those sent on assignment from ZiS or other machine-construction factories. Even at ZiS, established workers constituted something less than 10 percent of the total on 1 January 1933, as the AMO-ZiS work force increased more than tenfold during the First FYP, jumping from 1,798 workers in 1928 to 19,329 workers (including ITR) in 1932. Furthermore, rapid expansion continued through the 1930s, when the size of the work force grew to 37,000 in 1937, at the end of the Second FYP, and to 40,000 by 1940.[52] The expansion of the work force at SiM was not nearly so

Table 3.2. Expansion of the SiM Work Force During the First FYP

	Workers	White Collar	Total Staff
KORNAKOVSKII			
1928	5,051	560	
1929	5,082	742	
1930	8,355	972	
1931	10,042	1,112	
1932	8,073	1,415	
GARF			
1928/29		5,000	8,000
1929/30		6–7,000	10,000
1931		8,000	12,000
1932		10,000	15,000

Sources: Kornakovskii, "Zavod 'Serp i Molot,'" p. 194; GARF f. 7952, op. 3, d. 282, l. 11.

dramatic, and thus the weight of established workers and patterns of job segregation persisted much longer. Technology was an important part of the
equation, as there were few jobs that women were excluded from at ZiS, and
no hot shop where peasant-workers were segregated.

In the First FYP, the SiM work force either doubled or tripled, increasing
from 5,000 to 10,000 or 15,000, depending how the work staff is counted.[53]
Table 3.2 compares two sets of figures. After the layoffs in 1933, the work
force, waged and salaried, stabilized at roughly ten thousand for the remainder of the decade. Thereafter, the annual influx of recruits roughly
matched the number of workers leaving (retirement, quits, firings, transfers). In this equilibrium environment, breaking through older segregated
patterns of employment was far more difficult than in a factory like AMO-
ZiS, where expansion of the work force was continuous and dramatic
through the 1930s.

At AMO-ZiS, from the very beginning of the First FYP, new recruits were
assigned jobs in a much less segregated pattern than at SiM. In part, this
greater degree of integration came about because there was less prejudice
against employing women on the various mechanized and automated jobs
typical of an auto plant; it was thought that women would perform well on
the assembly line. More fundamentally, however, it stemmed from the fact
that the assembly-line jobs were entirely new, and there were no customary
patterns of recruitment and male work culture that had to be overcome.
Likewise for the peasant-recruits. In the new factories on the Soviet periphery, such as GAZ (Gor'kii Auto Plant), as the Niznyi Novgorod auto plant was
renamed in 1936, and the MMK, where the work force grew even more
rapidly, I would hypothesize that the pattern of integration was still more
pronounced at the outset, and any segregation between shops or occupations that the thin layer of skilled workers brought with them from Moscow
was more easily overcome.

Conclusions

Three broad conclusions emerge from this study of recruitment patterns
and initial job placement at SiM. First, recruitment was generally an enterprise responsibility and was generally spontaneous and unplanned. The enterprise took what it could get at the factory gate, and workers came by word
of mouth from the village or from friends or family in Moscow. Second, while
recruitment of new workers was comparatively easy at a large plant in the
capital city, holding onto the new recruits was a more difficult problem.
Turnover, as we will see in the next chapter, was forcing the SiM and other
factory administrations to recruit over and over again. Third, at a factory like

SiM, recruitment initially followed traditional patterns of shop and job seg-regation, with peasants in subordinate positions in the hot metallurgical shops, and women in subordinate positions in the cold shops. Soon, how-ever, these traditional occupational patterns would change, partly because of new technologies, partly because of the social mobility of youth, but mainly because the sheer numbers of new workers meant that the aristocrats' tight control over the work process (and labor market), under the rigid appren-ticeship system would yield to new patterns of placement and training.

Archival documents show that detailed plans were drawn up for some enterprises, indicating what type of labor was needed and from which social groups and geographic regions the new workers should be recruited.[54] Such plans were rarely effective, however and, in practice, enterprises took anyone who showed up at the factory gates. As Tevosian noted in 1936 (he was di-rector of the trust Spetsstal' and thus the intermediary official between the director of SiM, Stepanov, and the commissar of heavy industry, Or-dzhonikidze), not much had changed since the First FYP. In 1936, as in 1933 or in 1930, he noted, labor recruitment at SiM was still spontaneous (*samotekom*).[55]

The best description of how enterprises hired workers in the First FYP comes from a discussion in the council of the Metalworkers' Union on the Krasnyi Putilov plant in Leningrad. The boss of the tractor department at Putilov, Plekhanov, told the meeting of trade-union officials: "Here is the pic-ture, comrades, of how we fulfilled the [production] plan. . . . From the point of view of the factory administration . . . [we must] do whatever is nec-essary in order to fulfill the tractor program. . . . [They tell us] 'If you need workers—hire them. [If] there are no workers—hire people at the gate. [If] you need overtime—take however much you need.' Everything is [to be] given."[56]

At this same meeting, the discussion centered on labor turnover, the bane of the factory recruitment organs. A blacksmith from the tractor de-partment explained that high labor turnover in his department could not be blamed on the so-called rolling stones (*letuny*), contrary to what party leaders and the press constantly reiterated. He listed several factors, such as lack of housing, which were causing labor turnover, and then he explained, "We get a new worker from the village, he does not know our task, does not know our enterprise, everything seems awful to him, he works for one month, and then he leaves. If we educated him, he would understand, and would stay to work."[57] Contradicting the official line, this worker saw the peasant-recruit as a victim rather than as villain. The problem of labor turnover made rational and planned labor recruitment impossible during the First FYP. This was the source of the urban "quicksand society," but the labor turnover *(tekuchest'),* which was perceived by the regime to be an unmitigated evil was ephemeral and would partially correct itself after 1933.

A Crisis of a New Type: Labor Famine

From mass unemployment, to labor deficit, to widespread labor famine—this was the trajectory of the inversion of the labor market caused, first and foremost, by the scale of the regime's program of new construction and superindustrialization. This inversion threw the Stalinist leadership and economic policymakers alike into a state of confusion and then utter panic during the First FYP. Indeed, as the deficit turned into famine, the industrialization drive was on the verge of collapse. That it did not can be explained, first and foremost, by the decision of the combined Plenum in January 1933 to halt all new construction projects and complete all current construction projects, to lower growth targets for the Second FYP, to "assimilate" technology, and to put a temporary freeze on enterprise hiring.[58]

The labor market inversion was so extraordinarily rapid that, for a time in 1930, each of these two opposite imbalances, unemployment and labor shortage, could be found simultaneously in different sectors or branches of the economy, or in different geographic regions. The inversion perplexed Soviet policymakers and threw the economists working in the Commissariat of Labor (Narkomtrud, NKT), VSNKh, and VTsSPS into disarray. They began to carefully examine the pay scales and lack of material incentives caused by irrational variations in wage payments and bonuses.[59]

The labor market inversion has also wrought havoc with historical explanation. Soviet historians have universally interpreted the sudden inversion as the triumph of the planned economy in guaranteeing full employment. Non-Soviet historians have generally interpreted it, on the contrary, as a beneficial albeit unplanned side effect of the Stalinist policy of superindustrialization.[60] I would suggest a different reading, based on the factory newspaper, workers' memoirs, and archival documents from the PR and SiM.

Rather than a healthy, full employment economy, either by design or accidentally, the Soviet economy quickly veered from a labor market troubled by chronic rural underemployment and high urban unemployment rates under NEP, to an even more troubled "shortage economy," in which production was slowed or even stopped by labor deficits, supply deficits, and deficits in equipment and machines.[61] This was a permanent feature of forced industrialization, with stoppages so widespread by the end of 1932 that it was comparable to massive unemployment in the capitalist economy.

By the end of 1932, shortages, and particularly the labor shortage, were threatening to halt industrialization, and the economy was in a profound crisis, on the verge of collapse.

The regime acted decisively in January 1933 to reduce its output targets and growth rates for 1933 to 13 percent. It was a year for completing the projects already begun and for "mastering technique."[62] In fact, in 1933, there would be layoffs from bloated enterprises and the rate of industrial growth was closer to 5 percent.[63] When hiring resumed again in late 1933, it was on a much more modest scale, and would remain so through the rest of the decade. Still, it remained a labor-shortage economy.

As the Hungarian economist Janos Kornai has defined it, the "shortage economy," or the "resource-constrained" Soviet-type economy, differs fundamentally from the "demand-constrained" market economic system, precisely in that it inverts the relation between supply and demand. This means that:

In a resource constrained economy, after the transitory historical period of absorption of labor, full employment becomes permanent. This is one of the most important achievements of the socialist economy. At the same time, chronic labor shortage emerges as one of the manifestations of resource shortage....

Full employment is not brought about by specific economic policy measures aimed at increasing employment, and not even by planning which envisages labor-absorbing input-output combinations. An explanation of the phenomenon must be looked for in the institutional conditions. It is in consequence of the soft budget constraint that demand for resources grows almost insatiable. Demand for resources, including demand for labor, must necessarily grow as long as it does not hit the supply constraint.[64]

The documents support Kornai's analysis and show that the elimination of unemployment in the First FYP was really an unplanned labor shortage, that by 1932 the labor shortage was a far deeper crisis than any putative crisis of NEP caused by high unemployment in 1928, and that the regime did not anticipate the problem, nor did it understand how to respond to it until after it had declared the First FYP successfully completed at the end of 1932. This can be documented through employment statistics, workers' memoirs, and in the policy debates and the decrees of the state and party organs. However, it can be traced and documented best through Stalin's speeches at the Sixteenth Party Congress in June 1930, and in his speech before chief administrators and factory directors on 23 June 1931, which subsequently became known as the "Six Conditions of Victory" speech. The latter speech was the most important statement Stalin ever made concerning labor policy and social policy.

The initial reason for the regime's failure to anticipate a labor shortage was, in all likelihood, the high unemployment level in 1928. The failure to understand the serious nature of the problem persisted after 1930, when unemployment was officially eradicated, probably due to the belief in almost unlimited labor reserves among the three subaltern groups: peasants, housewives, and youth. Finally, the failure to recognize the impending crisis in 1931 and 1932 can probably be best explained in the language and ideology of the Stalin leadership itself. They denounced "wreckers" who were sabotaging policy implementation and recalcitrant "class aliens" who were worming their way into the working class and disrupting production. Then, in "Six Conditions of Victory," Stalin shifted the blame, claiming that the peasant was no longer interested in migrating to the city and the factory since the *muzhik* now had such a "good life" on the *kolkhoz*. The passage, which came under his first "condition" outlining the policy of *orgnabor,* was one of his most notorious.

We tore out stratification by the roots in the countryside, and thus we also overcame that mass poverty which chased the peasant from the countryside to the city. Finally, we supplied the countryside with tens of thousands of tractors and agricultural machines, smashed the kulaks, organized kolkhozy, and gave to the peasant the possibility of living and working like a human being. Now, one can no longer call the countryside the "step-mother" of the peasants. Precisely for this reason, because it no longer is the step-mother, the peasant has now settled in the countryside, and … the spontaneous flow of labor power to the city no longer exists.[65]

As Arutiunian pointed out, this was pure nonsense, since 4.5 million peasants went on *otkhod* in 1931, amounting to at least one-sixth of the adult male peasant population. As Stalin spoke, the USSR was, indeed, in the midst of a peasant migration of historically unprecedented proportions. Arutiunian argued that the regime implemented the Passport Act at the end of 1932 to keep the peasants from swarming into the cities, proving Stalin to have been wrong.[66] We might add what he could not write in 1964, that by the end of 1932, peasants were swarming into the cities in a desperate attempt to avoid starvation.

Stalin's analysis, again blaming the peasants, deflected blame from the dual sources of the labor deficits: the scale of the industrialization drive, with its insatiable need for construction and production workers; and the long-term problem of an institutional culture of "soft budget constraints" which made labor hoarding inevitable. The two factors were interrelated during the First FYP, when the drive gave birth to the soft budgets that Kornai found under less hectic conditions of industrial growth in Hungary during the

1960s. Stalin's search for an explanation reflected the mounting frustration of the leadership.

Even as the crisis deepened in 1932, Stalin, the planners, and policymakers thought that the labor reserves could meet the needs of industry and could be recruited with the proper administrative measures. They were relying on estimates of rural overpopulation, which ranged anywhere from 5 to 30 million persons.[67] Furthermore, according to one estimate by labor economists, the number of women who could be brought from the unpaid urban household sector of the economy into its wage labor sector was around 5 million.[68] The reserve of youth, it would seem, was not less.

The leadership, policymakers, economists, and planners were, during the First FYP, all still thinking in terms of the NEP experience, when peasants, women, and youth had waged a somewhat desperate struggle merely for the right to register as unemployed persons at labor exchanges. In fact, as the history of the PR and SiM show, they were right in these assumptions. Peasants, women, and youth remained anxious to find factory work, and entered the factory labor force in record numbers. Yet there never seemed to be enough new recruits to meet managers' demands for new workers and for cadre during the First FYP. The crux of the problem was not sheer numbers; they fulfilled and overfulfilled planned targets for staff, as was frequently noted and criticized. Rather the crux of the problem was turnover and training of personnel and establishing a reliable and productive work force.

It is worth noting here the relevance of Moshe Lewin's methodological breakthrough for labor recruitment. Not only was the Stalin regime improvising its industrial policy and its labor policy, but it was forced to do so in the context of a society and of worker behavior that it did not understand, but which it had to adjust to. The regime's totalitarian aspirations were more a reflection of its frustrations in this process of adjustment than they were of its ability to control the labor market or replace it with a planned distribution of workers. The problems and the solutions were, in some ways, similar to that of establishing the workday on the *kolhoz* and the *kolkhoz* brigade. The "draconian labor laws," were crude tools in attempting to deal with a society and labor force that were responding rationally (as Filtzer argued) to the inverted labor market.

Still, again following Lewin, this was not a weak regime or one without ability to implement its policies. After some major shifts, which included Stalin's "Six Conditions" speech, and the decisions in early 1933 to switch from new construction to "assimilation," the regime's industrialization drive was consolidated and would resume in a more consistent way in 1934. The labor market would remain inverted but the labor famine disappeared until the Second World War. With the crisis behind it, the regime would ultimately succeed in putting together a new industrial labor force and productivity would increase, albeit slowly. The regime's new labor policy and its efforts at recruiting workers were far more successful, however, than its *kolkhoz* policies, because it would be able to take advantage, albeit unwittingly, of the subaltern rural and urban workers' very widespread desire to engage in wage labor in the factories, particularly given the dismal alternative for many, on the *kolkhoz*.

4

ATTACHING WORKERS:
THE STICK, THE CARROT, AND THE
LABOR MARKET

The labor problem in Soviet Russia in 1930, as in Great Britain a century before, meant, first and foremost, finding new workers. Closely related was the problem of holding onto these recruits. The problem of *tekuchest'*, or labor turnover, from the standpoint of the Soviet regime, was rooted in petty bourgeois indiscipline, and especially in peasant values and attitudes. The peasant-migrant would supposedly wander from plant to plant in search of the "long ruble." They were pejoratively described in official jargon as *letuny* (rolling stones), *prebezhiki* (labor deserters), *rvachi* (self-seekers), and sometimes *prikhlebitel'ei* (freeloaders, or persons who had falsified documents or their status in order to live in factory housing or gain access to closed shops even though they no longer or never worked at that factory). The regime responded with a series of new regulations, decrees, and resolutions, under the rubric of "tightening labor discipline," which were aimed at "attaching" the new recruit to the factory, the shop, and even the workbench.[1] A cluster of such draconian labor laws, as they have rightly been labeled outside the USSR, were issued during the First FYP, and were the regime's disciplinary stick in the battle against labor turnover.

Stalin called *tekuchest'* the bane or curse of Soviet industry in his "Six Conditions" speech and offered, as a complementary approach to the draconian laws, the carrot of sharply differentiated wages. In this chapter, after briefly reviewing Schwarz and Filtzer on the "stick," I elaborate on the neglected "carrot" in Stalin's approach. In both sections, I argue that the Soviet labor market was not suppressed during the 1930s and that workers and managers were responding to changing trends in wages and in employment. The chapter then concludes with a cyclical theory of the Soviet labor market under Stalinism, from 1929 to 1953, which would explain why neither the stick nor the carrot was effective in reducing labor turnover until after 1933. It would also explain why a second cluster of draconian labor laws were legislated after 1938.

The Draconian Labor Laws and Their Impact

These laws have been described in detail in Solomon Schwarz's work, and he imputed to the regime the intention of replacing the free labor market with a system of compulsory labor by assignment. The impact of these laws has been reexamined by Donald Filtzer, who found that particularly those laws requiring the firing of tardy or absent workers were widely circumvented by management-worker collusion. This, he argued, caused a cycle in which the regime would attempt to close off loopholes, threatening to prosecute managers as well as workers. Filtzer's revisionsism followed Lewin's methodological breakthrough, in that the labor laws were the mirror image of the even more draconian *kolkhoz* regulations. What remains unexplained, however, in both Schwarz's and Filtzer's accounts is why the labor laws were bunched in two clusters, in 1930–32 and again in 1938–40, and what happened in between.

Schwarz traced three themes in the first cluster of laws. First, the unemployed workers registered on the labor exchanges were to be assigned jobs and expelled if they did not take them. This meant the conversion of these exchanges, by early 1931, into job assignment bureaus. Second, the regime sought to eliminate any dereliction of work duty, that is, unexcused absences or tardiness, requiring first the firing of workers for fairly trivial incidents, then expelling workers from their apartments and depriving them of ration cards. This series of laws culminated with the threat of prosecuting managers who did not fire recalcitrant workers. Third, a series of regulations, beginning with proposals for a "work book" in early 1931, and culminating with the Passport Act of 27 December 1932, were aimed at tightly regulating, if not controlling, the hiring of workers. For Schwarz, the work book law of December 1938 and subsequent law of 20 June 1940 meant the end of the labor market.[2]

Schwarz noted that the immediate objective of the Passport Act was to halt the influx of peasant-migrants, as the regime had called for a freeze on hiring for 1933. The long-term objective, however, was to prevent those workers who had quit jobs and those who had been fired from jobs from being re-hired by their enterprise or others. Schwarz concluded that the act "practi-cally wiped out the workers' freedom to move from job to job," adding that "labor turnover began to drop substantially."[3]

Schwarz noted, in passing, that the effectiveness of these laws and of the Passport Act in reducing labor turnover was connected to the decision to lay off workers in early 1933.[4] In other words, the threat of firing had teeth when jobs were not so easily found. In his first chapter, on the composition and growth of the Soviet working class, Schwarz claimed that total employees were supposed to be reduced by layoffs from 22.9 million at the end of 1932 to 21.3 million at the end of 1933, but that the actual decline in 1933 was 600,000.[5] He also noted, without drawing conclusions on labor market im-pact, that the projections in the Second FYP called for a major shift from two-thirds rural recruitment to two-thirds urban recruitment, but that actual new hirees during the Second FYP numbered some 2 million less than antici-pated.[6] Then, in his third chapter, on the labor relationship, he moved from a discussion of the first to the second cluster of draconian laws, without draw-ing any connection to the labor force trends that he had discussed in the first chapter, or to the labor market trends that he had discussed in the second. Yet, as I will argue below, an explanation for the lack of new legislation after December 1932, and for the legislation of new labor laws in December 1938, is to be found in the shifts in the labor market, which closely followed the shifting political decisions and imperatives of the regime over the course of the decade.

The second cluster of draconian laws, starting with the introduction of the work book on 20 December 1938, is introduced by Schwarz as if the regime was merely picking up where it left off six years before with the Pass-port Act.[7] The work book law indeed seemed to reiterate the Passport Act, and it was followed, a week later, by a law requiring the firing of workers for three disciplinary infractions (truancy or tardiness) within a single month and requiring that the worker give one month notice before quitting a job. This 28 December 1938 law was also a reiteration of the first cluster of tru-ancy laws. Something new was proposed in the most infamous of the dra-conian laws, that of 20 June 1940, which legally abolished the right to quit a job; henceforth, legal work transfers were only to be by managerial authorization. Schwarz concluded that "employment ceased to be a free contractual relationship . . . it became a relationship founded on the principle of compulsory labor."[8] The final act was the 2 October 1940 law establishing State Labor Reserves that would supervise registration and vocational training of youth in a reorganized FZO, completing the process of eliminating the free labor market in Schwarz's account.[9]

Oleg Khlevniuk has shown that the implementation of the law of 20 June 1940 was not so consistent in time or place as Schwarz had assumed. Much along the lines of Filtzer's revisionist approach to worker-management collusion, Khlevniuk argued that while the law was a powerful new intervention of the state, aiming at asserting greater control in the labor market, it was likely to be circumvented with managerial complicity whenever and wherever the regime relaxed its legal vigilance. Managers would certainly continue to rehire workers whenever they could do so without prosecution, given the severe labor shortages of the times.[10]

Filtzer's account of the first cluster of draconian laws shifted the focus from the intent of the laws to their impact. He argued that strike activity died out in 1933, and the only forms of protest workers could then muster were work-to-rule strikes, slowdowns, and quitting or indiscipline. Truancy and labor turnover were effectively reduced, he argued, because the managers who ignored the law and hired new workers could themselves face prosecution. He also noted, merely in passing, that the labor shortage in 1930 made enforcement of such laws virtually impossible, but this reference to the context of the labor market, as in Schwarz, was never sufficiently integrated into his account. His discussion of the second cluster of laws suggested that workers and managers had already learned in the first cluster how to circumvent them, and they applied this "training" to dealing with the even more draconian legislation on the eve of the war.[11]

Two empirically documented patterns emerged in Filtzer's careful sifting through Soviet published data on firings and on labor turnover. First, he argued that "in the wake of the laws of 1930–32, the incidence of both truancy and job changing, or turnover, fell considerably and remained more or less stable until late 1938." Second, he claimed that enforcement of these laws was relaxed somewhat after 1932, but he also noted: "This is not to say that the law of November [15] 1932 [firing for a single day of unjustified absenteeism in one month] was not being enforced. In 1934 . . . 22.3 percent of the industrial work force was discharged for truancy; in 1935, 18 percent, in 1936, 17 percent."[12]

These Soviet data, as Filtzer has reproduced it, require some serious rethinking about the relationship between the labor market and state intervention. First, Filtzer has emphasized the absurdity of the situation in which workers were intentionally using the truancy laws to get fired since voluntary quitting was, by law, supposed to be a violation and managers were not supposed to hire those workers who had quit prior employment. Of course, they were not supposed to hire truants who had been fired either, so it is still unclear how these laws worked in practice. Filtzer himself noted that the rates of discharge given for 1934–36, of 17–22 percent, are probably exaggerated because many of those fired were counted twice.[13] Even reduced to take this factor into account, these extraordinarily high figures still support his claim that workers were intentionally violating the truancy laws as a way of recouping their labor mobility since their legal right to quit was in doubt after 1932.[14] This kind of irrational legal morass, in which draconian antitruancy laws contradicted draconian antiquitting laws, in part at least, explains the second cluster of labor laws in 1938–40: to eliminate the loopholes.

More significant, however, are the conclusions that we might draw from Filtzer's data on truancy, firings, and especially on turnover rates in relation to state intervention. His data on all three clearly show a rising trend in 1930–32, a declining trend in 1933–37, and a rising trend again in 1938–40. Remarkably, this was precisely the pattern of clustering of the draconian laws and their enforcement: they were decreed and enforced stringently in 1930–32 and 1938–40, whereas they atrophied in 1933–37. Thus, we might conclude that state intervention had the opposite effect as intended, but a better explanation, I would argue, is that both state intervention and labor indiscipline were rising when the labor market inversion was reaching famine conditions. The labor market was decisive. Filtzer's all-union data, and data from SiM, support this contention, which neither Schwarz nor Filtzer asserted.

Citing Soviet sources, Filtzer suggested that the rate of turnover in Soviet industry increased from 115.2 percent in 1929 to 152.4 percent in 1930 and then declined slightly, to 136.8 percent in 1931, 135.3 percent in 1932, and 122.4 percent in 1933. In 1934, the rate fell considerably to 96.7 percent, in 1935 to 86.1 percent, and in 1936 to 87.5 percent. After 1937, he argued, the rate of turnover began to increase again.[15] Elsewhere, Filtzer presented the same picture with Soviet data organized in terms of average length of days on the job, showing that "the average Soviet worker changed jobs once every eight months in 1930, every nine months in 1932, every fourteen months in 1936 and 1937, every seventeen months in 1938, and every thirteen months in 1939."[16]

These data confirm my contention that high turnover and draconian laws were clustered in the same patterns, even if the turnover showed a slight decline in 1931–33. What is striking is how high the turnover rate remained despite the draconian labor laws in those three years. What will become clear below in my discussion of labor market cycles, is that these shifting clusters of indiscipline and draconian laws were a direct reflection of sudden and sharp shifts in the labor market, with the inversion gap widening toward labor famine in 1932, narrowing in 1933–37, and widening again in 1938–41.

Turnover figures would vary, of course, from enterprise to enterprise, but tracing the evidence for SiM reaffirms these all-union patterns. In the First FYP at SiM, the figures were less than 100 percent, probably because it was an older factory. Kornakovskii, using the Central State Archives, calculated labor turnover at SiM during the First FYP (see table 4.1). He found that it was highest in the metallurgical shops—the open hearth, the rolled metals, the sheet metal, and the model-forge shops. These were the shops in which peasant-migrants congregated, and in the yearly reports prepared for the administration, they most frequently listed returning to the village to agricultural work as their reason for leaving. However, a lack of housing for the peasant-migrants, not their so-called peasant mentality, was a central obstacle to the *orgnabor* campaigns and a major cause of peasants returning to the village.[17]

It is not clear that labor turnover was decreasing at SiM after 1930, as Kornakovskii's data suggest. The archives present a confusing picture. One source indicates that the rate of turnover was cut in half during the second half of 1931. Another shows that in the first quarter of 1932, 4,455 workers were hired and 4,349 left.[18] These last figures for 1932 are well over 100 percent, and thus, it seems likely that the rate of turnover was rising at SiM throughout the First FYP.

An article titled "He Who Does Not Work, Shall Not Eat," which appeared in *Martenovka* on 18 November 1932, was typical of the party's mood three days after passing the law requiring immediate firing for one day of unexcused absence from work. It blamed rapid turnover on workers and managers who were violating Soviet law. At SiM, during the second quarter of 1932, the article noted, 2,244 workers were hired while 2,068 left, and in the third quarter of 1932, 2,400 were hired while 2,477 left. This was more than

Table 4.1. Average Annual Turnover at SiM

	1928/29	1929/30	1931	1932
Number of workers	5,082	8,355	10,042	8,013
Number who left	2,338	7,854	8,121	6,417
Turnover	46%	94%	81%	80%

Source: Kornakovskii, "Zavod 'Serp i Molot,'" p. 230, based on GARF f. 7952, op. 3, d. 201, l. 52; d. 202, l. 15; d. 208, l. 41.

four times the rate of turnover in the first half of 1930. The article concluded that the resolutions stipulating that a worker fired for labor indiscipline could not be hired again for six months in any plant, and requiring immediate firing for one day of labor absenteeism, were being blatantly violated at SiM. In some cases, workers had been absent for eight days in succession without cause and were still not fired. In other cases, workers intentionally stayed home in order to be fired, so as to be able to legally move to another enterprise. SiM hired workers in violation of the six-month provision.[19]

According to E. I. Gaidul', perhaps related to I. P. Gaidul', the former party committee secretary at SiM and the former party committee secretary of the Proletarskii *raikom*, writing in the metallurgy journal in 1936, the turn-around in steel occurred in 1933 and 1934. He noted that in 1931, labor productivity in heavy metallurgy actually fell 2.6 percent but wages increased by 18.6 percent. In 1932, productivity increased by 15 percent, but wages increased far more rapidly, at a rate of 28.9 percent. Finally, for the first time in 1933, the correlation was reversed, as labor productivity increased by 10 percent, and wages only by 6 percent; and in 1934, this positive trend continued. In analyzing these figures, Gaidul' reached the conclusion that "for heavy metallurgy, 1934 was the breakthrough year."[20] It was in many branches of the economy.

The key factor was the stabilizing pattern of incremental labor recruitment during the Second FYP, rather than the frenzied labor recruitment of the First FYP. This pattern emerges clearly in *Martenovka*. In an article published on 24 September 1934 (p. 2), A. Rubanov noted that in 1933, SiM reduced its staff by 1,500 people, cutting the total plant work force from 11,000 to 9,500. Yet the factory had a higher rate of plan fulfillment in 1933 than in 1932, in spite of the fact that the plan for 1933 called for a 25–30 percent increase in output. Rubanov drew the obvious conclusion that prior to 1933, SiM had superfluous workers, who merely got in one another's way.

The reduction of the work force in 1933 at SiM would be permanent, and after 1933 labor productivity continued to increase. This fact was applauded by the commissar of heavy industry, S. Ordzhonikidze, in his speech "Questions of Labor" at the Seventh All-Union Congress of Soviets held in February 1935. Ordzhonikidze, who was widely perceived to be Stepanov's patron, praised the Makeevskii and SiM plants:

We are the only country in the world with the seven-hour work day, but we do not fully use these seven hours. The correct organization of wages will serve as the best linchpin for the growth of labor productivity. Thus, where wages are organized correctly, we have striking results. Take, for example, two plants: the Makeevskii metallurgical plant and the Moscow plant, SiM. At SiM, in four years the net product has increased by 82 percent, while the work staff has been reduced by 22 percent. Labor productivity has grown by 34 percent. This is the result of good [managerial] work in the organization of production and in setting aside [wage] funds for the leading occupations. The average earning of a worker in the marten-ovskii shop at SiM, in the third quarter of 1934, was 261 rubles, and in November of 1934 it was 271 rubles. However, a steel smelter of the eighth razriad [the highest paid] received 550 rubles for the third quarter and 705 rubles for November. An apprentice smelter earned 350 rubles in the third quarter and 374 in November ... this [wide differentiation of wages] is why Stepanov is able to raise simultaneously productivity of labor and its pay.

We have the same thing in the Makeevskii plant. Here, Comrade Gvakhariia succeeded in proving that he has the cheapest iron in the country, and the highest wages.[21]

This set the tone for a round of self-congratulation at the congress on the part of the SiM administration. The boss of the *martenovskii* shop, the young engineer M. N. Korolev, noted that his shop's output increased by 18 percent in 1934 as opposed to 1933, with *fewer* workers. All the workers in this shop had passed the *tekhminimum* exams, and the shop was producing almost six tons of steel per hour, which was very close to the technical limit. However, Korolev noted, costs were too high, at 122 rubles per ingot of iron and 144 rubles per ingot of steel.[22] Tarlinskii, superintendant of the rolling-metals shop, attributed the high costs to *prostoi* (idleness).

The chief engineer, Marmorshtein, claimed that the big improvement in 1934 output over 1933 was attributable to the fact that 1934 was the first year in which the plant did not shut down in August. Uninterrupted production, he argued, allowed for an increase in output while production workers were reduced from 7,606 in 1933 to 7,171 in 1934.[23]

Finally, Stepanov, the Red Director, was more modest in summing up the discussion. He noted that despite successfully fulfilling the plan, the SiM plant was still running at a loss, at least according to planned prices. In terms of market prices, he claimed, many of the shops in the plant were profitable. However, the objective he set was not only to meet the plan's targets for output, but to reduce the cost of steel ingots to not more than 125 rubles each. Citing Ordzhonikidze's speech at the congress, Stepanov blamed the catastrophic accidents in the rolling mill shop, and resulting worker idleness, for the continued high costs of production.[24]

The coincidence of declining turnover, declining absenteeism, rising labor productivity, with lessening enforcement of the labor laws, on the one hand, and stabilization of recruitment of new workers, on the other, is too strong to have been merely accidental. According to the evidence from *Martenovka*, turnover began to decline substantially at SiM sometime after 1934. An article entitled "The Factory Is Not an Entry Courtyard" shows that labor turnover was down considerably both in absolute and relative numbers in 1936 when 3,197 workers left and 4,397 new workers were hired. By the end of 1936, according to this account, the total number of workers was only 7,806, and so, depending on the method of calculation, the annual rate of turnover was about 50 percent.[25] Then, in 1938 and 1939, articles in *Marten-ovka* once again became more strident about the problem of labor turnover, indicating that the rate was increasing once again.[26] No surprise in that, since Stepanov's entire management team had been purged.

Thus, the relative success in reducing labor turnover at SiM after 1933 was a function of several factors. First, the size of the work force declined in 1933 and then did not change much over the rest of the decade, remaining constant at about ten thousand total wage workers and salaried employees. Recruitment was moderate, and mainly to replace retirees, which meant a slow and steady pattern of hiring. Second, this steady rate of increase meant that it was easier to attend to the needs and concerns of the new workers on the shop floor and that it was easier to train them. Third, while housing problems persisted, they were gradually alleviated after 1933, as was the famine crisis of that year. The experience of SiM shows that feeding the work force and housing the new workers adequately was the first and the most fundamental prerequisite for successfully "attaching" a factory work collective. The clusters of draconian laws and their tight enforcement was a reflection of the shifting labor market, as were indicators of labor indiscipline, such as turnover, truancy, and labor productivity.

Neither Schwarz nor Filtzer, by any means, entirely ignored the labor market in explaining these trends. Schwarz, as noted, covered aspects of the labor market trends in his second chapter, where he argued it was being eliminated by the state; Filtzer, too, noted the impact of the layoffs in 1933 and the subsequent improvement in economic conditions. He concluded his section on the First FYP:

In the middle of a severe famine it would have been surprising if the threat of loss of ration privileges and housing did not have some effect. But the economic recovery of the mid 1930s itself soon nullified the utility of these sanctions. At the same time it made the regime more tolerant of forms of misconduct which a few years earlier it had deemed a threat to its industrial policy . . . the regime shifted its attention away from overt violations of "labor discipline" and towards the much more pressing question of raising productivity. Although turnover and absenteeism remained high, the elite accorded them relatively low priority until late 1938, when it again sought to whip the working class into line through repressive measures.[27]

Then, Filtzer noted the impact of the draft and impending World War on rising turnover.[28] Despite such instances, however, in Filtzer's account even more than in Schwarz's, the labor market remained strictly in the background, and the extraordinary coincidence of the rising labor turnover and the institution of the draconian labor laws, in two distinct two-year clusters, is not sufficiently explained, let alone connected to the labor famine. Likewise, the extraordinary fact of the five-year hiatus of decline in the level of labor turnover and the coincidence with no new labor legislation, is not sufficiently explained. The key factor in accounting for these coincidences, as I argue below, was the labor market.[29]

Turnover and Wage Incentives: Stalin's "Six Conditions" Speech

The second regime strategy was the carrot of wage incentives, an attempt to convince workers to stay on the job, work hard, train and study, and raise their skill and wage rankings. This policy evolved partly out of the failure of the draconian laws, and partly due to the exigencies of the Stalinist political struggle against the legacy of Old Bolshevik leadership in trade unions. While in the long run this would prove to have greater impact than draconian laws in shaping industrial labor relations, it had no discernible, immediate impact on reducing labor turnover after 23 June 1931, when Stalin introduced the new strategy in his "Six Conditions" speech. That again, was because of the impending labor famine.

Stalin's first condition, organized recruitment or *orgnabor,* as we have seen, was a call for bringing the peasant *kolkhozniki,* by contract, to the factory, since they were supposedly now reluctant to leave their idyllic life on collective farms. His second condition, wage differentiation or an end to "petty bourgeois egalitarianism" (*uravnilovka*), would, he claimed, eradicate the bane of labor turnover.[30] Stalin's foray into the ideology of antiegalitarianism here contradicted not only Marxism on the necessary diminution of social stratification under socialism, but also his own assumptions about rooting out class stratification in the countryside. Like Bentham or Mill, rather than Marx, Stalin's assumption was that individuals would act rationally so as to maximize their income and thus would respond to wage incentives, making for the most productive labor force and society. Furthermore, Stalin grossly distorted the record on prior Soviet wage policy, which had vacillated between the conflicting objectives of equality and efficiency since 1917 and had never been strongly egalitarian.[31]

Less famous than Stalin's antiegalitarianism but ultimately just as significant, if not more, were the elements in this speech that proposed a type of ersatz social contract. Elaborating on the second condition, Stalin called for improvement of workers' living standards, which was, at least potentially, a very different emphasis than wage differentiation. It was potentially quite egalitarian, but beyond that it defined a new relationship between state and society. He argued that the Soviet worker now expected a higher living standard and that since the state was demanding an unprecedented level of labor productivity, it was obligated to meet the worker's desire to "live with all his material and cultural needs answered, including consumer goods, housing, and cultural activity."[32] Stalin's subsequent four conditions continued to suggest elements of this social contract. By eliminating *obezlichka,* that is, by holding managers accountable under one-man-management, by integrating technically educated Soviet worker-promotees with the old bourgeois specialists into the new Soviet technical intelligentsia, by putting an end to specialist baiting, and by instituting cost accounting (*khozraschet*) in industry, he was both elevating the authority and the responsibilities of the managers and the ITR and justifying their higher salaries and status as a new factory-based elite.[33]

Stalin's speech had followed a litany of complaints from factory managers and articles by economists, all lamenting the rising level of labor turnover. These complaints noted wage irregularities and irrationalities as a cause of turnover. Stalin politicized this issue, blaming egalitarianism rather than wage irregularities.[34] Despite sharp adjustments in the wage scales in the fall of 1931, establishing wider wage differentials, the problems of labor hoarding, labor turnover, and irrationalities in the distribution and organization of workers in industry continued to plague enterprises and exacerbate the problems of recruiting workers. In an important article published in the newspaper of VSNKh on the first anniversary of the "Six Conditions" speech, N. Ivanov claimed that the *orgnabor* system had been a great success for coal mining, heavy metallurgy, forestry, and at the construction sites, but that the system had not reduced labor turnover. *Otkhodnichestvo* continued to plague these branches of the economy.[35]

Ivanov noted that often the *kolkhozy* had properly organized the recruitment process in the village, but that once the peasant-recruits arrived at the mine, construction site, or factory, there was no guarantee that they would be housed or fed. There was no organization at the plant that was accountable for their welfare, and frequently the trade unions and party organs failed to take on this responsibility. No sooner had the peasants arrived than they were packing their bags.[36]

Ivanov then turned to the problem of labor turnover, linking it to labor hoarding and again showing his disregard for regime ideology.

But [in the past year] very little was done so as to organize the distribution of recruited labor power in production. Our enterprises, even now, are characterized by huge superfluous labor power, and this circumstance, to a great degree, sharpens the problem of tekuchest'; if you will, it is the soup in which the harmful bacilli of tekuchest' develops.

Our workers today have grown to such a degree that they can no longer accept disorganization in production. Often groups, even of the best cadre, move from shop to shop, from plant to plant, searching mainly for more satisfying work, where they can more effectively apply their efforts. Even among the samozakrepivshchikhsia [self-attached workers, that is, workers who voluntarily agreed to "attach" themselves to the factory, i.e., not to leave], you often find 'psychological tekuchest' . . . when the worker . . . is ready at a moment's notice . . . to leave the plant.

The average person usually does not understand this phenomenon. [This is a thinly veiled critique of state ideology.] He sees only self-seekers, rolling stones [shkurniki, letuny], who come to the plant [only to get] special work clothing and consumer-good cards, etc.,[and then move on to another plant].

Each enterprise, at any moment, will take any workers it can get, regardless of skill level, and regardless of their real need. Our factories and mines are insatiable [in their demand] for workers and are not at all selective in satisfying their bottomless hunger.

The struggle for the first condition of Comrade Stalin can hardly be completely effective, while the number of production workers [at enterprises] remains entirely limitless, while we have [such] open or hidden superfluous labor.[37]

I have quoted this passage in its entirety, because it contradicted state ideology and exposed the realities of Soviet inverted labor market relations and of labor hoarding during the First FYP in ways that anticipated Kornai's "economics of shortage." Instead of the official line, which attributed high labor turnover to self-seeking behavior, and especially to peasant attitudes, Ivanov had pinpointed labor hoarding and disorganization in production as the basic causes of turnover and the sources of recruiting problems (an argument which I will elaborate below). Then, sounding a more orthodox note, he concluded that the causes of labor turnover were petty bourgeois egalitarianism and the failure of the trade-union committees to "attach" cadre to their shops.[38]

Another official explanation of problems with rising turnover through 1931 and 1932 was the failure to root out petty bourgeois egalitarianism. Indeed, despite the strictures of the "Six Conditions" speech and the new and much wider wage differentials instituted in the fall of 1931 in iron and coal, and after that in other branches of industry, there was little real change in wage differentials before 1934, and differentials actually continued to decline slightly until that year, after which a rapid and continuous expansion of wage differentials lasted until the Second World War.[39] One explanation was the erratic effect of the progressive, piece-rate wage schemes, which Stalin himself had insisted on. Intended to further widen wage differentials, this system of premiums actually made the ratios between rankings on the wage scale *(tarifnyi razriad)* largely irrelevant, reintroducing wage irregularities, or even wage egalitarianism. *Martenovka* called attention to this problem:

Because this year in many metallurgical plants there was a lot of worker idleness due to the lack of supplies of coal, coke, iron ore, etc., the application of progressive piece rates had a greater negative effect on the earnings of workers in the leading occupations in production. As a result, we got a lowering of the level of wages of the production workers in the metallurgical shops in comparison with nonproduction workers and workers in the metal-finishing shops . . . that is, the result was the opposite of the goals and tasks of the wage reforms. This equalizes the pay of the production workers with that of support workers, resurrecting the previous uravnilovka, and causing turnover among highly skilled steel worker-metallurgists. In the past months, there were cases of skilled workers leaving the blast furnace and open hearth shops to take jobs in other metal-finishing shops.[40]

Furthermore, workers and managers would find ways to consciously exploit the piece rate systems to raise wages (see chap. 6). Widening the wage differentials after 1934 may or may not have reduced labor turnover, but only in the context of the labor market.

The labor market never disappeared during the 1930s, regardless of draconian laws, but the economic system was too crude to influence peasants and others to come into the factories based on wage differentials and bonus incentives. They went where there was food and housing.

Labor Market Cycles, 1929–53

While the labor market remained inverted virtually throughout the Stalin years and, for that matter, for the remainder of the Soviet era, it did not remain for long in the chaotic state of the First FYP era. The extent or degree of disequilibrium in the labor market fluctuated with the phases of economic cycles of Stalinism. Even during the most chaotic years of the First FYP, one can already detect the outlines of a new and more stable economic system. The question that must be asked is: How was the quicksand society of "early Stalinism" solidified, thus becoming the stable, indeed, the highly sclerotic social order of "mature Stalinism"?[41]

By the end of 1930, the industrialization drive had brought about an inversion of the labor market. In 1931, in virtually every branch of the economy, managers were complaining about a shortage of labor power and skilled workers. Enterprise directors were stuck on a treadmill, for the more they recruited, the more recruits they needed, as turnover increased. Or, they were sinking in the "quicksand society." Or, their factory gate was becoming a "revolving door."[42] The problem had reached the breaking point by late 1932, when hiring more workers only brought diminishing returns on investment and, in some enterprises, even a diminishing total output. Workers were literally getting in each other's way in some factories, while at others, directors and bosses were pleading for more recruits so as to finish construction and finally go on-line, often months or years behind plan. Skilled labor was in short supply in virtually every factory. It was a labor famine, and the party leadership, belatedly responding to this crisis in the first months of 1933, temporarily halted urban in-migration and recruiting by instituting internal passports and by issuing a hiring freeze.[43]

The decision to reduce target growth rates annually from 21 to 22 percent to 13 to 14 percent, to halt new construction and complete existing construction projects, and to concentrate on the more mundane task of "assimilation" of technology, adopted at the combined Plenum of January 1933 was decisive.[44] The hiring freeze of 1933 demarcated a major shift in the labor market, ending the labor famine. From 1934 to 1940, instead of the working class expanding by annual increments of 20 percent or more, as occurred during the First FYP, the annual incremental expansion was almost constant at 10 percent. This is a highly significant finding, suggested by Vdovin and Drobizhev, that deserves more attention than non-Soviet historians have given it.[45]

There were no new signs of a labor deficit until the end of the Second FYP. Sonin's data on *orgnabor* notes that 1937 saw the actual numbers of recruits fall to one half of the projected and anticipated total numbers.[46] The deficit emerging in 1938 became worse in 1939 and 1940, sparking the new cluster of draconian laws and a new round of high labor turnover. It was initially, in part, a consequence of the purges, which generated their own form of turnover and chaos. Soon, however, the labor deficit reflected the state's attempt to begin shifting the economy toward militarization, without sacrificing the FYP goals. The strain on the economy was too great, and it was felt first, once again, with the inverted labor market. With the exigencies of the draft, the labor deficit was headed back toward a labor famine. Obviously the demand for labor became infinitely elastic during the war.

I would propose that we can divide industrialization under Stalin into two twelve-year cycles, and that the fluctuations in the labor market paralleled the phases of each cycle. The first cycle spanned the years 1928/29–40, the second, 1941–53. Each began with four years of hectic economic restructuring, which I would call phase 1, in which the demand for labor was insatiable and in which the labor market inversion reached crisis proportions. In each instance, this was followed by a one-year hiatus (1933 and 1946). Then came seven years of comparatively steady and moderate economic growth, or phase 2 (1934–40 and 1947–53). In each cycle, phase 2 growth consolidated the as yet unrealized potential of the massive investment of the first phase. These economic cycles were never acknowledged by the regime, and they had no apparent reflection in the FYPs. With the onset of the Second World War, however, the regime reverted to a strategy similar to the First FYP, and so, the first cycle then became a model, after the fact, for the second cycle.[47]

While it might seem far-fetched to compare the First FYP program with the Second World War evacuation of factories, the two eras were, in fact, strikingly similar in their impact on the economy and society.[48] In each case massive population migration shook the very foundations of rural society, while undermining any stable sense of community in cities. The Soviet Union appeared to be a country of wanderers, a quicksand society. In both cases the population was being directed toward the east, but it was wartime evacuation that finally succeeded in changing the regional population balances to the advantage of the east according to plan. Thus, again, the result was seemingly according to plan, since the objective since the Frist FYP had been to move population to the east, but that result was achieved for other reasons.

In phase 1 of each cycle, the regime conceptualized economic tasks primarily in terms of constructing (or relocating) more than one thousand key or "shock" enterprises. These targeted enterprises, once so designated, took precedence over everything else, and they gobbled up all the available resources, raw materials, supply, and personnel. Construction or reconstruction took precedence over production, growth was extensive rather than intensive, and waste and labor hoarding were endemic. In both eras, the largest projects for new construction (or relocation) were concentrated on the geographic periphery of the USSR, which meant in the Urals or further to the east. In both eras, the priority in investment and construction was in Sector A, meaning that the new factories would produce mostly machines and tanks rather than consumer goods.[49] Rationing of consumer goods replaced the retail market in both eras and continued through the hiatus year and into phase 2. The legacy of phase 1 in the first cycle was a mass of unfinished construction and plants that had yet to be brought on-line in 1933; in the second cycle, more than 1,500 newly functioning plants were relocated in 1941 in the Urals, Volga, Western Siberia, Kazakhstan, and Central Asia. Meanwhile, more than 32,000 enterprises were devastated or emptied during the years of conflict on Soviet territory, in European Russia, the Ukraine, Belorussia, and the Baltics.[50]

The labor market mirrored these developments, as the demand for labor skyrocketed beyond whatever population reserves were available for mobilization both in 1928/29–32 and 1941–45.[51] The inverted labor market chaos was caused, during the First FYP, by doubling the existing wage and salary labor force, which leaped from 11,599,000 in 1928 to 22,804,300 in 1932, whereas the plan envisioned a total of 15,763,700 on 1 October 1933.[52]

During the Second FYP, as we have seen, growth was less than expected and that continued into the Third FYP so that the total labor force was at 31.2 million in 1940. It fell precipitously to 18.4 million in 1942 and then climbed back up to 27.3 million in 1945.[53] With the Red Army draft absorbing so many factory workers, it was necessary to hire new production crews to replace them at the bench. Women, children, and pensioners became the core of the Soviet working class, replicating the pattern of recruiting the subaltern labor reserves during the First FYP.

Finally, in both eras, during phase 1, labor turnover was enormous. During the war, however, this turnover was dictated by military draft. Then, in the one year hiatus following both the First FYP and the Second World War, the labor market momentarily reverted to a buyer's market in favor of the enterprise managers, as some workers were laid off in a downsizing in 1933, and as children returned to school and pensioners left the labor force (as did some women), making way for the returning veterans in 1946. In each case, this proved to be a mere hiatus, and hiring was resumed again in 1934. In 1946, hiring of new worker-recruits never stopped, while the hiring of Red Army vets was the most intensive form of labor recruitment for several years.[54] Unlike the Second FYP, however, hiring during the Fourth FYP exceeded planned levels, and with returning veterans we might guess that labor deficits were less severe after 1948 than in 1938, despite the cold war.[55]

In each cycle, after the brief hiatus, a less sharply inverted labor market reappeared. During the seven-year phase 2, there was more moderate growth because new investment, new construction, and new hiring were at a moderated tempo as compared with the stormy first phase of the cycle. The regime's objective became assimilation, which in both eras began with putting factories on-line after completing construction or reconstruction.

While the First FYP and the Second World War were unique in the extremity of the state's demand for labor power, the resulting labor famine, and the chaos generated by uprooting people in their millions, each created a lasting legacy of an inverted labor market with fairly high labor turnover. Historians have focused almost exclusively on these elements of continuity in Stalinist industrialization, that is, high labor turnover and draconian labor laws, while generally ignoring the fact that after the hiatus in both cycles, phase 2 saw the end of the labor famine and reduced turnover. Also, with the sound and fury of the draconian labor laws, shock work and Stakhanovite socialist competitions, the significant social stabilization during the second phase of the cycle has been largely overlooked.[56] Nor does the alternative theory, of a sudden "great retreat" or "Thermidor" coming with the end of Cultural Revolution in 1931, account for the most important features of this period of emerging social stability, mistakenly attributing it to the revenge of the *ancien régime*.[57] Rather, it was the social consolidation of phase 1 chaos, parallel to the regime's shift from all-out construction to the assimilation of existing plant and technology.

Ten percent annual increments to the industrial labor force, which Vdovin and Drobizhev found for 1934–40, was not disruptive and reduced turnover considerably from its peak during the frenzied hiring of 1930–32. This permitted the organization of stable work brigades, the specialization of work in the brigade, and improved division of labor between the brigades. It permitted some labor training, usually on the job. Furthermore, so long as hiring remained incremental rather than frenzied, the labor market in these normal years was not so inverted as to require various forms of compulsion in order to uproot people, or mobilization schemes to distribute them, or the enforcing of the draconian labor laws to attach them to the bench.

Quite the opposite, it could be said that this level of expansion with the mildly inverted labor market afforded plenty of opportunities for those who wanted industrial jobs. It guaranteed full employment for the urban population, brought into being the dual wage-earning household as women continued to find employment in increasing numbers, absorbed peasant in-migration to the cities, absorbed youth graduating from urban schools, and reduced the incentives for turnover. In all these respects, the labor market of 1934–40 was socially stabilizing. The same would be true after the Second World War, from 1947 to 1953.

The problem of labor turnover has not been adequately contextualized in such terms of the Soviet labor market fluctuations, despite Filtzer's comparison with German and American figures for turnover, which were also very high prior to the Second World War.[58] Turnover, while it seems to have been high throughout the Stalin years, was under control in phase 2 of each cycle. Part of the reason that historians have tended to overlook Soviet labor market cycles when considering the problem of labor turnover was that the regime was so obsessed with the problem from the time of Stalin's "Six Conditions" speech that the sources are filled with the term *tekuchest'*. Furthermore, this obsession failed to consider that the regime's own strategy of all-out industrialization was only possible with very high labor turnover and also made it inevitable. Several factors were important in this respect.

First, highly skilled and experienced workers were required to leave their workbenches and factories, where many had worked for up to twenty years, to become the skeleton crews for the new factories on the periphery. Thousands were sent across the country on assignment (*komandirovka* or *stazherovka*), which might last for several years. The strategy of assigning workers from the pilot factories to the new satellites necessitated a great deal of labor mobility and hence, labor turnover, among the most highly skilled workers.

Similarly, the evidence strongly suggests that many of the most skilled workers were being promoted to positions as foremen or as technicians, and in some cases even to shop boss or shift boss.[59] Such rapid promotion of rank-and-file workers *(vydvizhenie)*, generated some occupational mobility, which meant workers moving from one shop to another, or from one factory to another, or from one city to another. More significant in numerical terms were the masses of new recruits who came into the factories during the First FYP. Their mobility, both social and geographic, was absolutely essential for the success of the industrialization drive, but it also generated very high labor turnover rates until the dust had settled in 1933.

The construction and mining industries were frequently called "conveyer belts," because they were known to be an intermediate step for millions of peasants who would move from field to factory. What was a conveyer belt if not a mechanism for encouraging and facilitating labor turnover? From the standpoint of the regime, they provided the peasant-recruits with the experience that would prepare them to deal with the factory system and urban life. Once a new factory had been built, the factory administration would generally attempt to keep the construction workers and put them to work in production. They may or may not have succeeded, but in either case, it was measured as labor turnover. To recruit new workers meant to generate labor turnover, although the regime could only see its negative aspects.

Labor turnover deriving from these sources, I would suggest, could be called "flexible" or "positive" turnover. How much of the labor turnover during the First FYP could be legitimately classified in this way is impossible to determine. Certainly, a great deal of the labor turnover of the First FYP was negative because it served no useful economic purpose, even though, as Filtzer has argued, it was perfectly rational, market-oriented behavior from the perspective of the worker. He was right to emphasize that skilled workers with lengthy tenure seemed no less prone to switch jobs than peasant newcomers. Such turnover was caused by workers' never ending trek from one factory to another, from one industry to another, or from one region to another, always in search of better housing, a steady supply of food, or higher wages. Stalin and the regime would blame this on peasant-migrants, in search of the "long ruble," but it seems to have been universal.

Another important source of negative turnover was shop-floor conflict between bosses and workers. In the absence of real trade unionism and of a legitimate process of negotiation and conflict resolution, worker-management conflict in the First FYP frequently led workers to vote with their feet.

While the Soviet sources and historians have neglected them, probably a more frequent cause of shop-floor conflict, and hence of negative turnover, was also conflict between workers, and in particular, between established workers and newcomers, between urban and rural born, and between generations and genders.[60] One such incident involved Dinamo workers out at Sokolinaia Gora, the new factory barrack "suburb" built on the far eastern edge of Moscow. Dinamo workers decided to burn the bedding set aside for some SiM peasant-recruits who were to move in. These recruits promptly returned to their village instead of accepting this type of harassment.[61] Instances of male chauvinism and harassment of female workers likely were a similar cause of negative turnover.

Negative turnover was often caused by enterprises attempting to outbid other plants for labor power by promising of higher wages or better apartments. This was called "pirating" workers. One such incident involved the AMO-ZiS and Dinamo plants.

Labor piracy is getting to be literally an everyday occurrence and a subject of unabashed, rather good-natured discussion. . . . At a conference in the offices of the People's Commissariat for Labor, the manager of the Dynamo Works actually bragged of his successes. According to him, the Dynamo Works challenged the AMO Works to a competition in improved labor piracy: "The AMO Works pirate our workers, and we repay them in kind. They took our lathe operators. Well, the boys stayed for a while and came back; five of them came back and brought a few others." Even study tours through plants are used for such treacherous Trojan horse methods. Plant managers have become suspicious of all such tours.[62]

Negative turnover was also frequently caused by worker disgust with mismanagement and with the general disorganization of production that characterized the First FYP Soviet factory. For example, enforced idleness (*prostoi*), which could be due to deficits in raw materials, breakdowns in machinery, or the interminable queuing for equipment, resulted in lowering of workers' wages and general demoralization.

Finally, as Filtzer emphasized, labor turnover was, in substantial measure, caused by the regime's very own draconian labor laws that were intended to halt labor turnover. When the plant administration was required to fire a worker for a single day of unexcused absenteeism, or several instances of tardiness, then, of course, labor turnover shot up. Workers who wanted to quit to take other jobs, but who were restricted by new regulations governing hiring, would purposely miss work in order to compel their foreman to fire them.[63] The stricter the enforcement of such irrational truancy laws, the greater the level of labor turnover.

Soviet labor turnover was spiraling out of control during the First FYP, for the three years 1930–32, and again, during the Third FYP, 1938–40. The cause, in each case, had little to do with peasant attitudes, or labor indiscipline, or resistance, or alienation, or with a sudden rise in material self-interest. The underlying factors were the lack of housing, the lack of food, and the labor famine, all caused by the industrialization-collectivization drive, the insane construction mania. During the Third FYP, the underlying factors were the impact of the purge terror and then the conversion of much of industry for war, followed by the draft. In the interim of the Second FYP, turnover declined and hovered at roughly 100 percent, about the same as NEP levels.[64]

Not only was that a tolerable level, but it was necessary given the rapid geographic and social transformations demanded by Stalinist industrialization. The regime's obsession with labor turnover as the bane of industrialization, and its failure to understand that workers' response in the labor market was highly rational in economic terms, again brings us back to Moshe Lewin's methodological breakthrough in which society exacts a price on the regime. His focus was on collectivization, but the same holds true for industrialization. This is very clearly visible through the impact of the labor market, which the regime failed to understand as a function of its own industrial policy, just as fundamentally as it misunderstood peasant behavior in the grain market as a consequence of its collectivization policy. It took the crisis of the dual famine of 1932–33, the labor famine and actual starvation, to bring the regime to its senses and make the minimal necessary adjustments in economic policy.

This chapter has reaffirmed the findings of economic historians who argue that there were markets and economic cycles even in the Stalinist type of planned economy, regardless of the plan's supposed transcendence of the "law of value." I argue that there was a vibrant labor market of a uniquely "inverted" type, which workers and managers understood well but the regime only poorly. The "Six Conditions" and Stalin's new policy of wage stratification was a belated and poorly implemented response, which in the context of Stalin's taut if not bacchanalian plan targets did not halt the slide toward the crisis of dual famine and economic breakdown during the First FYP. This experience suggests that, in the long debate among Marxists about the role of markets in a socialist planned economy, the "market socialist" perspective has proved to be more realistic and has great explanatory value when applied to historical and theoretical problems of Soviet economic development in the work of Bettleheim, Davies, Erlich, Jasny, Kornai, Nove, and Zaleski. All of these economists and economic historians have shown that effective planning must be based on market realities, not plans acting as directives.

Many of them have shown that the commands of the plan were often circumvented from below. It should be clear, from this experience and from the internal economic collapse of "actually existing socialism" of the Soviet type, which fell apart almost immediately when it had to confront market mechanisms, that the only fruitful path for economic development during the historical era that Marx had called "socialism" is one in which plans are based on market realities.

5

TRAINING WORKERS:
FROM APPRENTICESHIP TO
MASS METHODS

Historians of Soviet education have emphasized the revolutionary polytechnical ideals developed by Krupskaya and Lunacharsky and then traced their impact after 1917.[1] The primary and secondary curriculum reforms reflected these ideals during the years of War Communism and NEP, and then they saw a final flourish, much to the dismay of Krupskaya and Lunacharsky, with the closing of universities, colleges, and secondary schools during the so-called Cultural Revolution. The Cultural Revolution, in what is now the conventional view, yielded to traditional principles of education with the Great Retreat of 1931, when grades and exams were restored, as were colleges and universities, and when the school curriculum shifted decisively away from the polytechnical ideals and returned to classical education. By the end of the decade, "high Stalinism" meant increasing emphasis on Russian national culture and a new conservatism. Children wore uniforms in the classroom, and girls and boys were segregated.[2]

In defining the Cultural Revolution as a short episode in class struggle politics that began with the Shakhty trial in March 1928 and ended with

Stalin's attempt at a reconciliation with the technical intelligentsia in his "Six Conditions Speech" of June 1931, Sheila Fitzpatrick argued that the regime's underlying fear was dependence on Old Regime specialists and its objective was training a new Soviet technical intelligentsia, recruited from among the working class. Such were the "worker-thousands," contingents of young workers selected from the factory bench to attend *rabfaky* (literally, "workers' faculties"). These were crash programs of higher education in applied science and technology that were run by the factories themselves, absorbing some of the function of the Institutes of Higher Learning (VUZy), which were mostly defunct.[3] As many as 150,000 workers were recruited in this campaign, roughly half of them party members.[4]

After graduating, the majority of these workers were placed in technical positions (ITR) or managerial posts. They became known as the upwardly mobile, "promotees" or *vydvizhentsy*. In Fitzpatrick's interpretation, promotion of workers into the Soviet elite had become a substitute for the original Bolshevik vision of eliminating elites and classes altogether, almost immediately after the October Revolution.[5] The phenomenon of First FYP *vydvizhentsy* was, therefore a first systematic attempt to apply this principle to a broader social elite, to the whole of the technical intelligentsia. From this perspective, the terror of 1937 provided an avenue for a new political elite, consisting of a select cohort taken from among these First FYP *vydvizhentsy*, to leapfrog ahead in rather spectacular fashion.[6] This interpretation of the terror is hardly new; variations on it date back to Bukharin's conversation with Nicolaevsky in 1936 and, more importantly, to Merle Fainsod's prosopographical-generational approach.[7] Fitzpatrick was right, however, to emphasize the role of education, because it elucidates aspects of the new elites' attitudes and values, and in particular, it helps in explaining the almost unthinking loyalty of the new political elite to the "general line," however it zigzagged under Stalin.[8]

The emphasis on education also provides an important clue to some of the attitudes of the broader Soviet public, as suggested long ago in the neglected but highly significant findings of Alex Inkeles and Raymond Bauer in the Harvard Interview Project. They based their research on 764 long interviews and more than three thousand responses to questionnaires, all conducted with Soviet Second World War refugees (mostly in Germany), who had avoided repatriation to the USSR at all costs. They found that, regardless of social status, these ex-citizens of the USSR, even though they despised the Soviet regime, valued higher education and respected the Soviet occupational hierarchy because it was meritocratic and based on higher education.[9] The regime, unleashing its purge-terror against hundreds of thousands of professionals and highly educated persons, among others, would have to work hard at convincing a public that valued education and merit-based promotions, that it was pursuing these same objectives.

Respect for educational achievement and professional occupational status, therefore, must be sharply distinguished from respect for the Stalinist political elite, particularly after the purge-terror. Furthermore, the broad pattern of upward mobility of several hundred thousand factory workers, who were promoted into the ranks of the ITR and factory administration, must be very carefully distinguished from the upward mobility of a small cohort of these workers, a few hundred or perhaps thousand, who were appointed to top party positions. The first, I would suggest, was an upward mobility into an emerging middle class; the second meant becoming part of the regime.

Fitzpatrick's theory of upward mobility, however, had little relevance for the vast majority of workers at the bench during the 1930s, workers who would have no opportunity for higher education and who would not experience rapid personal promotion from workbench to technician status or to responsible positions as foremen, let alone into the party-state apparatus. I do not deny that some workers may have emulated the newly forming middle class, and many more may have wanted or expected their children to move into professional occupations and the middle class based on educational achievement. That, however, was far from fully endorsing the regime's mythology of *vydvizhenie*. Not only did most workers have no possibility of becoming members of the ruling elite, but there is no indication that they had any inclination to try to do so. Rather, at this level, we must separate out the regime mythology from popular attitudes, and we must separate popular values concerning education, which were overwhelmingly positive, from popular attitudes about the political elite, which almost certainly were not positive during the 1930s.[10]

The mythology of the *vydvizhentsy* was very similar to that of the "outstanding" Stakhanovites, another cohort of promotees who were elevated as cultural model-heroes a few years later. Such cultural mythology was influential among a relatively narrow circle of workers, but since the vast majority of workers lived (and worked) in conditions that were difficult, if not wretched, its impact on wider circles was limited. Particularly striking was the gap between the *meshchanstvo* cult of domesticity that the wives of leading Stakhanovites indulged in, while the average woman suffered under the dual burden of full-time factory work and full-time domestic work.[11] For most workers, the income, status, and power of either the Stakhanovites or the First FYP *vydvizhentsy* was not worth dreaming about. Upward mobility was the Horatio Alger myth of Stalinism.

Education, however, was not mythology. After 1931, it devolved onto two tracks, each of which had significant integrating effects, albeit in different ways. Secondary study in the ten-year school became the first track, geared to placing its graduates either for further study in the VUZ (college) or for immediate employment in white-collar positions. The seven-year school, followed by either the *tekhnikum* or factory-based vocational schooling (FZU), became a second track, a polytechnical training for factory technicians and factory workers. Some graduates of the FZU would go on to higher education; this was not widespread except during the Cultural Revolution, however, and it was not the primary function or purpose of the factory FZU.[12] Upward mobility, therefore, does not explain the broad impact of primary schooling and mixed secondary-vocational schooling during the 1930s. It was part of what I will call a *status revolution.*

From Exclusionary to Mass FZU

The FZU, a factory-based vocational school, was established in 1921 on the foundations of the prerevolutionary vocational training schools. At the beginning of the NEP era, in 1921/22, there were more than 3,000 FZU schools, with over 200,000 trainees, but the number declined to 2,097 in 1922/23, while the number of trainees fell to 146,100. As NEP years passed, a slow recovery meant that by 1928/29, there were 2,519 schools and 272,600 trainees.[13] As the FZUs were attached to the factories these figures reflect the closing and consolidation of factories under trusts in the first year of NEP, followed by the slow expansion in the number of factories thereafter.

The FZU, as the 1926 Protocols of the Central Committee of the Metalworkers' Union illustrate, was a lengthy and thorough training program modeled on a vision of polytechnical education and attempting to match or exceed the skill level of the apprentice. The program combined abstract, secondary-school education with hands-on experience on the shop floor and thus offered a new type of depersonalized alternative to the apprenticeship. Youth began the FZU course of study at age fourteen or fifteen, and the program lasted for three years, the first half in the classroom and the second half on the shop floor.[14]

Prior to the First FYP, the FZU was still apprenticeshiplike in that it was a small-scale program and exclusionary, that is, it was not a mass form of instruction. According to one source, on 1 April 1926, the Krasnyi Putilov plant in Leningrad, with 10,304 workers, had merely 348 FZU students; AMO had 1,323 workers but only 93 FZU students; and Dinamo had 1,418 workers with only 125 FZU students.[15] Table 5.1 presents enrollment at the three leading PR factories in Moscow, but gives slightly different FZU enrollment figures. It shows that the FZU was basically a male preserve in 1926, with an exclusionary function similar to that of the apprenticeship: reproducing the layer of skilled workers. The social composition of the trainees enrolled in the FZU changed very little during the 1920s. In 1923/24, 80.1 percent came from a worker's family; in 1928/29 the figure was 80.4 percent. Trainees from peasant families increased very slightly, from 7.6 percent to 8 percent in the same period, as did those from a white-collar family, from 7.2 percent to 8.5 percent.[16] This extraordinary continuity in the social origins of the recruits to the FZU might suggest what Veselov's standard Soviet history of the FZU failed to note, namely, that control or monopolization of the labor market was maintained by the unions on behalf of skilled workers during NEP through the FZU system as through apprenticeship.[17]

Restricting access to the labor market through the FZU was supported by management during the NEP years of tight labor markets. With the market inversion and the labor famine of the First FYP, however, this was intolerable from their perspective, and so the FZU was rapidly expanded and its gates were opened wide to all youth, urban or peasant, male or female. SiM provides a good example of the transformation of the FZU from exclusionary to mass vocational training. According to Sergei Filatov, writing as the SiM *partkom* secretary in 1931, the FZU had become a "smithy of young cadre" during the First FYP. While that phrase would become popular jargon concerning all Soviet factories, and especially steel plants, here it meant mass vocational training.[18]

When the FZU was founded at SiM in 1921 with merely ninety students, its curriculum resembled that of a secondary school more than a vocational school. Narkompros, the Commissariat of Enlightenment, disliked the FZU because it encroached on the commissariat's ideal of universal polytechnical education in the primary and secondary schools.[19] Ironically, it was the FZU during the 1930s that preserved the ideal of polytechnical education even as that ideal was being completely abandoned in the primary and secondary schools.

In the First FYP, the FZU was supposed to become the basic form of vo-

Table 5.1. FZU Enrollment in 1926 at the Three PR Plants

| | Trainees | | Admitted | | Graduated | |
	Male	Female	Male	Female	Male	Female
SiM	115	2	49	0	21	1
Dinamo	107	18	29	4	9	1
AMO-ZIS	64	16	13	4	26	5

Source: GARF f. 5469, op. 10, d. 222, l. 16.
Note: Trainees are already in their second year of vocational schooling; admitted are just starting out, newly enrolled.

cational training. At Dinamo, according to the 1930 collective contract, "the administration is obligated to train its labor force from youth, only by means of the FZU, although in exceptional circumstances, individual-brigade apprenticeships are allowed."[20] The Dinamo contract stipulated that teenagers, hired and trained in the FZU, were supposed to replace all retirees and were to make up 40 percent of the projected increase in the number of skilled workers in the plant.[21] That was a dramatic shift from the 8 percent quota for hiring teenagers which had been established by the trade unions during NEP.

The Dinamo contract reflected the resolutions of the Sixteenth Party Congress in June 1930, which stipulated that the FZU would become the basic source for supplying industry with qualified workers as well as the basic form of mass education.[22] In 1930 and 1931 there was some possibility that the FZS, the factory-based seven-year school, in conjunction with the FZU, as substitute for grades 8–10, might actually replace primary and secondary schools. The Komsomol had advocated this through the NEP years, in opposition to Narkompros (as Fitzpatrick showed), and maintained this position during the Cultural Revolution, when VSNKh also began to push for this same strategy.[23] The tenth anniversary of the founding of the FZU occurred on 9 April 1931, and VSNKh decreed that 20 April–1 May be established as a special "decade" for mass FZU enrollment. Noting the decision of the Sixteenth Party Congress, the decree called on the FZU to both train and then graduate 360,000 youth in 1931.[24]

Indeed, the FZU were highly successful in increasing their enrollment during the First FYP across the USSR, as table 5.2 shows. The problem was not in attracting recruits; it was in providing graduates for the factory in a timely way and with sufficient training, according to Filatov, writing at the time, and Veselov, writing thirty years later. SiM, according to Filatov, had graduated 3,000 trainees from the FZU by 1931, and 591 went on to work at Magnitostroi, Kuznetskstroi, and Uralmashstroi, training workers in eighteen occupations. He lamented this record, arguing that the FZU should have trained more workers, and attributed the problem to the length and breadth of the FZU curriculum.[25] The course of study remained almost as long as during the NEP era at two, or two and a half, years of study. Then the FZU graduate began work in the factory at the third or fourth *razriad* (rank), that is, at the semiskilled level, and well ahead of the other newcomers who were initially placed in the first or second ranks (unskilled). In some cases, at SiM, FZU graduates were immediately classified as skilled workers, placed in ranks 5–6 when they began to work on the shop floor.

A. N. Veselov, the Soviet historian of vocational education, agreed with Filatov's assessment of the problem. He argued, like Fitzpatrick, that during the Cultural Revolution era the FZU was effectively preparing youth not only

Table 5.2. The Growth of FZU and of FZU-Type Schools in the First FYP

	Number of FZU Institutions	Number of Trainees (in 1,000s)
1929/30	2,711	323.1
1930/31	3,265	584.7
1931/32	3,970	975
1932/33	3,900	958.9

Source: Veselov, *Professional'no-Tekhnichskoe Obrazovanie*, p. 279.

for factory work but for further study in *tekhnikumy* or even in colleges: "In 1932, 35 percent of students who were taken into VTUZs and *tekhnikumy* of the NKTP [the Peoples' Commissariat of Heavy Industry] were former FZU apprentices."[26]

The problem was that graduates were not being readied rapidly enough across the USSR for factory work. During the First FYP, FZUs provided a two-year program for mass occupations preparing trainees to start at the third or fourth *razriady*, a two-and-a-half- to three-year program preparing skilled "worker-universalists" of the fifth or sixth *razriady*, and a three- to four-year program preparing assistants to the *mastera* (foremen), that is, bench repair workers, setup workers, and other highly skilled workers. In 1929/30, 23 percent of the FZU students were enrolled in the two-year program, 68.8 percent in the three-year program, and 8.2 percent in the four-year program. In 1930/31, 36.5 percent were enrolled in the two-year program, and 62.5 percent in the three-year program.[27] Thus, the average length of study decreased only marginally during the First FYP as compared to NEP.

That there was a substantial lag between enrollment and graduation of trainees can be seen in the fact that in 1931, the FZUs at industrial enterprises graduated a total of 55,000 trainees, while enrollment was already 584,700 in 1930/31 and would peak at 975,000 in 1931/32. In the Second FYP, however, the lag time had been eliminated. In 1933/34 enrollment was down to 400,000 and in 1934/35 to 261,300, and yet, in 1934, the FZUs graduated 203,000 trainees, or almost four times as many as in 1931. In transport and communications, the FZUs graduated 12,000 in 1931 and 75,700 in 1934. In agriculture, they graduated 200 in 1931 and 20,000 in 1934.[28] During the First FYP, according to Veselov, little attention was given to the fact that some occupations required much less training than others. Filatov complained that the FZU, by failing to differentiate, kept many trainees in training too long.

The lengthy program of FZU study made it all but impossible to meet the demand in the First FYP, but instead graduated the most trainees in

1933–34, just when the need for them had greatly diminished, as hiring was frozen in 1933. In the long run, however, this did not matter much, because the industrial economy absorbed all the FZU graduates during the Second FYP and again suffered from deficits of qualified workers in most occupations by the end of the Second FYP.[29] In the immediate circumstances of the First FYP inverted labor market heading into the labor famine of 1933, this long lag time between enrollment and graduation in the FZU, caused by the two- to three-year program of studies, was a source of considerable anxiety.

One solution was to substantially shorten the FZU program, which, indeed, was reduced to six months in 1933, then restored to one-and-one-half to two years in 1935.[30] Still, data indicate that the FZUs would continue to fall short of planning targets for releasing graduates into the national economy until the FZO, the State Labor Reserves System, was instituted in October 1940. For example, at SiM, in September 1935, the FZU opened with an enrollment of only 126, whereas the plan called for a very modest 225.[31] For the whole of the economy during the Third FYP, the FZUs were expected to train 1.1 million new workers, but in 1938 and 1939, they had graduated only 159,500, or 18.8 percent of Gosplan's targets.[32] The response of the regime, in October 1940, was conversion of FZU into the FZO.

A second solution was to provide night schooling, with uninterrupted production work during the day. These supplemental classes included both classical education and vocational training or retraining. The worker became a worker-student, spawning a veritable alphabet soup of new acronyms for types of schools or classes. The polytechnical ideal was carried over into an unplanned system combining work, mostly on the day shift, and study, mostly on the second shift.

John Dewey at SiM

To fill the gap between the need for skilled workers and the number of graduates, more rapid means of training were devised during the First FYP. Night schools proliferated in conjunction with the so-called brigade-apprenticeship and hybrid forms of crash training on the shop floor (see below). Night-school classes were an attempt to provide vocational training for many newcomers who did not fit into the FZU age bracket and to retrain established workers in handling new machines, equipment, or methods of labor organization. At the same time, they were aiming at providing all workers with the equivalent of a four-year, primary-school education.

Already in the fall of 1925, SiM established an Evening Technical School (*Vechernaia Proftekhnicheskaia Shkola*) with fifty-six workers of various ages participating. The director of the school, Bolshakov, recalled that the school lacked room and equipment and had no program for training the unskilled workers who had enrolled. In 1930, this became the Evening Workers' School (VRSh), incorporating the Evening Technical School and the Workers' Technical School (RTSh). The VRSh had the dual task of training the unskilled newcomers, and of retraining skilled workers to handle the new technologies, as well as teaching reading and math. It was housed in a separate, three-story building in 1930, and trained workers for SiM and other factories, in many different occupations. Filatov, the *partkom* secretary at SiM, was a graduate of this school. It turned out many workers who became foremen or brigade leaders, *mastery* or *brigadiry*. The VRSh expanded even more rapidly than the FZU, from 56 students in 1925 to 2,400 by the end of 1930.[33]

Even with this dramatic expansion, SiM still found itself short of skilled cadre, and so the *partkom* decided to establish a unified training combine (*edinii uchebnyi kombinat*) that would house not only the FZU and the VRSh but also the *tekhnikum,* a type of technical high school, equivalent to grades 8–10, and the SiM steel institute, VTUZ, which trained technicians and engineers.[34] This was the predecessor to the "enterprise-school" and was supposed to combine the two tracks described above. The FZU was for youth, and the night classes were for adults who were illiterate, innumerate, or poorly educated, as well as for technical retraining. The objective was to provide a universal education, the equivalent of seven years of primary and secondary schooling, and vocational training for all. The two tracks reflected a wide sociocultural gap in the factories between youth and older workers, and between newcomers and established workers. The average level of schooling for the whole of the SiM work collective was 3.7 years, while for FZU students it was 6.6 years.[35]

Summarizing statistically, by September 1931, a staggering total of 11,350 persons, including 5,250 adults and 6,100 youth, were studying in the factory's various schools. The figures below show total enrollment in SiM training programs in September 1931. The FZS was a factory-run primary and secondary school, grades one through seven.[36]

FZS	3,100
FZU	3,000
RTSh	2,400
Tekhnikum	500
VTUZ	150
Correspondence classes	250
Shop and plant technical circles	200
Shop schools	2,000
Total	11,350

These figures would indicate that SiM was becoming a community center for primary and secondary schooling, as the FZS-FZU track was absorbing all primary and secondary education during the First FYP. It appears that children of factory workers attended these schools, although it is also quite possible that the FZS simply replaced city schools in the PR factory district altogether. Other sources provide slightly different figures for enrollment. According to *Martenovka,* on 20 December 1930 there were 1,500 students in the FZS, about 1,000 trainees in the FZU, 800 in the VRSh, 316 in the factory *tekhnikum,* and 60 in the several institutes of higher learning under the factory, preparing its graduates to be engineers (p. 1).

On 23 June 1932, the first anniversary of Stalin's "Six Conditions" speech, *Martenovka* ran a headline: "We Are Putting Your Proposal Into Action Comrade Stalin" (p. 1). This article claimed that 5,009 workers attended the factory's *proftekhkombinat* (the vocational-technical combine, apparently the successor to the unified training combine and the enterprise-school at SiM). Of these, 216 were studying to become engineers in the institutes (VTUZs), 397 were studying to become technicians in the *tekhnikum,* 1,738 were studying to increase their skills or to requalify for other occupations in the RTSh, and 2,658 were training in the FZU. Since the FZS was no longer mentioned, it had apparently been dissolved and reappropriated by local government, probably the *raion* soviet, as public primary and secondary seven-year schools.

A few months later, on 18 August 1932, *Martenovka* reported that 1,500 workers were supposed to have been enrolled in the *proftekhkombinat* during the week of 8–15 August, but that only a small fraction of this figure had been recruited. Targets were set for each shop to enroll workers in the RTSh, the *tekhnikum,* and the institute, but because of weak work by the "social organs" in the plant, these targets were not being met. A special plant commission was set up to expedite the enrollment (p. 4). Then, on 27 September 1932, *Martenovka* reported that instead of 1,200 workers enrolling in the RTSh, only 883 workers had enrolled, and only 650 had actually come to classes. Another problem: there were 2,700 trainees enrolled in the FZU, but only one hundred pairs of workers' boots had been ordered for them (p. 4).

These types of vocational programs and classes still did not exhaust all the new forms of training and education introduced in the First FYP Soviet factory. In the summer of 1930, the Combines for Workers' Education (KRO) and Supplemental Workers' Education (DRO) were founded, and on 30 July 1931 the Sovnarkom decreed a system of Production-Polytechnical Courses (PPK). The PPK had three links aimed at achieving the four-year, primary-school level and occupational specialization. At Dinamo in 1932, there were 763 students enrolled in PPK and 226 in the RTSh.[37] The KRO, DRO, and PPK seem to have not been important at SiM but were widespread in other factories.[38] Still another type of school, a substitute for the *tekhnikum* which did not involve full-time study, was the Factory Technical Classes (FZTK). The FZTK opened at SiM on 24 October 1930 and required uninterrupted work at the bench during the day and study at night. Courses were modeled on those given at the technical institutes run by Stal' and by VSNKh. They were also modeled on the SiM *tekhnikumy* and VTUZs, which produced metallurgist-technicians and metallurgist-engineers.[39] However, whereas the *tekhnikum* required two or two-and-a-half years of full-time study away from the workbench to become a technician, and the VTUZ required a similar period or even longer to become an engineer, the FZTK was organized on the principle of uninterrupted work-study.

The assumption that the FZTK graduates would measure up to the standards of the *tekhnikum* seems to have been another instance of unbridled Cultural Revolution optimism. *Martenovka* and archival sources never even mention the FZTK, which seems to have died before it ever got off the ground in 1931, whereas the *tekhnikumy* flourished and expanded over the course of the 1930s. During the First FYP the number of *tekhnikumy* tripled to 3,509 with 723,700 students at the end of 1932. After a brief period of decline in the mid-1930s, by 1939/40 the total number of *tekhnikumy* reached 3,733, with 945,000 students.[40]

This alphabet of acronyms reflects a proliferation of enterprise courses concerned with training and education. The pressure to consolidate them into a single center was very strong. When combined with the ideal of the Cultural Revolution, namely of eliminating the distinction between manual and mental labor, the result was the enterprise-school.[41] The idea had been endorsed as early as November 1929, at a Plenum of the Party Central Committee, which had issued the following resolution for establishing the enterprise-school.

(1) Attracting all, or at least the absolute majority of workers into study. (2) Combining uninterrupted work in production with uninterrupted study, while unquestionably fulfilling and overfulfilling all qualitative and quantitative indicators of the promfinplan. (3) A well-composed system of education from the lowest to the highest forms of study on the basis of the last word in elevating the cultural, technical, political, and military level of the worker. (4) Actualizing the organic connection of theory to practical work [between training and production]. (5) A decisive rejection of the old system of subjects, and the working out of a new system, . . . with new programs and methods of instruction. (6) Bolshevik tempos of mass preparation of cadre while improving the quality of the prepared cadre.[42]

These six points, however, were basically the same principles of the poly-technical school developed in the 1920s by Narkompros, and long advocated by Krupskaya and Lunacharsky.[43] They had also been the principles of the unified training combine established at SiM in 1930 to coordinate and inte-grate all vocational and technical training at the factory. The only thing that distinguished the new enterprise-school from the existing combine was that the enterprise-school was supposed to bring schooling to virtually the entire plant work force. That is, it was an attempt to apply the polytechnical ideal through the factory, a way of bringing established workers up to the level of the seven-year school and providing new workers with the same seven-year standard.[44]

VSNKh designated SiM as an enterprise-school following the Central Committee resolution of November 1929, and it appears to have been the first plant so designated in the USSR. It would not be until the 22 October 1930 issue of *Martenovka*, however, that the program for the SiM enterprise-school was finally announced. In the meantime, the unified training com-bine had already accomplished much of its objective by pulling together the different programs. The enterprise-school, in practice, would seem to have originated with more narrow objectives. At SiM, for twelve occupations, it was supposed to be able to train a new, unskilled worker to become an engineer over a six-year period, without the worker leaving the shop floor for any ex-tended period of time.[45] These ideas were developed by an engineer, M. S. Shokhor, whose role in the Cultural Revolution has not hitherto been ex-amined.

According to a document from the Central Committee of the Metal-workers' Union dated 1930, Shokhor, author of *Integralnaia Systema*, a book on vocational training, was directly involved in setting up the enterprise-school program at SiM.[46] He "believed that training and mastering technol-ogy could be accomplished without division into special subjects, without textbooks, but by special thematic means . . . with ties to direct experience. Such training, . . . he called the 'integrated system.'"[47] He distinguished his system from the Schneider method in America, with the claim that his sys-tem had the objective of completely eliminating the barrier between mental and physical labor, between "inside" and "outside" the classroom.[48]

While this might or might not have distinguished Shokhor's system from the Schneider system, it would appear to have borrowed heavily from John Dewey.[49] In fact, his objectives were virtually identical to Dewey's, although he claimed his system differed from Dewey's pedagogical theory of "gradual reconstruction."

Until the advent of the enterprise-school, Shokhor argued, higher-level technical education took place in *tekhnikumy*, VUZs, or VTUZs, which were either state schools under jurisdiction of the commissar of enlightenment and independent of enterprises or else were established by and subordinate to enterprises. The enterprise-school, he argued, offered a new "third path," a "socialist path of mass preparation of lower, middle, and higher worker cadres [under the] condition of uninterrupted work, participating in production with organized coordination of theoretical preparation [under] a single *promfinplan*."[50] This is vintage Dewey, minus the plan, since Dewey wanted the same melding of mental and manual learning and he wanted to make it possible for individuals to go on with higher education at any point in their work lives, that is to eliminate the hierarchy built into classes and tracks.

Shokhor argued that learning had suffered in the VUZs, the VTUZs, and in the *tekhnikumy* because topics such as mathematics and mechanics, on the one hand, and machine construction, or metallurgy, on the other, were taught in isolation from each other.[51] How he would overcome the gap between pure and applied science, however, was not clear in his account, which certainly marked a step backward from Dewey's ideas in this respect.

Shokhor's vision also had its practical component. He argued that the enterprise-school had to satisfy the need for cadre both at SiM during the First FYP (and for the whole of the period of socialist reconstruction) and at other plants. At the same time, he claimed the enterprise-school had to integrate four different objectives: uninterrupted production, uninterrupted study, organized rest and relaxation, and rationalization of daily life (*byt*).[52] Shokhor's project thus applied Taylorist notions of the use of time, popular concepts of industrial management during the First FYP, to leisure time in daily life, where it would be sorely needed since there would be so little of it under his program![53] With the principle of "uninterrupted" work, study was only possible at night and on weekends. Thus, the actual length of the workweek under the enterprise-school for worker-student was not thirty-five hours, as established by law, but rather thirty-five hours on the shop floor (when overtime was not required) and up to an additional twenty hours in the classroom. While this would strain the resources of the worker-student (and of families), it should also be noted that it would require a very large outlay in human capital investment on the part of the state through the enterprises to provide mass education.

Such an investment made sense, as factory directors and VSNKh administrators understood, because with the endemic hoarding of workers, enterprises would soon have too many unskilled workers and not enough qualified workers. That was the situation still at the start of 1933. Then the labor famine disappeared as new construction was halted, production targets were lowered, and enterprises were instructed to undertake some reduction of staff through layoffs. During 1933, as the newly trained FZU students began to graduate to the shop floor, and as workers studying at night were beginning to complete their classes, the increase in qualified workers marked the end of the labor famine.

Shokhor claimed that, using his method, the enterprise school could turn an unskilled worker into an independent *val'tsovshchik* (rolling mill operator) in the sheet metal shop in two years. After two months' training, the *chernorabochii* (unskilled laborer) would be promoted to second apprentice rolling mill operator, and then after two more months to first apprentice. After four more months, the apprentice would become an assistant, and after eight more months, a fully independent *val'tsovshchik*.[54] This was the model that VSNKh was looking for, and it would continue to dominate party and administrative thinking long after the enterprise-school had disappeared.

What was striking about this was Shokhor's continued use of the terms first and second apprentice, when the training process that he had envisioned was limited to merely two years. Thus, his system projected the end of the old apprenticeship training, which was ten to twenty years, for the top mechanics in a factory, such as a *val'tsovshchik* or a *stalevar* (steel smelter). It marked the opening of the top positions to a much wider circle of workers, many from peasant backgrounds, who would become the celebrated shock-worker heroes of 1932–35, and then the exceptional Stakhanovites of 1935–37. While his scheme for the enterprise-school methods was never implemented beyond SiM, and only briefly there, the ideal of rapid training became universal.

Not surprisingly, Shokhor the engineer was preoccupied with the training of the most skilled workers, who had control over the production process and enormous responsibility. But his emphasis on speed in training was compromised by the ideal of uninterrupted production by the worker-student. Shokhor detailed how the scheduling for the trainees of the enterprise-school would be arranged so as to maintain the production output of the plant. Depending on the needs and on the work schedule of the enterprise, the trainees would either face a five-day or a six-day workweek. With four days of work, one day of rest, and one day of study (4-1-1), three worker-trainees would be needed to cover every two work posts. With a regime of 3-1-2, two would be needed for each work post; and with 2-1-3, three workers would be needed for each work post.[55] Shokhor's enterprise-school was premised on the fact that fulfilling the enterprise *promfinplan* came first and was the prerequisite for the educational component from the standpoint of the factory director, his superiors, and the regime.

The enterprise-school and Shokhor's integral system were presented as the alternative to Lunacharsky's polytechnical unified school. That, presumably, was because of the "withering away" of schools, which would be replaced by the enterprise school. However, Shokhor's theory was identical to Lunacharsky's, and they both disappeared in mid-1931, as did the Cultural Revolution itself.[56] One of the last instances in which the enterprise-school was mentioned was in an article in the 6 August 1931 edition of *Trud,* where M. N. Shvernik asserted that it was the obligation of the trade unions to organize the enterprise-school. He praised the program at SiM. The shop (*tsekh*) schools and the program of technical study without interruption from production were a model for the development of the factory-based enterprise-school, he said. The production training combine, as developed at SiM, he argued, was an "intermediate form" (p. 4). As usual, however, Shvernik, VTsSPS, and the trade unions were lagging behind, and they were the last organs to adjust to the new party policy.

The enterprise-school, the integral method, and the polytechnical school were all doomed by mid-1931 primarily because they were failing to provide the enterprises with the skilled workers, the technicians, and the engineers that they required. In other words, they failed in practice to accomplish what the integration of theory and practice was to be able to achieve; a breakthrough in preparing qualified workers. Thus, the party leadership discarded both the theory and practice of experimental education and training.

What survived from the experimentation in the field of labor training and education during the First FYP was the incorporation of the polytechnical ideal in the FZU and the extensive network of educational, vocational, and technical courses offered at night or as correspondence courses, allowing workers to continue on the job while they pursued their studies. The rapid expansion and growth of these forms of vocational education in the First FYP carried over into the subsequent period. On the other hand, a return to classical education in the ten-year schools prepared a generational cohort for higher, especially higher technical, education in the *tekhnikumy* and the VUZs and VTUZs. This was restored in 1931 and expanded over the rest of the decade.

When Molotov summarized the results of the First FYP at the Combined Party Plenum of the Central Committee and the Central Control Committee, on 1 January 1933, he never even mentioned the enterprise-school experiment. Instead, he claimed that out of 2.5 million new recruits in industry in the First FYP, 2 million ended up in skilled jobs by the end of 1932, even though "the majority of them had no prior concept of benches, instruments, and machines"[57] Furthermore, he claimed that the number of workers who were enrolled in the *rabfaky* increased ninefold, in the FZUs fivefold, in the *tekhnikumy* fivefold, and in the VUZs and VTUZs by threefold, while the number of specialists per one hundred workers increased from 3.8 percent to 7 percent.[58] The Cultural Revolution ideal of bringing John Dewey to SiM was dead. It would live on only in the evening-school general education remedial classes as supplement to specialized training at night for workers. The significance of these classes was enormous.

The enterprise-school failed because it had nothing to do with the actual trends in both broad-based education and in vocational and technical training during the First FYP. Establishing the four-year level of schooling required textbooks, Stalin argued in 1934, and not "complex methods" and "complex" or "loose-leaf" notebooks.[59] His appeal to traditional methods of pedagogy for general education applied equally well in the primary and secondary schools and in the factory night schools and meant the elimination of the polytechnical radical ideal in this realm. Vocational and technical training, on the other hand, was becoming ever more specialized, and thus the integrated methods that Shokhor tried to introduce were bound to confuse rather than clarify either the theory or practice of labor organization and production technique. The solution was to bifurcate theory from practice, that is, general education from vocational training. A fragment of the polytechnical ideal was passed on in the factory night education for the masses.

Shokhor thought himself a visionary, and his vision was based on an engineers' appreciation of rationalization. He was a Taylorist in his attempt to micromanage the schedule of the worker-trainee, with a balance between work, study, and leisure activity. However, his production theory failed to take into account the specialization in production and the division of labor or how best to train workers under new conditions. Thus the enterprise-school did not survive, however, and neither did the old apprenticeship system of vocational training, a system that had dominated training methods in the factories from the era of Peter the Great until 1928. It disappeared during the First FYP, to be replaced by new mass forms of on-the-job training, the brigade-apprenticeship. The proliferating alphabet of enterprise night school programs would become a complementary aspect to crash on-the-job training.

The Brigade Apprenticeship: Mass On-the-Job Training

During the 1930s, while the FZU played an instrumental role in vocational training for youth, it was eclipsed numerically by forms of uninterrupted vocational training. I have already discussed night schooling, but it should be understood that it was developed as a necessary complement to on-the-job training schemes of a mass type: crash courses given to an entire brigade or an even larger aggregate of workers.

These crash, on-the-job training schemes began during the First FYP with the so-called individual-brigade apprenticeship and evolved during the Second and Third FYPs into the *tekhminimum* courses and then the Stakhanovite courses. Finally during the Third FYP, they were called simply production-training courses. They evolved in tandem, from the mid-1930s, with new qualifying exams (certification for rank) attesting to vocational proficiency.

The individual-brigade apprenticeship (*individual'no-brigadnoe uchenich-estvo*), which became numerically the single most significant form of mass training in the 1930s, must not be confused with the old system of apprenticeship that had trained skilled workers in Russian industry since the 1860s. As Veselov explains: "The concept of the individual-brigade apprenticeship is usually understood to mean training in an occupation by individual or group attachment of unskilled workers to a skilled and experienced worker. Giving of their experience and knowledge, the skilled workers instruct the trainees or the trainee for three to six months, teaching them the basic methods of work in that occupation."[60] While Veselov confuses the issue, since it was typically a means of apprenticing an entire work crew at once, and not the individual, the most important feature that distinguished this from the old individualized apprenticeship was its three- to six-month duration, as he notes. Veselov claims that about half of all new workers were trained in this way.[61]

This short and basic form of training was very different from the lengthy and intense one-to-one apprenticeship that most new recruits had endured in tsarist times and that carried over into the 1920s. Its paternalism, in which the power of the *master* over the apprentice was nearly unrestricted, is well known.[62] During the 1920s, the individual-brigade apprenticeship appeared as a complement to the lengthy master-apprentice relationship. In the 1930s, however, it became a mass form of basic training, converted during the First FYP into a three- to six-month crash course. It was no longer an apprenticeship; it had become, instead, a cursory introduction to the work station for an entire work brigade. The masses of recruits who were not able to enroll in the FZU were fortunate, during the First FYP, to get even this cursory, hands-on introduction.

The old system of individual apprenticeship died because it could not begin to meet the extraordinary demand for new labor power in the 1930s: it was less suitable than other forms of training for adapting to the new technology that was being rapidly introduced in the 1930s; highly skilled workers were spread too thinly across the USSR to provide one-on-one training; and finally the masses of youth coming to work in the factories had no patience for it. Part of their rebellion against lengthy individual apprenticeships took the form of the "shock-work brigades," which served as yet another form of mass training on the job (see chap. 6).

On-the-job training was given new form with a decree from the Council of Defense and Labor on 30 June 1932 that obligated economic organs to define those occupations which required workers to master a "technical minimum" in order to work on "complex aggregates, equipment and mechanisms, or to work at especially responsible or dangerous jobs." Workers had to pass special exams to work at such jobs.[63] To meet this requirement, the Komsomol initiated "technical circles" at the enterprise and began to issue "social-technical exams" on 17 October 1933. The State Technical Exams (GTE), introduced on 1 January 1936 in the Commissariats of Heavy and Light Industry, were modeled after these Komsomol exams.[64]

In 1935, the list of occupations requiring workers to have passed the technical miminum was substantially increased, until it included almost all job categories. The State Technical Exams were given on 1 January 1936 to over a million workers; about 90 percent of them passed, and some were immediately given greater responsibility and a higher wage ranking. By 1 October 1936, in all heavy industry, 40 percent of the workers had already completed study in technical circles or other technical courses aimed at passing these exams, and 24 percent were engaged in such circles.[65] They took many forms, including on-the-job brigade instruction and nighttime classes. By December 1935, when virtually every phenomenon in industry had to be linked to the Stakhanovite movement, the Plenum of the Party Central Committee made the technical minimum courses (*tekhminimum*) the first link in a new integrated system of technical training: "technical minimum courses for all workers; Stakhanovite schools and courses for all workers passing the State Technical Exams; courses for masters of socialist labor for worker-innovators; other, less widespread forms of technical training (special technical courses, *tekhminimum* at the second degree, courses for preparing new workers, etc.)."[66]

The first so-called Stakhanovite school was organized by a Stakhanovite, Iashin, at the Parizhskaia Kommuna shoe factory in Moscow in late 1935.[67] Stakhanovites were instructing groups of workers on how to apply their new work methods, and these training circles were now glorified as Stakhanovite schools. They were simply another on-the-job, brigade training program, which blossomed in 1936, supplanting the *tekhminimum* circles, and then atrophied in 1937, yielding to these same circles. In 1937, in industry and construction, there were 1,292,077 graduates and 518,232 students enrolled in *tekhminimum* courses, whereas Stakhanovite courses had 160,563 graduates and 79,409 students in 1937, and in 1938, these figures dropped to only 83,850 graduates and only 8,174 students. *Tekhminimum* courses at the second level had 154,802 graduates in 1937 and 137,950 students still enrolled at the end of the year. In 1938, they had 156,815 graduates with 117,899 still enrolled at the end of the year.[68] While some of these courses involved night schooling, the key element was hands-on training or retraining.

The term "individual-brigade apprenticeship" dropped out of usage, the *tekhminimum* courses replaced it, the Stakhanovite courses were added and then disappeared, then so-called production training was introduced in the shops at ZiS in 1939 or 1940. This crash training and retraining on the job was numerically the most widespread form of vocational training during the 1930s, and in conjunction with night schooling had an important impact on the millions of new workers who would have no formal apprenticeship, who were too old to enroll in the FZU or unable to because of lack of places, and who were just beginning to work in production.

The combination of night schooling and on-the-job vocational training was the only realistic possibility during the 1930s short of compulsory registration of seven-year graduates in the FZU, an expedient which would be adopted in October 1940 with the State Labor Reserve System. The FZU enrollments fell off in 1933, apparently because more and more youth were opting for the ten-year school and college, or the seven-year school and the *tekhnikum*. FZU enrollments only haltingly recovered during the Second and Third FYPs, in exactly the same way that *orgnabor* recruitment fell off dramatically in 1933 and then haltingly recovered.[69] A brief consideration of the ZiS plant on the eve of the Second World War illustrates how the night school and shop-floor crash training functioned as complementary programs, even with the introduction of the reserves and the compulsory assignment of labor.

Several documents from the Moscow City Archive show that, at ZiS, uninterrupted vocational training in night classes complemented on-the-job brigade instruction, which was called simply production training. These, not the FZU, remained numerically most significant as a form of vocational instruction as the war approached. A 1940 document shows classes that were open to new workers aged twenty to thirty-five years, or to experienced workers who needed retraining on new technology, or for a new occupation. The trainee was required to have completed seven years of basic schooling. Classes ran from three to six months and were full-time. Occupations such as milling and grinding would require four months of classes, lathe operation would require three months, and mechanics classes for stamping machines ran for six months. Workers were selected for such classes by their shop bosses, illustrating again the return of authority to the foreman.[70] These were classes for machine operatives, a new mass of semiskilled workers who were to be rapidly trained, and such short courses clearly illustrated the obsolescence of the protracted individual apprenticeship.

Training was also reorganized on the shop floor itself and simply called mass production training. It would be organized in one of three ways: individual trainees would be "attached" to a *master*-instructor (the old apprentice model without its duration); groups of trainees would be "attached" to a *master*-instructor of the shop section (*uchastok*): finally, an entire brigade of trainees would both work and study under a *brigadir* (the individual-brigade apprentice model.) In addition, complementary study classes were to be organized in each shop by a new and undefined organ, the OTO.[71] There was really nothing new in these three programs; they were merely variations on what, during the First FYP, was called the individual-brigade apprenticeship, with various forms of evening classes.

The document explains that remuneration would also be uninterrupted. The worker-trainees were to receive pay ranging from 150 rubles per month for beginners to 300 for workers who were requalifying. The *master*-instructor was to get 600–750 rubles per month, while the *master* of the *uchastok* received a 10-ruble-per-month bonus per worker-trainee that he supervised.[72] Uninterrupted training would be rewarded with uninterrupted pay.

Another document from AMO-ZiS provides a glimpse into how the factory tried to estimate its labor needs for 1940, as the war approached, and how it tried to plan to meet them, primarily through the uninterrupted vocational training programs. The expansion of the factory and of its filials in 1940 would require 4,000 additional workers. Natural loss (death, retirement, and draft into the army) was anticipated, based on the previous year, to be 12 percent of the work force or 4,190 workers. Thus, the plant's total need for 1940 was figured at 8,190 workers. Breaking down this figure by skill grouping, the document assumes that the demand for skilled and highly skilled workers of the sixth, seventh, and eighth *razriady* would be satisfied by promoting workers from the middle ranks who were taking technical courses in night school. The demand for workers of average skills, at the fourth and fifth *razriady,* was quantified at 3,940. Promotion of workers in the first three *razriady* were supposed to account for 2,000 of these; the FZU and *tekhminimum* classes would provide 500; and new workers trained in occupational courses would account for 360. Still, what the document called *nabor so storony* (hiring from outside) was supposed to account for 2,410 new workers of the middle ranks, or well over half.[73] These figures, of course, do not add up, but what is important is that they show that an absolute majority of the new workers in 1940, those who would staff the lower and middle ranks, would be newly hired and without training. That, again, left no option but crash on-site training and night school.

According to a shop-by-shop census taken at ZiS in 1940, there were 25,700 skilled (qualified) workers in the plant, of whom 23,600 had some formal technical training. The 2,000 without formal training were required to take the State Technical Exams and were expected to enroll in the *tekhminimum* courses. In addition, 2,000 new workers were expected to enroll in these courses and take the exam. The FZU, on the other hand, was only expected to have an enrollment of 810.[74] On-the-job training and night school were clearly the predominant forms of vocational training, and the FZU was far behind.

A census of worker-training at AMO-ZiS in 1940 gives precise occupational data on the trainees and a very clear breakdown of the numbers of trainees enrolled in three types of vocational training courses in 1938, 1939, and the first quarter of 1940. The first type were the *tekhminimum* courses, the second were "courses for raising skills," and the third were "courses for new workers." Over seven thousand were in the first, over fifteen hundred in the second, and over three hundred in the third.[75] These clearly remained the predominant form of training new workers as they arrived on the shop floor, as the FZU-trained contingent was less than one-tenth of this total.

Only when the war reached Soviet soil were training courses at ZiS substantially modified. Courses for preparing "universalists" were established in July 1941, and both the *tekhminimum* courses and the courses to raise skill levels were disbanded. The new universalist courses were set initially at six months and then shortened in 1941 and 1942, until they were two to three months.[76] The Stakhanovite schools continued to operate, and a new course for preparation of operators (*operatsionnikov*) was established. This course was primarily designed to train the new recruits who replaced men who were drafted. According to this document, they were the wives of workers, the children, and white-collar workers.[77] It is hard to draw conclusions about these data, because workers were being evacuated with ZiS equipment to Ul'anovsk, Cheliabinsk, and Miass in October 1941, and the sudden need for universalists may have had to do with the problems of coping with dismantling and setting up the machinery.

Surveying the all-union data on worker enrollment in the FZUs in 1937/38, and 1938/39, we can see that these schools accounted for only a tiny fraction of the total number of workers in training. The uninterrupted forms of vocational training assumed far greater numerical significance than did the full-time training offered in the FZUs. In 1937/38, across the USSR, there were 224,300 students enrolled in the FZUs, and in 1938/39, this figure increased slightly to 242,200; in the same years, the *tekhminimum* first-level courses alone had more than twice the enrollment and over five times the number of graduates.[78] Of course, this is not an entirely fair comparison, because by 1937, the FZU program was back up to one and a half or two years of study, while the program of the uninterrupted *tekhminimum,* and most other forms of uninterrupted vocational training, required less than half a year of preparation. However, so long as peasants and urban recruits over eighteen years of age made up the majority of the new recruits, the uninterrupted system of vocational training would inevitably have numerical predominance over the FZU.

It is not merely demographics that explains the predominance of the uninterrupted system. It was also preferred by the enterprise directors and administrators. In an era of rapidly changing technology, these directors were hesitant to invest in lengthy vocational training programs and instead wanted workers to become more versatile by acquiring a rudimentary, general, secondary education. They preferred the much shorter programs of on-the-job training supplemented by night-school classes because they were much less costly in time, in money, and in resources. The key fact, furthermore, was the constant pressure to meet the immediate demands of the *promfinplan.* For this, it was much more tolerable for managers to have their workers training at night or in short shifts, rather than in hiring FZU trainees who would not show up on the shop floor (at least not full-time) for one-and-one-half to two years. It was hard for managers to justify diverting funds—and workers and machinery and equipment—to extensive and lengthy vocational training programs, when they were struggling to fulfill the industrial-financial plan.

The problem that the Red Directors, like Stepanov and Likhachev, faced after 1933, and especially after the purge-terror and the onset of the Second World War, was not labor shortage *per se*; rather, as was true in 1931 or 1932, it was the shortage of qualified workers, ready and able to use the machinery properly or fit in on the assembly line. Likhachev probably paid little attention to sending out pushers (*tolkachi*) to recruit *kolkhoz* peasants, or to find city youth to enroll in the FZU. They showed up at the factory gate anyhow, and the FZU was too expensive and time-consuming as a method of training. Instead, at ZiS, Likhachev and his staff would hire thousands of new workers again on the eve of the war and would, rationally enough, put them into the crash training courses on the shop floor. That was the pattern which had been established during the First and Second FYPs and would continue into the war years. Contrary to regime assumptions, there was no need for additional *orgnabor* or FZU recruits.

Conclusion

Closely related to the problems of recruiting workers and of attaching them to a factory, a shop, and a workbench, was the problem of training and educating the new recruits. Vocational training simultaneously presented the state with both its greatest opportunity and its greatest challenge in developing a labor policy during the First FYP and afterward. Whereas recruiting the worker was a one-time event, and attaching was primarily a matter of threatening the recalcitrant workers with job loss or penal repercussions (or conversely, offering the incentive of higher wages), vocational training required that the state invest in the worker and make a long-term commitment. It also provided the state with a unique opportunity to influence new recruits.

For new recruits, vocational training in the FZU offered the potential for starting at the semiskilled or skilled ranks on the wage scale. Those who gained vocational training on the shop floor and at night school also had good prospects for rapid promotion. This was not upward mobility but was, instead, a status revolution because it was a universal phenomenon for newcomers.

Vocational schooling could help to reduce new workers' anxiety about technology and facilitate their adjustment to machinery and to the enormous shops and factories where they would work. This was no trivial matter, as memoirs make clear. Whereas the apprenticeship had traditionally been the way of making such an adjustment, vocational training and hands-on crash courses offered a potentially broader vision of the factory. Even more important, the new vocational training reduced the dependence of the new worker on older, male, established worker-instructors. Personalized authority was not being eliminated, as the resurgence of the foreman showed; however, it was mitigated through formal schooling and vocational training methods which were much more institutionalized. Not only that, but the recruits were training in groups, not as isolated individuals, which offered the opportunity to develop new solidarities in the training process itself. Cohorts of FZU graduates, or cohorts of those who passed the *tekhminimum* exams together after cramming in class, may have promoted a new shop-floor solidarity among cohorts of these newcomers.

Thus, formalized schooling and crash-training on the shop floor provided a widely generalized if not universal elevation of status. It was a mass *uravnilovka*, or rough equalizing, of the situation on the shop floor for established workers and newcomers, for peasant-recruits and urban workers, for women and men, and for youth and older workers. The irony of the situation was that, buried within the antiegalitarian message of the "Six Conditions" speech, with its emphasis on skills, training, education, and corresponding promotion and pay differentials or bonuses, was a powerfully egalitarian mechanism of transformation. The egalitarian polytechnical ideal of Lunacharsky, Krupskaya, and Dewey, thus, and quite ironically, triumphed in the Soviet factory, but without the innovative combination of mental and manual aspects of pedagogy. The workers were given separate courses, vocational and general primary or higher education, raising all of them to a new common level, the level of literate and numerate and qualified, that is, they became the new Soviet working class.

Such egalitarianism, while it indeed required enormous work and sacrifice on the part of this generation of factory workers, who worked one shift and often studied for half a second, was no mean feat for a country so strapped for resources, funds, and hell-bent on tempos of production.

The state had a vested interest in the success of vocational training. Stalin had stated, in his famous "Ten Years to Catch Up" speech, delivered on 4 February 1931, that "technique decides everything," and this became a regime slogan for the next four years.[79] In May 1935 he modified this, in a speech before the graduates of the Academy of the Red Army, stating that "cadres decide everything": "Thus, comrades, if we want to successfully overcome our famine in the field of people and achieve enough cadre for our country [who will be] competent to move forward the technology and to put it into operation, then we must, first of all, learn to value people, to value cadre, to value each worker. . . . We must, finally, understand, that of all the important capital in the world, the most important and the most decisive capital is our people, cadre. We must understand that under our contemporary conditions 'cadre decide everything.' If we have a multitude of good cadre in industry, in agriculture, in transport, in the army, then our country will be unconquerable. If we do not have such cadre then we will limp along on both legs."[80]

While Stalin's foray into human capital theory was decades ahead of Gary Becker, it was three years late in the Soviet context, where the "famine in the field of people" had struck in 1932 and 1933. By the time Stalin gave his speech, that crisis had been basically resolved, and the various forms of vocational training and higher education, both factory-based and Soviet-based, were already well established. Still, the shift in slogan was highly appropriate and significant, because it reflected the very large outlay in human capital investment on the part of the state to provide for mass education. That investment was critical in the status revolution.

With the endemic hoarding of workers driven by the desire to meet insane plan targets, as I have noted, enterprises during the First FYP would hire too many unskilled workers and not have enough trained workers. The situation by 1933, when the labor famine was at its worst, was a clear indication that the problem was not the failure of recruiting mechanisms, nor was it caused by labor turnover. Rather, it was the inability to train workers rapidly enough, given the unrealistic plan targets and the scale and scope of the new construction projects that was the source of the crisis.

The labor famine disappeared overnight during 1933 when new construction was halted, production targets were lowered, and enterprises were instructed to undertake some reduction of staff through layoffs. The shift in the regime's emphasis from recruiting, to attaching, and finally to training workers, was clear indication of the end of this phase. Artificially caused by politics, the labor famine was politically resolved in the January 1933 Plenum, much as the real famine would be resolved in the spring of 1933 with belated concessions on the household plot and marketing of surplus produce. What was left was a labor deficit economy, which could and would head back toward labor famine with the threat of war in the later 1930s.

Vocational training presented the unique opportunity, for the state, of breaking through the old apprenticeship system, which for generations had made new workers beholden to the older workers for many years of their productive lives and which had enhanced the authority and cultural influence of the older workers. It was an opportunity that the state could not afford to miss, since its own authority and prestige were at stake. By successfully training workers to fulfill responsible jobs on the shop floor, the state would greatly enhance its own authority in the eyes of these new workers and, at the same time, break the authority of the older generation. Some from that older generation would achieve upward mobility through promotion to foreman, technician, or other positions. But for millions of established workers, the regime would offer evening vocational retraining and general education, making them participants in the broad status revolution sweeping up the masses of newcomers.

The First FYP saw a shift in the regime's emphasis, from attempting to control recruiting and the distribution of labor through such mechanisms such as *orgnabor*, the "social roll call," and the FZU, to attempting to control *tekuchest'* with a series of increasingly harsh labor laws, to issues of training workers. This shifting was clear indication of its less than totalitarian objectives in labor policy. By the end of the First FYP, the emphasis was already on labor training. This would prove to be one very important aspect of the social stabilization (the subject of part 3 of this study). By raising expectations for job training and education, and then meeting them, the regime was building a reservoir of goodwill among the new recruits that was more likely than either the stick or the carrot to bring the type of labor-discipline and productivity that it wanted. So, too, it made for a positive transition for most of the established workers, who were able to adapt to new work methods by retraining and thus participating in this broad status revolution, rather than experiencing the transition as a negative phenomenon of "deskilling."

Education and vocational training were combined in the factory, on the shop floor, and at night school. This was a type of mass polytechnical egalitarianism which would, ironically, help give birth to the new Soviet working class by negating Stalin's antiegalitarian ideology.

R-R-R-R-REVOLUTIONARY SHOCK WORK AND SOCIALIST COMPETITION[1]

I n part 2 I argue that the repression/resistance paradigm misses the point of the Stalin regime's labor policy, which was concerned with the mundane tasks of recruiting, attaching, and training a new labor force. The regime's labor policy evolved *ad hoc* and smacked of utilitarian more than totalitarian objectives. The draconian laws and mobilization of labor came about because of social factors and labor market realities which the Stalin regime neither anticipated nor understood. First, the regime faced unique problems arising from the labor market bifurcation inherited from the *ancien regime,* in which labor aristocrats and subalterns were locked into traditional patterns of Russian and Soviet NEP industrial relations that were obstacles to the new industrialization drive, such as lengthy apprenticeships, the peasant-proletarian engaging in *otkhod* or seasonal migration, and the ghettoization of women in textiles and other light industries. Second, the regime faced the sudden inversion of the labor market once the industrialization drive was under way, spawning the problem of turnover that frustrated efforts to raise productivity. These two aspects of the labor market, historically unprecedented and absolutely unique in combination in 1929–30, yet another aspect of Soviet combined development, turned mundane and simple problems of the labor market into a central and difficult problem of state industrial, social, and labor policy.

This chapter concludes my discussion of state policy in part 2 and anticipates part 3 by introducing the perspective of the workers and the issue of workers' consciousness. Contrasting a "false consciousness"and state ideology of solidarity of the shock work and socialist competition movement with the new worker solidarities that emerged in the work brigade, partly because it was able to "routinize" shock work, I suggest that a new working-class consciousness was an inseparable aspect of Soviet working class formation, and that this consciousness was not at all according to official Stalinist ideology. This chapter opens up my discussion of workers' solidarity by starting from the vantage point of the state, whose prototypical shock-work campaigns of the First FYP spawned many such campaigns during the 1930s, the most famous of which was the Stakhanovite movement of late 1935 and 1936.

The repression/resistance paradigm analyzed these production campaigns as a form of social control and speedup and interpreted both shock work and Stakhanovism as strategies of social stratification and class fragmentation aimed at creating a labor aristocracy that would be loyal to the regime. The contingent identity studies by Hiroaki Kuromiya, Vladimir Andrle, and Lewis Siegelbaum (see chap. 7) went beyond this approach, finding various new workers' solidarities over the course of the decade. They were at times fostered by the regime's production campaigns; at other times or among other workers they emerged in reaction against the campaign; and in other circumstances, they evolved despite the regime's campaigns and intervention on the shop floor.

This chapter will approach the issue from a somewhat different standpoint, showing how a new solidarity, which was fundamental to stabilizing Soviet labor relations, was evolving among Soviet workers and foremen within the standard industrial work brigade. The work brigade emerged, in part, as a routinized version of the shock brigade. On the one hand, such routinization was inevitable because the regime attempted to make all workers shock workers or Stakhanovites, and in that sense of the term *routinization,* I mean a degradation or watering down of the movement, which, from my perspective, exposes it as regime ideology rather than social solidarity. Yet routinization signified a triumph for steady work routine and a stable work unit, the work brigade. It signified a triumph over the "storming" that was needed to meet the *promfinplan* each month or that accompanied the socialist competition campaigns, first of shock work and then of Stakhanovism. From the standpoint of the regime, that looked like a defeat, but as with so many other ironies of the 1930s, the triumph of the stable work brigade was a crucial step in improving labor productivity and an essential building block in working-class formation. In all these respects, I am using the term *routinization* in a strictly positive sense.

The work brigade replaced a medley of primary production units inherited from the past. It replaced the peasant work unit, the *artel'*, in which a peasant *starosta* directed the work of the group, which he had also recruited, usually from his village. It replaced peasants on *otkhod* who often came to a factory based on ties to a villager already working there, a *zemliak,* and then were assigned to work, again often together with a village-based team, under the direction of a *master',* who was a highly skilled urban worker with long tenure. It replaced work units that consisted of something like the old guild arrangement of artisans, journeymen, and apprentices, in which the *master* was the factory equivalent of the artisan and where he directed a work unit of subordinates, typically called first and second apprentices or assistants. These were usually boys or young men with family or village connections to the *master* under which they worked or to another skilled worker or foreman in the factory.

This medley of old work units, proliferating into the NEP years, was supplanted by shock-work brigades, and what emerged when these brigades were routinized were very stable, modern, factory work brigades. The modern work brigade was already emerging prior to shock work, but was strengthened by the proliferation and then routinization of the shock-work brigade. It would remain intact, if not strengthened, in the later 1930s after routinization of the next massive regime intervention—Stakhanovism. The work brigade meant a sufficiently defined division of labor such that labor turnover, even when it was high, did not undermine the overall organization of the brigade.

Shock work went through three distinct phases. The first phase, 1926–28, was characterized by scattered shock brigades, which were, it would appear, organized from below by groups of young worker-enthusiasts. The second phase began in January 1929, and saw the party leadership embrace these initiatives and then launch widespread "socialist competitions," transforming shock work into a production campaign and making it a cornerstone of state industrial and labor policy. The first shock-worker heroes appeared in this phase. With the new direction in labor policy after Stalin's "Six Conditions" speech of 23 June 1931, the regime moved shock work into a third phase, shifting away from the "heroic working class" and shock brigades to the individual "shock-worker hero." By 1933, routinization of the shock-work brigades had made them indistinguishable from ordinary work brigades, and shock work itself became thoroughly routinized, despite the rise of the most celebrated shock-worker heroes, who were the progenitors of Stakhanovism.

Shock Work as a Production Campaign: 1929 at SiM

Soviet historians have dated the first shock brigades to spontaneous initiatives coming from rank-and-file workers in the mid-1920s. Then, they suggest, these scattered shock brigades were transformed into a mass movement
by the party, which provided the "consciousness" and organization.[2] SiM offers no direct evidence on this since there was no first phase of shock work
at the plant, but that fact alone raises serious questions about just how genuine or at least how widespread such spontaneous workers' initiatives were
during this first phase.[3] The evidence at SiM shows that in 1929 there was a
transition to production campaigns with a wide proliferation of shock-work
brigades under socialist competition, following the regime's publication of
Lenin's article "How to Organize Competition" in January 1929. The article
sparked the first all-union "socialist competition," which is dated 5 March
1929, when the workers at the Krasnyi Vyborzhets metallurgical plant in
Leningrad issued a challenge in *Pravda* to workers from other metallurgical
plants.[4]

The first shock brigades at SiM were organized in response to this challenge.[5] SiM established a headquarters for the socialist competition, which
included N. D. Korotin, secretary of the party committee in the sheet metal
shop, and three sheet metal workers: Arsenii K. Gladyshev, soon to become
the first shock-worker hero at SiM; N. A. Mikhailov, a member of the SiM
writers' circle; and Misha Chernyshev, the shop steward. The headquarters
also included three rolling mill workers, Savel'ev, Ivanov, and Bykovskii, and
from the plant administration, A. I. Pogonchenkov and N. P. Gromov. The
headquarters totaled fifteen members of the factory work collective.[6] It is
clear that the shock brigades at SiM were organized by plant party, komsomol, and trade-union committees.

At a meeting of workers in the sheet metal shop held on 3 April 1929,
according to the accounts given by veterans of the shop, Gladyshev made a
dramatic speech, calling on all the SiM workers, the Serpomolotsy, to take up
the challenge of the Vyborzhetsy, the workers at Krasnyi Vyborzhets. Then a
young sheet metal worker and brigade leader, I. M. Romanov, volunteered
his brigade in the competition. Romanov, like Gladyshev, was destined to become a famous shock worker; according to his own recollections, however,
he stood up very reluctantly and only at the urging of "Uncle" Grisha
Bykovskii.[7] Next, the sheet metal workers at SiM, at the Lys'vensk plant, and
at the Dnepropetrovsk plant drew up a formal contract for the socialist competition.[8] It would appear, from these documents, that the Gladyshev and Romanov brigades were competing against each other as well as against
brigades from the other plants. It would also appear that production campaigns in the new shock-work brigades began in heavy metallurgy.

In May 1929, the movement spread from metallurgy to other branches of the economy when six of the Soviet Union's largest factories, encompassing 75,000 metal workers, signed a contract for socialist competition, led by the Kolomenskii ship building plant and the Red Putilov plant in Leningrad. Soon, over 2 million workers were under socialist competition, including 650,000 metal workers, 600,000 coal miners, and 450,000 textile workers.[9] This was no longer a matter of a few individuals, brigades, or factories, but a mass-production movement, mobilized by the party-state.

That fact was already becoming clear at the Sixteenth Party Conference (23-29 April 1929), where the Central Committee endorsed the maximum variant of the First FYP and sealed the defeat of the Right Opposition, while calling for the widest possible use of socialist competition. A resolution of the Central Committee from the conference, published on 9 May, entitled "On Socialist Competition of Factories and Plants," called for socialist competition, while cautioning against the spread of fictitious competitions organized by the party and trade-union committees: "It is also essential to forewarn all organizations against the danger of socialist competition being transformed into a paradelike roll call of organizations, without actual participation of the masses. The trade unions must assume the responsibility for leadership of the socialist competitions."[10] Indeed, as we shall see, the "paradelike roll call" was to be exactly the fate of the shock-work movement during its second and third phases, when it was routinized.

It was quite remarkable that, in the spring of 1929, shock work began in the sheet metal shop at SiM. This shop was, by all indicators, one of the least productive and had the highest level of absenteeism and labor indiscipline in the plant.[11] In the first half of 1929, this shop failed to fulfill its production plans for several consecutive months, and only 50 percent of its product was "first sort" in quality. Workers refused to come in on the weekends, and so only one of eight mills was in operation.[12] N. Mikhailov described the desperate situation in the shop at the beginning of 1929. For the first quarter of the economic year 1928/29 (1 October–31 December 1928), the plan was only 94 percent fulfilled. Workers were frequently "going to Semashko," the commissar for public health, which meant feigning illness.[13]

Yet this is where the shock brigade movement began at SiM. The socialist competition of the sheet metal workers was based on four criteria: fulfilling the production plan, lowering costs, improving labor discipline, and exchange of production experience with the sheet metal shops of other plants.[14] The competition led to the declaration, on 1 October, that the entire sheet metal shop was a "shock shop" and that all the sheet metal workers were shock brigaders.[15] The three most famous shock workers at SiM in

1929, Gladyshev, Monger, and Romanov, came from this shop, which sent Gladyshev, Bykhovskii, Savel'ev, Duplishchev, and Denisov to the First All-Union Congress of Shock Workers in Moscow in December 1929. The only other SiM workers at this congress were Podrubaev, from the model forge shop, and Kurochkin from the wire manufacturing shop. Smelters from the open hearth shop were conspicuously absent.[16]

That was no longer true in 1931, when a second surprise was the sudden shift in shock-work brigades and heroes in favor of the open hearth shop and away from the sheet metal shop. In 1931, the entirely new cohort of shock-worker heroes in the open hearth shop included Chesnokov, Ovchinnikov, Sveshnikov, Eroshkin, Grebeshkov, Sviridov, Brylkin, Il'in, and Povaliaev. Later, during the Second FYP, the leading Stakhanovite in the plant, Makarov, was also a steel smelter in the open hearth shop. Finally, even after the Second World War, most of the leading SiM workers who gained fame came from the open hearth shop. This included three apprentices under Chesnokov who won the Stalin Prize in 1950, and Viktor I. Diuzhev, who founded the first shock brigade of Communist labor, as they were called in the Khrushchev era, in 1958, also in the open hearth shop of SiM.[17] The generational shift after 1931 among these shock-worker heroes will be discussed in more depth below.

The most logical explanation for this shift from the sheet metal to the open hearth shop was the change in production priorities for the plant, as established by the commissariat (first VSNKh, and then NKTP), and by the Special Steels Trust (Spetstal'). Their priorities, of course, became the priorities of the Red Director, Stepanov, and of the plant administration. In 1929 and 1930, the priorities were reconstructing the sheet metal shop and expanding it. According to the *promfinplan* for SiM for 1931, the factory was to provide 50 percent of the sheet and shaped metal for AMO-ZiS, for the auto plant VATO no. 2, and for the auto plant at Iaroslavskii. The sheet metal supplied to VATO (the All-Union Auto Combine), was supposed to be increased from 200 tons in 1929/30 to 6,958 tons in 1931. In 1932, SiM was supposed to begin supplying sheet metal for the giant new auto plant in Nizhni Novgorod.[18]

In 1931 and 1932, however, the plant's priorities shifted, both for new products and for new investment. The new priority became manganese steel alloys and other alloys which, until then, had been imported from abroad and were necessary for many new industries. In 1927/28, only 4.1 percent of the plant's output was in high-quality steels, but by 1934, that figure had risen to 94.7 percent.[19] For the rest of the decade and then into the Second World War, the priority was on the open hearth shop, where new steel alloys were smelted. Production in this shop thus acquired an immediacy, a heightened sense of urgency, that came with the need to supply important new factories and new branches of the economy.

It is not surprising, therefore, that the demands first on the sheet metal shop, and then on the open hearth shop, created an environment conducive to the rise of shock brigades and worker-initiators and heroes. Priorities of VSNKh, under Ordzhonikidze, and of "Spetstal'" under Tevosian, were communicated directly to Stepanov. Tevosian was credited, in fact, with playing an important role in the development of high-quality steel output at SiM.[20] The Moscow Steel Institute conducted experiments with bimetallic steel at SiM.[21] Thus, the introduction of a new steel, or meeting some special order for a steel alloy, might lead the plant administration to declare them to be shock projects, and thus the workers involved became shock brigaders. The early history and subsequent development of shock-work brigades and heroes at SiM thus very clearly reflected the pressures and demands from the center.

The situation at AMO-ZiS was similar. Following the publication of Lenin's article, the first shock brigades were organized at the plant on 10 January 1929, and following the challenge by the Krasnyi Vyborzhets workers, the ZiS workers took on the obligation of reducing costs by 20 percent by 1 October 1929. The largest increase in shock-work brigades and participants at AMO came after the Sixteenth Party Conference. While noting that the shock brigades often fell apart as rapidly as they were organized at AMO, Soviet historians have focused on the role of Likhachev and the party, declaring the movement a success in 1929. In their highly formulaic account, a conflict between A. P. Salov and P. V. Mokhov over whether or not to install a new press in the spring shop was "class struggle," and the shock-work movement triumphed.[22]

Salov, who in this account supported a young innovator who defied Mokhov and who worked closely with Likhachev in installing the new technology, was soon rewarded with a new two-room apartment and, on 8 November 1930, with a cruise on the first Soviet passenger ship, the *Abkhazia*. Also on the cruise was a SiM shock-work organizer, Ivan Mikhailovich Romanov, like Salov a key figure in the plant conflicts over shock work and socialist competition during the spring of 1929. Alexander Petrovich Salov figures again in chapter 8 below, since he was also co-organizer, with Gor'kii, of "Val'tsovka," the ZiS literary circle. Salov discussed his novella, "Birth of the Shop," with Gor'kii in Italy when the Abkhazia docked near Capri. Later, he wrote a nonfiction account of the food supply base at ZiS. Salov worked at ZiS from 1924 to 1958.[23]

Beyond that, and more broadly speaking, shock work was expected to play a major role in transforming masses of new recruits into highly disciplined and productive industrial workers. A resolution of the Sixteenth Party Conference in April 1929 stated that "competition . . . must become the means of socialist education of the working class, particularly of the new workers—those who came from the countryside and from the petty bourgeois urban layers."[24] V. Kuibyshev reiterated this point at the First All-Union Congress of Shock Brigades in December 1929, when he said that the shock brigades were a means for reeducating the backward petty bourgeois elements that were being recruited in unprecedented numbers into the Soviet working class.[25]

And so it was, as isolated shock brigades were praised and rewarded and the party began to organize such brigades on a wide scale to wage "class struggle" for improving productivity in the factory. Converted into a mass movement, shock work and the shock brigade became a training method, a type of rapid orientation like the individual-brigade apprenticeship, which was providing the new worker with a very rudimentary form of training.

Phase Two: Every Worker a Shock Worker

In the Metalworkers' Union, the number of shock workers had grown dramatically by 1 January 1930, when approximately 35 percent were members of shock brigades and 60 percent were participants in socialist competitions. These figures were fairly representative for other unions also. On 1 November 1930, for all VSNKh industry, 48 percent of the workers were shock workers, including 43.3 percent of coal miners, 51.1 percent of metalworkers, and 48.8 percent of textile workers. Almost a year later, on 1 October 1931, the total for all workers in VSNKh industry was up to 62.1 percent: for coal miners, 44.2 percent; for metalworkers, 66.6 percent; and for textile workers, 60.7 percent. After that, recruitment leveled off. On 1 January 1932, for all industry, the 1 October 1931 figures hardly changed, as shock workers made up 64.2 percent of the total.[26]

According to data from SiM, the number of shock workers and brigades grew rapidly until mid-1931, and then declined rapidly after that. The figures for 1932 and 1 January 1933 given in table 6.1 are somewhat inflated because they include all participants in socialist competitions, non-shock workers as well as shock workers. The most spectacular growth in the numbers of shock workers occurred during the first three months of 1930, under the impact of the so-called Lenin Enrollment. The enrollment was announced on 21 January 1930, the sixth anniversary of Lenin's death, by the Central Committee of the Komsomol together with the All-Union Central Council of Trade Unions (VTsSPS). In the next three months more than one-half million new

Table 6.1. SiM Shock Workers During the First FYP

	Shock Brigades	Shock Workers	% Shock Worker
1 January 1929	43	370	6
1 January 1930	83	900	14
1 August 1930	321	4,200	52
20 September 1930	401	5,000	62
1 July 1931	1,154	10,257	82
1932	—	13,000	87
1 January 1933	—	8,126	72
1933	—	—	55.8

Sources: Figures for 1929–31: Filatov, *Partrabota*, pp. 58–59; 1932 and 1 January 1933 figures: GARF f. 7952, op. 3, d. 343, l. 29, and GARF f. 7952, op. 3, d. 282, l. 191; final figure (1933): trade-union census, *Profsoiuznaia Perepis'*, pp. 156–57.

shock workers joined the movement, and in the metalworkers', textile, and railroad workers' unions, the number of shock workers more than doubled.[27] There was a clear parallel to massive party recruiting of workers from the bench in the Lenin Levy of 1924, and then again, in 1930.

At SiM, shock-work recruitment in the spring of 1930 was hectic. One source indicates that on 1 January there were 900 shock workers, while four months later, at the Third Party Conference of the factory, on 10 May, the *raikom* secretary, Gaidul', claimed that SiM had 5,000 shock workers.[28] In four months, if these sources are credible, there had been more than 500 percent increase in participation. Archival sources, however, provide somewhat lower figures: 3,452 shock workers at SiM by 1 April and 4,089 by 1 June.[29] A report by the union secretary, dated 11 June, gives the figures shown in table 6.2. Even if these figures are accurate, the factory trade-union committee was probably unable to list all the new shock workers individually during the Lenin Enrollment, in January and February 1930. Work brigades, and even entire shops, were simply listed as "shock brigades" or "shock shops," and all the workers were included. This meant exactly the type of "paradelike roll call" that the party leadership had cautioned against in May 1929. It was a debasing of shock work.

The roll call also meant the routinizing of shock work, which became inevitable as participation in the mass movement was expected to become universal. On 5 April 1930, *Martenovka* ran headlines that read "Encompass All Workers in Socialist Competition Not Later Than May 1" and "By the First of May SiM Must Become a Shock Factory" (pp. 2–3). After such unrestricted enrollment, "false" shock workers and "fake" shock brigades were "exposed" and purged from the ranks. A checkup was organized at SiM in July 1930,

Table 6.2. Expansion in Shock Work at SiM, Spring 1930

	Shock Brigades	Total Shock Workers
1 October 1929	43	368
1 January 1930	83	891
15 February 1930	214	3,452
1 June 1930	297	3,567

Source: GARF f. 5469, op. 14, d. 193, l. 132.

shortly after VTsSPS and the TsK issued a joint decree calling for "self-checkup" on socialist competitions. That checkup was deemed inadequate.[30] Then a Temporary Control Commission (VKK) was set up for the Metalworkers' Union, which, on 20 July 1930, concluded that at SiM "many brigades were organized spontaneously and fell apart."[31] They had remained, since the Lenin Enrollment, on paper, as "fictitious" shock brigades.

The VKK's report concerning the Krasnyi Ok'tiabr steel plant on the Volga concluded: "Putting together the fact of 70–80 percent participation in shock work with the fact of not fulfilling the plan . . . testifies to the existence of false shock work."[32] In summarizing findings from the Vozrozhdenie and Imena Lenina steel plants, the report noted that "in particular shock brigades there was more idleness of equipment [*prostoi*], growth of absenteeism, and worse production indicators than in brigades without shock workers."[33]

The commission report, like the checkup at SiM, did not call for reducing the numbers of shock workers. Quite the contrary; the checkup, while it might purge some, was expected to be used as a mechanism for recruiting new and "genuine" shock workers. The report of the Metalworkers' Union concluded that shock work should be universalized, that is, that it should encompass 100 percent of the metalworkers.[34]

The evidence from these checkups suggests that a worker could become a shock worker by producing above the norm for a month or two and then retain the title even after producing at or below the norm thereafter. Or, during the Lenin Enrollment, it would seem that all volunteers were accepted among the ranks of shock workers, because the recruitment drive aimed at universal participation. The inevitable result was that the title became meaningless, as became clear on the eve of the Stakhanovite movement, on 1 July 1935, when a trade-union census of 4.6 million industrial workers showed that only 42 percent of shock workers were fulfilling their norms.[35]

Numerically swelling the ranks of shock workers constituted the first aspect of the regime's actions that led to the debasing and routinizing of the movement. The second aspect was the frequent alteration of the forms and functions of shock brigades and their subordination to the changing party-state objectives or campaigns of the moment. It was from such state impera-tives, however, that workers and managers would succeed in routinizing the movement in a positive sense, that is, by converting the shock brigades into functioning work brigades.

One of the first functions of shock work was mobilization of workers to participate in "counterplanning." The counterplans were often then incor-porated into the contracts for socialist competitions. In counterplanning, the shock workers and/or the workers contracting to socialist competitions claimed to uncover "hidden reserves," or untapped potential in their shop or factory, and suggested, on this basis, more ambitious plan targets. This ac-tivity, exposing the hidden reserves, always threatened to spill over into ex-posure of conservative administrators, ITR, specialists, or managers as well. That is, counterplanning was linked to purges of the specialists and of the economic administration during the First FYP. A typical example at the AMO-ZiS plant cited the administration's plan for 6,400 cars for the eco-nomic year 1930/31. Plant shock workers presented a counterplan (*vstrech-nyi promfinplan*) projecting 7,900 cars for 1930/31. Special shock days were set up on every tenth day in the plant to implement workers' suggestions and innovations to fulfill the counterplan.[36] The ultimate counterplan slogan, "Fulfill the FYP in Four Years," was attributed to the Lugansk Shipyard work-ers by Soviet historians.[37]

Two of the earliest forms of shock brigades were rationalization brigades and brigades of expediters, or *tolkachi*. As one trade-union report from AMO-ZiS indicated, "Rationalization brigades are being organized in every shop. They now gather workers' suggestions and inventions and implement them. The factory is always having difficulties and interruptions in the supply of metal and other necessary materials, and so the shock workers . . . organize brigades of expediters who go directly to the suppliers. . . . One brigade even went to VSNKh with a letter from the workers of AMO, asking for a guaran-tee for the supply of metal and for a metallurgical supply base, which the fac-tory does not have now and which threatens to halt production next year."[38]

Brigades of rationalizers and *tolkachi* were not necessarily shock-work brigades, but they often were.[39] On the other hand, *skvoznye brigady*, which might best be translated as "troubleshooting brigades," and *buksirnye brigady*, which is translated as "tugboating brigades," were the direct outgrowth of the shock brigade movement. According to a trade-union report concerning AMO, the VKK and such forms of shock brigades were widely used to deal with the problems of "bottlenecks." "To deal with particular problems of pro-duction, a frequent practice is to establish VKKs and shock brigades. For bot-

tlenecks [*uzkie mesta*] in the production process *skvoznye brigady* were organized, which immediately produced good results. . . . The *buksir* method has
become widespread within the factory, and in relation to outside plants."[40]
Such bottlenecks, caused most frequently by equipment failure or supply
lapses, were a plague in Soviet industry, causing slowdowns and shutdowns of
brigades, sections, and even of entire shops in most plants.

Shock brigades were also expected to help resolve discipline problems.
The movement, with its different forms of brigades, was seen as a panacea for
all labor and industrial problems. The same trade-union report from AMO-
ZiS explains how the shock-work brigades were to become a mechanism for
voluntarily attaching workers, that is, for reducing labor turnover attributed
to peasant attitudes.

In response to the appeal of the Central Committee on 25 September 1930, to strengthen
work discipline, competitions were held on how to resolve the problem of the letuny
[rolling stones], perebezhiki [labor deserters], and rvachi [self-seekers]. At AMO, 60 percent
of the workers promised to "attach themselves" [samozakrepivshchit'sa] to the factory until
at least the end of the First FYP. . . . After this appeal of the Central Committee, a tribunal
of leading workers was set up to deal with those who were ruining labor discipline.

In the first days after this appeal, thirty new shock brigades and six new *skvoznye
brigady* were organized at the plant.[41]

There were other, temporary forms of shock work and socialist competition with specific disciplinary functions. Special tribunals of shock workers
were established to judge and punish undisciplined workers, primarily by os-
tracizing recalcitrant workers on the shop floor, even boycotting them. Furthermore, VKKs were organized at a moment's notice to establish counterplans and conduct the self-checkups of shock work. Still another function
was *shefstvo*, a type of inspection over other factories, or even over agencies
of the state administration by appointed groups of shock workers.

Thus, in 1930, shock work was seen as the solution to any and all production and labor problems, and a shift in party policy had an immediate impact in the mobilization of new shock brigades, or in redefining the content
of the shock-work movement and the activities and forms of these brigades.
In other words, shock work, during its second phase, had become incorporated as a tool of state labor policy. This explains its multiplicity of forms,
which ultimately led to its thorough routinization in the cost-accounting
brigade.

Arguably the least regulated and most spontaneous new forms of shock
brigades were the production collectives and production communes. They
flowered briefly in 1930 and 1931, and in April 1931, a survey of 1.8 million

shock workers across the Soviet Union showed that 7.2 percent or 134,000 were members of collectives and communes.[42] They became officially anathema after Stalin's "Six Conditions" speech for spreading the evil of "petty bourgeois egalitarianism." Indeed, they did promote egalitarianism, according to documents from the Metalworkers' Union.[43]

The organization of communes and collectives at SiM and AMO-ZiS confirms this. One document dated 11 June 1930 indicates that at SiM there were four communes including 48 workers and thirty-three collectives including 248 workers.[44] Other documents indicate that a commune household, the first in the PR, was founded by Marusa Arushanova. She had come to Moscow from the Caucasus in 1928 and began working at SiM in 1929 in the wire manufacturing shop. She organized the first production commune in this shop and then in the dormitory where she and other young workers from SiM, AMO, and Dinamo were housed. Later, in 1930, Arushanova was chosen by the party as the organizer of the Women's Section in the factory.[45] It is possible that the communal living arrangements of these Komsomol workers formed the basis for the production commune.[46]

This wide variety of forms and functions of shock brigades, with the possible exception of the collectives and communes, far from demonstrating their vitality, is a most definitive catalogue of their decline from the regime's perspective. No longer the reflection of worker initiative or of autonomous worker enthusiasm, if they ever had been, they were converted into the instruments of state policy. The shock brigades were given new forms and new functions corresponding to every new direction or shift of emphasis in state labor policy.

This does not mean that factors "from below" were irrelevant in the changing forms and functions of shock brigades. The *skvoznye,* or troubleshooting brigades, for instance, almost certainly were a shop floor response to the bottlenecks and lack of coordination between different shops. At SiM, for instance, one account describes the formation of temporary troubleshooting brigades to smooth over intershop problems in production. These tended to become permanent as *skvoznye brigady.*[47] Subsequently, the rapid proliferation of these *skvoznye brigady* was certainly the result of the state's decision to organize them as a tool in the struggle to reduce idle time, which meant routinization. In other words, what might have begun as a workers' initiative "from below" was then promoted "from above."

Shifting the focus of the discussion, we can also trace the routinization of shock work by considering it as part of a tendency toward contractualization. The transition to the second (mass) stage of shock work was driven by socialist competitions that were based on formal contracts: contracts between workers and managers, contracts between different factories, contracts between different shops of a single factory, and contracts among shock brigades. These labor-management contracts established mutual obligations. On the one hand, management was obligated to supply the necessary raw materials, semifabricated parts, or equipment in a timely fashion and to make sure that machinery was in good repair. On the other hand, workers were obligated to fulfill or overfulfill output targets set by the plan. They were also both obligated, under some contracts, to lower costs, reduce defective output (*brak*), to eliminate idleness, and to combat absenteeism and other forms of labor indiscipline.

Some important features of the socialist competition contracts were foreshadowed by the annual collective contracts between union and management in the NEP years. By the First FYP, these contracts no longer reflected union input on behalf of the workers, but rather were a type of formal elaboration of management's and of labor's obligations, primarily in relation to the state. The socialist competition contracts were very similar documents.[48]

With Stalin's "Six Conditions" speech, itself an ersatz social contract as I have argued, contractualization in economic relationships developed rapidly. The contract for shock work and socialist competition evolved into a new and crucially important form of shock brigade, the final form, the cost-accounting brigade (*khozrazchetnaia brigada*). Cost-accounting brigades would incorporate most of the functions of the *buksir* and *skvoznyi* shock brigades, of rationalization and check-up brigades, and of counterplanning.

An excellent account of how cost-accounting brigades were supposed to function was provided by an economist, L'vov, heading the Production-Planning Department (PPO) at SiM. In addition to the general problems of implementing cost accounting, he deals with the particular problems of establishing cost-accounting brigades. He explains that the entire factory was formally placed on cost accounting on 1 January 1931. Implementing cost accounting at the shop level, however, proved to be very difficult. A coworker in the PPO observed that it was like "exploring uncharted earth; it was not clear how to begin or in what direction to move." L'vov blamed the problem on the fact that for each shop in the plant, "the budgets and tasks were all set from above, without . . . corresponding to their real capacity, but rather, deriving from the need to subdivide targets received [by the enterprise administration] from above [from the Commissariat]." Furthermore, the price figures in these plans were merely estimates, and some shops, like the service shop, had no budget. According to L'vov, it took all of 1931 to iron out some of these problems.[49]

A particularly telling summary of the same problems was presented in a resolution of the Central Committee Plenum dated 27 January 1932 and reprinted in the ZiS factory newspaper. Entitled "On Implementing *Khozraschet* at the Plant," the resolution concerned the auto industry and was based on theses to be presented at the Seventeenth Party Conference by Molotov and Kuibyshev. It assessed the situation in cost accounting as plagued by four basic problems:

The basic causes of the poor implementation of khozraschet in the factories are: (1) the absence of precise working out of instructions on the internalization of khozraschet and of uchet [accounting] at the level of the otdel [department], tsekh, and brigada by the factory administration; (2) lack of contracts between the otdel and the tsekh; (3) the failure to clearly define functional responsibility between various organs in conducting accounting work [the factory accountants (bukvaltery) were at odds with what were apparently factory planning organs, listed as the PPO and PEO] resulting in obezlichka [denial of personal responsibility] by these organs; and [4] the lack of help from VATO.[50]

This litany of errors indicates a basic failure in management in the plant. Introducing cost accounting through shock brigades meant mobilizing masses of workers to carry out from below what would usually be standard managerial functions. The same article noted seven specific problems at ZiS, all of which were obstacles in the effort to establish the cost-accounting brigades. First, many cost-accounting brigades were hastily set up, formalistically or mechanically. Second, the contracts establishing the brigades failed to specify what percentage of the achieved cost reductions would be put into a premium fund for the brigade. Third, premiums often were not paid out in a timely manner, severing the link between high output and bonus. Fourth, there was no calculation of additional pay to compensate the brigade for periodically working under difficult or abnormal circumstances. Fifth, a gap had developed between the shock brigades and the cost-accounting brigades, with the former having contracted for socialist competitions, while the latter had contracted to set up cost accounting. Sixth, there was some opposition from the administration to aspects of the new brigades. Seventh, where there were plant bottlenecks (such as the plant forge and the instrument shop), there were no new cost-accounting brigades.[51] This discussion, more clearly than any others, indicated that the shock brigade was becoming a standard work brigade, with some autonomy over work and pay issues.

Of these seven points, it is the fifth, the gap between shock and cost-accounting brigades, that is particularly significant for our purposes. While it was clear that the party leadership had decided that the cost-accounting brigades were a higher form of shock brigade and had begun to encourage the wholesale conversion of shock brigades to the new and supposedly more advanced form, it is also evident that it was not easy to organize the transition under Soviet economic conditions.

The new form of brigade was supposed to establish cost accounting effectively, that is, to be responsible for all the important economic indicators (both input and output) at the level of the brigade, so as to be able to accurately determine profitability at the brigade level. At the same time, they were supposed to organize and sign contracts for socialist competitions, just as the original shock brigades had. However, whereas the original shock brigades had organized socialist competition based on a single indicator, total output, it was much more difficult to organize competitions with multiple indicators, let alone for "profitability," notoriously hard to define in the context of Soviet enterprises. This criterion hinged on a myriad of factors beyond the control of the individual brigade, such as supply of materials, age of machinery, and effectiveness of factory management. Thus, the link between cost accounting and socialist competition was often only established in a formalistic or mechanical way, as the article noted. In fact, the new cost-accounting brigades did not necessarily have anything to do with shock work. They routinized shock work, and the cost-accounting contract routinized the socialist competition contract.

Eventually, the responsibilities and rights of the cost-accounting brigade were more clearly defined in the resolution of NKTP and VTsSPS of 27 July 1932. By then, however, discussion of these brigades was disappearing from the press. And that is no surprise, since the resolution listed the responsibilities of the cost-accounting brigade as including: (1) strengthening labor discipline and liquidating turnover; (2) raising labor productivity; (3) lowering cost; (4) improving quality of output, and reducing the percentage of *brak;* (5) better and more careful use of machinery and equipment; and (6) raising the skills of the brigade members. In addition, the brigade was supposed to fulfill and, if possible, overfulfill the production assignment.[52] That was merely a description of what any and all work brigades were supposed to be doing, and so the designation "cost-accounting" (like the designation "shock") was becoming redundant.

The resolution of 27 July 1932 further stipulated that the *brigadir,* the brigade-leader or foreman, was entitled to a 10–25 percent wage bonus for converting the brigade to *khozraschet* and that the brigade was entitled to a premium based on how much it economized. Savings were calculated by comparing the actual brigade expenditures with the norms for that production assignment. The resolution further specified that the premium could range from 20 percent to 60 percent of the economized funds and that it had to be distributed between the brigade members according to the production results and the skill level of each worker. The resolution concluded with a discussion of brigade-level control over the premium, which could be denied to irresponsible workers and their share given to shock workers. "The brigade can deprive individual members of all or of part of the premium, for absenteeism, *brak*, overexpenditure on materials, and the like, using the premium funds instead to further reward the best shock workers."[53] Clearly this was an attempt to increase differentiation of wages within the brigade, but at the same time, it was also an attempt to hold down the rising wage bill associated with shock work.

We can conclude that this statute on cost-accounting brigades, together with Lvov's description of how they functioned at SiM and the newspaper articles on AMO-ZiS, make it clear just how insignificant shock brigades and shock work had become by late 1931. The resolution of 27 July 1932 had specified that any work brigade could sign a contract with shop management to go onto cost accounting.[54] Shock brigades were redundant. Cost-accounting shock brigades were doubly redundant. Again, SiM provides solid evidence for this.

The *khozraschetnaia brigada* proliferated rapidly at SiM after June 1931, following Stalin's speech, and by 1 September 1931, 112 had already been organized. On 11 September 1931, a resolution on how to organize cost-accounting brigades was issued by VSNKh and VTsSPS, prompting further expansion at SiM. By 1 January 1932, there were 254 such brigades including 4,000 workers, or 38 percent of the work force.[55]

In January 1932, a checkup at SiM revealed, however, that only 112 of these brigades were legitimate. That was exactly the same number of cost-accounting brigades as there had been on 1 September 1931, before the VSNKh and VTsSPS resolution. The rest were only "paper" cost-accounting brigades, that is work brigades which continued to operate as they always had. By 1 February 1932, 142 cost-accounting brigades had been dissolved, and thus, only the original number of 112 remained, including 1,118 workers. This pattern of rapid expansion followed by an equally rapid dissolution, with only formal and not real compliance with a new policy, indicates, by 1931, the degree to which the shock-work movement was subject to control and organization from above. After the campaign to expose false cost-accounting brigades was completed, the number began to rise once again. At SiM, by 1 July 1932, there were 188 cost-accounting brigades, including 3,106 workers.[56]

Shock brigades had constituted the vast majority of the cost-accounting brigades, because they had already been involved in competitions and signed contracts that included many of the same indicators that were a part of the cost-accounting contract. Indeed, cost-accounting contracts were really only a conglomeration, an updated catalogue, of the various types of indicators used by the shock brigades, and socialist competition, since 1929. Combining them all under one general indicator of "economizing," a concept that was supposed to be similar to the capitalist firm's profitability indicator, this new type of contract and form of work brigade attempted to establish responsibility for all aspects of work within the brigade itself.

This evolving system of contractualization was an attempt to overcome irresponsibility and personal disinterestedness, or lack of responsibility, which Stalin called *obezlichka* in the "Six Conditions" speech. While it used many of the very same indicators that had been the basis for competitions in the past, the emphasis on care for machinery and equipment and on overall economizing of results, rather than merely on volume of output, marked a decisive break from the logic of shock work and socialist competitions. They were moving from the logic of storming to the logic of rationalizing, which required specialization and routinization of production activity in the factory. That meant the triumph of the stable work brigade.

The cost-accounting brigades at SiM seemed to disappear later in 1932 and 1933 as fast as they had appeared in 1931. After 1932, they were no longer mentioned in *Martenovka*. Some Soviet historians have argued that they disappeared because neither the enterprise as a whole, nor its various shops, was able to establish accurate cost accounting, and so the basic production unit, the brigade, also could not.[57] I have suggested that they disappeared because they were redundant. The work brigade was the routinization of the shock-work brigade, and the cost-accounting brigade was the intermediate form. With the decline of the cost-accounting shock brigade, the evolution of the shock brigade came to an end.

The multiplicity of forms and functions of the shock brigades from 1929 through 1931 reflected the rapidly changing policy objectives of the political leadership. These objectives were being redefined time and again in response to the deepening crisis of the economy precipitated by the rapidity of the industrialization drive and the inverted labor market. The changes in the organization of shock brigades culminated in the cost-accounting brigade, which was the most routinized shock brigade of all. Cost-accounting brigades borrowed from shock work only in that they also signed contracts with management similar to socialist competition contracts. It is difficult to see how effective accounting, that is, measuring output costs and values of production in rubles, would fire the imagination of Soviet workers and stimulate them to labor heroism. The mass shock-work movement, which on paper already comprised over half the work force, was effectively dead as a production campaign.

When the dust settled in 1932, what remained were the work brigade and a system of pay and responsibility that had evolved to the form of the cost-accounting brigade. In addition to being the final form of shock brigade, the cost-accounting brigade marked a transition to a new, third phase of shock work, in which control over the total brigade wage bill and the attempt to widen pay differentials to stimulate productivity were paramount. Shock work, as it existed in mid-1931, contradicted the objectives of Stalin's "Six Conditions" speech in at least two important respects. First, it did not promote wage differentiation and might even have tended to promote some degree of egalitarianism. Second, it did not help enterprise management in establishing wage discipline and cost accounting, but was instead an important factor in the chronic tendency to overspend the wage fund.

Shock brigades and socialist competition, not to mention the production collectives and communes, created an egalitarian tendency for two reasons. First, the total wage bill tended to increase substantially when most of a factory's work force was participating in shock work or socialist competition and garnering pay bonuses. This created generalized wage inflation and diminished the impact of the differentiated wage scales which the "Six Conditions" speech had wanted to establish. Second, the socialist competition contracts that shock brigades drew up with management often specified that the number of workers in the brigade, and the distribution of wages within the brigade, were to be left to the discretion of the brigade itself. Even piece rates and norms were sometimes set at the discretion of the *brigadir*, while management merely defined the task and the total pay that the brigade would receive for fulfilling that task.[58]

In other words, the shock brigade system left too many decisions to the discretion of the brigade itself; in particular, it gave the brigade too much autonomy in wage determination. Note that by July 1932, in the resolution on the cost-accounting brigade, this was altered and that new precautions were adopted to ensure that both base wage and premium pay within the brigade corresponded to Stalin's antiegalitarian wage policy. Even more important, the wage overspending effect of shock work and socialist competition was finally reigned in by the cost-accounting brigade, whose efforts to reduce total costs and establish some indicator of profitability, rather than merely maximize total output, finally put Soviet industrial relations firmly on the road to the stable work brigade. The work brigade would have some room for autonomy, but the experiment with shock brigades had proved that, left to themselves, brigades and brigade leaders might well find ways to further their collective interests at the expense of regime objectives.

Summing up, the debasing of shock work and socialist competitions through the near universalization of the shock worker and the routinization of the shock work brigade as it evolved was simultaneously the triumph of the standard and the universal work brigade, the *brigada*, as the basic production unit or work team in the Soviet factory. This was a victory for improved organization of labor and rational patterns of labor exertion, a victory for the workers, foremen, managers, and technicians achieved in opposition to the shock work–socialist competition movement, which was the central aspect of the regime's labor and industrial policy and ideology during the First FYP. It was a victory over "storming," which the Soviet regime attributed to peasant habits, but which was, instead, a built-in monthly, quarterly, and annual feature of meeting the *promfinplan*. It was also a victory over "storming" as performing heroic labor feats to complete the construction of a new factory in record time, a central aspect of the shock-work movement. It was a victory over "counterplanning," another aspect of shock work, with its assumption that "bourgeois specialists" were hiding potential reserves. It was a victory over the regime's obsession with exposing "class aliens" among the workers, that is peasants or petty-bourgeois urban elements who were accused of "worming" into the factory merely to gain a secure income, food, and housing, while putatively disrupting production. Finally, it was a victory over socialist competitions as speed-up.

Yet the triumph of the work brigade as the basic work unit was also a triumph for the regime, despite its ideology and policy of shock work, in overcoming long-established and long-outdated traditional models for the work unit. Three models inherited from the *ancien regime* persisted, in modified forms, during NEP. The apprenticeship model in which a *master* supervised assistants usually called first or second apprentices was nearly univeral in metalworking, even if the FZU had modified it. The peasant *artel'* model, in which a *starosta* from the village or again a skilled *master* from the factory supervised a work unit consisting of peasant boys and men from a single village, was still widely practiced in the construction industry, in mining, and in some branches of production such as iron and steel. Finally, for lack of a better term, the segregated model, in which women machine operatives worked individually on highly specialized machines under the supervision of male foremen and under the control of male mechanics who repaired, altered, and set up their machinery, was still widely practiced in textiles. The new standard Soviet work brigade, as it emerged during the First FYP, replaced these with a much more socially integrated unit, with different rules of promotion, type of managment, and organization of tasks. Thus, the factory brigade work unit was becoming a social melting pot, the central theme of chapter 7.

Phase Three: The Rise of the Shock-Worker Hero

Falling between the stormy years of the shock-work campaigns of 1929–31 and the Stakhanovite campaigns of 1935–37, the third phase of shock work came with the shift in policy that began with the "Six Conditions" speech. Some historians have seen 1933 as the momentary triumph of the party's right wing and a prelude to the purge-terror.[59] Whether or not there was a split between moderates and hard-liners, by 1933, in face of the crisis that I have called the dual famine, the leadership had reduced its investment targets and its targets for annual industrial growth rates. The slogan of 1933 became "mastering" technique, and the main objective became completing construction of the hundreds of unfinished new plants and putting them on-line, rather than building still more factories. Stalin, in a speech at the combined Plenum of the TsK and the TsKK on 7 January 1933, called for the slowing of industrial growth in the Second FYP to an annual level of 13–14 percent, as compared with an annual average of 22 percent during the First FYP.[60]

The shift in the shock-work–socialist competition movement following Stalin's "Six Conditions" speech was subtle and not easily discernable until it reached fruition in the Stakhanovism of September 1935. Essentially, it was a shift in emphasis from the heroic working class to the individual shock-worker hero. Simultaneously, it was also a shift in the role and social type of the shock-worker hero. The shift was subtle because there was considerable continuity. Shock brigades were not disbanded but rather were preserved as a formality, and the number of shock workers remained high in 1934 and 1935. In addition, the idea of the worker hero was not new to shock work. From its inception there had always been shock-worker heroes, and there was record breaking, so it was not immediately obvious, in 1932 or 1933, that these were heroes of a new type. That became clear with Stakhanov's record in 1935.

The new shock-worker hero broke the cultural hegemony of the skilled workers, whom the Soviets called *kadrovye* (core or cadre workers) and "hereditary" workers, and whom I have called the "established" workers. The new shock-worker hero was youthful, relatively inexperienced, often from a peasant or nonworker background, and was, above all, a record breaker who broke the mold of apprenticeship. This new figure moved to the center stage of state labor policy and was promoted more flagrantly than the old heroes. The new heroes represented something different, in their attitude toward both production and consumption. On the shop floor, the first shock-worker heroes had become famous as instructors, not as record setters. The new wave of shock-worker heroes, far from instructing others, were busy refuting their would-be instructors. In the community, their conspicuous consumption and attempt at a middle-class lifestyle was an equally sharp departure. This pattern emerged clearly at SiM.

The first shock brigades at SiM are inseparably associated with the names Gladyshev, Monger, and Romanov. They became the three most famous SiM workers during the First FYP, and all three achieved unionwide name recognition. They all worked in the sheet metal rolling shop (*listoprokatnyi tsekh*) and, by 1929, had very long work tenure and industrial experience. Gladyshev and Monger, who came from workers' families, had worked at SiM since 1908 and 1909 respectively. Romanov, who was the son of peasants and came to SiM in 1922, dated his industrial experience back to 1910. These three workers exemplified what Soviet historians have called the *kadrovyi* or hereditary proletariat.

Arsenii Konstantinovich Gladyshev was the most famous worker in the history of SiM. He became known throughout the plant in 1929 as the organizer of the first shock brigade in the sheet metal shop. He was born in 1897 in Tul'skaia Gubernia, and following in the footsteps of his father, he went to work in the sheet metal shop of the Guzhon plant in 1908, when he was eleven years old. He was a participant in the October Revolution in Moscow, when as a Red Guard he joined in the assault on the Kremlin under Priamikov's command. Later, he became a soldier in the Red Army and fought through the Civil War. He was involved in the suppression of the Savinskii uprising in Iaroslavl. He then headed a food requisition detachment, and in 1921, after the introduction of NEP, he became an "extraordinary plenipotentiary" for the collection of the bread tax. In 1922 he was demobilized, and on May 3 of that year, he returned to SiM. He immediately resumed work in the sheet metal shop, where he worked without interruption through the NEP period.[61]

Gladyshev made a rousing speech at a shopwide meeting on 3 April 1929 in response to the challenge issued by the metallurgy workers of the Kranyi Vyborzhets factory in Leningrad as published in the 5 March 1929 edition of *Pravda.* Gladyshev promised that he would organize the first shock brigade in the plant, which would help to transform the sheet metal shop from the "turtle" into the "airplane" shop of SiM. The sheet metal workers of SiM contracted to a competition with the sheet metal workers of the Lysvensk and Dnepropetrovsk plants, beginning on 9 April 1929. That competition had four criteria: completion of the production plan, lowering costs, labor discipline, and exchange of production experience with the sheet metal shops of the competing plants.[62]

Following that speech, Gladyshev's brigade began to set new production records, increasing the production of sheet metal from an average of 150 pieces per shift to an average of 200–210.[63] This performance was surpassed by Romanov's brigade on 6 March 1930, which set a new record by rolling 330 units of thin tin plate.[64] Gladyshev's brigade started the record mania, and Gladyshev became the symbol of the shock-work movement in the plant, its first worker hero.

For the economic year 1929/30 (1 October 1929–31 September 1930), Gladyshev's brigade produced at 113.31 percent of the plan, the highest figure in the plant. This record was all the more remarkable in that it was set in the face of frequent turnover of personnel. Turnover in Gladyshev's brigade, however, was a positive indicator, because it meant promotion. His original shock brigade included Korotin, Khromylin, Kormilkin, and Kiselev. All of them began as unskilled or at best as semiskilled workers at the third or fourth rank on the wage scale. Of these, Korotin became superintendent of the rolling steel shop, Kiselev became a shift boss in the sheet metal shop, and Kormilkin became a *brigadir,* heading up a twenty-man brigade.[65] Korotin and Kiselev, who were promoted from the bench to commanding positions in the plant, were exceptional at SiM, where Stepanov staffed his management team primarily with college-educated professionals (see chap. 9).

Gladyshev and six other workers represented SiM at the First All-Union Congress of Shock Workers held in Moscow in December 1929. Five were from the sheet metal shop (Gladyshev, Bykhovskii, Savel'ev, Duplishchev, and Denisov), while only two came from other shops, Kurochkin from the wire producing shop, and Podrubaev from the model-foundry shop.[66] Podrubaev would become well known for initiating the first cost-accounting shock brigade at SiM in March 1931, but only Gladyshev would achieve all-union fame.[67] Early in 1930, *Izvestiia* ran an article describing the main events in Gladyshev's life. He received considerable further national exposure when he was elected as a full voting delegate to the Sixteenth Party Congress in June 1930. Soon after the congress, he was awarded the Order of the Red Banner of Labor, and then the Lenin Prize, both of which brought him banner headlines with his photograph in the all-union press. Gladyshev's fame, however, seemed to diminish after 1931, and as the 1930s wore on. He was mentioned less and less frequently in the factory press, and he apparently played only a secondary role as a Stakhanovite, a title he acquired in 1936. He became a shift boss in the sheet metal shop in the later 1930s, and he died in 1944.[68]

Thomas Monger was born in 1871 in England, where he became a sheet metal worker at the age of fourteen and later became a welder and then a rolling mill operator. At age twenty-six he became foreman of his rolling mill, and at thirty, the director of a sheet metal factory in England. In 1909, Monger came to Russia along with a group of English workers and technical experts recruited by Guzhon to establish a rolling mill division at the plant. He quickly established a reputation as a rationalizer and an outstanding worker.[69] Under Soviet rule, in 1918, he was made shop superintendent of the sheet metal shop. He was the only one of the foreign workers at Guzhon who stayed after 1917.

Monger was known throughout the plant for his excellent understanding of production technique and for his intensity at work. He was also equally well known for his broken Russian with a strong British accent and for his imperious attitude toward his apprentices. In describing Monger, coworkers and apprentices always seemed to link the two, as if his British accent was relevant to his treatment of his apprentices. To them, Monger's arrogance was inseparably linked with the fact that he was from the West and came into Russia at the invitation of a foreign-born capitalist, in order to apply his technical expertise in the backward Russian Empire. Many resented his power as superintendent.

Even Romanov, who came to admire Monger during the shock-work movement, admitted in an interview some fifty years later that when he came to the shop in 1922, he was irritated with Monger.[70] In another account, Nikolai Mikhailov described Monger's arrogant behavior: he rejected many of the new workers sent to his shop, impetuously threatening to resign or leave the plant if they were not transferred to another shop. After 1929, however, according to Mikhailov, Monger changed his attitude. Inspired by the enthusiasm of the shock workers, he allegedly began to show patience with the young workers and even came to respect their methods of work.[71]

Monger received the Order of the Red Banner of Labor on 28 February 1931. He had been a leader in promoting the shock-work movement, when he became known as one of the best instructors in the plant, apparently overcoming the linguistic and other obstacles that had antagonized the workers. The first history of SiM, a short account published in 1935, credited him with training the entire sheet metal shop, including technical personnel, in the techniques necessary to produce sheet metal for cars.[72] An incident in 1929, in which he was disparaged by a few workers, saw the work collective rally around him.[73]

Monger had gradually gained the acceptance of the SiM workers as a genuine proletarian-internationalist, according to these accounts, by his example as a boss who was constantly trouble-shooting (repairing or inventing) and who was an untiring instructor, generous with the men in passing on his experience. He became known across the USSR as a model of proletarian-internationalism, in 1935 or 1936 he fell victim to antiforeign hysteria and returned to England, although it is not clear if he was expelled or requested repatriation.[74] More important, he was less and less prominently featured in

Martenovka after 1931, and like Gladyshev, his role in the factory seemed to diminish, even as his all-union reputation was growing.

According to his autobiographical account, Ivan Mikhailovich Romanov was born into a peasant family in Moscow Province, in the Maloe Korovino, near Riazan, in 1897. At age thirteen, he went to St. Petersburg where he worked as a laborer. In 1916 he was drafted. He fought in the Red Army on the southern front during the Civil War, then was involved in suppressing the Kronstadt uprising in 1921. While serving in the Red Army, Romanov later explained, he talked with a fellow soldier who had worked at Guzhon prior to the Revolution and by 1920 decided to apply for work there. After demobilization, he was on a waiting list at the Moscow labor exchange and was assigned to the plant in October 1922.[75]

Like any common laborer who came to the sheet metal shop, Romanov was assigned by Monger to work as an assistant to a skilled worker. He became a welder-assistant to the rolling mill operator, Bykovskii. Uncle Grisha, as Grigorii Bykovskii was called in the sheet metal shop, had a reputation as a fine instructor but, like Monger, one who would not tolerate any indolence. Bykovskii, according to Romanov's account, was one of those rare *master* workers who generously passed on his knowledge to a curious young apprentice. However, Romanov was less enthusiastic about Monger and his way of dispatching new workers to their jobs, noting his strong British accent. Asking a fellow worker about him, he learned that Monger was from England and a *byvshii,* or prerevolutionary person associated with the management or ownership of the plant.[76]

Monger apparently followed Romanov's progress and promoted him several times. With only four years of general education, Romanov enrolled in night school. He was promoted to welder after a few years. In May 1926, he became the first assistant to the rolling mill operator and then enrolled in the metallurgical *tekhnikum.* Soon he became a brigade leader, the youngest *brigadir* in the sheet metal rolling shop.

Romanov's studies in the *tekhnikum* were cut short after two years by the birth of his daughter and by the new demands of the shock-work movement. Romanov was volunteered by Uncle Grisha to engage in the socialist competition with Gladyshev in April 1929. Romanov described the event as follows:

The third of April 1929 is a day that I will remember for my entire life. On that day, at the shopwide meeting, we decided to respond to the challenge to a socialist competition, posed by the workers of the Krasnyi Vyborzhets plant. Just before this meeting, the shop party committee had already met. I was not yet a member of the party and learned about this from Arsiusha Gladyshev, who asked me directly, did I intend, as brigadir, to support the party cell. What could I say; it was a terrible obligation at first to accept such a responsibility. After all, I had only recently become a rolling mill operator. . . .

At the meeting, Gladyshev said the first word. He spoke heatedly, agitatedly, and as a result, not entirely consistently. I do not remember the entire speech, only the very end: "Let's get rid of the self-seekers and the absentees and turn this shop into the leading shop." And then he announced that his brigade, from now on, would be a shock brigade. Then he waited to see who else would accept the challenge, and he looked right at me. Uncle Grisha Bykovskii was standing next to me. He elbowed me and asked if I would take up the challenge. I only managed to nod my head when Gladyshev, seeing this, announced to the whole shop: "Here, Romanov and his brigade accept the challenge."[77]

Despite his doubts, Romanov's brigade went on to become the leading brigade in the shop by 1930, establishing the record of 330 pieces of sheet metal in a single shift, on 6 March 1930. In recognition of his accomplishments for the year 1929/30, in November 1930, Romanov and German Bebchuk, a rolling mill operator at mill no. 250 and member of the plant literary circle, were sent on a monthlong cruise around Europe with 257 shock workers on the first Soviet-built passenger ship, the *Abkhaziia*.[78]

Romanov's greatest achievement, however, was his success in training a new generation of young rolling mill operators in the sheet metal shop. He thus established what became known as the Romanov school, producing such outstanding sheet metal workers as Mishkin, Diuzhev, Nurulin, and later Iakovlev and Shliakhov.[79] Romanov remembered that his first trainee, Nikolai Mikhailov, had become a Soviet minister. After the Second World War, the most famous graduate of the Romanov school was Viktor Diuzhev, who founded the first "shock brigade of Communist labor" at SiM in 1958. This wrested leadership in socialist competition from the open hearth shop, reestablishing the leading role of the sheet metal shop in the plant for the first time since 1933. Romanov's impact was long-lived.[80]

Romanov was promoted later in the 1930s and became boss first of the Cold Division and then of the Hot Division in the sheet metal shop. Much later, from 1957 to 1961, he served as a people's representative to the Supreme Court of the USSR.[81] While he remained a highly respected figure in the shop and throughout the plant for the rest of the 1930s and the Second World War, his fame, like that of Gladyshev and Monger, appeared to diminish after 1931. As a boss and an instructor, he was no longer directly involved in setting production records. Instead, the focus shifted to the open hearth furnaces, where a new generation of worker heroes began setting records and quickly surpassed the first generation.

These three workers, Gladyshev, Monger, and Romanov, can be said to have constituted the first generation of shock-worker heroes at SiM, and their fame rose through phase two of the shock-work movement. They shared many similarities of social background, and their careers followed similar patterns. They came from working-class families (except Romanov),

they learned their trade through lengthy apprenticeship, they had long production experience before they became worker heroes and record setters.
They demonstrated a long-standing commitment to Soviet power, and their
political commitment was reconfirmed when they became founders of the
shock-worker movement in the plant. They trained large numbers of new
workers in their shock brigades, beginning in the First FYP and then
throughout the thirties. They were promoted to managerial positions, and
while they remained well-known figures in the plant through the 1930s, they
were soon superseded by a new generation of shock-worker heroes.

Romanov's students, and those who apprenticed under Monger or in
Gladyshev's brigades, never achieved recognition as record breakers or as
worker heroes until Diuzhev's success in 1958. Not only did these three first-
generation shock-worker heroes fall out of the national spotlight, but they
even receded to the background in the factory, as did their trainees. They
were replaced, in 1932–33, by recognition of an entirely new cohort of shock-
worker heroes. This new cohort was not trained by Gladyshev, Monger, or
Romanov, because they were steel smelters, not rolling mill or sheet metal
workers. Chesnokov, Grebeshkov, Eroshkin, Sveshnikov, Ovchinnikov,
Brylkin, Il'in, and Povaliaev came to comprise the second generation of
shock-worker heroes at SiM. They were all smelters working in the open
hearth shop. They achieved fame by setting individual smelting records for
a single shift during a socialist competition for heavy metallurgy announced
by Ordzhonikidze for 1933.

The second generation quickly achieved plantwide recognition. S. V.
Chesnokov, the leader in the Ordzhonikidze competition, became the first
Izotov worker in the plant.[82] T. G. Grebeshkov blazed his own path to become a leading smelter within five years, despite resistance from old-timers.
G. M. Il'in, another record setter, would be named Red Director of SiM in
1938, when Stepanov fell in the purges. G. Sviridov was soon rewarded with
an Order of Lenin, and I. Brylkin was credited with an important innovation
in the smelting process during the socialist competition of 1933. Their
records in the 1933 competition became known unionwide.

What united these workers and sharply differentiated them from Gladyshev, Monger, and Romanov was their social origins. They were almost all
young, from peasant background, and relative newcomers to industrial production. I. Brylkin proved to be the one partial exception, in that he came
from a worker's family and began to work at SiM during the NEP period.
Born in 1912, he followed in the footsteps of his father, Leontii Vasil'evich,
who had been smelter at the Guzhon plant since 1907, and enrolled in the
FZU (vocational school) at SiM in 1924 at age twelve. Still, he was only eigh-

teen, and had only worked for six years at SiM, when he became one of the emerging new group of worker heroes.[83]

Grigorii Markelovich Il'in "came to the plant . . . as an ordinary brick layer, and now he is a leading *master* at a blast furnace, who has traveled abroad and brought new ideas back to the plant."[84] He was born in a peasant family and came to Moscow as a wage laborer at age fifteen. In 1918 he enlisted in the Red Army, and in 1921 he began to work at the Guzhon plant. He became the best bricklayer of the shop, was promoted to a *master,* and went on a *komandirovka* to Germany. On his return he worked with the engineer Korolev and developed a new technique for the construction of Marten furnaces. He was honored with his first order in 1935.[85] Il'in was an active participant in the Ordzhonikidze competition of 1933, when he established his reputation as one of the leading smelters in the plant and across the USSR.

Timofei Gavrilovich Grebeshkov first came to the plant in 1930, an eighteen-year-old peasant-migrant. Like most peasants, he followed a relative into the plant. His cousin Mikhail found a job for him in the open hearth shop as an unskilled laborer. There, an old-timer, a *master* smelter, recruited Grebeshkov to his brigade and put him at a job opening and closing the furnace door. This was easily learned and required no particular skill, but despite Grebeshkov's pleas, the old-timer refused to teach him the smelting trade. Grebeshkov enrolled in a night technical school at the plant and as soon as possible moved to another brigade, where he apprenticed under Nikita Abramovich Dronnikov, one of the best smelters in the plant. After five years, Grebeshkov began to smelt steel independently, and by the Second World War he had become one of the best smelters in the plant.[86]

Semen Vasil'evich Chesnokov followed a similar career path, although his social origins are not known. In 1921 he left Irkutsk for Moscow and came to SiM, beginning his tenure as a *chernorabochii* in the open hearth shop. Chesnokov labored as apprentice to the experienced smelter and brigade leader Korovin, who repeatedly told him to be patient when he asked about smelting techniques, insisting that it took a minimum of twenty years to become a smelter. Chesnokov refused to accept this, and their argument became widely known throughout the shop and the plant.

A sort of experiment was set up as a two-year trial in which Chesnokov would try to master the art of smelting. While continuing to work in Korovin's brigade, he attended night school. Soon, he progressed from simple assistant to *dubler-praktikant* (understudy-probationer). Korovin, who had only worked on two types of open hearth or blast furnaces in his long production tenure and who never had any technical training, refused to discuss questions of technology or production with Chesnokov and reacted angrily when Chesnokov suggested the use of new instruments that could rationalize the smelting process. In 1929, at the conclusion of the two-year trial period, Chesnokov smelted his first batch of steel independently. He had become a competent smelter after five years as an assistant and two years of experimental training, which combined the theory he learned at night school with the practical experience he gained on the job.[87]

Chesnokov, by 1930, was the youngest master smelter in the plant, and he joined the party in that year. He read constantly on labor organization, and in 1932, began to take notice of Izotov's techniques and records in coal mining. Chesnokov, Eroshkin, and Povaliaev began to compete in rationalizing the smelting process and brought the record down to five hours and forty-five minutes during the all-union competition in 1933.

After the war, Chesnokov helped in automating the smelting process, and in 1949 he won the Stalin Prize, along with his apprentices Subbotin, Mikhailov, and his younger brother, Nikolai Chesnokov. As with Romanov, his apprentices would later say, "We are from the Chesnokov school."[88] While the term *apprentice* was, thus, still used in the later 1930s and after the Second World War, it meant something very different than when Chesnokov began his apprenticeship during the 1920s. Significantly, Chesnokov was only the second cohort shock-worker hero who became well known as an instructor, and this took place only much later, fifteen years after he became a record breaker. The second-generation worker heroes were first and foremost record breakers, not instructors or *brigadiry* or *mastery*. The first-generation heroes were already at least foremen, if not shop bosses, when they set the records and were first-rate instructors.

Another leading participant in the 1933 competition, Filipp Ivanovich Sveshnikov, and his assistant, Aleksei Il'ich Ovchinnikov, became leading *skorostniki* (speedsters) during the Second World War in the open hearth shop. This was the aftermath of Stakhanovism. The second generation of shock-worker heroes which emerged in 1933 almost immediately became known as the leading Izotovtsy. Then, in rapid succession, they formed the core group of *otlichniki* (outstanding workers), then Stakhanovites, and finally, during the war, of *skorostniki*.

There were other new worker heroes from other shops who emerged in 1935 or later. The rolling mill operator, I. A. Makarov, became the plant's leading Stakhanovite and the sole SiM representative at the First All-Union Congress of Stakhanovites. A list of leading Stakhanovites during the war includes the rolling mill operators Shcherbakov, Turtanov, Dorozhkin; the welders Abrosimov and Matrenkin; and the roll-forging workers Sukhinin, Ermakov, and Shchegolev. However, it also included the smelters Sveshnikov,

Povaliaev, Chesnokov, as well as two new names among open hearth workers, Shibanov and Lysakov.[89]

While many of these were new names, the most respected and well-known heroes of the later 1930s remained the same second-generation worker heroes who rose to prominence in 1932–33. This was true of Stakhanov himself and for the first and leading cohort of the Stakhanovite movement in the fall of 1935, including Busygin, Faustov, and Velikzhanin in auto, Fillippov and Smetanin in shoe manufacturing, Odintsova and the Vinogradova sisters in textiles, Gudov in machine construction, Demchenko in sugar beet harvesting, and Krivonos, the railway engine conductor. Many of them had already become record breakers prior to 1935.[90]

Most of these original Stakhanovite heroes were of the same social type as the second-generation shock-worker heroes of 1932–33. They were from that same generation, hired into the factory or mine only during the First FYP; they were young, relative newcomers without any work tenure or experience in industry, frequently from a peasant background, and only arriving in the city when they began mining or factory work. They were quick to enroll in night school, become literate, and technically literate after enrolling in night vocational courses.[91] They set out, on the shop floor, to defy old-timers and break records and the mold of apprenticeship.

The shift in social type in the second-generation worker hero can best be explained in terms of the regime's changing labor policies and the dramatic changes in the composition of the factory work force during the First FYP. After June 1931, the regime needed a new social type in its new generation of heroes, and it set about finding them. The regime began actively and consciously to search for worker heroes who would serve as relevant models for social emulation, especially for the mass of new peasant-worker recruits. Rather than a "heroic working class" the regime was now looking for individual worker-heroes, in the aftermath of Stalin's "Six Conditions" speech. The cohorts at SiM show the differences.

Comparing biographies of first- and second-generation shock-worker heroes at SiM, four distinctions stand out. First, there was a radical reduction in production tenure prior to becoming a worker hero. Second, there was a complete change in training methods that radically reduced both the length of the apprenticeship and the extent of dependence of the apprentice on the *master* to learn existing or new production techniques. Third, most of the second generation persisted as leading worker heroes at the bench throughout the 1930s and into the war period, whereas the first generation was promoted into management and quickly lost its heroic-worker status after the First FYP. Finally, and most significantly, the social profile of the first and second generations was completely different. Each of these points of comparison deserves some further elaboration.

First was the sharp contrast in production tenure. Whereas the first generation had more than a decade of work experience and training before they became production heroes, the second generation, with few exceptions, began to work at SiM only during the First FYP. In other words, they dated their employment to 1929, 1930, or 1931. This simple fact had profound implications. It meant that, in 1933, the second generation of worker heroes shared this common experience with the 45.8 percent of the workers at SiM with two years tenure or less and the 55.1 percent with three years or less. It also meant that these heroes were very young, a highly relevant fact when, according to the 1932–33 trade-union census of 9,151 workers at SiM, the average age was 27.4 years.[92] Their youth meant that most had come to SiM without prior factory work experience.

For a regime in search of models for emulation for masses of new workers, for peasant-migrants, women, and youth, this second generation of heroes was eminently more suitable than the first. They were living proof that it was possible to rise from the ranks of the newcomers to the pinnacle of the factory work force within a couple of years. The older generation were a living testimony, rather, to the old system, in which it took a decade or more to become a skilled worker under an arduous and highly personalized apprenticeship.

The second factor, the change in the methods of training, was directly related to the first factor. The rise of a new generation of worker heroes to the top, despite their very short production tenure, required drastic changes in the methods and the time required for training during the First FYP. The regime was, essentially, discarding the apprenticeship system, although the term would continue to be in use through the 1930s. The new shock-worker heroes were icons of adaptation, absorbing classroom education and vocational schooling and adapting rapidly on the shop floor to the new technologies and organization of labor (described in chap. 7).

The second-generation shock-worker heroes exemplified the success of the new system of training, just as the first generation had exemplified the old system. They demanded rapid training and, like Chesnokov, they wanted to assume unsupervised personal responsibility for the top job in their occupational category as rapidly as possible. This often brought them directly into conflict with the older *mastery*, like Korovin, who were still trying to train them under the apprenticeship system. The conflict between Korovin and Chesnokov was symbolic of a widespread conflict between generations in Soviet industry, a conflict that was played out in a battle over training methods, and that was widely reflected in the worker memoirs and literature of the period. Again, the regime misinterpreted this as class struggle, claiming that older workers were jealously guarding their monopoly over production methods and knowledge as they had under capitalism.

The new generation of shock-worker heroes successfully resolved their personal conflicts with the older generation by decisively breaking the power of the *mastery*, by discrediting the old apprenticeship system, and by setting out personally to demonstrate the superiority of studying technique in the factory schools. Hiroaki Kuromiya argues that this was a "crisis of proletarian identity" and that young shock workers were able to use the title *shock worker* to great advantage in such conflicts with "cadre" workers with long production tenure.[93] The shock brigade itself, particularly once it had become routinized, also provided a type of on-the-job training. It became an important mechanism in the transition to the new system of brigade apprenticeship. Thus, the conflict over shock work, which the regime described as class struggle, was often a conflict over training new workers as well as over introducing new production technologies and with it techniques and organization of labor.

The conservatism of the *kadrovye*, and particularly of the *mastery* or the factory artisans who were the instructors, was already under assault in the first stages of shock work. Even the first-generation shock-worker heroes, although they themselves were *kadrovye*, discarded many of the traits typical of the social group from which they had risen. They pushed for technological innovations and changes in the organization of labor, for shock brigades, and for socialist competition. They devised new methods of training workers that accelerated the old apprenticeship system, even while preserving some of its attributes. However, they were still themselves the products of the old system of training, and they still perpetuated some of the aspects of the traditional individual apprenticeship system. This was the real meaning of the Romanov school; Romanov was an outstanding *master* who commanded the respect of many apprentices. Despite his remarkable achievements, for most of the new workers, he was much less likely to serve as a model for emulation than were the new cohort of shock-worker heroes in the open hearth shop.

The third change was in the differing pattern of promotion of first- and second-generation shock-worker heroes. Whereas most of the second generation, among them Chesnokov, Grebeshkov, Eroshkin, Sveshnikov, and Ovchinnikov, were still working as steel smelters in the open hearth shop on the eve of the Second World War, the first generation were all in mid-level managerial positions. The first generation ceased to set production records and instead became well-established managers with a particular aptitude for instructing new workers, during or shortly after the First FYP. In this respect, they came to symbolize the fate of their entire generation, the generation of established workers from the 1920s. The most successful of them were promoted into management, while others made the transition into the ITR or to responsible positions involving the setup and repair of machinery. Once they were promoted to mid-level managerial positions, however, they were largely forgotten as worker heroes. They could no longer serve as models for the rank and file, the newcomers to production work.

Certainly not all of the second-generation heroes remained on the shop floor. We have noted the spectacular promotion of G. M. Il'in to replace Stepanov as plant director in the summer of 1938. Even in such a case, however, the fate of these second-generation heroes was different than that of the first generation. Il'in vaulted over the shop-level managerial strata, all the way to the summit of plant management. Others would vault into the all-union level of economic administration. Whereas Gladyshev, Monger, and Romanov saw their fame diminish after moving into mid-level management, Il'in and the most famous Stakhanovites saw their fame increase after they left the workbench or the mine. Again, Il'in was a symbol for the new recruits, although, as I suggest below, it is open to question how widespread was the desire among these new workers to emulate such symbols.

The fourth and most important distinction between the generations of worker heroes was their radically different social profiles. The first generation were *kadrovyi* proletariat. They were generally from urban workers' families. They had long work tenure by 1929 and learned their trade through long apprenticeships gradually becoming the most skilled workers, and then instructors, and then managers. In many basic respects, despite their willingness to innovate, they remained part of the culture of the established workers.

Workers of the second generation, on the other hand, arrived at SiM during the First FYP, were still very young and relatively inexperienced in industrial work, and were predominantly from a peasant background. Following a *zemliak*, like Grebeshkov, they were recruited as peasant-migrants had been typically recruited for decades, into the open hearth shop, where they would be performing the heaviest, hottest, and dirtiest tasks. Feeling constrained by lengthy apprenticeship, they sought new methods to acquire skills and technical knowledge, both through shock work on the shop floor and through the FZU or the night courses organized by the factory. They used every opportunity to jump ahead in the production process. They became record breakers very quickly, usually within two or three years after having entered the factory gate. Unlike the first-generation shock-worker heroes, they were generally too busy setting production records during the

1930s to occupy themselves with training new workers. The decline of the shock brigade and the first-generation heroes went hand in hand with the rise of these individualistic record setters, who were determined to succeed. They relied on formal technical schooling at night and rapid-fire, self-taught, hands-on experience on the shop floor to become the new leaders of the socialist competition movement. Individual feats of labor heroism now replaced brigade records, and heroic individuals now replaced the heroic working class. They were becoming the living examples of a new Soviet Horatio Alger mythology, of upward mobility.

Moving from the factory to the home and the community, one notices an equally fundamental transformation. The lifestyle of the worker hero and of his or her family was changing quite dramatically. The shock-worker heroes of the first generation appear to have had modest lifestyles, and their family life was simply not a matter of public knowledge. The shock-worker hero, after 1932, was being molded into a model in community life, in family life, and in party life. They were supposed to flaunt their new wealth, and many did.[94]

Conclusion: Stakhanovism and Running the Script in Reverse

Stalin, when his policies had gone awry, was a past master at scapegoating lower-level party cadres who zealously promoted his policies. The "Dizzy with Success" fiasco of 2 March 1930, in which he blamed the political amateurishness of the party rank and file for *excesses* in implementing collectivization policy, was perhaps the first indication of how he would operate. His taunt of "R-r-r-revolutionary" should be thrown back at him. Shock-worker heroes, and the new labor policy and industrial relations of the Stalinist system, were based on simplistic, Horatio Alger myths and the belief in popular emulation (envy) and material self-interestedness. They appealed to the basest popular instincts of social jealousy and envy and were as far removed from any type of revolutionary politics or strategy of development as could be imagined. They were also far removed from the egalitarian premise of Communist Saturdays in Lenin's "Great Beginning," which is why the regime resurrected his unpublished notes for "How to Organize Competition." Whereas the "Great Beginning" essay had emphasized egalitarianism and the spirit of self-sacrifice, the "Competition" essay emphasized accounting and discipline by which workers would monitor themselves.

This chapter has argued that neither shock work nor Stakhanovite labor heroes per se could have much impact in improving labor productivity or labor organization. Instead, the shock-work brigade yielded, through routinization with its mass proliferation, with its wide varieties of forms, and above all with the actions and reactions of workers, to the stable work brigade. The work brigade was the building block to a new type of labor relations that was replacing various inherited forms of work organization, including the *artel'* and village-based work units following either *zemliachestvo* or *orgnabor* recruitment paths, lengthy forms of individual and personalized apprenticeship, and gendered segregation. The new brigade was the building block to what might be called an ersatz industrial relations system.[95] Routinization of the shock-work brigade, which decidedly came from below, was a victory for sanity, a victory for a type of modern Soviet industrial relations.

The shock-work movement bifurcated during its third phase. For the rank and file shock workers and shock brigades, the movement was routinized, whereas for a new and comparatively thin layer of worker heroes, shock work brought plantwide, and sometimes unionwide, recognition and considerable privileges. This third phase continued until it overlapped with the beginnings of Stakhanovism in September 1935. Stakhanovism seemed to run through the same phases, only in reverse order from shock work.

Stakhanovism began with the individual heroes, who were in principle no different from previous worker heroes. Then, there were Stakhanovite brigades (and decades, or ten-day stints), then Stakhanovite shops (and months), and then Stakhanovite factories (and the year 1936).[96] Thus, the trajectory of the regime's ideology from 1935 to 1941 was the mirror image of 1929–35, in that it went from worker heroes on single shifts, to heroic brigades for ten-day stints, to the heroic working class for the year 1936. Obviously the shock-work movement was a prototype for the subsequent Stakhanovite movement, since they were both based on production campaigns under the rubric of socialist competition.

Periodizing shock work and Stakhanovism in this way helps to clarify a number of issues, such as the relation between labor heroes and the rank-and-file shock workers and Stakhanovites, and the relationship of both of them to other workers. The focus in this chapter has been on the three phases of shock work at SiM. They were not rigidly defined, as there was some degree of overlapping. Already in the first phase, some individual workers were celebrated in the press as shock-worker heroes, and even in the third phase, new shock brigades continued to form spontaneously, especially among enthusiastic youth who went off to construct new factories on the frontiers of the Soviet Union. Nonetheless, these were the exceptions to the characteristic form of shock work predominant in each phase. The same could be said of the phases, in reverse order, of Stakhanovism. The entire "long" decade, 1929–41, was a tug-of-war between a regime bent on production campaigns and a working class and class of factory administrators, ITR, and white-collar staff bent on establishing stable new forms of labor organization.

Soviet workers, acting increasingly as a class, would find ways to make use of these regime-sponsored campaigns, not to gain upward mobility as individuals, but rather to facilitate the broadly based status revolution that I discussed in chapter 5 and will elaborate in chapter 7. New workers took advantage of the shock work or of the Stakhanovite movement to become accepted as Soviet workers, in stable work brigades and in the new Soviet working class.

Part 3

Site of Social Stabilization
The Urban Factory Community

1

THE FACTORY AS SOCIAL
MELTING POT

This chapter is a tentative effort to develop a theory of Soviet working-class formation, with the emphasis on a dual process in the factory that I will call *homogenization-redifferentiation.* I begin by reviewing the three recent studies of Soviet workers that I grouped as contingent identity approaches and reconsidering the Soviet triumphalist school in an attempt to rethink Soviet working-class formation and consciousness in terms of social solidarities and homogenization. The second section examines existing all-union data and data from SiM and ZiS on wage stratification and sociooccupational segregation. Here I argue that in the Soviet factories one saw a deep structural process of working-class homogenization during the 1930s, accelerated by a shallow new wage differentiation, or redifferentiation. The third section considers the politics of labor recruitment and the shift in regime ideology and policy, from blaming the class "aliens" to training the recruits and attempting to integrate them into the new Soviet working class.

Contingent Identity and Reconceptualizing the Soviet Working Class

The contingent identity school, as I indicated in chapter 1, was a school only in the sense that each historian showed the limited nature or the fleeting patterns of workers' social identity during the 1930s. The works by Hiroaki Kuromiya, Vladimir Andrle, and Lewis Siegelbaum were all revising, on the one hand, the simplistic assumptions of the Soviet triumphalist school in which the Soviet working class marched in linear fashion from one victory to the next and, on the other, the equally simplistic antithetical assumption of the repression/resistance paradigm, in which there was no working class or workers' social identity at all, just isolated individuals facing a powerful if often inept repressive regime. Discussing the different approaches to identity in the works of Kuromiya, Andrle, and Siegelbaum, I will continue my focus from the previous chapter on the rise of the stable work brigade to the exclusion of many other important issues that they raised.[1]

The central theme in Kuromiya's study is the politics of class struggle as the driving force in mobilizing state and society in the push of the First FYP for superindustrialization. Kuromiya clearly showed that there was both a popular social basis for a class struggle against technicians, engineers, economic experts, managers, administrators, and the party's right wing, and also how the Stalin regime was able to channel the energy of a new cohort of young, skilled shock workers to force through its industrialization drive and to undermine its political opponents. Less clear, however, was how the class struggle could have resolved the social and economic crises that he calls, respectively, the "crisis of proletarian identity" and the "crisis of 1930."

Kuromiya' did not really explain how the class struggle, especially as it was conducted through the shock-work movement, could have redefined proletarian identity. If the economic crisis of 1930 was followed by the "restoration of order" during 1931, then that was presumably because the regime had shifted its politics, although Kuromiya never clearly explains the shift. Was the regime abandoning or downplaying the class struggle approach for a more conservative one? Where did that leave shock workers and the cadre in the "crisis of proletarian identity"? Was it the shock-work and socialist competition movement, with its class struggle politics, or was it, rather, the abandonment of these mobilization politics that resolved the social "crisis of proletarian identity"? With the new conservatism in 1931, who were "cadre workers"? Were they now a combination of skilled old-timers and younger shock workers?

Andrle's study provided one potential way of answering these unresolved issues and suggested a more lasting if limited type of workers' identity, by looking at how "modern" work practices and labor organization evolved during the Second FYP (1933–37). Shifting his emphasis from mobilization movements and their politics to the brigade-level, day-to-day aspects of "shopfloor interactions," he showed how a new solidarity among workers would emerge in the work unit, through compromise between the workers and foremen, production staff specialists, and managers. In their daily activity, Andrle argued, Soviet workers, technical staff, and line management developed a modern industrial relations system, not at all dissimilar to that existing under industrial capitalism.

In part, the differences in Kuromiya's and Andrle's approaches simply reflected the sharp shift in the regime's approach to the politics of production from the First FYP to the Second FYP. In the Second FYP, the regime shifted from new construction to putting the new factories into operation. The regime's new slogans in 1933 were either "master technology" or "assimilation" in industry.[2] For the next two years, the campaigns of shock work and socialist competition atrophied, and then, apparently impatient again, the mobilizations were revived in September 1935 under the new guise of Stakhanovism. In the meantime, as Andrle argued, the work "bargain" within the production unit was firmly taking root.

In Andrle's account, the work bargain meant that the production effort and level of remuneration were negotiated in such a way that workers and managers alike understood what a fair days' work and a fair days' pay were and established this sense of balance in the work unit. Even after the onset of Stakhanovism, he argues, these emerging patterns of work-group negotiation over the production process would persist.

What Frederick Taylor had deplored as workers' "soldiering," and what D. Roy later described in less pejorative terms as a labor-management compromise bargain, or "the fix," was becoming institutionalized in the Soviet factory, according to Andrle, notwithstanding the regime and Stakhanovism.[3] The work routine, once established, would withstand the regime's attempts to destabilize it and to push for higher output norms with its new mobilizations. Attempts to use the Stakhanovite movement to increase work norms, which had been derived through extensive shop-floor practice, would fail, and the movement would be "managerialized."[4]

Andrle's study should be credited for explaining that mobilization strategies such as shock work and Stakhanovism did not promote a modern work rhythm based on the industrial clock, that is time orientation rather than task orientation. Such campaigns, instead, obstructed a modern work rhythm, by resurrecting the very "peasant" task orientation that the regime had denounced as backwardness. Time orientation was becoming prevalent among workers in the Soviet factory through the daily negotiation over norms and wage rates, and not because of the Stalin regime's putatively modern "rationalization" ideology, which was betrayed by its draconian labor laws and its various mobilization schemes.[5]

In the end, however, Andrle never raised the question of Soviet working-class formation or consciousness, or of how the identity that he saw emerging on the shop floor might or might not have carried over into community life outside the factory gates. Workers, in his account, were developing a strong but narrow consciousness shaped within their work unit, contesting norms and wages, but apparently without any broader vision. This was a contingent workers' identity, not in the sense that it was shifting, like Kuromiya's "crisis of proletarian identity," but rather in the narrowness or limited scope of the workers' vision.

Siegelbaum's history of Stakhanovism takes us from the shop floor to the community, and back again, in a case study of massive and continuous regime intervention into the production process from late 1935 until late 1937. He traces the origins of Stakhanovism back to shock-worker heroes, running through Izotov and Izotovism in 1932 and 1933, and the *otlichniki* in 1934 and 1935. He also traces the twists and turns in division of labor and recombination of tasks in coal mining prior to the night of 31 August 1935, when, under special conditions and a new division of tasks, Stakhanov's record was set.[6]

Stakhanov's record and a new cohort of record breakers would emerge "from below," according to Siegelbaum, because local party officials and journalists were responding to the clear signals coming "from above." The regime then mobilized the Stakhanovite "decades" or ten-day stints, Stakhanovite "months," and finally the Stakhanovite "year" of 1936, attempting to turn from heroes to a new mass movement. Siegelbaum is skeptical, however, that the shift from a few model heroes or "outstanding Stakhanovites" to mobilization of a mass Stakhanovite movement translated into any new surge in labor productivity, or signified any real improvement in the rationalization or organization of labor.[7]

Siegelbaum then takes us beyond the shop floor to consider the lifestyles of "outstanding Stakhanovites," and the impact of their patterns of conspicuous consumption. He is skeptical that these patterns had much influence among wider layers of the working population, emphasizing in particular the discrepancy between the cult of domesticity encouraged among the wives of the outstanding Stakhanovites and the "dual burden" that was the lot of most urban women during the 1930s. His concluding chapter shows how the attack on "stodgy" engineers and managers began with Stakhanovism and ended only with the conclusion of the purge-terror. By then, he says, Stakhanovism had already seen considerable "proliferation," which "inevitably led to the debasement of the category."[8]

One could draw widely differing conclusions concerning working-class formation and consciousness depending on what one chose to emphasize in Siegelbaum's study. On the one hand, it would be possible to highlight the divisiveness of the regime's policy among workers and its fragmenting, if not individualizing, impact. First, he notes, there was a wide gap between a few hundred "outstanding" and a mass of "ordinary" Stakhanovites. Second, the clear distinction between rank-and-file Stakhanovites and the non-Stakhanovites, two mass categories, was significant. Being a Stakhanovite often meant having improved access to scarce consumer goods and apartments, as well as meant higher wages.[9]

In analyzing these divisions, however, Siegelbaum rejected Trotsky's "labor aristocracy" approach, as adopted by Schwarz and Filtzer, and his account offered a much more convincing discussion of class fragmentation. He argued that Stakhanovism fostered a new type of worker individualism, but parted with Deutscher, who attributed such individualism to peasant values. Siegelbaum, like Deutscher, argued that Stakhanovism provoked opposition from the workers who preferred work solidarity to individualism, and this contradiction was reflected in the attacks on Stakhanovites on the shop floor. Stakhanovites and non-Stakhanovites thus was a meaningful distinction for understanding Soviet workers' self-identities in 1936.[10] These conclusions, it would seem, indicate yet another type of "fleeting contingent identity," since the distinction between Stakhanovites and non-Stakhanovites would lose its significance just as quickly as it had arisen, when in 1937 the movement was "on its way to being marginalized."[11]

One might, however, draw very different conclusions from Siegelbaum's study, putting aside the divisiveness and individualism of Stakhanovism and emphasizing that Soviet workers defended themselves quite well—as individuals, as work brigades, or collectively as a class. It is clear in Siegelbaum's account that Stalin's formula for norm revision, applied in the spring of 1936 and again in the spring of 1937, caused considerable anger among workers against Stakhanovism. Stalin's formula in February 1936 called for new norms that would split the difference between existing norms and new records set by the outstanding Stakhanovites since September 1935. While this was a naked speed-up, its impact was to thin the ranks of the Stakhanovites, since the workers who could overfulfill these new and higher norms dropped significantly. The resulting mass attrition of Stakhanovites contradicted the regime's stated goal of turning it into a mass (if not universal) movement.[12] The outcome was Stakhanovism's rapid atrophy, as the workers were thus "negating" the regime's intervention into the "politics of production" on the shop floor rather than mobilizing through Stakhanovism, as the regime had intended.

Whether one emphasizes divisiveness and individualism or collective opposition to regime intervention, Siegelbaum's study clearly shows that the Stakhanovite label was shifting, and that it was fleeting. With norm revisions and monthly fluctuations and disruptions in the typical Soviet factory, today's

Stakhanovite was tomorrow's non-Stakhanovite, and therefore its impact on workers' social identity was necessarily short-lived. Taken together, the three studies by Kuromiya, Andrle, and Siegelbaum, with the shifting or the contingent worker identities that they described, provided a solid foundation for tracing the emerging Soviet work brigade and its lasting influence on workers' consciousness through the decade, despite the regime's periodic massive intervention into shop-floor relations and attempts to destabilize the "fix." My discussion of the routinization of the shock brigade, I believe, sets the stage for understanding this new work culture and brigade solidarity.

The legacy of shock work and Stakhanovism was the triumph of the stable work brigade and the growing ability of the working class, whether participating in the movement or not, to defend its own interests as a class vis-à-vis the state. Rather than active or passive opposition to the party-state, what was emerging was a new concept of the "class interest," extending beyond the work brigade and defining what the working class could legitimately be asked to produce and what it could also realistically hope to extract from the regime as compensation. The "bargain" as it evolved in the work unit was, thus, writ large, defining the relationship of the working class to the state. Shop-floor trends in the work brigade were extended beyond the boundaries of the shop, to the factory, and to the Soviet working class. In this way, Stalin's ersatz social contract was gradually becoming operative from below. But, was "Stalinism" becoming operative? We can answer with a qualified yes, as Stalinism came to terms with a new Soviet working class by shifting from class struggle ideology to an inclusive concept of the new Soviet working class and by adopting a vision of the state negotiating the terms of work and community life with this new working class.

This answer, I believe, must be framed in terms of the process of Soviet working-class formation and potential for class solidarities during the 1930s. Class solidarity would integrate workers, not necessarily in ways that the regime understood or directly controlled in accordance with its ideology, but in long-lasting patterns in the factory and in the community, which would stabilize Soviet urban society and industry until the late 1980s. The new class solidarity would be based on the incorporation of masses of peasant-recruits, women, and youth, which was its defining characteristic during the 1930s.

Analyzing this process of class formation in the factory and community, the themes of this chapter and the next, requires some reconsideration of the largely neglected Soviet historical school, in particular the much more sophisticated work that was published after Stalin's death on the Soviet working class. Discarding its triumphalist teleology, one must take seriously its findings on the numbers (recruitment), social composition, and changing social outlook of the Soviet workers, all topics in which this literature developed some important insights since the 1950s. Some of these findings have been incorporated in the studies by Kuromiya, Andrle, and Siegelbaum, and also in several important articles by John Barber.[13]

The Soviet school under Stalin began with the linear, teleological assumption of a working class triumphant from 1917 through 1945. The workers who had made the revolution were, in this scenario, still leading the Soviet Union to victories in socialist construction during the 1930s and would defeat the Nazi war machine. These simplistic assumptions, in particular the notion that a "core working class" remained intact throughout the dramatic events of the Civil War, NEP, and then the 1930s, were challenged and revised by Soviet academicians after the Stalin era. Worthy of mention in this respect are three seminal monographs by Sonin (1959), Shkaratan (1970), and Vdovin and Drobizhev (1976), but there were a number of other significant works as well.[14] These three Soviet studies revised the picture of a triumphant working class, retaining the outcome but making it nonlinear, that is, by discarding teleological or whiggish assumptions. They showed, with ever increasing clarity, the dramatic changes in the social composition of the industrial work force during the 1930s, no longer hiding the fact that by the end of the decade, nothing was left of the "revolutionary proletariat" of 1917. In Sonin's work, the scale of the social transformation of 1929–41 was, for the first time, clearly outlined.

By taking into account deaths and retirements (which historians of the Stalin era ignored, thus inflating the weight of cadre proletariat through the 1930s), Sonin showed that the new recruits (primarily peasants) already constituted over half the industrial work force by 1933. During the later 1930s, however, working-class formation took shape primarily on the basis of working-class (urban) self-reproduction, and this shift, he argues, accounted for the preservation of working-class values. The shift from rural to urban recruitment was explained by the shifting forms of labor recruitment, that is, by the declining role of *orgnabor* and the increasing role of what he called "enterprise-organized recruitment," which was attracting mainly urban recruits and school graduates. On the eve of the war, he notes, State Labor Reserves coordinated the process of recruiting urban youth. After seven years of primary schooling, they were then given a year or two of vocational schooling in the FZO and then assigned work in a factory.[15] Since "simple reproduction" of the urban population was still inadequate for the needs of industry, however, the "expanded reproduction" of the working class required population resettlement. This meant urbanization, to be sure, but increasingly, especially after the Second World War, it meant "territorial redistribution" rather than peasant in-migration. Population was shifting to the Urals and Siberia. For Sonin, therefore, the dominant trend in the later 1930s was toward urban working-class self-reproduction, rather than recruiting peasant-migrants, which, as I noted in chapter 1, augured a fundamental and significant historical shift in the process of Russian and Soviet working-class formation. Sonin assumed an identity of interests and values between the urban factory recruits, particularly the urban seven-year-school graduates and workers' wives and children who became factory workers, and the Soviet cadre proletariat, with long work tenure. In this way, he retained the Stalin-era triumphalist conclusions even while abandoning its teleology.

Shkaratan's monograph, the work of a maverick sociologist whose formative years were post-Stalin, rejected these triumphalist conclusions, and thus provoked considerable controversy. He discarded the Stalinist categories of "forming workers," "cadre workers," and "labor aristocracy," and he argued that the values of the Russian prerevolutionary proletariat and of the revolutionary proletariat of 1917 were not reproduced during the 1930s, but instead, that a new type of working class evolved.[16] While he would not use the phrase "working class of a new type," since Stalin had coopted it in his discussion of the 1936 constitution, that was precisely what Shkaratan found. This argument anticipated John Barber's perspective and my own.

Classes under socialism, Shkaratan asserted, were "losing [their] class traits and acquiring characteristics of an associational society." In other words, society was becoming increasingly homogeneous. Drawing conclusions contrary to the Stalin school, he argued that dispossessed peasants, artisans, and others from non-working-class backgrounds posed absolutely no challenge to the Soviet regime in the factories, and therefore there was no class struggle. The regime's categorization of workers as "forming," "cadre," and "labor aristocracy," was an artificial construct for the political purposes of waging this class struggle. Shkaratan suggested that "aristocracy" was irrelevant, while the distinction between "forming" and "cadre" was losing most of its significance. The working class, and Soviet society as a whole, was becoming more homogeneous.

On the other hand, Shkaratan challenged the widely accepted assumption, under Stalin and since then in the USSR, that socialist construction necessarily promoted social homogenization. He noted that, under Soviet-type socialism, as workers lost class traits based on ownership functions, they were at the same time becoming increasingly differentiated by new and nonownership criteria, of which he emphasized education, scientific knowledge, new techniques and technology, "cultural level," and level of responsibility in the production process.[17]

This apparent contradiction in Shkaratan's work between the declining ownership basis of social differentiation within the working class and within Soviet society as a whole, and the rising education-knowledge basis for social differentiation, is well worth exploring. It is the foundation for what I would suggest was a dual social process dominating the 1930s, homogenization-redifferentiation. By interjecting the "Six Conditions" speech and the new wage differentiation during the 1930s, which Shkaratan noted but did not emphasize, as the precursor to the type of knowledge- and skill-based social differentiation that Shkaratan found in his sociological studies of the Leningrad working class during the 1950s, we can show how these apparently opposing trends were historically mutually reinforcing.

Shkaratan's rejection of Stalin's triadic categorization of the working class and his discussion of declining ownership criteria and social homogenization were accepted, in part, by Vdovin and Drobizhev and subsequently by other historians, but his innovative arguments on increasing social differentiation under Soviet-type socialism provoked hostile responses from the Soviet academic establishment in the late 1960s. His approach to social differentiation was based on empirical evidence from his own studies and from Eastern European sociological studies in the 1960s. Despite his strong rejection of Weber's multivariate approach to classes, and his even more strident rejection of "functionalist" conceptions, his approach to social differentiation resembled the modernization perspective of Inkeles and Bauer, with their "social class" analysis of Soviet society. They found six class groups, from elite on top to *kolkhoz* peasants and camp inmates on the bottom, and they stressed education and skill as key factors in this social differentiation.[18] Shkaratan's theory, like that of the Hungarian sociologist Hagedus and the Polish sociologist Widerszpil, was moving toward a Weberian concept of class and away from a strictly Marxist conception, despite his disclaimers. It was, particularly with its emphasis on scientific and technological revolution, an Eastern European variant of modernization class theories.[19]

In part, the contradiction between homogenizing structural tendencies and functional differentiation in Shkaratan's analysis could be explained away as a matter of historical sequence. His argument on functional differentiation is more relevant to the post–Second World War era with its scientific revolution, than to the 1930s, when the structural social homogenization that he described in terms of the "discarding of class traits" was more important. Still, both aspects of his argument are extremely important for understanding the process of class formation during the 1930s and have been instrumental in shaping my own thinking of it in terms of a dual process of homogenization-redifferentiation. The differentiation that Shkaratan found in the 1950s and 1960s had its origins in the factory during the 1930s, as I will show in the section below, but was a shallow, new type of differentiation, hence a redifferentiation. Such redifferentiation was accelerating the deep processes of homogenization in Soviet society as a whole and particularly in its most dynamic social class, the urban industrial working class.

This can best be conceptualized in terms of *external* and *internal* labor markets, a distinction developed in the context of the union and non-union sectors of the U.S. economy in the 1950s and 1960s by Dunlop, Kerr, and especially Doeringer and Piore (see chapter 1, n. 8). In the Soviet context, the homogenizing trend was predominant in the external labor market and redifferentiation in the internal labor market. Both trends, I argue, caused the rapid disintegration of the sharply bifurcated Russian "dual" labor market which Soviet Russia had inherited and which was perpetuated into NEP.

The homogenizing trend in the external labor market meant that at the enterprise gate or the personnel department *(otdel kadrov)*, where most hiring occurred, social origins no longer mattered. Enterprises were generally hiring all who came to their gates, and there was virtually no institutional obstacle to those moving from one type of industry to another. These "ports of entry" into the factory, in Clark Kerr's terminology, were suddenly wide open. Obstructions that had for centuries been the defining factor in industrial work for peasant-migrants, women, and youth, had suddenly disappeared. Peasant origins, gender, and age no longer meant inferior status on the shop floor. The dual labor market, sharply bifurcated between aristocrats and subalterns, also disappeared, with striking impact.

Equally dramatic transformations were also taking place in the internal labor market. Here, "redifferentiation" predominated as new job definitions saw a proliferation of specializations and new criteria for placement and promotion. This replaced the traditional pattern of assigning jobs strictly by a worker's ascribed status, when a new worker was hired through traditionally regulated "ports of entry," which meant that a *starosta* or *master* could place one in a subaltern position that persisted throughout one's career. The new internal labor market brought the disintegration of a sharply polarized industrial work force and the end of traditionalism, ascribed status, and the vagaries of personal dependency in the assignment of jobs. New forms of dependency, in the form of party connections, did persist during the 1930s, but the overall tendency was toward a more specialized division of labor on the shop floor.

Vdovin and Drobizhev, following Shkaratan's critique of the class struggle ideology of the triadic Stalin formula, adopted a dual strata categorization, "forming" and "cadre" workers, for the whole of the 1930s. They accepted Shkaratan's argument that strict ownership criteria of social stratification used by Stalinists was losing its significance during the 1930s, but found no evidence for new sources of stratification. Where Vdovin and Drobizhev went beyond Sonin or Shkaratan was in the striking clarity of their approach to the issue of working-class formation. They showed that new recruits were still 50 percent peasants after 1933, and that the numbers of women among the recruits increasd to 50 percent, but correctly concluded that new recruits were less significant after 1933 than before.

Following Sonin and Shkaratan, Vdovin and Drobizhev also focused on the key issue of proletarian self-reproduction. They would adopt a new approach, however, noting a diminishing proportional weight of the new recruits in the industrial work force after the First FYP. This is a highly important finding, that has been largely overlooked. They were the first to note the significance of the hiring freeze and short-term layoffs of 1933 and to emphasize the more stable pattern of labor recruitment after 1933, as opposed to the chaos of the First FYP influx. They showed that, after 1933, the most important issue was not where the new recruits came from, but rather their very diminished significance in the overall picture of working-class formation. Whereas during the First FYP new recruits to the work force had averaged over 20 percent of the existing work force annually (it doubled in four years, 1929–1932), from 1934 through 1940, the new recruits had averaged 10 percent annual increments to the existing work force.[20]

Thus, they virtually reconstructed (without noting it) Sonin's poorly developed argument about the shift in the working class from rural to urban-based recruitment (or a shift to increasing self-reproduction) during the Second and Third FYPs. Since peasants still comprised roughly 50 percent of the new recruits for the years 1934–41, the claim of working-class "expanded self-reproduction," Sonin's fundamental argument, was not valid. Furthermore, his arguments about population redistribution (to the east) as a rising trend replacing urban in-migration in the later 1930s were wrong, since most recruits in the Urals and Siberia were also peasants. What was valid in Sonin's approach, which Vdovin and Drobizhev clearly showed, was that the new recruits, urban or rural, were no longer the dominant social factor in the factory after 1933. In other words, they showed, if we were to use Sonin's application of Marxist terminology to the demographics of class, that "simple self-reproduction" of the working class was of greater significance after 1933 than "expanded reproduction" based on peasant recruits. (These are my conclusions concerning Sonin, not those of Vdovin and Drobizhev, but they follow directly from their work on class formation.)

Vdovin and Drobizhev also went beyond Sonin in attempting to salvage triumphalism in cultural terms rather than in terms of a "genetic" argument about working-class formation by self-reproduction. They approached the cultural development of the working class from three angles, arguing that new recruits were converted into cadre, not as Lenin expected, in ten years, but in three to five years under Soviet conditions during the 1930s.[21] In accounting for this acceleration, they stressed worker education and "enlightenment" under "positive" impact of Soviet ideology and political culture. Under this rubric they included disciplinary labor laws, the socialist competition movements, vocational training, education, and *agitprop*. Second, they argued that skilled workers at the bench, especially shock workers and Stakhanovites, helped to train the newcomers on the shop floor rapidly by sharing their work experience and knowledge of the work process, with a degree of generosity that had never been possible under competitive capitalist labor market conditions. Third, they invoked material self-interest, that is, Stalin's policies, to explain why the newcomers were anxious to find jobs in the factories and to stick with them, quickly acquiring work skills and improving their pay ranking. In a related argument, they also invoked moral incentives through rewards such as honoring workers with the Order of Lenin or the Order of the Red Banner of Labor, or with the title of shock worker or Stakhanovite.

This approach by Vdovin and Drobizhev meant a refocusing of the question of working-class formation in terms of the politics of culture, and it offered what might be called a Soviet institutional approach to class formation and class consciousness. In the end, this was not very convincing and was the weakest part of their study, but that was because of the circumscribed answers that they provided, largely in terms of the ideology and policy of the Stalin regime, and not because the questions that they posed were the wrong ones.

A more convincing explanation of how the Soviet working class was reconstituted during the 1930s, in terms of attitudes toward the regime, was clearly outlined in an unpublished article by Barber, which built on these Soviet studies as well as on extensive research of his own. Barber retraced the rapidly changing composition of the Soviet work force in the three prewar FYPs, suggesting that a "new Soviet working class" was indeed, in the process of formation during the 1930s.[22] He also suggested why the dramatic changes in the composition of the work force were likely to have generated considerable support for the regime among some layers of both the new workers and cadre workers and why, among the other layers, there was likely to be political apathy rather than hostility to the regime. Barber continued with this theme, approaching it from somewhat different angles in two subsequent published articles on the labor market and on workers' living standards. The first explained how the combination of wide job availability and considerable flexibility in applying the draconian labor laws in practice meant a favorable situation for workers in the labor market. The second showed why, despite sharply falling living standards during the First FYP, most workers were, again, not likely to turn against the regime.[23] These articles began to develop an argument about class consciousness. In this chapter, I will elaborate and build on the idea that some strata of workers were attracted to the regime's program or policies, while the vast majority were at least neutral or not hostile to the regime. In rethinking the question of class formation and solidarities during the 1930s, I will suggest that ideas of class inclusiveness and of a class interest were clearly emerging in the very process of class formation and fundamentally shaped workers' attitudes vis-à-vis the regime.

The Factory as Social Melting Pot

The Soviet factory became a "social melting pot" in that three distinct social groups with distinct cultures—peasant-migrants, women, and youth—were integrated in Soviet society in some historically new ways during the 1930s. While I see the process as strikingly analogous to the American pattern of ethnic integration in the factories and in some communities during the 1920s and 1930s, I do not mean to suggest that the Soviet case was primarily a matter of integrating the diverse ethnic groups or the nationalities of the USSR.[24]

The data that I have been able to gather, primarily from the First FYP and at the factory level, suggest these trends, but are by no means exhaustive. To show conclusively that there was such social integration, one would have to consider other types of personnel data at the factory level, data at the all-union level, and at all the intermediate levels, including *glavki*, combines, trusts, and the industrial branches, corresponding roughly to the trade unions. The ideal approach would be to trace, over time, the changing patterns of employment for the four major substrata of the working class that I have identified in this study: established workers and, among the newcomers, peasants, women, and youth. The objective would be to see in which occupations, geographic regions, and branches of industry, segregated patterns of work units were yielding most rapidly or least rapidly to integrated patterns. Alternative approaches would be to trace individual worker's life histories as representative cases.

Nothing like this has been attempted, in large part because of the lack of access to factory-level and other data and the lack of knowledge of its existence. In the 1930s, as sociology was crushed by Stalinism, serious factory-level, industrywide, or all-union surveys were fewer and fewer. Increasingly, such surveys as were conducted were for internal purposes of the party and sought to show differentiations so as to illustrate how the party was attracting the best elements of the working class.[25]

Soviet published data on the work force from the 1930s divided workers either according to four skill categories or according to the eight ranks on the *tarifnyi razriad*. The fact that ranks 1–2 were defined as unskilled, ranks

3–4 as semiskilled, ranks 5–6 as skilled, and ranks 7–8 as highly skilled workers, with some occasional data on the pay differentials between the ranks, is the sum total of information that the regime generated.

Given the paucity of data, few historians or social scientists have attempted seriously to consider the issue of differentiation in Soviet society since the Second World War, let alone for the 1930s. The Soviet economists Rabkina and Rimashevskaia examined decile wage ratios for the entire national economy of the USSR and concluded that the ratio of highest to lowest decile narrowed slightly from 3.33:1 to 3.16:1 in the years 1930–34 and then widened substantially every year until 1946, when the gap reached its widest extreme at 5.43:1. Their findings spelled out the basic trends that Bergson had suggested long ago.[26]

While this indicates that Stalin's antiegalitarian wage policy was slow to be implemented but then began to take effect in the mid 1930s, it tells us very little about social stratification, since actual earned wages corresponded only remotely to the decile wage ratios.[27] In the Brezhnev era, Mervyn Matthews and Murray Yanowitch, both following the lead of Soviet sociologists, began focusing attention on the problems of wide pay differentials and Soviet poverty, suggesting that there were some strata that qualified as poor within a more widely stratified society than had been previously recognized. They also found starkly negative indicators for much of the *kolkhoz* peasantry.[28] However, their findings, as was true for Soviet sociologists, were more concerned with the ways in which education and training impacted on individuals and their career choices and opportunities than with the degree to which peasants, or women, or youth had been integrated into the occupational structure.[29]

The only serious study of social differentiation over the long scope of Soviet history was Alistair McAuley's study of women's wages, based on all-union census data from 1917–79, which goes beyond mere wage differentiation to consider the problem in terms of degrees of vertical and horizontal segregation. His method of tracing desegregation of Soviet women in the work force along both the horizontal and vertical axis is very useful. Ghettoization in particular occupations or branches of industry (horizontal segregation) must be distinguished from lack of upward mobility (vertical obstruction). McAuley found that from 1917 to 1939 women made substantial progress in breaking through barriers along both axes. From 1939 to 1979, however, women were collectively bumping up against what is now called a glass ceiling. His periodization, which follows closely from the years of All-Union Census, raises a number of interesting problems that lie beyond my scope here.[30]

What is most significant was his finding that there was increasing job integration of women from 1917 to 1939. One might question these findings for lumping together the era of revolution and civil war, NEP, and industrialization-collectivization (1917–1939), as governed by the single trend toward integration and greater equality for women. Instead, I suggest that from 1917 to 1928 the record was mixed in integrating women in skilled industrial occupations and metalworking, whereas from 1929 to 1941, substantial inroads were made that opened job categories and entire branches of industry that were, until 1928, mainly male preserves. McAuley's outline indicates the broad trends. Furthermore, his method of analyzing desegregation along horizontal and vertical axes is also, in theory, readily applicable to other social groups, such as peasants or youth. That is precisely what is needed, both with all-union and with disaggregated factory-level data, which could trace the history of selected work brigades and the life history of selected workers in order to establish the extent and patterns of homogenization of formerly subaltern social groups in the new Soviet working class.

Working with the same method, along horizontal and vertical axes, enough information exists on SiM to show that considerable vertical integration occurred, while integration along the horizontal axis was less rapid and thorough during the 1930s. The only Soviet study to address the problem of patterns of social differentiation and segregation at the factory level during the First FYP happens to be based on SiM, the manuscript by Igor L'vovich Kornakovskii, "Zavod 'Serp i Molot,' 1883–1932: Opyt Istoriko-Sotsiologicheskogo Issledovaniia."[31]

Kornakovskii's research clearly shows that prior to the industrialization drive, there was sharp horizontal segregation at SiM and very little upward mobility for peasants or for women. Virtually all the peasant-recruits went into the hot metallurgical shops that smelted the steel or rolled it into suitable forms, while most of the urban recruits, young men and some women graduates from high school, went into the cold shops. The cold shops made metal products from the iron or steel, such as cable or wire.

Peasant-workers were not only expected to be stronger and more tolerant of intolerable conditions in the hot shops, but it was assumed that they would only work in limited stints and then return to the countryside. As seasonal workers, it was expected that they would prefer to earn higher wages in the hot shops and suffer the hellish working conditions in limited stints. One might question if these peasant-migrants, many of whom remained as seasonal workers until 1930, were really a subaltern group at all. Wages were historically highest in the hot shops, so as to attract the seasonal migrants to perform the most arduous labor. Regardless of these higher wages, however, such workers had no prospects for promotion and remained subalterns.

During the 1930s, as seasonal employment ended at SiM, pay scales were kept higher in the hot shops to reflect exertion and strain. Whereas the seasonal workers of imperial and NEP times could not aspire to promotions, since they lacked continuous work tenure, that changed dramatically in the 1930s at SiM. Peasant-migrants coming to SiM could no longer work seasonally after 1930, when the factory discontinued its August shutdown and went onto year-round production. Furthermore, peasant-migrants working seasonally at SiM in construction declined in significance after 1932, when the massive reconstruction of the First FYP was concluding. These workers, if they stayed, became permanent workers in the hot shops. Their pay was initially higher than for urban recruits in the cold shops, and, more important, for the first time they would gain promotions just as rapidly as the urban-born established workers and newcomers in the cold shops. The peasant-recruits were no longer kept at the bottom of the vertical status scale. Their segregation in the hot shops no longer looked like a discriminatory pattern or ghettoization.

Horizontal segregation of the peasant-recruits in the hot shops persisted through the First FYP. A rough breakdown of SiM workers showing the distribution of youth, peasants, and of workers whose prior occupation was not income producing (that is, primarily students and housewives) was constructed by Kornakovskii for the seven most important shops in the plant in 1932, employing 73 percent of SiM workers. His sample was 7,391 workers, not including white-collar workers, FZU trainees, and MOP (support personnel, nonproduction workers). In table 7.1, based on several of Kornakovskii's appendices, youth were defined as ages seventeen to twenty-two. Peasants were defined as those workers whose father's occupation was given as peasant. Lacking data on the shop distribution of female workers, workers whose prior occupation was nonremunerative (primarily housewives and students), has to serve as a very unreliable proxy.

Kornakovskii's data do not allow us to clearly separate women, peasants, and youth at SiM by shop since they were, in substantial measure, overlapping categories. It is impossible to draw any conclusions about degrees of segregation of women. The only firm conclusion that can be drawn is the bifurcation of rural and urban workers in hot and cold shops, where it can be seen that peasant-recruits are concentrated in the top three shops in this table, the hot shops, while urban workers are concentrated in the next four in the table, the cold shops. Thus, during the First FYP, old patterns of social segregation persisted at SiM. All the evidence suggests that it was the attempts of newcomers to break through on the vertical axis, not on the horizontal, that were the primary sources of shop-floor tension and of social conflict between newcomers and established workers during the First FYP that unfolded under the rubrics of apprenticeship versus vocational training and cadre proletariat versus shock workers. (See chapters 5 and 6.)

Table 7.1. Social Distribution of SiM Workers by Shop

	I	II	III	IV	V
HOT SHOPS					
Prokatnyi (rolled metal shop)	1,165	15.8	23.3	61.8	25.7
Listoprokatnyi (sheet metal shop)	505	6.8	19.9	60.3	24.2
Martenovskii (Marten, or open hearth shop)	619	8.4	19.9	65.7	19.2
COLD SHOPS					
Staleprovolochnyi (wire shop)	1,237	16.7	40.5	52.0	27.4
Pressovyi (pressing shop)	1,050	14.2	48.5	54.5	30.2
Fasonno-liteinyi (form-casting shop)	526	7.1	28.2	52.3	28.5
Kanatnyi (cable shop)	285	3.8	36.1	40.8	40.1
Total SiM	5,387	72.8	32.6	56.2	29.4

Source: Compiled from appendices in Kornakovskii, "Zavod 'Serp i Molot,'" pp. 446–50 and unpublished data provided by Kornakovskii from GARF f. 7952, op. 3, d. 214, l. 1.
Note: Column I: total workers for each shop; column II: percentage of the work force for each shop; column III: percentage of youth; column IV: percentage of peasants; column V: percentage of workers whose prior occupation was nonremunerative.

The trends toward integration or the persistence of segregation along the horizontal axis, that is whether peasant-workers continued to labor primarily with fellow villagers in hot metallurgical shops, or with a wide variety of people in cold as well as in hot shops, cannot be answered without making use of a type of source that has not yet been available to researchers: the factory personnel cards. With these cards, one could place individual workers over their work career at specific workbenches and thus reconstruct the composition of the various work crews in terms of the social origins of their members, and how that changed over the decade of the 1930s. The personnel cards were issued to every worker in the USSR in the late 1920s, and while these records do not exist for SiM from the 1930s, they exist for many other plants through that decade.[32] However, there is some limited data available concerning vertical integration.

The degree to which newcomers were able to move from unskilled ranks up the ladder to skilled ranks can be discussed in terms of some aggregate wage-scale statistics for SiM and ZiS. Whereas Soviet historians have used data from the *tarifnaia setka* (wage scale) and changes in *razriad* (rank category) to try to demonstrate that there was a clear secular trend of increasing level of skill for the whole of the Soviet working class in the 1930s, I will use them to show a less spectacular trend: namely, the rise of a homogeneous, semiskilled work force that was replacing the polarized working class of the dual labor market.

Two objections immediately come to mind when using the wage scales as Soviet historians have, to show a secular trend of rising skill levels. First, in 1932, the first *tarifnyi razriad* was essentially discarded, and as part of a general wage increase accompanying the wage reforms, new workers began their careers at the second *razriad*. This, of course, changed the entire scale and inevitably diluted skill rankings, although it had no impact on the remaining differentials. Second, and more significant, these skill rankings were continuously diluted by the changing definition of jobs as given in the wage-skill handbooks, the *tarifno-kvalifikatsionnie spravochniki*. The handbooks were inevitably changed with the new technologies, although there were constant complaints during the 1930s that they were not being revised quickly enough to keep pace with changing job definitions and technologies.

Generally speaking, we could assume that as mechanized and even automated processes spawned proliferating job definitions and categories, there was a creeping skill inflation built into the wage scale. Thus, the scales serve as very poor indicators of real changes in skill levels, but much better indicators of changes in status. In other words, what was classified as semiskilled work in 1934 might have been only marginally more skilled than the same work that was classified as unskilled in 1932. However, what was important was that a status revolution had occurred in those two years in the bottom ranks of the work force.

Following the conventional classification used in the 1930s, as I noted above, Soviet workers were divided by skill into four categories: unskilled, semiskilled, skilled, and highly skilled. At SiM, by these criteria, in 1932, in the final year of the massive recruitment drive, 45 percent of the work force was unskilled, 39 percent semiskilled, 14 percent skilled, and 1.9 percent highly skilled.[33]

After the hiatus year 1933, when almost 10 percent of the workers at SiM were dismissed, the situation changed fundamentally. By 1934, only 14.6 percent were unskilled (or about one-third of the 1932 percentage), 52.3 percent were semiskilled, 27.6 percent were skilled, and 5.5 percent were highly skilled.[34] These figures unambiguously and strongly confirm the middling tendency of the SiM work force in the aftermath of the great recruitment drive of the First FYP. While we cannot draw any specific conclusions from this concerning the status of peasants, women, or youth, it is clear that if only 14.6 percent of the work force in 1934 was still unskilled, then all three groups saw substantial vertical progress into the semiskilled ranks. Again, I would emphasize, that was an improvement in status more clearly than in skill levels.

Examining the wage scales at AMO-ZiS, the same general middling trend can be observed, but with even greater salience. Table 7.2 shows the distribution of AMO-ZiS workers by *tarifnyi razriad* in absolute numbers: the vast majority of new workers who were hired in 1931 came in at the second *razriad,* while none started at the first *razriad.* Furthermore, the rapid growth in the third and fourth *razriady* meant rapid promotion and also probably the placing of some newly hired workers directly into these semiskilled ranks. Since the data available for 1932–33 are in percentages, converting the figures for 1930 and 1931 (the total row) yields the following percentages for comparative purposes. In 1930, 42.5 percent of the workers were ranked in the second *razriad,* while 20.7 percent were ranked in the third. By 1931, 50.7 percent were ranked in the second *razriad,* and 24.4 percent in the third. Combining the two, in 1930, 63.2 percent of the AMO-ZiS work force was categorized on the border between unskilled and semiskilled, in the second and third *razriady,* while in 1931, fully 75.1 percent were in these two categories. Note, also that in this one year, 1931, the AMO-ZiS work force increased by over 150 percent. It was the year that the new shops went on-line.

A volume of published documents on Soviet industrialization gives comparable data on the next two years, 1932 and 1933, at AMO-ZiS. They show that the average worker's ranking on the *tarifnyi razriad* rose from 3.0 in 1932 to 3.2 in 1933. However, more indicative of the middling tendency are the figures for *razriad* distribution shown in table 7.3 (in percentages).

Thus, comparing 1932 to 1931, we see that the percentage of workers in the second *razriad* has dropped dramatically from 50.7 percent to 31 percent, and then it fell again, in 1933, to 28.2 percent. The percentage in the third *razriad* held almost constant at 23 percent. Thus, it is worth emphasizing that by 1933 the percentage of unskilled workers was already consider-

Table 7.2. Distribution of AMO-ZIS Workers by Tarifnyi Razriad, 1930–31
(in absolute numbers)

Firm	Year	Unskilled		Semi-Skilled		Skilled		Highly Skilled		Total
		1	2	3	4	5	6	7	8	
AMO-ZIS	1930	96	1,719	838	533	453	260	139	2	4,040
AMO-ZIS	1931	52	5,538	2628	1,128	736	392	197	1	10,672
Filial	1931	65	236	150	93	76	59	32	0	711
Total	1931	117	5,774	2,778	1,221	812	451	229	1	11,383

Source: TsGAOR g. Moskvy f. R-414, op. 4, d. 27, l. 1.

Table 7.3. Distribution of AMO-ZIS Workers by Tarifnyi Razriad, 1932–33
(in percentages)

Year	Unskilled		Semi-Skilled		Skilled		Highly Skilled	
	1	2	3	4	5	6	7	8
1932	14.6	31.0	23.4	14.7	8.7	4.8	2.5	0.3
1933	9.3	28.2	23.5	16.7	10.4	5.0	2.3	0.5

Source: Industrializatsiia SSSR, vol. 3, p. 425.

ably lower than at the beginning of 1930, that is, before the plant began its threefold expansion of the work force, in the process of "sewing the coat around the button" as Likachev put it. Whereas in 1930, 42.5 percent of the workers were in the second *razriad,* by 1933 the percentage had fallen to 28.2.

If the most rapidly expanding *razriad* categories in 1930–31 were the second and third, then clearly, the most rapidly expanding categories in 1932 and 1933 were the fourth and fifth. The fourth fell from 13.1 percent in 1930 to 10.6 percent in 1931 and rebounded back to 14.7 percent in 1932 and to 16.7 percent in 1933. Likewise the fifth was at 11.2 percent in 1930, fell to 6.1 percent in 1931, and then increased to 8.7 percent in 1932 and 10.4 percent in 1933. In sum, the ranks of the semiskilled and skilled workers were expanding most rapidly after 1931.

One anomaly at AMO-ZiS, however, concerns the first *razriad,* where, for some reason, very few new workers were placed in 1930 or 1931, the percentage dropping from 2.4 percent to 1 percent. In 1932, however, that figure increased considerably to 14.6 percent. Even though the level fell to 9.3 percent in 1933, this still remained much higher than the 1930 and 1931 levels. This is peculiar, because in most enterprises, prior to 1932, the evidence suggests that most new workers were placed in the first *razriad,* while in 1932 and after, most were placed in the second. Thus, the situation at AMO-ZiS seems to be the opposite of the general trend.

Despite this anomaly, AMO-ZiS still fits the general trend if we lump the first two or three *razriady* together. The total for *razriady* 1 and 2 was 44.9 percent in 1930, 51.7 percent for 1931, 45.6 percent for 1932, and 37.5 percent for 1933. By 1933, the percentage of unskilled workers was thus considerably lower than in 1930, despite the fact that the work force had already tripled in size. For *razriady* 1, 2, and 3, the totals were 65.6 percent for 1930, 76.1 percent for 1931, 69 percent for 1932, and 61 percent for 1933, showing precisely the same trend. Therefore, no matter where one draws the boundary between unskilled and semiskilled, and despite the ZiS anomaly with hiring into the first *razriad,* there was clearly a very sharp rise in the percentage of workers defined as unskilled in 1931, followed by an equally sharp decline in 1932 and 1933, until it was, once again, lower than the 1930 level.

These figures show that if 1932 was the pivotal year, then 1933 was the year of mass promotion such that by the end of 1933, the new workers already had been absorbed into the work force and made the transition to modern production methods on machines and conveyer belts, in the sense that they had attained a semiskilled status. It is obvious that the hiring freeze of 1933 was essential in this process; however, it was the slower and steadier pace of hiring over the remainder of the decade that consolidated these trends. As Vdovin and Drobizhev indicated, the ratio of workers with production tenure of less than one year fell to 10 percent in 1934 and stayed remarkably stable at that level for the rest of the decade. As production tenure rose, on average, so too did the level of skill ranking.

Published sources and archival sources do not provide comparable data for SiM or AMO-ZiS in the mid to later 1930s. However, one study of labor organization in Soviet assembly-line industries asserts that for the whole of the Soviet auto industry, the average *tarifnyi razriad* increased from 3.0 in 1931, to 3.8 in 1937, to 4.21 in 1938.[35] Furthermore, this study shows percentage distribution of all Soviet auto workers by *razriady* (see table 7.4).

Obviously, then, there was a drastic change from 1931 to 1937 along the lines that were predicted, from unskilled to semiskilled, while from 1937 to 1938, the ranks of both unskilled and semiskilled thinned somewhat, and the ranks of the skilled and highly skilled increased. The most striking figure, however, was the reversal of the percentages between the unskilled and semiskilled categories. Whereas in 1931 almost half of all workers were in *razriady*

Table 7.4. Distribution of Auto Workers by Tarifnyi Razriad, 1931–38
(in percentages)

	Unskilled (1–2)	Semi-Skilled (3–4)	Skilled (5–6)	Highly Skilled (7–8)
1931	49.5	33.1	14.4	3.0
1937	26.1	48.0	20.3	5.6
1938	18.4	42.6	29.1	9.9

Source: Boltianskii, p. 95 (citing *Voprosy Ekonomiki* 10 [1950]: 49).

1–2, by 1937 almost half were in *razriady* 3–4. While pay differentials between the first and eighth ranks were being widened, the social trend was toward a bulge in the middle ranks, confounding Stalin's antiegalitarian wage policy.

In the post–Second World War years, efforts to reclassify workers by revising the wage-skill handbooks would slightly lower the average ranking level. It fell from 4.5 to 4.1 among a sample of 1,480 workers chosen, apparently, from the Stalin auto plant and the GAZ plant, as an experiment in simplifying the handbooks and clarifying what tasks each ranking required.[36] With the changes in production and machinery, unless the handbooks were constantly updated, there was a built-in inflationary bias. Still, these very partial data show that, after rising sharply during the Second FYP, the average ranking level achieved by 1938 did not change much in the next decade. That may have been caused, in part, by the Second World War chaos, but it also reflected stabilization of the First FYP cohort of recruits.

Thus, the Soviet work force, in the 1930s, was undergoing the same type of middling transformation that had been changing the work force in the United States, Germany, and to a lesser extent Britain and France, since the turn of the twentieth century. While we can be certain that it was overwhelmingly peasant-migrants, women, and youth who were filling the ranks of the new mass semiskilled occupations and the middle ranks of the wage scale, pinpointing variations within these three large groups would only be possible with different data than the *razriad* aggregates used here. The solution to this problem, as with the problem of horizontal segregation, is to be found in the personnel work cards, a type of source which, until now, has been little used.

Individual personnel work cards (*lichnye kartochki*) were issued for each new hiree at SiM from 1925 until at least 1978 by the plant personnel department. The cards for SiM from 1930 to 1941 were lost during the evacuation of the plant in October 1941, but are available for 1941–58. Kornakovskii and Slavko have used them to show the changing gender composition of the wartime and postwar SiM work force. By the end of the Second World War, women constituted 56 percent of the SiM work force; however, by 1958, they were only 15 percent, which was far less than their 24.2 percent at the end of 1932 and closer to the 13.5 percent figure of women at SiM in January 1917.[37] This finding would seem to reaffirm McAuley's all-union findings of a positive trend prior to the Second World War and a negative trend thereafter.

Working with other factories where the *lichnye kartochki* still exist for the 1930s, one could go beyond the general findings presented here on the First FYP, based on limited *tarifnyi razriad* data, and begin to determine with some degree of precision how the patterns of vertical and horizontal segregation were changing during the 1930s. One could trace the work history of individuals and reconstruct the work aggregate or *brigada,* demonstrating the extent to which workers from similar or different social backgrounds were lumped together in 1929/30 as compared with 1932/33, or in 1941. Instrumental for reconstructing a career path would also be the "work book" *(trudovaia kniga),* required by law of each worker from December 1938, and in theory providing the worker's prior employment history, detailing occupations, skill and wage levels, and places of employment from the first day of employment.

Until this type of study can be undertaken, however, use of crude factory-aggregate data by *razriady* indicates the general trend, which was a status revolution in which millions of new workers became semiskilled or cadre workers in roughly the period that Vdovin and Drobizhev suggested, that is, three to five years. Furthermore, anecdotal evidence concerning the employment of peasants, women, and youth points in the same direction. Whereas the regime presented it as evidence of upward mobility, or the "forging of cadre" (see chap. 8), I have interpreted it as a status revolution along the vertical axis. Finally, the rapid proliferation of jobs in the wage-skill handbook during the 1930s is further evidence of the proliferation of occupational categories, suggesting that there was a sharp and sustained process of job specialization and skill redefinition taking place in the 1930s and that the mass of new workers moved very rapidly into the ranks of the semiskilled. Again, this evidence points toward a status revolution.

The more troubling question concerns the horizontal axis. The anecdotal evidence and the available data concerning peasants and women tend to indicate persistence of segregation during the 1930s. While this no longer applied to branches of industries or factories as a whole, it seems to have still applied to the gendered distribution of jobs between shops in a steel plant like SiM. However, the integration of women into machinist and assembly line jobs at an auto plant like ZiS may have meant an unprecedented degree of horizontal integration of women. As vertical obstacles to promotion were removed, however, it appears that such segregation no longer entailed discriminatory wage or promotion patterns. Furthermore, it is quite possible that peasants or women preferred to be placed in a work brigade or shop in which they predominated. The segregated job distribution patterns may have been preserved into or through the 1930s not only by the assumptions of bosses and personnel departments, or by protective legislation concerning women, or by seasonal migration patterns, but also by the links of villagers who came into the factory together or of women who perhaps knew their coworkers from life in the community.

My two working hypotheses have also become my tentative conclusions based on the available evidence from SiM and ZiS. First, the newer the plant and industry and the more processes mechanized or automated, the greater the proliferation of semiskilled job categories, and the greater the speed and thoroughness of both vertical and horizontal integration by social origin. Second, the patterns of vertical and horizontal integration greatly favored youth, and it was the shift in generational composition of the work force that broke down many of the barriers confronting both peasants and women in industry during the First FYP.

The study of personnel cards from other areas of Russia would probably show that integrative trends, along both horizontal and vertical axes, were strongest in new developing regions on the periphery (Urals, Siberia), a bit less strong in the intermediate center (Moscow, and perhaps the Donbass), and were weakest in the oldest industrialized zones (the west and Petersburg). At least, I suggest that would be true for peasant migrant-workers; perhaps the patterns of integration for women were different.

The Stalin regime assumed that Soviet society was becoming increasingly homogeneous during the 1930s, putatively the objective of socialism, even while its strategy of encouraging differentiation was acclaimed for stimulating labor productivity. Sonin, Vdovin and Drobizhev, and even Shkaratan, with his anti-Stalinist approach, had all uncritically absorbed both of these seemingly contradictory assumptions. In an important way, I am arguing, both were true, because the predominant trend was toward a deep structural social homogenization, while a relatively superficial type of differentiation, a redifferentiation was being established based on occupation, rank, and pay, which ironically would foster homogenization.

The new differentiation was superficial or shallow, first, because the dominant trend was a mass status revolution from the unskilled into the semiskilled and skilled job rankings. That was a middling trend rather than a polarizing trend. It was also superficial in a second sense, that job categories and ranks were wide open and accessible, not rigid and defined for a worker's lifetime during the 1930s. That meant job mobility, much greater movement between occupations, and the breakdown of patterns of work based on ascriptive status on the shop floor. The notion of peasant's work, of women's work, and of youth's work was being undermined in the SiM steel plant. It had all but disappeared in the ZiS auto plant next door.

The Politics of Labor Recruitment and Working-Class Formation

The Stalin regime, having launched the industrialization drive, saw the many "hostile," or "alien," or "petty bourgeois" social elements being swept into the Soviet factory. These included urban and rural artisans, whose shops were closed in 1928/29, and white-collar workers fired from Soviet state institutions in 1929 and 1930, and NEPmen (traders, petty entrepreneurs) who were driven out of business. Indeed, one might assume that workers from such origins must have come into the factories with grievances, and it would be easy to leap to the conclusion that their sense of "moral economy" had been violated, that like early nineteenth-century artisans in England they were prone to opposition or even to Luddism, which the regime would call "wrecking." Nothing like that appears, in fact, to have happened.

The same applies, on an even wider scale, to the 8.5 million peasant-recruits to wage and salaried work during the First FYP. The regime had distrusted them more than any other social group, not only because most were defined as petty bourgeois by the Marxist category of property ownership, but even more because of the cultural gap between city and village and the traditional, antirational, indeed "backward" values that the regime ascribed to the peasantry. During the last years of NEP, the regime had labeled peasant-migrant workers as "self-seekers" and denounced them together with the urban petty bourgeois elements for trying to "worm" their way into the factories in order to take advantage of the special privileges and benefits granted to factory workers. There were campaigns to remove peasant-migrant workers on *otkhod* and shift to employing only permanent production workers.

Then, with the inversion of the labor market in 1930, peasants were again labeled self-seekers and rolling stones, but in that context they were blamed for the opposite types of negative behavior. They were accused of trying to avoid factory work or of moving from job to job, always looking for the "long ruble," or persisting with seasonal migration instead of settling down in the city. This blatant contradiction in the ideological arsenal had nothing to do with the peasants; it expressed the ambivalence of the regime.

As we have seen, by June 1931, Stalin was blaming the peasants for not migrating readily enough from the *kolkhoz* and the village, in the midst of the most rapid urbanization in human history. Peasants' behavior, prior to 1930, when they were accused of trying to worm into the factories, and after that when they were accused of trying to avoid the factory, was, in both instances, assumed to be petty bourgeois, self-seeking, and irrational. This set of regime assumptions was used to account for virtually all the negative features of Soviet industrial and labor relations during the First FYP. Labor indiscipline, tardiness, absenteeism, turnover, and drunkenness, all of which increased sharply after 1929, were attributed to the peasant-worker. Labor productivity fell far behind planned increases and even began to decline in 1932, and the blame was placed squarely, once again, on peasant attitudes. Where there were signs of worker opposition to the draconian labor laws or to shock work, the same peasant attitudes were again invoked as the explanation. Not only was this a reflection of the regime's frustration in labor policy, but it was antithetical to the objective of integrating peasants and turning them into reliable Soviet industrial workers. Waging the class struggle by blaming, scapegoating, and punishing these new recruits had the opposite effect. It drove many out of the factory or from job to job.

The regime was caught in a bind in that its First FYP construction program depended on progress in recruiting peasants and making them productive workers. As I suggested in chapter 3, the dual objectives of bringing peasants into the factories so rapidly, while at the same time trying to counteract or even negate their allegedly petty bourgeois and backward culture, left the regime with only two realistic options. First, it could try to structure the factory environment so as to turn peasants into class-conscious, pro-Soviet, *kadrovye* workers as rapidly as possible. Second, it could try to supplement the new peasant-recruits with supposedly more reliable recruits from the two urban labor reserves, the wives and children of male factory workers and other urban residents. This was the regime's dual strategy of the First and Second FYPs, and there were no other options.

To make this strategy successful, the class struggle discourse and labor relations practice directed against "class aliens" had to be dropped in favor of a discourse of a "new Soviet working class," an all-inclusive discourse. Instead of scapegoating new recruits, integrating them became the obvious objective. The shift occurred between 1931 and 1936, beginning with the "Six Conditions" speech and concluding with the Stalin Constitution. It was a broad ideological shift in the regime's social and labor policy. One important component of the shift was the attempt to individualize the measure of output and to structure pay accordingly. That meant treating each individual recruit not in terms of her social origin, but rather in terms of her daily output, effort, or exertion. Ironically, wage differentiation promoted social equity.

The regime adopted a dual strategy. It set out to transform peasants, housewives, and youth, as well as former artisans, NEPmen, white-collar workers, Red Army veterans, and others into cadre workers by providing them with training and political education in the factory schools or, where that was not possible, by giving them shop-floor training, including the individual-brigade apprenticeships. Furthermore, the regime expected shock work and socialist competition to foster a new work ethic among the recruits and at the same time hoped that the many social activities organized by the *zavkom* and the *partkom* would begin to transform the peasant-recruit into an urbanite. According to the most influential Soviet account, that of Vdovin and Drobizhev, these policies succeeded in transforming the new recruits into *kadrovye* workers in three to five years.[38] My findings on a middling tendency confirm that.

The second strategy was to recruit as many urban workers as possible in order to dilute the impact of the peasant-recruits and disperse them among the more "class conscious" elements. However, from the standpoint of the party leadership, the wives and children of factory workers were not necessarily reliable social elements either, and their level of "proletarian consciousness" was highly suspect. Housewives in particular, by virtue of their social isolation, were seen as a potentially conservative social element, and it was suspected that they would not adapt well to the factory environment. Youth, by virtue of primary and secondary schooling, were expected to adapt more quickly. However, the demographic situation guaranteed that not until the Third FYP could urban society begin to hold its own by matching rural recruits to the industrial work force. Even with the comparatively very moderate Second FYP recruiting, some 54 percent of the new recruits were peasants.[39]

The best information available on recruits during the later 1930s comes from a document of Gosplan's Labor Department which in August 1940 was assessing labor-power needs of the economy and the potential of the FZUs to meet them. The total number of workers and white-collar employees in all branches of the economy increased over the Second FYP from 22,942,800 to 26,989,500, and in industry from 7,999,700 to 10,111,700. According to Gosplan, in industry the FZU graduates accounted for 1.4 million, about 1 million were housewives or other urban "resources," and about 2.5 million came from the countryside.[40]

The Gosplan document showed that its Labor Department anticipated an increase of 7.9 million workers and white-collar employees during the Third FYP, of which 2.92 million were to be in industry. Obviously frustrated by the fact that more than half the labor recruits during the Second FYP were from the peasantry, the document emphasized that 7 million urban youth and housewives were the still large untapped labor reserve for the future. Decrying the fact that only 30 percent of the FZU trainees were young women, the document also noted that in 1938 and 1939 the FZU prepared only 159,500 new trainees for industry, rather than the 1.1 million called for by the Third FYP. That was less than 20 percent of the plan for those years.[41] Obviously the document should be seen in the context of prewar preparations, with its emphasis on bringing more women into the work force. It was also clearly a justification for the soon to be established State Labor Reserves and the conversion of the FZU to the FZO. Nonetheless, we can safely conclude that while there had been a shift toward urban working-class self-reproduction during the Second FYP, it was not nearly so rapid as the regime had expected and wanted, or as Sonin has claimed. Nor would the situation change in any fundamental way during the Third FYP.

In the politics of recruitment, the Soviet leadership was trapped by its own ideologically based constructs and its simplistic dichotomies—proletariat/peasant, pro-Soviet/anti-Soviet—which only obscured the real social conflicts that were raging on the shop floor during the First FYP. Blaming the peasants and class aliens for anti-Soviet attitudes, they simply made those conflicts worse. The shift from a class struggle discourse to a class inclusive discourse was the only realistic option for overcoming the very real social tensions on the shop floor.

In the First FYP, there was sharp social conflict on the shop floor that could not be understood in terms of the regime's categories. Not only were workers divided between urban and rural cultures, but gender and generation were also important fault lines. All the new recruits had very different life experiences than the established workers, those who dated their work tenure back to the NEP period or earlier. All three new social groups (peasants, women, and youth) would develop grievances against these established workers, who held the superior positions in the factory.

Furthermore, the regime's categories failed to consider conflicts or cultural differences among the peasants, women, and youth themselves. As I have already suggested, youth and youth culture provided a link that helped to span the gap between the other two social groups, since young men and women, from rural or urban families, were likely to train together in the FZU. Still, the life experiences of urban housewives and of peasant-migrants were so different from each other, as well as from that of the established workers, that some clash was inevitable. It is quite likely that they initially preferred segregation by shop or by occupation, since at least that put them within a familiar social group, if not among friends, family, or acquaintances, as they entered a very unfamiliar work environment. A desire to integrate may have developed roughly during the three to five years that Vdovin and Drobizhev hypothesized for cadre formation. Or the struggle may have been for "equity" in terms of vertical mobility rather than in terms of horizontal integration.

Social realities on the shop floor during the First FYP were further complicated by the fact that the categories peasants, women, and youth were themselves aggregates and were overlapping aggregates. Youth were as often as not peasant-migrants, and so, lumping them together with urban youth as a single social category is not very useful in understanding patterns of group identities and shop-floor attitudes or cultures. Did a young peasant-recruit, if she was enrolled in the FZU, tend to identify with her fellow trainees in outlook, or with her fellow villagers? Either sense of self-identity (or both) was certainly possible.

Similarly, young and usually single women coming into the factory FZU do not fit neatly into either category of youth or women. Their life experiences were substantially different than that of housewife-recruits, or of women textile workers with long work tenure, because theirs was the first generation of girls that had nearly equal access to primary and secondary schooling to boys. They were, perhaps, more likely to identify with their youthful male counterparts than with older women, who were married and had children. On the other hand, these young women, like older women, initially at least faced discriminatory patterns of job distribution, with reduced access to skilled jobs and lessened chances for promotion. The labor laws for protecting women inevitably had this effect. So did the legacy of the past, where few women had worked at SiM or AMO. Furthermore, all women faced the same struggles with male chauvinists in positions of authority.

Obviously, the 8.5 million peasant-recruits to the work force during the First FYP were not a single social category. Regional, ethnic, religious, and national traits divided them in many ways. Minority nationalities, such as the Tatars at SiM, clearly faced different problems than the Russian, Ukrainian, or Belorussian peasant-recruits. Even among Russian peasants, the regional distinctions remained very important, since they grouped themselves in a factory, whenever possible, on the principle of *zemliachestvo*, or *artel'*, that is, by village. The party relied on this principle in recruiting peasant-workers through *orgnabor* and by trying to attach them to the factory. The party recognized this as an organizing principle when it seemed useful, but failed to consider what impact it had in shaping the peasants' attitudes and group identities on the shop floor and in the urban community.[42]

On the other hand, the regime's disaggregation of the peasants in class categories, which included landless-proletarian (*batraky* or *bezloshchadnye*), poor (*bednaky*), middle (*serednyaky*), well-to-do (*zazhitochnye*), and wealthy or capitalist (*kulaky*), did not correspond to actual peasant groupings or attitudes in the work place at all. The "dekulakized" became a social group at many factories by virtue of performing compulsory labor in the "resettlement" colonies. However, the distinction between *edinolichniky* and *kolkhozniky* (individual households and collective farmers) that became so important after the collectivization drive began in 1930 seemed to have no real importance in how peasant-recruits responded to the shop floor.

Finally, the Soviet regime's categories provided no concept or space for the established workers, provoking what Kuromiya has called a "crisis of proletarian identity." The category "cadre workers" was hopelessly ambivalent in the Stalinist politics of the First FYP. *Kadrovye rabochie* in some contexts meant "hereditary workers"; in other contexts it could also mean "core" workers sent from a pilot plant to set up production in a new satellite plant; in other contexts it meant workers with long work tenure in industry; and yet in other contexts it meant the new shock brigades, the avant-garde of the working class. Finally, it could mean all qualified or skilled workers, an ambivalence which I have already noted. Reconciling these very different concepts of *kadrovyi* was impossible.[43]

Rather than the Soviet manichaean dichotomies—proletarian/nonproletarian or pro-Soviet/anti-Soviet—I would postulate a very different dichotomy of salient worker identities on the factory floor. Consisting of two large aggregate categories, these were the newcomers and the established workers. By the last day of 1932, when the First FYP ended, these two groups were numerically equal in the Soviet factory. The newcomers included all those who came into the factories after 1 October 1928, when the First FYP began, most prominently, the three groups of incoming labor reserves. The established workers included all those who had begun their industrial employment prior to that date. (An alternative dividing point would be 1925/26.)[44]

Obviously, the category of established workers is an aggregate. It included workers of all ages, some of whom were hired before 1917, while others were hired during NEP's last years, the so-called first two years of reconstruction, 1926–28. It included both "hereditary proletarians" and first-generation workers from the village. It included male *metallisty* and female *tekstil'shchiki*. In comparison with the newcomers, however, it was a much more homogeneous social group regardless of these very real distinctions.

While the dichotomy between newcomers and established workers is an oversimplification, it is, nonetheless, a construct that explains most of the conflict and social tension in the factories and cities during the First FYP. Furthermore, it corresponds to how Soviet workers thought of themselves during those years, with the newcomers constantly doubting their own proletarian credentials because the regime and the established workers were constantly questioning their proletarian credentials. By the end of the First FYP, or the first two years of the Second FYP, workers no longer were identifying themselves in terms of this dichotomy. The newcomers had put it behind them. They were factory workers and, as the next chapter will show, Muscovites. That was the single most significant social development of those chaotic years and the single most important factor in the transformation of labor and industrial relations.

Archival sources and newspapers show that there were serious conflicts between the established workers and the newcomers during the First FYP, although from these sources it is hard to determine how widespread these were. Conflicts occurred over job assignment and distribution, training and apprenticeship, and concerning distribution of housing. There was also conflict over claiming the leading role in the shock-work–socialist competition movement. The labor policy of the party-state, which usually supported the established workers, vacillated, at times favoring "storming," the work culture that it attributed to peasants but that most frequently came from the young newcomers, the youth.

More important, the labor policy of the regime, like all its social policy during the industrialization-collectivization drive, was based on the faulty premise of class struggle, which profoundly exacerbated social tensions everywhere and among all classes, strata, or groups in society. The archival and published sources reveal a clear and incessant pattern of class struggle policy. What has not been clear to non-Soviet historians was the extent to which real social conflict was disguised and distorted through these regime lenses. Rather than focusing on interest groups in the Cultural Revolution who used the class struggle to their advantage, my focus has been on how the regime's policy exacerbated the inevitable social tensions on the shop floor, tensions caused by crash industrialization in the context of crash collectivization. While I have argued that class struggle policies were deemphasized after the "Six Conditions" speech, the regime never abandoned them in Stalin's lifetime. The major theme, after 1931, became "class inclusivity," while the minor theme became "class struggle." That balance, which allowed for frequent zigzags, persisted right up until 1953.

In essence, Stalinist labor policies during the First FYP were shifting from exclusive definitions of working-class culture to an all-inclusive one. Stalin's "Six Conditions" speech could be accurately described as the "wager on the skilled" and, like Bukharin's statement to peasants in the "high NEP" of 1925, it was an open invitation to the established workers to "enrich themselves." That was, however, only one part of the ersatz social contract. The broader aspect of that social contract was an invitation, open to all the subaltern social groups, to become part of the new Soviet working class. Worded in the language of individualism and differential remuneration, it launched a status revolution, and ironically, a broad status revolution and social homogenization that was critical in working-class formation.

That was the only political option available to the regime, given the poor results of more than two years of class struggles against imaginary enemies, in which it mistook social conflict between the established workers and the newcomers for political opposition.

1. *Martenovka,* 23 June 1932, p. 1. Headline: "Your Instructions, Comrade Stalin, We Are Putting Them Into Life." Inside the photo montage, Stalin's "Six Conditions" are enumerated and briefly evaluated.

2. *Martenovka,* 20 April 1936, p. 1. Headline: "Greetings to the First Conference of Bolsheviks of the First of May District." Photo: Khrushchev, Medbard, Kulikov, and Filatov (the former party secretary at SiM). In 1936, the Proletarian District was divided into two, and SiM fell within the new First of May District.

3. *Martenovka,* 6 July 1935, p. 3. Headline: "Architectural Reconstruction of 'Serp i Molot' by the Architect M. E. Zil'bert." Photo: Design for the main entry to the factory. This neoclassical entryway was never built; the main entrance was a modest doorway into the personnel department.

4. *Martenovka,* 6 July 1935, p. 4. Headline: "Our Factory Will Look Like This." Like the neoclassical entrance, this monumentalist reconstruction was never built.

5. *Martenovka,* 24 January 1935, pp. 2–3. Headline: "Above Our Marten Furnaces Flashes the Victorious Banner; In 1935, Give Our Country More Metal, Cheaper, and of Better Quality." Photos: top left, Ordzhonikidze, commissar of heavy industry, on the phone; center left, Stepanov, Red Director of SiM; bottom left, SiM party secretary Rubanov; center right, M. N. Korolev, *nachal'nik* (superintendent) of the open hearth shop; bottom right, a leading smelter in the open hearth shop.

6. The first Soviet car, the AMO-F-15, 1924. The banner reads: "Each new car will strengthen transport and in that way solidify the brotherhood of all peoples living in our state."

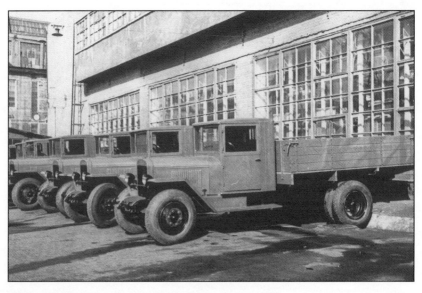

7. The ZiS-5 flatbed trucks in the factory courtyard, circa 1935.

8. The "quality brigade" in the form-casting shop, first furnace, SiM, April 1931: Korestelen, Semekov, and Klenin. Photo courtesy of GARF (f. 7952, op. 3, d. 349, no. 10).

8

THE FACTORY AS COMMUNITY ORGANIZER

In accordance with the Stalinist ideology of the First FYP period, the Soviet factory was supposed to become a "Bolshevik fortress." During the First FYP, however, it looked more like a sieve. Workers were coming and going so rapidly that the factory personnel department could not keep track of the payroll from month to month. As the previous chapters have suggested, that was an economic problem of an inverted labor market heading toward a labor famine in 1932, but the regime saw labor turnover as political resistance and attempted to convert the sieve into a fortress under its draconian labor laws. The idea of the factory as a Bolshevik fortress, of course, was part of the class struggle ideology.

The regime's ideology began to shift in 1931 from class struggle to ersatz social contract, and with this shift, the metaphor of the factory as Bolshevik fortress, would yield to a new metaphor, the factory as the "forge" of the "new Soviet man." The most widely read Soviet novel of the 1930s and the work that was the prototype for socialist realism, N. Ostrovskii's *How the Steel Was Tempered,* embedded this same metaphor in its title. The forge metaphor was bound up with the regime's shift to the idea of labor heroes and the belief that they would reflect the new social psychology of the masses under socialism.

In opposition to the two Stalinist slogans of "Bolshevik fortress" and "forge of the new Soviet man," two mutually exclusive visions of the Soviet factory and urban community emerged from within Soviet society itself. The first was a nightmarish vision of the factory and modern urban community as a type of totalitarianism, in which everyone was observing and reporting on the behavior of fellow citizens to the party-state organs. The second suggests that factory patriotism became widespread among workers as the factory was understood as a sort of socialist institutional building block, a benign factor in the life of its workers that, while it had obligations to the state in terms of production, had a duty to workers and their families to provide them with cradle-to-grave security. Yet another theory might be called that of the "total institution," something like Foucault's Panopticon, in which these negative and positive elements of control might be combined in ways that workers only partially perceived. My theory of "community organizer" borrows from but rejects these.

My theory, as suggested in chapter 7, is that Soviet workers, engineers and technicians (ITR), and managers, through engaging in conflicts and in cooperative efforts, as well as in unconscious ways, were turning the factory into a social melting pot internally and into an urban "community organizer." The stong tendencies toward working-class social homogenization were furthered, I will argue, as the workers themselves attempted to create an urban factory-community. I am attempting to outline a theory of human agency in which Soviet society, not the state, was shaping itself. Between the Soviet party-state and population there emerged a strong intermediate institution: the factory-community. While it was obviously a creation of an unprecedented program of forced collectivization and industrialization, and while it met the regime's demands for output, how that urban factory-community took shape was not understood, let alone controlled, by the Stalin regime. Rather, it was tolerated after the fact, then partially incorporated in a totally revised ideology of class in socialist society. It was shaped, within limits, by society.

Housing and Transport

The construction of housing, grocery stores, public baths and pools, sports clubs, day-care centers, and public transportation for the population of Moscow lagged far behind the growth in the city's industry and of its working population during the First FYP. This fact was never publicly acknowledged by the regime in 1929 and 1930. Finally, at the June 1931 Party

Plenum, a plan was introduced for the reconstruction of Moscow, and party leaders acknowledged what every Muscovite knew, namely, that none of the social facilities had kept pace with Moscow's industrial reconstruction or with the total growth of the city's population.[1]

The construction of new housing in the PR, as in the rest of Moscow, was lagging far behind the construction of new factories and the increase in city population during the First FYP. This was also true of transport, schools, shops, and parks. In the mad rush of industrialization the factories were being built by peasant-migrant construction workers, who were housed in nearby barracks. Many stayed on to work in the new factories, others left for new construction sites, and some probably stayed on in the PR to build the permanent apartment buildings that replaced most of the barracks during the Second and Third FYPs.

The housing fund, in thousands of cubic meters, increased for all of Moscow from 12,598 on 1 January 1929, to 14,415 on 1 January 1933, to 15,012 on 1 January 1934. That was a total increase of only 14.4 percent for the whole of the First FYP, and of 4.1 percent for 1933. Meanwhile, the city gained over a million new inhabitants, its population jumping, in those same years, from 2,319,000 to 3,600,000.[2] The situation in the PR was even worse, since the population more than doubled during the First FYP.

The increase in the housing stock in the PR was slightly above average for the city. From 739,000 cubic meters on 1 January 1929, it increased to 912,000 cubic meters on 1 January 1933, and then to 960,000 cubic meters on 1 January 1934. This was an increase of 23.4 percent for the First FYP and of 5.3 percent for 1933. Only the Stalin District, with a 37.4 percent increase in housing stock for the First FYP and an 11.2 percent increase for 1933, had a faster rate of growth.[3] However, this was hardly satisfactory when the population of the PR more than doubled in the same time period.

The Party Plenum in June 1931 admitted that new housing and other essential amenities lagged far behind the in-migration of people to Moscow. The Plenum resolution stated that: "The development of the city's facilities is lagging behind the increase in workers and working population of the capital and lags behind their needs. This lagging is especially heightened by the serious inadequacies in the work of the Moscow utilities. Precisely because of these inadequacies, gaps have appeared in our tram network, [there have been] housing shortfalls, poor results in road construction and in underground work, unsatisfactory sanitary conditions in the city, etc."[4] In response to these problems, the Plenum adopted a program for massive reconstruction of Moscow, that in three years was supposed to provide new housing for 500,000 people. In addition, the plan was to build enough new cafeterias, cafes, laundries, and day-care and nursery facilities to accommodate the new population.[5] However, in the year and a half following the Plenum, the city's population increased by almost a million, making the plans immediately obsolete. The 1935 General Plan, which envisioned a city of 5 million by 1945 and set that as the city's permanent limit, did much better than its predecessor in providing for the population of the city, since population growth was so much slower and steadier in the Second and Third FYPs. Whereas 1930, 1931, and 1932 saw more than 500,000 migrants settle annually in Moscow, from 1 January 1933 to 1 January 1939, the population increase was only about one-half million, from 3.6 to just over 4.1 million.[6]

The absence of any plan prior to June 1931, and then the failure of the first citywide plan to resolve the problems caused by Moscow's explosive population increase during the First FYP, invariably forced the factory administration to take an active role in providing housing for its workers. Otherwise, it could not hope to successfully recruit workers, halt labor turnover, and train the new recruits, that is, put together a reliable work force. The significance of the enterprise in housing construction during the First FYP can be quantified. For Moscow as a whole, 3,696 new apartment buildings were constructed, and 206 existing buildings were considerably expanded. The municipal government (city and *raion* soviets) built only 290 of these, RZhSKT (Workers' Housing Construction Cooperative Trust) built 197, and private construction accounted for 1,105. On the other hand, enterprises and institutions (hospitals, universities, offices) built 2,310, accounting for almost 60 percent of the total.[7]

In the PR during the First FYP, 354 new apartment buildings were completed, but there is no information on how many of these were built by enterprises.[8] Anecdotal evidence suggests that the enterprises, first among them SiM and ZiS, were heavily involved in this construction.

In 1926–27, prior to the First FYP, construction began on four new four- to six- story apartment buildings at Dangauerovka, and at the Rogozhskii Poselok, and along Vorontsovskaia Ulitsa.[9] (See map 4.) At about the same time, new construction began on the Dubrovka housing project at the Peasant Gate Square, just to the east of the Dinamo plant, south of SiM and north of AMO. According to Lapitskaia, who published a history of the Trekhgornaia Manufaktura Moscow textile plant based on the Gor'kii interviews, the Dubrovka housing project in the PR was typical of new workers' housing in that it provided, on average, 5.5–6 cubic meters per person. Poletaev, writing much later, mentioned it as well.[10] According to the encyclopedia, between 1925 and 1928, twenty-five new five-story apartment buildings were constructed there.[11]

Both Dubrovka and Dangauerovka would serve as models of workers' settlements, and photos of the latter appeared in Soviet publications during the 1930s.[12] Far from serving as a model, however, these communal apartments were made available only to the established workers during the 1920s, and new rooms were held in reserve for shock workers during the First FYP. As noted in chapter 3, two hundred shock workers were given new rooms at these settlements in late 1930, while over eight hundred more were waiting in line. In fact, most peasants could only dream of living in permanent communal apartments such as these when they first arrived in Moscow, as the vast majority were housed in factory barracks, often in wretched conditions. Gradually during the 1930s and then again after the Second World War, such communal apartments became typical for Moscow factory workers.

Peasant-migrants coming to SiM, as I have noted, were housed in barracks constructed by SiM at Novogireevo, Sokolinaia Gora, Reutogo, and Sortirovochnaia. Whereas the apartment housing at Dubrovka and Dangauerovka was relatively close to the plant, the new barracks went up on the far eastern edge of Moscow or beyond the city limits, making it hard and time-consuming to get to work, given the inadequate transportation network.

According to one archival document, 1,500 peasants that SiM had recruited in 1931 in so-called organized recruitment were housed in barracks at Sokolinaia Gora, which had no running water, no means for boiling water, and almost no electricity. Sokolinaia Gora was the name of a hill at the eastern edge of settled Moscow. The forest beyond was soon converted into the "Stalin Park of Culture and Rest," which became the Izmailogo Park. (See map 4.) Four new barracks were built there in June–December 1931 to house SiM's peasant recruits, and then two more new barracks were completed early in 1932.[13]

In March 1932, reporters from *Martenovka* and the journal "Culture and Lifestyle" *(Kul'tura i Byt)* wrote a scathing account of conditions at the SiM barracks at Sokolinaia Gora (*Martenovka*, 30 March 1932, p. 4). Almost a year later, on 2 February 1933, a front-page article noted that there was hardly any heat for the barracks at Sokolinaia Gora, a complaint continued on 20 October 1933 (p. 4). Nor were conditions much better at the other SiM barracks at Sortirovochnaia, Reutov, and Novogireevo, place names that trace an arc to the east of the factory along the Shosse Entuziastov (see map 4). In these districts, permanent communal apartment buildings, *kommunal'ki*, gradually replaced the barracks during the Second and Third FYPs. According to a 1939 trade union report 2,500 SiM workers and their families out of a total of 9,642 still lived in what were called "dormitories," or glorified barracks (*Martenovka*, 24 May 1939) at these four locations. The factory's goal was to transfer them into rooms (i.e., separate rooms in a communal apartment), and the report noted approvingly that eighty families had been moved to a new apaprtment building on Kuskova on May 1, and that many others would soon move into new seven-floor apartment buildings on the Shosse Entuziastov.[14]

The 26 February 1932 edition of *Martenovka,* which devoted the whole of page 4 to problems of housing SiM workers, showed clearly that there had been a transfer of authority for providing housing from municipal institutions to the enterprises. SiM was supposed to build six new buildings in 1932 to house workers. The factory had already prepared the blueprints, but Mosgorplan (Moscow City Planning) had still not ratified them. This put the factory in a difficult position for procuring construction materials and for gathering the building, because in a month the construction season would begin. The buildings would be run by the workers' cooperative, RZhSKT, with workers paying shares, which ranged from five to one hundred rubles, depending on the number of family members and on the size of the family's wage packet. Evidently the egalitarian impulse had not been entirely extinguished.

Municipal responsibility for housing was still a factor in the district. The PR *raisoviet* was building communal apartments in 1932 on Bol'shaia Kommunisticheskaia Ulitsa. One SiM worker suggested that it should assign 450 apartment units to SiM workers. He complained that 400 FZU trainees at SiM were without housing, and the article suggested that the *raisoviet* should build a temporary dormitory for them.[15] In a letter to the editor, a woman working at SiM complained about three new buildings that were being constructed for SiM workers. Apparently the designers had "forgotten" about building communal showers, kitchens, rooms for day care and kindergarten, and even bathrooms in these buildings.[16] Obviously, such buildings were virtually uninhabitable, but under the circumstances of the housing crisis, people quickly moved in anyhow.

At AMO-ZiS, during the Second and Third FYPs, conditions were similar. On 1 January 1932, ZiS housing covered 4,434 square meters and served only 660 occupants. By 1 January 1939, factory housing covered 87,000 square meters and served 19,740 occupants. The factory built very little housing for its workers until the last year of the First FYP and in the Second and Third FYPs. The plant constructed apartments along Avtozavodskaia and Velozavodskaia Streets and in the Kolomenskii settlement, but still could not keep pace with the rapid growth in the number of workers at the factory. As a result, there were fewer cubic meters per person in 1939 than before the First FYP began.[17]

As Kuznetsov's memoir explained, the second reconstruction of the plant, undertaken in 1933, required appropriating 200 hectares of adjacent land at the expense of other enterprises and of existing workers' housing.

These were demolished, so that new shops could be built for ZiS, and according to Kuznetsov, some ten thousand workers had to be resettled into new apartments, some of which were to the east of the plant and others to the south, across the river in Kolomonskoe.[18] In April 1936, the ten city districts were divided into twenty-three, and the PR was divided into three districts. The new PR ran north-south along the river and was dominated by ZiS and its housing. SiM fell in the new Pervomaiskii Raion. (See map 3.)

Thus, each factory was left to improvise, negotiating with the *raisoviet* or the Moscow Soviet for space, materials, and funds, and taking over the task since these municipal authorities could not meet the demand for housing and were not directly concerned with the situation of the factory workers. Red Directors like Stepanov and Likhachev used their pull in economic administration or established connections with construction trusts, by-passing municipal authorities and procuring the construction materials and workers to build the housing, stores, and perhaps even schools for their workers. This pattern of factory responsibility for housing workers became well established during the First FYP.

The First FYP was thus a time of improvisation in housing, which for most workers translated into living in barracks or in overcrowded communal apartments, the *kommunal'ka*. These had bath and kitchen facilities that were shared by an entire floor, while a family of four was fortunate to dwell in a single room. Frequently the room was subdivided by curtains or a furniture partition to make a space for kin or fellow villagers or even strangers. This communal existence, typified by the barrack, the dormitory, and the *kommunal'ka*, is an important factor, perhaps the foundation, in Alexander Zinoviev's theory that Soviet communism was merely an urban variant on Russian peasant communalism of the *mir*. (This idea will be considered further below, but then rejected in favor of a theory of an emerging urban proto-community.)

Matters were no different with transportation for factory workers and other inhabitants of the factory communities of Moscow during the First FYP. As it underwent massive construction and reconstruction, entire sections of the PR were really nothing more than muddy construction pits. There were few paved roads, and trams and horse-drawn cabs were the major means of transportation within the *raion*, as they were throughout the city.

The inadequacy of transportation within the PR and the SiM settlements that spread into the Stalin District (Stalinskii Raion) was graphically illustrated by several incidents in 1934, concerning the Novogireevo project, where the SiM *fabzavkom* and *partkom* had recently built nine new apartment buildings housing 940 people, of whom 700 worked in the plant. The workers were apparently satisfied with these new apartments, which were larger, brighter, and cleaner than their previous homes. However, they had to walk two and a half kilometers to the tram stop for transportation to the plant. One kilometer went through woods, where it was muddy and dark. Hooligans gathered here and robbed the workers. On 20 November 1934 at 9:00 P.M., the best roller in the rolling steel shop and the winner of several premiums for his shock-work records, Comrade Fokin, had his new coat, suit, and boots stolen when walking through these woods.[19] This was the most egregious case affecting SiM workers, but transport from Sokolinaia Gora and Reutogo was not much better.

After the Fokin incident, five workers from SiM sent an open letter, published in *Martenovka,* to the plant director, Stepanov, calling attention to the lack of transportation to their settlement at Novogireevo. They complained that the idea of running a bus line to Novogireevo had already been proposed, but that nothing had happened. They claimed that it would require a directive from Stepanov to get action. They suggested a bus line from the Kuskovo Highway to their new settlement, which was, at the time beyond the city line, not so far from the old Sheremetev Kuskovo estate.[20]

The situation had not improved much, according to a letter to *Martenovka* in early 1935 that described living at Novogireevo "like living on an island." Later in 1935, the situation evidently still had not improved, because workers always walked through these woods in groups of ten for protection against hooligans. It was not until 1939 that *Martenovka* reported that a tram line had finally been completed out to Novogireevo.[21] From peasant barracks to permanent apartments, connected by tram to the city—such was the pattern of the three prewar FYPs in Moscow. Novogireevo was the last SiM settlement to achieve urban status.

The situation was similar at Sokolinaia Gora, another housing district for SiM workers in which barracks were thrown up in the First FYP and remained completely isolated because of a lack of public transportation. As *Martenovka* described it in 1932: "The Sokolinaia Gora district is completely removed not only from the factory, but also from cultured and enlightened society, where there are theaters and cinemas. The barracks are far away, and the lack of trams force the workers to stay in their barracks [when they are not at work]. Going to and from work, the workers spend more than an hour on the trip; [many also spend another hour going back] for lunch, leaving no time for relaxation."[22]

Not only was intradistrict transport poorly developed; it was also very thin. The PR as a whole was geographically and physically isolated from the rest of Moscow in unique ways. The two rivers, and the factories themselves, blocked access to the city's center. The PR remained unique in Moscow in its degree of isolation from adjoining city districts. The Zamoskvoretskii District to the west of the PR across the Moscow River, and the Baumanskii District to its north and west, the route to the Moscow city center, were inaccessible because bridges across the Iauza and Moscow Rivers for pedestrians and cabs hardly existed. As late as 1934, a Dinamo worker complained that to get into Moscow, the workers had to traverse the ZiS plant and cross by the bridge running from the plant into the city. He called on the party to consider building a new bridge.[23]

The isolation of the PR from the rest of the city was nothing new. It was symbolized in a famous incident during the February Revolution, the shooting of I. T. Astakhov, a steel worker who was leading a column of Guzhon workers across the Iauza bridge.[24] The workers had to cross the bridge to reach the city center, and army units from the nearby barracks blocked their way briefly at the bridge. AMO and Dinamo workers faced similar obstacles in trying to reach the city center when the Revolution began.[25]

This geographic isolation changed only during the later 1930s. Until then, access to the center of the city remained limited to two bridges crossing the Iauza and connecting the PR to the Baumanskii District (one railroad and one highway) and two others further south, crossing the Moscow River and connecting the PR to the Zamoskvoretskii District, the Novospasskii Bridge, constructed 1909–1912, and the Danilovskii Bridge.[26] In 1938, the two Ustinskii bridges were built, one above the other. The Bolshoi Ustinskii crossed the Moskva and linked the PR to the rest of the city via what was then known as the Kirov District and what had been the Zamoskvoretskii; the Malii Ustinskii crossed the Iauza River, connecting the PR to what was then the Krasnogvadeiskii District. The Novospasskii Bridge was also completely rebuilt with steel in 1938. This immediately made all of the PR accessible by car or bus and ended the isolation of the district.[27]

Some workers commuted to SiM from outside of the PR, although the means for commuting from other parts of the city were very limited. It was probably easier for peasant-workers commuting in from the villages in Moscow Province to the east of the city on the train that stopped right at SiM's door en route to the Kursk Railroad Station. This was an important, modern type of symbiosis between village and city, replacing the seasonal migrant worker with the daily commuter. But it is impossible to know how widespread this was during the 1930s. However, workers could not live on the western side of Moscow or in the city center and work at SiM, because there was no connection to other railway lines at the Kursk Station and there were no direct trams running from the factory district to the city center.

At the June 1931 Plenum, where the reconstruction of Moscow was first proposed, the party passed a resolution calling for the construction of an inner-city electric train line linking the Northern, October, and Kursk lines to the center of the city.[28] This may have helped commuters at SiM in the later 1930s, but more likely it was not until the Moscow metro was extended into this district and linked to these same train lines, during the Second World War, that they could realistically make the commute. Even then, on 1 January 1943, the opening of the metro station Avtozavodskaia meant that ZiS and Dinamo workers had immediate access to the rest of the city and, via the circle line opened in 1952, to all the city railroad stations. But that stop was several miles from SiM, and the metro did not come out to SiM until 1979. The station Ploshchad Il'icha, with direct access to the SiM plant, was opened in December 1979, as were the Avtomotornaia, Shosse Entusiastov, Perovo, and Novogireevo stations along the Kalininskaia Line, which connected these communities, the site of SiM settlements since the First FYP, to the factory. The Kalininskaia Line also connected the factory and these communities to the rest of the city and its metro at the final stop, Marksistskaia, adjoining the Taganskaia stop on the circle line, and also on the Zhdanovsko-Krasnopresnenskaia Line.[29] Finally, then, only in the 1980s, did the SiM factory workers of these eastern districts of the city have rapid access to work and to the city center and other sections of the city. By that time, however, the pattern of settlement of the factory's work force was much more dispersed throughout the city (see map 5).

The June 1931 plenum also resolved to build a new circular tram line along the Kamer-Kollezhskii Val, thus linking the city's *raiony,* one to the other, along a northern route.[30] This, too, however, would have only limited use for workers traveling to SiM from other areas of the city, because it would bring them in a wide arc and deposit them well east of the factory. Until paved roads and bridges were completed in the PR in the late 1930s, and until ZiS manufactured the first Soviet buses, workers would have to rely on their feet and on the tram network to get to work, and they remained largely cut off from the rest of the city.

Thus, for SiM, Dinamo, and ZiS workers, and also for many of the construction workers who built more than one dozen new factories in the PR during the First FYP and then stayed to work in these factories, the PR was more like a *kotlovan,* a "foundation pit," than a city during the First FYP.[31] The influx of a new peasant-migrant population would strain every aspect of the district's infrastructure. While we might imagine that longtime residents were deeply bitter about this disruption of their community life and the continuing isolation of the district from the rest of the city, whether the peasant migrant workers were similarly dissatisfied is not clear. They had no urban experience with which to compare it.

The PR may have been a high-tech zone in terms of the designs for its factories, but it was more like a frontier city springing up on the Siberian steppe for those who had to live there amidst the construction sites and the foundation pits. Whether they were living in the Dubrovka, Dangauerova, Vorontsovskai Ulitsa, or Rogozhskii Poselok, all built during the mid to late 1920s in what soon became the PR, or in the new barracks that were quickly thrown up during the First FYP farther to the east in the PR and in the Stalin District, where most of the peasant-recruits were housed, SiM workers were living in a second Moscow, a peripheral or industrial Moscow, not to be confused with administrative, central Moscow.

This new industrial Moscow of the PR was not, however, an overgrown peasant village as the area had been prior to 1929. The Guzhon factory and Dinamo had been built at a gateway and monastery where medieval fortifications had been erected against the Tartars, and the AMO plant was constructed in the woods along the Moscow River known as the Tiufelevaia Roshcha at the Spaskii Gateway; but these were merely place-names by the 1920s, as the gateways and the woods had long since disappeared and only the derelict monastery remained.[32] During the First FYP, the remaining open space in the PR was under construction, but by the later 1930s, it was mostly under buildings, roads, or parks.

More important, whereas the Rogozhsko-Simonovskii District, prior to 1917, had been inhabited primarily by the "fourth estate," that is, peasants living in the city with work passes, by the 1930s, peasant-migrants were settling in the city permanently. The Passport Act of December 1932 was not the same as the work-pass required for peasant *otkhodniki* under serfdom and until 1905. The act gave permanent urban status to those peasants who had migrated to work in Moscow prior to December 1932, that is, a passport and a living permit (*propusk*) for a dwelling space.[33] After the hiatus of 1933, when some population was driven out of the city (who, it would appear, were the most recent peasant arrivals not entitled to the passport and perhaps did not have full-time work), the in-migrants of 1934–41 found obtaining a passport fairly routine if they had employment. The Passport Act was initially a means of restraining peasant migration into the cities during the famine, and after that, primarily a means of conferring Soviet "citizenship" status, that is, the right to urban dwelling, on the peasant-migrant. The tsarist passport system was, by contrast, a means of perpetuating the peasant status of urban factory workers who may already have been second-generation city dwellers. The parallels between the two types of legal restrictions have long been emphasized, but the differences were at least as significant.

One might object that the barracks set up on the outskirts of the PR and the Stalin District during the First FYP seemed to promise the same, transitory existence for the 1930s as that of the peasant-migrant who had populated the Rogozhsko-Simonovskii Districts in imperial times. In the flux or "quicksand society" of the First FYP, it certainly looked that way. That flux, however, during the 1930s, was a question of the settling-in of the new inhabitants. They were moving, in waves, from the barracks to the new permanent apartment housing built during the Second and Third FYPs. The barracks were a revolving door, not because of turnover, where peasant-migrants were headed back to the village, but because they were finding and occupying permanent apartments just as rapidly as they could. Although the apartments were crowded, they were better than the barracks.

Even if the inhabitants of the *kommunal'ka* had to share bath and kitchen with up to a hundred coresidents, and even if their room was partitioned, simply obtaining it meant a decision to settle permanently in the city. It also usually signified the desire to raise a family in the city, since it was families who typically applied for and received rooms in the communal apartments. The fact that a considerable number of families endured barrack life for a year or more before moving to a *kommunal'ka* testified to their determination to stay in the city.

This marked a fundamental break from the historical pattern of peasant migration, ending the "bird of passage" mentality of the subaltern Russian peasant-migrant workers. Previously the peasant-migrant had lived with only one foot in the new urban world, since he expected to return to the village. Michael Piore defined transcontinental migrants to America as "birds of passage," but Mikhail Tomskii meant the same thing when, at the 1926 Seventh Trade Union Congress he called the Russian peasant-migrants "guest workers."[34] The Stalin regime continued in that tradition, but used more pejorative labels, in calling the peasant-migrants "self-seekers," "grabbers," "rolling stones," and unleashing the "class struggle" against them. The irony, however, was that the regime was unleashing the class struggle just when the peasant-migrant was, at last, settling in the city and abandoning the idea of returning to the village.

In part, of course, that was because collectivization was so dramatically transforming the village. In part it was because of the sudden wide availability of construction and factory jobs which were, themselves, becoming permanent. Thus, instead of the split family and the rural-urban economic symbiosis of agriculture and wage labor in industry, either husband, wife, and children were all migrating together and settling in Moscow, or unmarried and mostly young peasant men and women migrated to Moscow and then married in Moscow, establishing their family life in the city. The historical confusion over *otkhod* during the First FYP, which reflects the regime's inability to distinguish at the time between seasonal and permanent migrants, is also a reflection of this fundamental transition (see chapter 3). *Otkhod* meant seasonal and permanent rural-urban migration. During the First FYP both were encouraged, but the migration that was expected to be seasonal was instead becoming permanent.

The transition from seasonal migration and seasonal factory work to permanent city life and full-time factory work was symbolized in two roughly concurrent events. First, most peasant-migrants began wage employment with a seasonal or permanent stint in what were called "conveyer" jobs, that is, in mining, forestry, and especially in construction. Construction became year-round work during the First FYP only because of the industrialization drive, and even then, it still required workers to migrate from site to site, perpetuating peasant migratory traditions. As the new and reconstructed factories went "on-line" *(pusk),* typically toward the end of the First FYP when construction work was completed, most of these peasant-migrant workers would become full-time and permanent production workers in the new factories which they had just built. Second, the official celebration of the auto factory going on-line, and Likhachev's use of the metaphor "sewing the coat around the button" on 1 October 1931, encapsulated the transformation of the entire economy and the work lives of millions of peasants who were becoming full-time factory workers. The *pusk* of the Moscow auto plant on that day, celebrated with Ordzhonikidze and the renaming of the AMO plant as ZiS, the Stalin Auto Plant, thus marked an important and symbolic moment for the regime, for the factory, and for the new workers and especially the former peasants.[35]

The Factory as a Food Distribution Center

After housing and transportation, the supply of food was the single most important variable limiting the pace of urbanization, and hence also of industrialization. Like housing, food supply came to be assumed, by default, primarily as the responsibility of each enterprise. As food became increasingly scarce in cities and in the countryside in the latter part of the First FYP, culminating with the devastating famine of 1932–33, the social feeding network *(set' obshchestvennogo pitania)* became not merely a convenience, but a critical resource for the survival of workers and their families. Access to the factory food supply network, for some peasant-migrants, meant the difference between life and death. The passport law of December 1932, which halted in-migration from the countryside and forced some recent arrivals to Moscow to return to the villages, thus condemned many would-be migrants from desperate rural areas to starvation, since they could find no food on the destitute *kolkhozy* or in neighboring villages or towns.

Until July 1930 there was not a single cafeteria or buffet at SiM. Workers apparently brought their own lunch with them, but about fifteen hundred went to the cafeteria at the Rogozhskii Market, crossing over the railroad tracks and then waiting in long lines. Apparently the cafeteria was dirty, and the workers called it the Obzhorka, the "Gluttony."[36] According to an archival document, in July 1930 this market cafeteria was converted into a closed SiM factory cafeteria, available only to factory workers, and each factory shop was now instructed to open its own buffet. Whereas SiM had only one cafeteria for its ten thousand workers in 1930—and workers had to wait forty-five minutes in line and then eat their lunch standing—by 1932, the plant had built a new kitchen that prepared the food for eight cafeterias, including one dietetic cafeteria, and twenty buffets.[37]

One source attributes the decision to install factory kitchens, cafeterias, and buffets to the party leadership.[38] That is clearly not what happened. The document claims that the Sixteenth Party Congress in June 1930 already recognized that the distribution of consumer goods and food for most workers was grossly inadequate. While it is true that these supply problems were mentioned at that congress, the resolutions adopted clearly show that the leadership did not make this issue a party priority. Rather, the congress shifted the responsibility to the trade unions, who were blamed for these problems.[39] Party leaders, in June 1930 and after, did not anticipate the ways in which enterprises would take on organization of factory kitchens and "closed stores" for distribution of food supplies.

Opening new cafeterias and buffets at SiM was no guarantee that the food was edible or the service efficient. There were frequent complaints about the quality of the food and the chefs who prepared it. In 1932, a *Martenovka* article exposed "fake cooks." In 1934 in the rolling steel shop, workers complained that they were wasting all their lunch break waiting in line, only to receive kasha every day, while the open hearth workers complained about "black eyes" in their soup.[40] Nonetheless, with famine stalking the countryside in the winter of 1932–33, and with a severe deficit of food supplies in the cities that year, the SiM cafeterias and buffets[41] offered incomparably better access to food than other urban inhabitants had. The cooperative and municipal network of food stores and cafeterias that served the Moscow public had longer lines and much less food.

The development of cafeterias and buffets at AMO-ZiS followed a similar pattern. Until 1929, there had been a single cafeteria, which was first located in the barracks and then was moved to the basement of the administration building. It could serve relatively few workers. In the First FYP, a new central cafeteria was built, which was eventually capable of serving nine thousand people daily. After that, cafeterias were built in four shops, and buffets were opened in ten. Toward the end of the Second FYP, a *kombinat* was established to handle food preparation at the AMO-ZiS plant. By 1940, the factory had twelve large cafeterias and fifty buffets, employing 1,350 people. This was the equivalent of a mid-sized enterprise—a food factory within an automobile factory—that was feeding a substantial portion of the PR. The head chef, K. G. Karavaev, was known and respected in the plant.[42]

Cafeterias and buffets were not the only food services that the factory provided for its workers. SiM established a special closed grocery store and ensured its own supply of fruits and vegetables by creating its own vegetable garden and by taking control of collective farms and "attaching them" to the plant. This was sanctioned, indeed encouraged, from above: "The party directive that each factory set up its own food shop, with its own food product base *[prodovol'stvennaia baza]* found a response in the worker collective at SiM. In Reutov, twelve kilometers from Moscow, the first SiM vegetable garden was established. SiM workers put in 7,000 work days there. . . . Thus the basis for an independent food product base was established. At the beginning of 1932, SiM was *given the sovkhoz, Moscow Vegetable Trust*. . . . All of 1932 was dominated by the struggles for widening the food product base, for rabbit breeding, for fishing, for milk firms, for pig breeding, etc."[43]

Factories not only were "given" state farms (*sovkhozy*) in this way, but they were also encouraged to adopt collective farms (*kolkhozy*) under so-called *sheftsvo* arrangements, putatively to provide them with extra workers in peak periods such as sowing and harvesting and with skilled mechanics who knew how to repair tractors and other machinery. However, the factories, which were supposed to be repaid in produce, took so much that they seemed to be plundering their attached farms.[44]

For example, in the contract establishing SiM *shefstvo* over the Mozhaiskii District in Moscow Province, the peasants in several *kolkhozy* were obligated to set aside thirty hectares for gardening for SiM and to provide the factory with 16,500 poods of cabbage, 3,000 poods of table beets, 7,300 poods of carrots, 3,000 poods of cucumbers, 33,000 poods of potatoes, 100,000 poods of lettuce, 800,000 poods of tomatoes, etc.[45] The contract even stipulated how many hectares were to be allocated for each crop. Contractualization thus spread from factory to *kolkhoz*, and the factory became not only a community organizer but also a *kolkhoz* organizer.

Similarly, early in 1933, the ORS (department of workers' supply) at AMO-ZiS was given direct control over five state farms that provided cattle, fowl, rabbits, vegetables, and fruits for the factory workers. The Vas'kino state farm, for example, set aside 5,000 hectares of land for vegetables, as well as cattle and rabbits for the AMO-ZiS factory workers. As the factory history accurately describes this, "The *sovkhoz* was converted into a solid food product base for the factory."[46] Apparently the idea of setting up "food product bases" for factories originated at a conference held at SiM. It was reported in *Pravda* and then spread to other large factories throughout the USSR.[47] The factory thus became a procurement agency.

The AMO-ZiS worker, Salov, who founded the first shock brigade in the plant, and who met Gor'kii and was a founder of the writers' circle at AMO, described how the plant began to collect grain procurements (*zagotovki*) both from *sovkhozy* and *kolkhozy* directly for its own ZRKs (closed workers' co-operatives).[48] The factory thus relieved the state of one of its most difficult tasks vis-à-vis the peasantry and at the same time guaranteed that food reached urban factory workers first.[49] In his brochure, *The Organization of Workers' Supply,* Salov also described how problems of corruption and em-bezzlement in the ZRK led to its elimination. The work of the ZRK was re-viewed at AMO-ZiS following an ordinance of the Central Committee and the Council of Peoples' Commissars dated 4 December 1932, establishing the ORS (Department of Workers' Supplies). There was a complete purge of ZRK employees. The ZRK staff of 350 was found to have included 48 *byvshchii* (NEPmen, that is, petty bourgeoisie, or tsarist officials), who al-legedly were cheating workers and providing poor service. Salov blamed these "former" elements even for the long lines at the ZRKs.[50]

The problem, however, was not merely with the ZRK staff. Of the 22,000 workers and family members who were "attached" to and served by the ZRKs at AMO-ZiS, fully 9,125 were "freeloaders" (*prikhlebately*) who no longer worked at the factory. Many of these, Salov claimed, had been construction workers at the plant in 1929 and 1930. Plant reconstruction was completed on 1 October 1931, and most of these workers had moved on to other con-struction projects. However, they were still using AMO-ZiS facilities and stores.[51] They were thus purged from the ranks of employees on the lists in the new ORS, which incorporated ten stores, ten grocery booths, a depart-ment store, two stores for industrial consumer goods, and others.[52]

While food was the most important commodity, it was not the only type of consumer good that was falling under the control of the factory distribu-tion network at this time. In October 1930, by decree of Kaganovich, then party first secretary of Moscow, SiM took over Mostorg Univermag No. 20, a department store in the PR. It became a closed store, only serving SiM work-ers and their families. The closed distribution system stipulated that: "To re-ceive goods, each worker and white-collar worker of our factory receives from his shop or division a special book, which lists his/her last name, salary, and number of family members." This entitled the family to purchase goods at the closed stores. For deficit goods, special coupons (*talony*) were issued to workers through the workplace. In all, the store served 43,000 people.[53]

A flourishing illegal trade in these booklets and coupons sprang up at SiM, just as it had at ZiS. A headline on page 4 of *Martenovka* on 3 September 1930, "The Distribution Book Cannot Be in the Hands of the Class Enemy: Strengthen Workers' Control Over the Activity of the Cooperative; Repress the Speculators and Wreckers; Liquidate Speculation in Coop-Books and *Talony*," indicated that the problem was widespread. In addition, the article mentioned that the nephew of the chef was carrying factory food home illegally, and the person in charge of one of the buffets was cheating on the quantity he served to each worker at lunch and absconding with the rest in order to sell it outside the plant. Finally, the article noted, service at the SiM ZRK was poor, because it was supposed to serve 8,000 workers, but it only employed 160 people.

Already by the end of 1930, the closed distribution network was the predominant form of consumer goods distribution in the PR, but it still did not meet the needs of all the workers, let alone of the rest of the community. This was made clear by Gaidul', the *raikom* party secretary, at the Fourth Party Conference at SiM held late in December 1930. He noted that in the *raion*, nineteen closed distribution stores served 93,000 people, while the remaining nine (presumably open distribution stores) served 64,000 people, including many workers who had no access in their plants yet to closed distribution stores.[54] What these figures do not show is that inventory was generally much larger at the closed distribution stores than at the open stores in the community. The greater the store's inventory, the less time spent and wasted standing in line. In addition, the special advance ordering system (*zakaz*) and better service offered by the closed stores greatly reduced time in line. This was no small advantage.

Thus, what was essentially a two-tiered system of consumer product distribution went into effect. It had evolved spontaneously, largely by factory initiative, and was then endorsed, after the fact, by the regime. The endorsement, when it came, attempted to organize the factory food distribution system in a new all-union system. A resolution of the Party Central Committee and the Council of Peoples' Commissars, "On Widening the Rights of Plant Administrations in the Matter of Supplies for the Workers, and on Improving the Card System," was passed on 4 December 1932. It stipulated four measures. First, for "group I enterprises," the ZRK were to be put directly under the control of the plant administration, which was to incorporate them into a new "division of supplies for workers" (ORS). Second, for other enterprises in large-scale industry and railroads, the ZRK was to remain a consumers' coop, but the enterprise director was to sit on its board of directors. Third, a high-level commission including Kaganovich, Mikoian, Piatakov, Shvernik, and three others, was to report to the Council of Peoples' Commissars within three months with a plan that would outline how to supply those enterprises without any ZRK with foodstuffs. Fourth, the procedure for issuing books and coupons was to be tightened up.[55]

Elaborating on this fourth point, the resolution explained that the books and coupons were to be issued only to workers and their families, by name and number, in order to prevent misuse. They were to be issued by the accounting office in charge of wages and distributed by the cashier in each shop. If a worker was dismissed or left an enterprise, they were to be returned to this cashier. Finally, it stipulated that speculation in these items would result in criminal prosecution. A new type of coupon was to be issued on 1 January 1933.[56]

Whatever the myriad problems and inefficiencies of the system, by the end of the First FYP, SiM workers ate their lunch at the factory cafeteria, had their morning coffee or tea (if there was any) at the shop buffet, and frequently purchased food from the same buffet to take home for dinner. Furthermore, the worker purchased food for her family at the factory ZRK, and then after 1932 at the factory ORS. Whereas in America this type of company store generally had a poorer selection and higher prices than in other communities, in Moscow they had a greater selection of goods and at the same or lower prices than the often rancid state groceries, or "fruit and vegetable stores," which were open to the public at large. They had much lower prices than the peasant markets that were legalized in May 1932.[57] Most significant, with the order department and closed shops, factory workers did not have to waste hours in line every week to get food. They could order in advance and pick up their food at the factory.

The Factory as Cultural Center

Soviet factories were almost always short of funds and almost always lagging behind the workers' demand for facilities, not only for housing, transport, and food, but also for health care, sports, and cultural facilities. The situation was particularly acute in the First FYP, but it improved in the Second and Third FYPs. SiM, however, had established an impressive record as a center for health care even prior to the FYP, which it would build on during the 1930s.

Under Guzhon there had been only one doctor's assistant *(fel'dsher)* at the plant.[58] In the mid-1920s, the first Soviet factory polyclinic was organized at SiM.[59] Then, a network of smaller clinics or first-aid stations *(zdravpunkty)* was established, serving the various shops of the plant. Despite its leading role in the 1920s, the medical care at SiM was judged to be inadequate for the factory collective in November 1934, according to an article in *Martenovka*. The article praised the medical staff of the polyclinic for going out to Sokolinaia Gora or Novogireevo to provide medical care for workers in their barracks. But it noted that the clinic lacked the basic medical supplies needed to treat many illnesses and that sick people had to travel to other medical clinics, such as at Solianka or Petrovka, to get medicine. The article noted that the journey was likely to make the patient sicker.[60]

According to *Martenovka*, the source of the problem was a lack of space at the polyclinic to store the necessary medicine. Two or three doctors worked in one office, also for lack of space. The article also complained that the polyclinic was not included in the budget of the factory administration. At Dinamo, GPZ-1, and AMO-ZiS, the polyclinics were included in the administration's budget and were in much better shape. ZiS was building a new 2.5-million-ruble polyclinic.[61] Soon after this article, the SiM administration absorbed the polyclinic's budget from the municipal authorities, just as it absorbed housing and even transport budgets from municipal administration.

By 1959, to look far beyond the First FYP, the SiM polyclinic had evolved into a medical-sanitary section (*medsanchast'*) with six *zdravpunkty* and thirty-five cots. It also administered a central medical laboratory at the plant, a division for tuberculosis, a dentistry division, and a dispensary with one hundred cots at Kuchina.[62]

The AMO-ZiS plant also became a medical center, not only for its workers, but for the community. At AMO, in the aftermath of the Revolution, there was a single *fel'dsher*, A. I. Ivanov, who was both skilled and conscientious. Eventually he became a full doctor. In 1929, a factory polyclinic was built, but it soon proved to be inadequate. The clinic was expanded only in 1940, and a medical *kombinat* was established at the plant, with a surgery division, an X-ray division, a therapeutic division, a physical-therapy division, and others. Four laboratories were established at the plant, and a filial of the medical *kombinat* was opened in the workers' district at Kozhukhov. *Zdravpunkty* were set up in all the important shops. The surgeon E. N. Dmitriev and the therapist S. M. Etingon became well known in the plant and Ivanov received the Order of Lenin.[63]

Another essential service that factories had to provide as they began to employ more and more female workers in the First FYP and throughout the decade, was crèche (*iasli*) and day-care (*detsad*) facilities. At SiM there were *iasli* for infants and *detsady* for young children, and the fee that parents paid for enrolling their children was graduated according to income.[64] On 4 June 1936, Director Stepanov proudly announced that the administration, together with the trade-union committee, had set up a camp for workers' children at Mozhaiska. Three hundred children were already at the camp, and Stepanov urged that the plant needed to use its funds to set up more *iasli* and *detsady* so that the wives of workers and ITR could be recruited and become cadre workers in the factory. He suggested that the plant set up a separate department to administer the various programs for children.[65]

At AMO-ZiS by 1940 there were 2,000 available places for infants and young children at the factory crèches and kindergartens. This must have still been grossly inadequate for a work force of 39,000, but it marked a big improvement over the First FYP. For schoolchildren, there were young pioneer camps that served thousands, and the plant built a "children's city" in the nearby village of Miachkovo.[66] The factory thus assumed a large part of the responsibility for child care until the child reached seven years and began schooling.

Beyond health care and day care, virtually all other essential services in the life of the workers' family, including insurance, workers' compensation, rest homes, and vacation resorts with excursions, were provided by the factory, primarily through the activity of the plant trade-union committee, the *fabzavkom*. The Soviet factory thus became a cradle-to-grave institution, fulfilling (even if far from adequately or in a timely way) the promise of socialism to provide all its citizens (at least urban citizens) with a social safety net and a minimum standard of welfare. This was the workers' expectation, and it became the factory's responsibility.[67]

I would suggest, however, that the factory's Red Director and management, and its union and party committees, went beyond these social welfare functions and began to assume the role of "community organizers." Furthermore, they did so in a way that fundamentally and permanently transformed the semirural and semipeasant aspects of all Russian cities, including even Moscow, with its long-term reputation as the peasant-city or overgrown village. The factory provided the foundations, not merely the foundation pit or *kotlovan,* for a new urban community. It provided housing for the unified family that broke the decades-long practice of peasant seasonal migration and the split family. It provided remedial primary and secondary education, vocational training, and higher education for some in the FZU and night schools. It became the center of culture, sports, and organized leisure in the community, the foundation for a new proletarian lifestyle. While the labor aristocracy of imperial Russia and the established workers of the 1920s had created their own urban lifestyle, this was the first time in the history of Russia and the Soviet Union that a mass, urban, proletarian lifestyle or culture was taking shape—urban protocommunity.[68] A sketch of the leisure activities of the emerging protocommunity is suggested by the discussion of factory clubs, palaces of culture, writers' circles, and sports.

The Astakhov Club at SiM, named in honor of the victim from the February Revolution, met in an obsolete building during NEP while the administration wrangled over funds for constructing a new one. As early as 1927, there were suggestions to relocate the Astakhov Club, and an architectural plan for a three-story building was drawn up. Nothing came of these plans, however. On 15 May 1930, *Martenovka* ran an article, "Enough Chatter: We Demand the Rapid Construction of a New Club Building" (p. 4). It noted that only 300,000 rubles had been allocated, while to complete construction of a new building would require 1.1 million rubles. On 28 May 1930, *Martenovka* insisted that the designs for the new factory club had to be completed by 5 June 1930 and that construction had to be completed by 1 July 1931 (p. 1).

Almost a year after the building was supposed to have been completed, *Martenovka* published an indignant letter from a dozen old-timers at SiM (2 June 1932, p. 4). They implored and convinced the presidium of VTsSPS, convening at that time, to put the Astakhov Club on the agenda. The workers demanded to know where the funding and resources for constructing the factory club would come from. The twelve signed their names and the year in which each had come to work at the Guzhon plant.

On 9 July 1932, workers from SiM sent a letter to Shvernik, the head of VTsSPS; to Tevosian, the head of Spetstal'; and to Bulganin, head of the Moscow Soviet, asking why the club was still not completed after twenty-three months of construction (p. 3). The building was finally finished shortly thereafter, because shock workers and Komsomol worked voluntarily as construction workers on weekends and during the workweek, after work hours.[69] That was much more rapid, but also more amateurish than the showcase Palace of Culture at ZiS.

The workers at AMO-ZiS lacked adequate facilities for their club until the Palace of Culture was built in 1931–37. The Vesnin brothers designed it—the last constructivist building to be erected in the Soviet Union, and one of the most successful. It became a favorite for tours of foreign trade unionists and for speeches.[70] Furthermore, it functioned not merely as the new center for the factory club, but as a new center for cinema and theater and much else of interest to the broader working class community of the PR.

Few other Soviet factories could boast such facilities by the end of the Second FYP, and in fact, the Palace of Culture was unique. Construction of these new buildings for the workers' clubs at SiM and AMO-ZiS, even if only very belatedly, showed that these were two of the most important enterprises and of course, they were in the capital city. Furthermore, it showed that the directors, Stepanov and Likhachev, had the prestige and the influence that was needed to get the funding for such projects.

The factory club became the first cultural and sporting center of the new urban protocommunity. It was a center for the worker-correspondents and editors to produce the factory newspaper and wall-papers. It was also the center for newly organized literary circles, Val'tsovka at SiM and Vagranka at

AMO-ZiS. During the First FYP, the well-known writers Leonid Leonov, Aleksandr Bezymenskii, Viktor Gusev, and Nikolai Ognev attended meetings of Vagranka.[71] The Val'tsovka circle included Mikhailov, Shipilin, Shvedov, Pandul, Krutianskii, Gudkov, Tanatov, Iasenev, and others.[72] From these circles emerged the editors for the factory newspapers, *Martenovka* (Shipilin and Tanatov), and *Dognat' i Peregnat'*, and also the committees in these factories organized for writing the "history of plants and factories" project. Maxim Gor'kii headed this project and was frequently at the two plants. (See bibliographical essay.)

Gor'kii came to the ZiS plant on 1 June 1928 to meet with the worker-correspondents, including A. P. Salov. Soon afterward, on 2 October 1928, *Vagranka* was first issued, the mass-circulation newspaper at AMO. (On 1 January 1932, it was renamed *Dognat' i Peregnat'*, "Catch Up to and Surpass," and after the Nazi invasion, it was reissued as *Stalinets*.)[73] Two years later, in November 1930, Gor'kii was in Italy, where he met with touring Soviet shock workers on the cruise ship *Abkhazia,* and there he read Salov's manuscript for the novel *Rozhdenie Tsekha.*[74] This meeting, Gor'kii later noted, was important in his decision to return to Moscow in 1931 and in his determination to assemble teams of workers and writers to conduct interviews and collect memoirs in preparation for writing the history of the factories.

Writers' collectives played a major role in the cultural life of these factories, as did other forms of literary culture. TRAM, a "theater of working youth," was organized at AMO-ZiS in 1930. At the outset, it was merely a brigade of nine young people, but within two years it included 265 workers. TRAM performed in Leningrad and other cities.[75] Later, the factory opera staged versions of the classics of socialist realism, Ostrovskii's *How the Steel Was Tempered* and Sholokhov's *Quiet Don.* From the theater at AMO-ZiS, twenty-two performers eventually became professionals, and the factory theater itself became semiprofessional.[76] This was a type of fusion of "high" and "low" culture, of fusion of classical literary form with a folk-culture plot, signifying, perhaps, a new "middlebrow" culture.[77]

That does not mean, however, that "heroic workers" were being "forged," as Ostrovskii's novel suggested. Rather, attendance at TRAM productions showed that a mass, urban, proletarian culture was in the process of formation. The new middlebrow culture of the theater and cinema, was, by all accounts, highly popular among workers, as were the socialist realist novels themselves. So were "lowbrow" light films, or entertainment. So, too, were classical ballet, music, and professional theater, for which the workers had preferential access through ticket distribution in their factories under the *bron* or quota. It was the cinema, however, that was ideally suited to this new middlebrow culture, and the club at SiM and ZiS, particularly at the ZiS

Palace of Culture, provided cinema that was among the most widely attended in the city.

Popular culture meant, however, mass participation. Beyond amateur theater, operas, choirs, and reading circles, there was also mass worker participation in chess and sports such as football at the Astakhov Club at SiM. From such club activities emerged teams for football, hockey, basketball, and other sports. In 1938, the SiM football team, Metallurga, placed first among all trade-union teams and third overall in the USSR.[78] Competitions among factory sport clubs provided the foundation for the modern Soviet sport system, from the *spartakiada,* a sort of semiprofessional competition, to the fully professionalized clubs with their fans and all-union competitions. The all-union soccer league was organized during the 1930s based on these semi-professional factory clubs. Later, during the 1960s and 1970s, the club teams participated in international and Olympic competitions.[79]

The factory became a community organizer in a political respect as well. The factory administration, the *partkom* and the *zavkom,* organized frequent political meetings, lectures, and discussions at the factories. At both SiM and AMO-ZiS, meetings were held in the First FYP to organize MOPR (a voluntary organization that would lend assistance to the proletariat abroad); to discuss elections to the Supreme Soviet, the Moscow Soviet, and the *raion* soviets; and to discuss important political issues as well as issues of industrial output.

The prestige of the factory and the conscious identification of workers with the factory was enhanced by the visits of nationally famous political leaders such as Ordzhonikidze, and by cultural figures, such as Gor'kii and Krupskaia. Ordzhonikidze frequently spoke at AMO-ZiS on political themes and often came to discuss problems of production.[80] On 1 October 1931, when some of the first reconstruction was declared to have been completed, and when Likhachev gave his speech calling the reconstruction of the plant "sewing the coat to the button," Ordzhonikidze and Iaroslavskii also gave speeches. After 1937, when the new Palace of Culture was completed at AMO-ZiS, Krupskaia and Kalinin gave speeches there, while important foreign Communists such as Maurice Thorez and Georgii Dmitrov also addressed the auto workers.[81]

Similarly, factory prestige was greatly enhanced when, at the Seventeenth Party Congress in February 1934, Ordzhonikidze singled out Stepanov and SiM for the most efficient use of the open hearth furnaces. "Go and learn from Stepanov, comrade metallurgists," he concluded. Again, on 5 March 1934, Ordzhonikidze praised Stepanov and SiM in a speech delivered at the conference of Shock Workers of Heavy Metallurgy. Then, in February 1935, at the Seventh All-Union Congress of Soviets, Ordzhonikidze praised SiM for its unique record of increasing net product by 82 percent in four years while reducing the work force by 22 percent. He attributed these successes to proper management, in particular to organizing production well and to establishing proper wage scales. At the same congress, Tevosian also praised SiM for successfully making the transition from a producer of nuts and bolts to high-quality steels that were needed by many new Soviet industries.[82] All this, of course, greatly enhanced the plant's reputation throughout the USSR, and it certainly had an effect on its workers.

The converse was also true. The factory gained national recognition by sending its leading shock workers, engineers, and managers to the Kremlin for well-publicized meetings with Stalin or Ordzhonikidze or to attend party congresses or sessions of the Supreme Soviet. Gladyshev was elected as a full voting delegate to the Sixteenth Party Congress in June 1930. And in December 1934, a number of SiM workers were elected to the Moscow Soviet, including A. S. Rubanov from the open hearth Shop, E. R. Ukhanova from the sheet metal shop, G. N. Cherepanov from the open hearth shop, and I. Ia. Parshin, from the rolling mill shop.[83]

On the last day of December 1934, thirteen of the country's leading directors of heavy metallurgy met with Stalin, Molotov, and Ordzhonikidze. Among the most well known were Zaveniagin, director of Magnitogorsk; Bardin, director of Kuznetsk; Makarov, director of the Stalinskii plant; Gvakharia, director of the Makeevskii plant; Treidub, director of Krasnyi Ok'tiabr; and Stepanov, director of SiM.[84] The press reports of this meeting were bound to have positive reverberations back on the shop floor at these plants and in the PR community.

Ultimately, however, I would emphasize that it was in everyday life, rather than in the festivals and celebrations linking the factory collective to the regime leaders, that the factory exerted a powerful pull in founding a new urban protocommunity, in integrating the peasant-migrants, housewives, and youth in ways that had never before been possible in Russian and Soviet history. This is hard to extract from the Stalin-era press and archives, governed as they were by finding various types of "model" citizens, workers, wives, and so forth, who were expressing regime platitudes. Even they, however, provide some important clues about processes taking place on a wide scale.

One theme that could help us in understanding this type of integration was workers applying the ideals of shock work and Stakhanovism to everyday life—using sport as a metaphor for production and factory production as a metaphor for rationalizing daily life. Two striking examples of this type of thinking were published in articles in *Martenovka* in 1935. The first, from the 24 January edition, was a short article from a woman basketball player, Bogdanova-Kramm, entitled "Both in the Shop and in the Stadium, We Are Shock Workers." Bogdanova-Kramm was a worker in the carding machine shop at SiM, and her vision of the basketball court and the shop floor as analogous fields of activity in which shock methods were applicable, was indicative either of her own worldview or that of the regime. She was applying the model of factory work to sports, or perhaps, of sports to factory work, which surely illustrated the affinity of the "fast break" and "storming." "When I was still a young woman, I began to play basketball with the work-collective of the SiM plant. My years in the club I remember with great joy. . . . I am not only a good sportsman. I am a shock worker in production and have received premiums. I quickly mastered production technique in the carding machine shop. . . . Now, even though I am pregnant, I play basketball" (pp. 2–3). On the one hand, this woman, it would seem, was not at all typical in that she played ball while pregnant, she went by a hyphenated last name, and she was a female shock worker. Still, this article gives some indication of how the factory was serving as a model in daily life in the mind of at least one shock-worker "enthusiast."

Bogdanova-Kramm's model was one of abnormal exertion, effort, and heroism. This was one vision of shock work and Stakhanovism, a "storming" at work applied to sports. The other vision was of rationalization of work and a modern time-orientation in production, which might then be applied to leisure, family life, and community life. This idea was developed by another highly atypical figure, one Zosim Ivanovich Chernyshev, a shock worker who, it would appear from his account, published in *Martenovka* on 11 March 1935, was also deeply involved in child rearing in his household. His speech, which was an attempt to convince the factory to send his youngest daughter to summer camp, raised a number of broader issues.

Chernyshev's ideas on the father's role in child rearing, as much as Bogdanova-Kramm's discussion of women in sport, reflected the continuing impact of the ideals of 1917 on changing sex roles in the family and society. His speech also presented the idea of rationalizing household chores along the lines of rationalizing factory work. This was useful, since most families had limited time and resources to devote to child rearing in the hectic life of Moscow during the 1930s, where both parents were usually working. It was a prescription for orderly and disciplined family life, which the party was enthusiastically promoting by 1935, contrary to many of the ideals of 1917. Chernyshev's account showed the affinity of these rationalization ideals with what might be called a Moscow variant on the Europeanwide emergence of a proletarian family.

In the crowded rooms of the *kommunal'ka*, women and men, more than half of them born in the village, were creating a Soviet variant on the modern proletarian family.[85]

The Factory: Forge of Soviet Man, Total Institution, or Community Organizer

The regime's obsession with factories as the building blocks of the new socialist economy was reflected in the way it implemented the First FYP, which was, in essence, a plan to build or to reconstruct roughly fifteen hundred factories. Beyond that, the plan was expendable. I suggested above that the factory was glorified in the official discourse, first as a "Bolshevik fortress," and then increasingly as a "forge of cadre." The latter theme was linked to an old idea in Russian revolutionary literature, prominent in both Chernyshevskii's *What is to be Done?* and in Gor'kii's *Mother,* which described how "new women" were "enlightened" and became conscious agents of change, Vera Pavlovna in her cooperative workshop and the mother in the revolutionary movement. In the socialist realist novel of the 1930s, the process of enlightenment shifted back from revolutionary situations to production in the factory, where ordinary workers were transformed into outstanding worker-heroes who were "sprouting like mushrooms before our very eyes" in the language of the times. This ideal was best captured in the semiautobiographical character of Pavel Korchagin, hero of N. Ostrovskii's *How the Steel Was Tempered.* Not only the steel was tempered, but more important, worker heroes and worker cadre were tempered. That happened in Ostrovskii's novel, to be sure, through the myth of class struggle on the shop floor, but the novel also suggested other explanations for how the cadre were tempered. Increasingly, however, the emphasis was on factors such as training and education and upward mobility, which was central in the "forge of cadre" ideal, Pavel Korchagin. This became the central mythology of the Stalin regime.[86]

The antithesis to this romanticized Stalinist image of the worker-hero was developed in various negative utopian visions of the Soviet system, among the most interesting being Alexander Zinoviev's and Andrei Platonov's. Zinoviev's negative utopia was first presented in his two famous novels and then developed in his nonfictional account, *Kommunism kak Real'nost'* (Communism as Reality). His idea was that in Soviet urban society, "communalism" was an extension of the peasant *mir,* and it was based on village culture in which everyone knew practically everything about other villagers. This was, under Soviet conditions, replicated in the "urban village," particularly the *kommunal'ka.* Soviet citizens were encouraged to spy on each other and to denounce suspicious or anti-Soviet citizens. While an improvement over totalitarian theory in that such communalism does not deny social bonding altogether, Zinoviev's theory still preserves the core of the totalitarian idea, namely, destruction of individuality. Factory and urban community are mechanisms of social control, employing the "nosy" culture of the village to provide observation, control, and denunciations for the state in "modern" urban guise, but based on peasant traditional culture.[87]

This theory, it would seem, marks an advance over the ideas of Trotsky, Timasheff, and Berdiaev, all of whom saw Soviet Communism under Stalin as resurrecting key aspects of tsarist Russia, but failed to explain why the population accepted this mold. Indeed, one might legitimately ask if any urban community was possible under conditions in which the worker was attached to the factory, either by means of draconian laws or by means of the cradle-to-grave welfare functions of the factory. Was not this factory-community really a second, urban serfdom, comparable to what some peasants called the second rural serfdom on the *kolkhoz?* The same idea of the total subordination of the individual personality has been invoked even more stridently in the now widely popular, "antiheroic," negative utopian literature of Platonov, which was written during the Stalin years. Platonov's "Kotlovan" presents the common workingman in the industrialization drive as "antihero," so alienated from human needs that he becomes a wanderer. This was his only escape from the official life, that is the barrack life of the construction workers and the communal apartment life of the factory workers, which established new urban communities of total (or totalitarian) control with no room for individual dissent, thought, or behavior. I have invoked Platonov's "Kotlovan" to describe the PR during much of the First FYP, when it was little more than a "construction pit"; however, his alienated antihero seems no closer than the regime's worker hero to representing the average worker during the 1930s as she emerges from the archives and the factory press. The problem with this approach is that it denies the possibility of new urban social solidarities.

A third theory of the factory, building on its usurpation of the role of social security net and welfare provider, its cradle-to-grave organization of workers' lives, might emphasize the power of "factory patriotism," a phenomenon noted by many historians of the imperial Russian workers' movement.[88] The similarities of the role of the Soviet factory in 1930s and the factory in Imperial Russia are immediately obvious, particularly as providers of barrack-type factory housing for peasant-migrants. Workers frequently identified themselves as "Guzhontsy" prior to 1917, or as "Serpomolotsy" after 1922. However, whereas factory patriotism in 1917 would be the strongest example of "negative integration" in European history, culminating in the workers' control movement of 1917, factory patriotism of the 1930s, it could be argued, was a type of "positive integration" with its patriotic pro-Soviet content.

Finally, a fourth theory of the factory in Soviet society might be suggested, based on Foucault's idea of the prison as a total institution of social control. Such control, in the context of the Soviet factory, might have been achieved on the shop floor by the daily measuring of output performance and assigning a wage value to it, or by the daily structuring of leisure activity by the factory organizations, or through the daily packaging of the news in the factory press. On the other hand, social control in the Stalinist factory was periodically established by resort to exceptional methods, such as the mass-production movements or the terror, geared to stimulate sudden "leaps" in output by strengthening discipline in a more conventional sense than Foucault's usage. The two aspects, mundane daily regulations, what Foucault called "discipline," on the one hand, and the use of mobilization and/or terror as coercion, on the other, might be called a twentieth-century variant of "panopticism," which Foucault defined as "the technique . . . of coercion."[89] There are a number of respects in which this theory is appealing.

First, Stalin's ersatz social contract, as I have argued, was an attempt to combine the principles that Bentham advocated in Panopticon, principles of defining tasks, measuring output, and then calculating wages accordingly, together with a crude and simplistic view of material self-interest, which incorporated something like Bentham's or Mill's utilitarianism. Stalin's emphasis on accounting and personal responsibility in "Six Conditions" spurred a decade-long attempt to use "observation" in the factory to find correct relations of norms to wages.[90] This was not far from Bentham's ideal of using the penal institution as a test case of social control and of the total internalization of external authority. The norm and wage system in the factory, geared toward internalizing the same sense of constant surveillance, paralleled this Panopticon ideal.[91]

It might be argued, however, that widespread use of penal labor, both in the *gulag* and in non-*gulag* factories during the 1930s, with origins in Makarenko's pedagogical theories and his juvenile labor colony for delinquents, suggests a more primitive type of social control in which overt external authority was omnipresent. Rather than Panopticon, and despite Makarenko's theories about redemption through labor, the *gulag* was perhaps, the modernized version of pre-Panopticon forms of capital punishment.[92]

One instance in which Foucault's discussion of Panopticon and observation seems directly relevant was in Sergei Filatov's evaluation of the meaning of Stalin's "Six Conditions" speech for the SiM plant. As the SiM *partkom* secretary, Filatov, noted, "Comrade Stalin's speech, to a great degree, is directed at us, at our plant. It was as if Comrade Stalin had walked around in our shops, saw all of our inadequacies, and then figured out how to handle them and explained it all in his speech."[93] Filatov's statement could be regarded as mere toadyism, typical of the times in that respect, but it also indicated a type of fear-respect for authority that should not be lightly dismissed.

Evidence of the factory as a total institution might be found in the dissemination of the news in *Martenovka,* which provided a daily account of factory output that was read with varying degrees of interest and enthusiasm in the community. It was hard to avoid the hype, which was also recorded in all-union newspapers such as *Trud, Pravda,* and *Izvestiia,* as well as in citywide papers like *Vechernaia Moskva* and *Rabochaia Moskva* (later *Moskovskii Bolshevik.*) The public was informed of competitions between brigades of smelters at SiM, in the all-union competition announced by Ordzhonikidze, and people would bet on whether Chesnokov's brigade or Turtanov's or Puchkov's would be the first to smelt six tons of steel per hour for an entire work shift.[94] How widespread the interest in such competitions was outside the factory is hard to gauge, but the anecdotal evidence suggests it was considerable.

Once the Stakhanovite record mania began in September 1935, the radio gave out hourly reports on the progress of individual record-breakers, and wives of Stakhanovites congratulated or reprimanded their husbands at the door of the apartment, already well aware of whether or not they had set a new production record on that shift. These were the box scores of Soviet society, or perhaps a better analogy would be to the stock market reports from Wall Street. There were times when, for a ten-day period *Martenovka* would run a headline every day showing how much SiM had produced the previous day and how much the plant still had to produce in order to fulfill the *promfinplan* for the month. Similar headlines periodically gave progress reports on the quarterly plan, yearly plan, and FYP. Brigade production records were front page news in *Martenovka* in the first stages of shock work, and then the focus shifted toward individual production records in 1933, a trend which continued with Stakhanovism.

Thus, the factory as an institution was potentially a strong force which could unify its work collective, their families, and the surrounding community by organizing almost every aspect of community life and of leisure activity. When the Red Director, the management team, and the *partkom* and *zavkom* were effective in meeting the basic needs and demands of the workers, both on the shop floor and in the community, then the factory realized its potential as a powerful unifying social force, a community organizer. But was it a total institution?

One type of evidence that might support that view came from the conception of "insiders" and "outsiders," which was very much linked to the ideal of the factory as Bolshevik fortress. Those who had worked in the factory for years were, with a few exceptions, the "insiders," or in Russian, *nashi* (ours). Others, the "outsiders," were *chuzhie* (aliens). Insiders had rights and privileges, beginning with an apartment, access to closed stores, a factory club, and a place in the FZU for son or daughter. Outsiders would try to gain these privileges illegally; they would try to buy or forge identification papers or coupons to purchase goods in closed stores, or they would try to remain in factory housing even if they had quit their job at the factory long ago. These were, of course, the regime's categories, but they had strong resonance in the First FYP factory, the sources suggest, especially among many of the established workers, who often felt besieged by the flood of newcomers.

Outsiders, in the broadest First FYP definition, could include peasant-recruits, seasonal migrants in particular, who flooded the city and strained its resources while their work was unskilled and their work habits less than regular. They could include housewives and even youth. They could be defined as "*kulak* agitators," like Uskov in the SiM wire shop, who was "exposed" in *Martenovka* on 10 February 1931, for hiding the fact that he had owned 670 hectares of land before the Revolution. He also, apparently, opposed the lowering of the piece rates in 1929 and was expelled from the factory (p. 2). They could be former artisans and shop owners, or NEPmen, or white-collar employees who were dismissed in various antibureaucracy campaigns. They could be gangs of hooligans who robbed workers on the trek back to the apartment from work, or black marketeers, or drifters. Outsiders could also include communist foreign workers and engineers, whose "partyness" was always suspect, and nonparty experts whose expertise was distrusted, as was that of the Russian specialists with Old Regime standing, for political reasons.

As the First FYP's social chaos yielded to Second and Third FYP's social stabilization, the masses of peasants, women, and youth who had been recruited during the First FYP were in the process of becoming insiders as surely as the established workers. The difference was that the category of outsiders was now very sharply restricted to "enemies of the people," with the new politics of working-class inclusivity. The regime justified this shift in the Stalin Constitution by redefining the peasantry and the Soviet intelligentsia, as "working" or "laboring" classes, as cotoilers with the working class in the project of socialist construction. That meant that the new recruits of the First FYP were insiders by 1936.

Insiders/outsiders; it was a manichaean worldview that served a potentially important psychological function as an escape valve for social anger and tension on the shop floor and in the community. Established workers and newcomers, sharply divided though they were during the First FYP, would soon both identify with their factory and could both begin to direct their anger elsewhere, at "outsiders," "aliens," indeed, at "enemies," fictitious though they might be.

The manichaean worldview was also, potentially, a powerful force in shaping the popular mentality outside the factory, where the label "outsiders" was applied to "enemies" of the polity and community. The Stalinists claimed, with increasing stridency in 1936 and 1937, that the party-state organs were plagued by outsiders, that is by traitors, saboteurs, and enemies. This worldview shifted readily from the class struggle ideology of the First FYP to a nonclass discourse of spies and wreckers in the purge-trial-terror of the Second FYP. In this sense, the idea of Bolshevik fortress was perpetuated into the terror.

The factory as community organizer, however, suggests a different perspective than the four presented above, synthesizing aspects from all of them while emphasizing yet a different dimension. The regime's discourse of Bolshevik fortress and forge of Soviet man, and the antiheroes of dissident literature, seem to be the least useful since neither accounts for integration of new workers into the working class. The issue of continuity of the 1930s with Imperial Russia under something like factory patriotism, as I have suggested, fails to take into account the totally different content of factory patriotism during the 1930s, when it seemed to fuse with Soviet patriotism. The theory of factory-based communalism and of the factory as total institution are more sophisticated and require further evaluation.

There are two fundamental problems with the assumptions of the communalist school for the historian. First, the factory was not the *mir* because its production activity was increasingly specialized, whereas the *mir* (and the *kolkhoz,* despite its attempt to set up factory-type brigades) organized peasant farming according to what Durkheim called primitive "mechanical" solidarity and what I will describe in chapter 10 as "gang labor."[95] Second, while the barracks were indeed a type of urban village, a shantytown, the *kommunal'ka* was not. It was not a replication of the village. The shift to permanent communal apartments signified the end of seasonal migration, and for the first time in Russian or Soviet history, it meant the possibility of an urban family life for the peasant in-migrant, then of an urban protocommunity, and gradually a community life.

The *kommunal'ka,* despite the plethora of jokes that it has occasioned in literature and in oral culture, was a great improvement over the barrack and the dormitory in fostering privacy, individualized space for the new workers, especially peasant-migrants, and urban family life. Given the number of in-migrants and the regime's priority on investment in factories, there was no alternative. To be sure, sharing the kitchen and bath replicated certain aspects of the barracks and everyone got to know each other's business. Yet, overcrowded and inadequate as they were, the communal apartments were fundamentally important in the transition from seasonal peasant-migrant worker to permanent urban working class. They meant the end of the split family.

Paraphrasing Durkheim's argument on the division of labor and specialization, I suggest that a new sense of urban community could only arise with the end of barrack communalism and the rise of the urban proletarian family. When workers were living cheek-by-jowl in barracks, or crammed together behind curtains or partitions in a single room of a communal apartment, such forced communalism disrupted family life, caused substantially high levels of divorce, alienation, and anomie, and preempted any real possibility for an urban community. There was a paradox in that primitive communalism had to disappear before a sense of individual privacy, and with it of an urban community, could begin to develop. The parallel to Durkheim's ideas on labor process is strong, in that Durkheim argued that primitive "mechanical" solidarity had to disappear with modern labor specialization before "organic" solidarity could take root.

That the modern urban community has much less kinship-based and village-based cohesion than did the barrack communalism based on *zemliak* or *artel'*, does not mean that anomie was widespread or that alienated antiheroes of Platonov's type were typical. Whether in Chicago or in Moscow during the 1930s, communities were emerging in which people chose their friends and associates according to their interests and activities. Of course, they chose within limits imposed by impersonal processes such as urbanization and industrialization, governed by market factors in Chicago and by state policy in Moscow. Anomie and alienation were more likely, I believe, to plague the barracks, despite the continuities to the peasant village.

The theory of the total institution is closer to what I have in mind by a social melting pot and community organizer than these other three theories, but it too has a number of drawbacks. It would be easy to reject Foucault's theory on the premise that the factory was more of a sieve than a Bolshevik fortress during the 1930s and therefore could not be a total institution. But, on these grounds, one would have to reject the idea of a community organizer as well. However, as I have argued, labor turnover was an exaggerated phenomenon and was an obsession of the regime under labor famine conditions, which slowed or disrupted but which did not prevent social transformation in the factory melting pot and urban protocommunity.

My problem with the total institution approach for the Soviet factory is that it suggests a process of social control from the top down, in which the "object" only becomes "subject" by internalizing what Foucault called discipline. While that may well have worked in Panopticon or in the *gulag*, one would be hard-pressed to illustrate how this explains worker behavior in bourgeois society or in Soviet society during the 1930s. Michael Buroway's study of how such internally (worker) driven consent operated shows that "observation" was also a two-way street in the capitalist factory and that what was internalized by the worker was not the ideal of the manager or stockholder about production, but a sense of equity bargain.[96] Andrle showed similar processes at work inside the Soviet factory.

I am not suggesting that factory and community were autonomous from the party-state. This clearly was not a case of negative integration, but neither was it a case of positive integration, if by that we mean something like Panopticon.[97] The resolution of ubiquitous social conflict in the First FYP, that is, the process of integration of the newcomers at work and into a new urban community, was the central drama of Stalinism during the 1930s and once again after the Second World War. Rather than negative or positive, perhaps it was a parallel or social integration, which percolated up to the regime's leaders via the Red Directors and caused the shift in ideology to ersatz social contract.

9

THE RED DIRECTORS TRANSFORM
SOVIET INDUSTRIAL RELATIONS

T hus far I have been describing the changes in the factory and in the urban community without squarely addressing the question of why these changes took place, or rather, of who was pressing for them. Obviously, the party-state strategy of forced industrialization and collectivization changed Soviet Russia, and so state initiative looms large in the background as a powerful driving force in the events described here. Urbanization, and even something like what Marx, Durkheim, and Weber thought of, in very different terms, as modernization seems to have been the result. Such broad, impersonal forces, by themselves, however, explain very little about the agents of social change. As I have been at pains to show, it was the actions and aspirations of workers, both the established workers and the newcomers, that to a large extent shaped the new urban society and industrial system, and which slowly but inexorably forced the Stalin regime to back away from its class struggle politics of production. Had the regime not reached some kind of consensus with the new workers, in what I call the ersatz social contract, the industrialization program would have collapsed. It was on the verge of collapse in late 1932.

In this chapter, by turning the focus of inquiry to managers, and in particular to the Red Directors, I suggest that they were the first to shift away from class struggle politics, as they moved away from their posture as radical industrializers and adopted a rather conservative posture as organization men. They advocated the class struggle to win the battle to rebuild SiM and ZiS, but after that, it was of no use to them. They were the first to see its negative impact on the shop floor, and so they shifted from blaming to training the newcomers and from the shock-work assault on records to the stable, cost-accounting work brigade.

Stepanov Builds His Management Team

The single most significant figure in pushing through the reconstruction of SiM was the Red Director, Petr Fedorovich Stepanov. Prior to 1917, Stepanov was a lathe operator at the Bromlei plant, a machine-construction plant located across the Moscow River from SiM in the Zamoskvoretskii Raion, which was renamed Krasnyi Proletarii after the Revolution. Veitsman was then the director of the Bromlei plant and was, ironically, also technical director of Gipromez (State Institute for Design of Metallurgy Pants) and Stepanov's main opponent in 1929 over the issue of rebuilding SiM *in situ*. Stepanov became an active participant in the strike movement in 1917 and a leading figure in the plant trade-union committee in that year.[1] He joined the party in 1919 and was appointed as the Red Director of the Podol'sk textile plant, where he replaced Miliukov. By 1925, production at the Podol'sk plant was restored to its 1913 level, and Stepanov was credited with this and promoted, becoming Red Director of SiM, which was also just reaching its 1913 level of output.

Arriving at SiM on 15 April 1925, as his unpublished memoirs in the archives dated 9 June 1932 indicate, Stepanov had considerable doubts about his ability to manage a steel plant, since his work at Bromlei and as Red Director at Podol'sk gave him no familiarity with technology and work organization in producing steel. Stepanov noted that when he arrived, the plant had 2,800 employees and that his main concern was with the ITR, who were all carried over from Guzhon days. The head engineer left just as Stepanov was arriving. His immediate concern was that only two open hearth furnaces, the fifth and the seventh, were functional.[2]

Furthermore, the collective contract for 1925 called for a 13 percent reduction in piece rates (*ratsenki*) throughout the plant and a reduction of 23 percent in the rolling steel shop, putting most of the workers there in a foul mood. Stepanov was warned that the rolling mill workers were "anarchists," prone to conflict with management. He claimed the problem was that they were underpaid. The SiM collective contract was part of an all-union campaign, in which many plants were being called on to reduce their piece rates by 17–18 percent. Stepanov discussed the matter with the departing Red Director, Burdachev. He talked with the president of the plant trade-union committee, Iakovlev, and with the party secretary, Khleptovskii. The rate issue was adjudicated in the plant RKK (Rates Control Commission), which met, Stepanov tells us, for two months in his office, and it came as no surprise to Stepanov that the workers were quite upset when it apparently sanctioned this reduction in their piece rates.[3]

Stepanov, however, was even more concerned about putting his administrative team in order. He described the plant administration in 1925 as "a mess," and began what he called a "search for cadre." He noted that he "preferred working with young engineers rather than with old ones because they were easier to train in the new [work] methods." He was particularly upset about the disastrous condition of internal transportation within the plant: "I went to Malyi Iaroslavets and asked the controller on the railroad if there wasn't a young engineer who could come to work managing railway transport at SiM. He asked, 'and what will you give me?' I answered, 'an apartment in Moscow.' He said he would send someone. I left him my card . . . later a young transport engineer came to SiM. It was Beliaev. He took the first steps in organizing transport."[4]

Some years later at SiM, when he spoke at a workers' evening at the plant, Stepanov recalled the difficult situation that he faced back in 1925:

This is what I remember of the collective when I came to the plant. My first impression: virgin soil. People [who were] open-hearted, unspoiled, unpolluted; a wonderful group. I came at a very difficult time; the work norms were being revised. Some of my comrades here— Mironov, Zaitsev, Novikov—remember that time well. Roman Iakovlevich Tuzeforich was my right arm in the TNB [Technical Norming Bureau].

There was an interesting meeting at the plant—the entire collective [work force] was at the meeting because [of concern about] the norm revision. In fact, the collective was in my office, while I was [out of my office and] on the shop floor.

. . . When several of the norms had been revised, the rolling mill workers came to my office with their tongs. My assistants gathered around to defend their director—they feared excesses. But, I must say, there were no excesses. I remember one of the rolling mill workers (from the floor: Bogoslavskii) came after me with the tongs. This was a huge man—next to him, I was a pigmy. So, I said to him: "You could kill me [with your bare hands]; why bother with the tongs?" He laughed, and said: "Out of habit." The people [narod] are good; rough, with simple upbringing and uneducated. . . . I decided that this was a good place to work, a challenge. I [had worked] in the [Bromlei] machine construction plant . . . there it was like a section of Europe, but here, it is not only Eurasia, but simply Asia.[5]

Thus, from the perspective of the skilled Russian machinist who became a Red Director, "Western culture" was the *sine qua non* of industrialization, and the working conditions at SiM were primitive, hence "Asiatic." His thinking on culture was shaped by his work experience.

We face the question [at SiM] of speeding up the training of workers. I detected a very sharp difference between engineers and workers here [at SiM]. At machine-construction plants, the situation is different in this respect. At these plants, when necessary, a skilled worker can substitute for a master, a master can substitute for the shop boss [nachal'nik tsekha] because this is an educated person, able to read blueprints, etc. But here, when there is a disaster, they [all] run to the engineer. He comes [to the scene of the accident] and does not know what to do.

Before us lies a large field of activity in the sphere of raising the cultural level of our workers. Work with high quality steel demands culture, knowledge. Here, we still have a lot of work to do.[6]

These passages are remarkably revealing of the mind-set of a skilled Russian machinist who became a Bolshevik and a Red Director. For him the peasant-worker was Asiatic Russia, while the hereditary working class was urban and European Russia; the gap between them was essentially a cultural dichotomy rather than a function of the dual labor market, hiring and training practices and customs, or the prejudices of managers and foremen. Even more important than displaying Stepanov's cultural prejudices, this passage shows that the dual labor market had become institutionalized as a cultural chasm.

Stepanov related this autobiographical information at a meeting of the plant collective in 1932. He was very astute in this retrospective appraisal of the situation that he had faced in 1925. He realized that he had to immediately find a way to diffuse workers' anger over the sharp reduction in piece rates; the problem of training workers whom he saw as mired in the "Asiatic" culture of the plant was a long-term project. In fact, it is likely that he did not understand this cultural gap so clearly in 1925 and that it only became apparent over the intervening seven years.

Stepanov's 1932 speech was rich in its reflections on the problems that he faced as Red Director, and he clearly diagnosed the problem of shop-floor power. He recalled that in 1925, real power was held by the trade union's shop deputies, rather than by his shop superintendents and subordinate line managers. Of course, in 1932, when the party line of *edinonachalie* was already firmly entrenched, it was easy for Stepanov to blame the parallelism of the trade union or of party committees for interfering with the tasks and prerogatives of management.[7] His assessment, however, should not be dismissed for this reason.

Stepanov claimed that he tried, initially, to win the trade union shop deputies to his side by promoting some of them onto his management team. He appointed Vaitsev as superintendent of the supply shop, Shchepalov as boss of the bolt shop, and he made Pozdukov the boss of the very important rolling steel shop. He made these appointments in consultation with Martynov, the head of the *zavkom*.[8] By his own account, however, we can see that Stepanov must have grown impatient with these men, because he soon moved from this strategy to training and promoting what he would call "his own people."

The common characteristics of "his" people, the new cohort that Stepanov appointed, was that they were young, they were almost all new to the SiM factory, and they had no background as industrial workers but were graduates of institutes of higher education, mostly as engineers. As Stepanov put it,

We have put youth in [charge at] fairly important positions. . . . Neither the youth nor the old-timers know [how to run the machinery], but it is better to teach the youth than the elderly. . . . It is worth the expense to train the youth. . . . I believe that in training new cadres, we took the right approach. I remember how a stazher, Korolev, came [on temporary assignment] to the open hearth shop. He stayed and now is the boss of the shop. In the rolling steel shop—Marmonshtein. He was promoted to engineer, and then to the boss of the shop. He can produce any kind of rolling metal. You [also] remember Sagaidak, Shebaturin, and others. In the sheet metal shop [we have] Gromov and Pogonchenkov. Pogonchenkov I forcibly transferred to the sheet metal shop. . . . He protested loudly. . . . Gromov also protested loudly when I transferred him. . . . The results in the sheet metal shop showed that a series of serious technical problems had been resolved. We have wonderful youth developing here.

In the model-forge shop, there were no engineers. The only specialist . . . was a *praktik* . . . [so] I threw Andreev, who was working [managing] in the Martenovskii shop, into the model-forge shop. He complained for a long time, but I stood my ground, and now Andreev has developed significantly. Karmazin is also an excellent engineer. We sent most of our young engineers abroad . . . now we have a fine group of young specialists.[9]

In this passage, in which he reiterates his reason for shifting toward youth, Stepanov was defining the new leadership team that he had already put into place, in most shops by 1930, and which still occupied these positions, with some additions and a few subtractions, until late 1937 and early 1938.[10] Each personally owed his appointment directly to Stepanov, and subsequent events would show that they were strongly loyal to him. Following Ordzhonikidze's "suicide" on 18 February 1937, most of Stepanov's men were removed at SiM, predicating the fall of Stepanov himself. Criticism of Stepanov began to appear in *Martenovka* in April 1937.[11] Surprisingly, he was not actually removed until April 1938, and even after that he retired, survived the war, and died of natural causes in Moscow.[12]

Unfortunately, I have not been able to find more biographical information about Stepanov's new management team.[13] It is clear, however, that none of them were workers at SiM or at other plants before they were appointed as chief engineers or shop bosses. Furthermore, one can make a well-educated guess from these passages in his comments that Stepanov was looking for young engineers right out of the VUZ or *rabfak* to put into top managerial and technical posts. He was looking for "specialists," and obviously was very proud of the fact that most of his team had been sent to Western Europe to learn the latest in steel technology. He was not looking for *praktiki,* that is, workers without higher education who were frequently placed into responsible positions as assistants to engineers or even as engineers in the helter-skelter days of the First FYP, based on the state policy of promotion of the *vydvizhentsy.* Stepanov's new appointees might well have come from working-class families, but the important issue is not so much their class origins, as their lack of prior work experience and their success in higher education.[14]

Stepanov's argument was that new technology was rendering past experience largely irrelevant, and therefore he wanted to train the younger men rather than retrain the older. This made sense for many reasons. Not only would the younger men likely adapt more easily to the new technology, but their education was essential for the engineering tasks that the Red Directors were confronting virtually every day in the new and reconstructed factories. This was also Stepanov's golden opportunity to put "his" men into authoritative positions, and he and Likhachev, and other Red Directors, acting after 1929 under the auspices of the party doctrine of *edinonachalie,* moved swiftly.

The young men whom they chose to staff their new managerial teams were crammed with text-book knowledge but lacked shop-floor experience, and a Red Director such as Stepanov or Likhachev well understood that they faced daunting new challenges and pressures. They also realized that such young men would not necessarily find it easy to give orders to older veteran workers and foremen, let alone to communicate with new recruits who had neither higher education nor factory experience. Nor was their job made any easier given the tense atmosphere created by a regime hell-bent on fulfilling plans, quick to label failure as sabotage, and quick to blame "class aliens" and foreign specialists for failures or accidents.

The successful Red Directors found various ways to put the new management team at ease. They could shield them from regime pressures in many ways. They could aid them in dealing with difficult technical problems by hiring competent staff, engineers and technicians who could follow instructions and even improvise when needed. Most important, however, the Red Directors could draw on their own experience on the shop floor, first as former workers and then as managers, to find ways to facilitate the interaction of these new men with old-timers and new workers alike, and with a formidable group of foremen and lower-level technician-*praktiki* who lacked formal education. They used their own personal prestige, authority, and ability to foster worker respect for the young specialists and to minimize and then finally eliminate the specialist baiting (*spetseedstvo*) unleashed in the Cultural Revolution. That is how the Red Directors built loyalty among the young managers, shop and shift superintendents, and engineers that they had appointed. This was the great achievement of the Red Directors like Stepanov and Likhachev and their key to success during the First FYP and after.

Furthermore, successful Red Directors would find the language and the management style to become the link between the regime and their own management staff. For their management staff not only lacked the factory experience necessary to communicate readily with workers and foremen at the bench, but also lacked the political experience necessary to communicate with the regime leaders and with the party apparatus. Stepanov and Likhachev drew on their own considerable experience within the party, which included difficult assignments during the Civil War, to speak the language that the regime leaders would understand. Indeed, they would "speak Bolshevik," to use Kotkin's term, and thus protect their management team from Cultural Revolution and class struggle politics unleashed by the Stalinists, from above, or by radical shock workers, from below. Many of the old-regime specialists at SiM and AMO-ZiS, on the other hand, would fare poorly during the Cultural Revolution. That was probably because they opposed the Red Director in the battles over plant reconstruction in 1929, but we can see that at SiM, it was also because of Stepanov's preference for youth.

Stepanov and Likhachev, as skilled mechanics, could also speak in a language that the foremen, the skilled workers, and established workers at SiM and ZiS understood. That was important, especially since many established workers felt that they were under siege, squeezed by new technologies and young engineers and bosses, on the one side, and by the "invasion" of "Asiatic" peasant-recruits, on the other. But it was equally important for the directors to be able to communicate with these same peasant-recruits. Stepanov was painfully aware of the problems of recruiting and holding onto new workers, and so it was in his interest both to try to meet the needs and to speak the language of the incoming workers, and to prevent the old-timers from lording it over them. We could take the fact that Stepanov labeled them as "Asiatic" as Russian chauvinism or racism, and dismiss his problems of integrating these workers as invented, fabricated, or mythical social construct. Since, however, almost all the peasant-recruits at SiM were Russian, and with the exception of a Tatar contingent none could be considered "Asiatic," we might better interpret his statement as reflecting Stepanov's perception of a the dual culture in his factory. There was the culture of the established workers, and the multiple and very different cultures of the newcomers. Thus his dichotomous thinking was insightful, since he had to confront the clash of these two cultures on a daily basis.

Another big concern for Stepanov and Likhachev was to try to thoroughly understand the production process in their large and complex plants. Over and over again, both in unpublished memoirs of engineers and superintendents in the archives from the Gor'kii Project and in the published memoirs about Likhachev collected in the volume *Direktor*, engineers and managers with higher education praised Stepanov and Likhachev for their willingness to learn and their capacity to master difficult technical problems. Both were willing and anxious to learn the new technology and technical language of the young professionals whom they had hired. Stepanov and Likhachev, themselves workers with low levels of education, were not at all complacent. They respected the role of education in promoting science and technology and made an attempt to understand it.

While the upper-level plant management and the director's managerial team were highly educated, the middle and bottom layers of management were not. The *brigadir* who often was promoted to head a specialized grouping of brigades under the section or *uchastka*, and their *praktiki* were all without higher education or specialized technological knowledge and were promoted directly from the bench to these lower and mid-level managerial posts. Most were, like the Red Directors themselves, established workers, rehired in the early 1920s as industry was restored, with work tenure dating back to pre-1917. Rushed into these positions with the industrial expansion of the First FYP, their own personal experience and long apprenticeship was no longer relevant for the newcomers. They, too, would look to the director for guidance. The Red Director was equally dependent on them for the effective implementation of his decisions and for establishing an intermediate link between his new management team and the worker on the bench. Initially called *master*, and then more and more frequently called *brigadir*, the coherence of the work brigade depended on their establishing an effective relationship with the work team. As the shock brigade yielded to the cost-accounting brigade, and merged with all the other brigades simply as the most basic work unit, the *brigadir* became a central figure in the production process.[15]

In appointing foremen, Stepanov followed just the opposite tactics of personnel recruitment from his top managerial appointments. He wanted to promote workers from the bench, and he had no choice but to do so, given the numbers of *brigadiry* required by the rapid proliferation of work brigades and the limited relevance of book knowledge for the problems encountered at this level of production. This was a less spectacular type of promotion than the *vydvizhenie* of the regime's ideology, since these foremen often worked in the shop themselves. On the other hand, many of them apparently spent much of their day procuring supplies and equipment for their work brigade, foraging around the plant or joining "expeditions" to other plants for this purpose. The established workers filled the ranks of the new foremen.[16]

When he arrived at SiM in 1925, therefore, Stepanov had a separate agenda for the lower-level appointments to his staff, called *mastera* at the time. Again, he was looking for political loyalty, but here he would rely on Communist Party membership, in conjunction with the lengthy work tenure of the established workers. He described his initial problems in forging a politically loyal staff in the following:

When I came to the factory, I was the only Communist in management. I had nobody to consult with. The factory administration resembled an institute. . . .

The most difficult thing [was that] in the shops there were no *mastera* who were party members. One must say that the old *mastera* were very flexible . . . they quickly sent young [challengers], who were uncultured, packing. I decided to choose the master from among the party membership. It was impossible to do this surreptitiously . . . [so] I took another route. I asked the old *mastera* to train Ponomarov and others and then put them on the other shifts . . . the money tempted them, and so they taught him. Now Ponamarov is [a master and the] boss of his workbench. And once one party member became a *master,* that broke the ice, and it became easier for others in the future. Youth began to feel that it was possible for them to become a master, and this began to show in their work. Our Soviet cadre began to develop. The majority were trade-union representatives, worker-correspondents for Martenovka, and party activists. Now, as a result [of these policies], the non-party *master* is an exception.

Thus, a new type of manager, a new working-class technical intelligentsia has formed and grows.[17]

Stepanov was trying, it is clear, to promote young party members who were also workers at the bench to become the new foremen. He immediately realized, however, that to train them, he would have to rely on established *mastera*, that is the leaders of the old labor aristocracy, who themselves had all undergone long apprenticeships and had long experience at the bench. More important, there were sizeable numbers of party members among the established workers, and Stepanov would have to rely on them to fill the ranks of the proliferating *brigadiry*.

The social gap between foremen, old or young, and the young professional recruits at the top of his management team could not have been wider. The foremen needed remedial secondary education at night school during the 1930s; the managers graduated from the institutes and came directly to the factories. The foremen worked with their hands; the managers were "mental" workers, closely tied socially and culturally to the factory ITR. The foremen were promoted from the ranks; the managers were outsiders brought in. It required considerable skill, or cultural diversity, on the part of the Red Director to bridge this gap.

Stepanov, as we have seen, was not hesitant during the First FYP to use the class struggle against superiors such as Veitsman who blocked his proposals for the reconstruction of SiM. He also appears to have been anxious to remove many older, nonparty specialists who still dominated the ITR and plant management on the eve of the First FYP. These included figures such as List and Sattel', who were accused of wrecking. However, even though he was very anxious to replace the old, nonparty specialists with his own men, there is no solid evidence that Stepanov ever believed that any of these old specialists were wreckers. In his memoirs, he blames the three major fires at the plant in 1925, 1926, and 1927, first on the fact that these shops were housed in wooden structures, and second, on the fact that they had faulty electrical lines. After the fires, rather than blaming anyone, Stepanov noted, "we slept without undressing."[18] This clearly contradicted the party line on wrecking, which Gaidul' and Filatov had applied with such zeal at SiM. Stepanov apparently tried to limit the politics of the class struggle to defeating opponents who blocked his proposals.

Stepanov's push for reconstruction initially depended not on the old trade-union officials, who he felt undermined his authority, nor on his new management team, who were just arriving and still unknown in the plant. Rather, he was dependent on the party committee in the plant. The three leaders of the campaign for reconstructing SiM *in situ* were the *partkom* secretary, Gaidul'; his assistant and subsequently *partkom* secretary, Filatov; and Stepanov.

Gaidul' and Filatov used the issue of reconstruction to assert their control over the *partkom* and the *raikom*. They purged the plant *partkom* and then used that base to purge the *raikom*, linking up to the new Stalinist leadership on the *gorkom* and *obkom* (city and province party committees) under Kaganovich. Vasilii Bogatyrev, who had become party secretary at SiM in August 1928, when he replaced Semen Ivanov, was an easy target. Gaidul' and Filatov attacked Bogatyrev by linking him to the *raikom* first secretary, Pen'kov, who was a supporter of the "rightist" Moscow Province first secretary, Uglanov.[19]

Pen'kov supposedly was able to persuade the novice, Bogatyrev, that the line of the Right Opposition was the "general party line," in other words the position of the Stalin leadership. He allegedly had tried to consolidate his hold at SiM when he came to the plant on 9 May 1928 to address a closed Party Plenum with 509 party members attending. At the Sixth Plenum of the Moscow Party Committee, in the fall of 1928, a representative from the Rogozhsko-Simonovskii District, Comrade Chanke, accused Pen'kov of operating in a secretive and arbitrary manner. Pen'kov was removed by the Fifth Plenum of the MK and MKK (Moscow Committee and Moscow Control Committee) on 10 October 1928, when Roman Davidson was appointed as the new first secretary of the *raikom*.[20] This offered a fine opportunity at SiM for a determined and rising young Stalinist careerist like Gaidul'.

I. P. Gaidul' was born in 1900. During World War I he worked at the Baltiiskii factory in Petrograd. He then joined the Red Army, and he served and was wounded twice in the Civil War. He continued service in the army until 1926. Then the party demobilized him and sent him to the Sverdlov Communist University for two and a half years. Finishing at the university in 1929, he was assigned to do party work at SiM.[21]

Arriving at SiM, Gaidul' was immediately put in charge of an *ad hoc* party committee to plan for the plant's reconstruction. He staked his career on immediate reconstruction of SiM *in situ,* asserting that this was the only plan consistent with rapid industrialization and the First FYP. He replaced Bogatyrev as *partkom* secretary shortly after arriving at the plant. In August 1929, he gave his speech accusing administrators of wrecking. By the beginning of 1930, Gaidul' was working closely with Krylenko of the OGPU, to put together the case for wrecking against List, Sattel', Mattis, and Babadzhan. On 4 March 1930, at a mass meeting of 7,000 workers, Krylenko and Gaidul' accused them of wrecking, with their plan to phase out SiM. They also blamed this group for the fires of 1925, 1926, and 1927, and for the explosions in the wire mill and the rolling metal shop in the spring of 1929.[22]

From then on, Gaidul's rise was rapid. Gaidul', Stepanov, and Gladyshev were selected as the three representatives from SiM at the Sixteenth Party Congress in June 1930. Speaking at the congress on 1 July on behalf of the SiM party organization, Gaidul' called for the expulsion of Rykov, Tomskii, Bukharin, and Uglanov from the party. When Davidson was promoted to become a secretary of the Moscow *gorkom* on 6 October 1930, Gaidul' was promoted to the position of first secretary of the Proletarskii *raikom,* replacing

Davidson. Gaidul' held this position until 18 October 1933, when he was blamed for covering up or protecting the corrupt circle of officials at GPZ-1 who were held responsible for the scandal there. He was forced to resign.[23]

Working closely with Gaidul' at SiM was another rising young Stalinist star, Sergei Filatov. Filatov was born in 1905.[24] His father worked on the Tsaritsyn railroad line, and from age nine Filatov had worked in the fields as a day laborer while attending primary school. In 1919 he joined the Komsomol and served on a *gubernia* committee. He fought during the Civil War and in 1921 was moved to work in the Cheka. In 1922, he was demobilized and moved to Moscow. Later that year, he became an electrician at the textile plant Spartak.[25] Here, in 1923, he joined the party and became secretary of a party cell, and then president of the trade-union committee. Then he was promoted to the Moscow Committee of the Komsomol.[26]

Next Filatov rejoined the Red Army where he carried out party work in 1927–28, and then he returned to Moscow and began to work at SiM in October 1928 as an unskilled laborer in the model-forge shop.[27] When administrators found out that he had some experience as an electrician, they moved him to work on servicing motors in the steel rolling shop. Filatov worked on the third shift and was unanimously chosen by this shift as secretary of the party cell. Under Filatov, the cell became one of the most active in the plant, successfully recruiting many members and leading the shock-work–socialist competition movement.[28]

Filatov was named head of the organizing-instruction division of the plant *partkom* in February 1930. When Gaidul' was promoted to *raikom* secretary in October, Filatov replaced him as the *partkom* secretary.[29] Together with Gaidul' and Stepanov, he had led the assault against the "Rightists." His tenure as party secretary, however, was short-lived. By the time Gaidul' was disgraced, in 1933, Filatov's name had disappeared from the SiM party committee records, and one A. Rubanov was, by then, secretary of the SiM *partkom*. While it is unclear what happened to Filatov, he would not figure again at SiM, and Rubanov was so inconspicuous that he was never mentioned in *Martenovka* or in the Central State Archives.[30]

The rise of both Gaidul' and Filatov was rapid, and their immediate impact was substantial on the issue of massive reconstruction of SiM. They mobilized support for reconstruction in the party apparatus and among the work force, thus allowing Stepanov and his team to break through opposition in Gipromez, Mashtrest, and other layers of bureaucracy by giving voice to their claims in the all-union press and reaching the top regime leaders. The party apparatus in the plant thus played a decisive, albeit short-term role. After Gaidul' and Filatov, the SiM *partkom* came under the control of the Red Director.

The long-term influence of Gaidul' and Filatov at SiM was minimal. They were gone by the end of the First FYP, and their successor seemed to have been wholly compliant to Stepanov, perhaps even hand-picked by him. Thus, the *partkom* was subordinated to Stepanov's team of young managers and engineers. By the end of the First FYP, the factory triangle (managers, party committee, and trade-union committee) had yielded to the dominance of the managers under the leadership of the Red Directors. This was, indeed, a type of *edinonachalie,* and it was built on a system of patronage, a system which was also proliferating throughout the party-state bureaucracy.

Stepanov was no less an industrializer and was no less enthusiastic about reconstructing SiM than were Gaidul' or Filatov. He believed that SiM had no future as a producer of small finished products such as nails and bolts. He thought that the only way to make the plant useful in the industrialization drive of the First FYP was to begin to produce new types of steel that would be in great demand in the future. His objective was to tie SiM's production to the machine-construction industries, which he expected to grow very rapidly.[31] His thinking was right on target for the transformation of Moscow into a "metal" city, and for the integration of metalworking industries around SiM and AMO-ZiS in the new PR.

This was the position of Tevosian, Ordzhonikidze, and Stalin as well. Thus was established the crucially important personal link, indeed a patron-client relationship, between Stepanov and Commissar Ordzhonikidze. Ordzhonikidze had replaced Kuibyshev as the commissar of VSNKh in November 1930, and after 5 January 1932, when VSNKh was split into three commissariats, he became commissar of the most important, NKTP.[32] Tevosian became one of Ordzhonikidze's most competent and trusted deputies. After 1931 he worked closely with Stepanov and was frequently a participant in experiments and technical decisions at SiM. This close personal link determined the fate of SiM, to its great advantage, until Ordzhonikidze's power was undermined in late 1936.[33]

Initially, Stepanov relied on Filatov and Gaidul' to spearhead the attack against the old specialists inside and outside the factory who were not in favor of the reconstruction of SiM. Fighting the battle of his life as a young Red Director, with only four years at SiM, Stepanov's politics coincided neatly with those of the Stalinist leadership. He needed all the help he could get from these young Stalinist party men in the plant and Moscow party organs. However, by 1931 when the reconstruction of the plant was guaranteed, he no longer needed Filatov or Gaidul'. He needed party men who would take orders from his new management team and implement the type of industrial relations that he wanted.

Filatov and Gaidul' soon left on promotions, and Stepanov secured the low-profile party secretary that he wanted in the plant. All the while, he was quietly building up the authority of his young engineers and managers and a strong cohort of foremen below them. He based his power and authority for the duration of his tenure as Red Director on his own management team. Ivan Alekseevich Likhachev at AMO-ZiS built a very similar type of management team during the First FYP. The two Red Directors became such quintessential organization men that it seems hard to imagine that they had initially gained stature as radical industrializers. The important issue, I am suggesting, is not whether they had substantial room for maneuver or were tightly constrained by the party-state, but rather, the shift in managerial style from radicals to organization men.[34]

Mr. Director: Ivan Alekseevich Likhachev

The conflict over reconstruction at AMO followed a path very similar to the conflict at SiM, except that the dispute was even more dramatic and involved American as well as Soviet specialists. It culminated with Likhachev presenting his case before the Politburo in January 1930. Until that moment, his opponents appeared to have had the upper hand, ensconced as they were in the trusts and also in the special reconstruction agency, URRA, which had been established at AMO in 1929. Unlike Stepanov, however, Likhachev did not rely on any important plant party leaders. From the outset he relied on the young specialists of his own management team to make his case both to party leaders and to the factory collective and the larger public.

Without question, Likhachev himself was the dominating figure in the reconstruction of AMO-ZiS, and from the outset, his management team of new young engineers and well-educated young bosses spearheaded the campaign. He was appointed Red Director at the end of 1926 and served in that capacity until 1939, surviving the Great Terror.[35] Then he was promoted and became the commissar of mid-level machine construction (which included auto manufacturing) in 1939, but after one year he was reappointed Red Director at ZiS. In 1941 at ZiS, he supervised evacuation of the plant to Ul'anovsk on the Volga and then the third reconstruction of the plant after the Second World War. He remained there as Red Director until 1950, when he was again promoted into the Auto Ministry. He became minister of auto transport and highways in 1953, the post that he held until his death in 1956.[36] After he died, and as part of destalinization, the auto plant was renamed ZiL (the Likhachev plant) in his honor.[37]

Likhachev's was a unique case of continuity as Red Director at a single Soviet factory for the better part of twenty-five years. Stepanov had thirteen consecutive years at SiM, which was already quite exceptional, since on average in the mid-1930s, directors were moving laterally from one plant to another or were promoted or demoted every two years or less.[38] Then, in 1937 and 1938, the Great Terror caused even more rapid movement. For directors such as Stepanov and Likhachev, who had very close connections to Ordzhonikidze,[39] the terror usually meant the end of their careers. Surprisingly, both Stepanov and Likhachev survived the terror, and Likhachev never faced the humiliating discrediting campaign at ZiS that Stepanov was subjected to at SiM. Both were promoted, Likhachev becoming commissar and Stepanov onto the staff of a glavk in steel manufacturing. In most cases, deprived of their support base in their factories, such ex-directors who survived the purge-terror were then appointed as directors at much less significant plants.[40] Stepanov was forced into retirement shortly after having been "promoted" to the glavk in 1939. The fact that Likhachev returned to ZiS after a short stint as commissar was a sign of the extraordinary trust that the Stalin regime had in him. That, however, did not protect his factory management team, which appeared to suffer the same mass purging in 1937 that SiM experienced.[41]

During his long career Likhachev received the Order of Lenin five times and the Order of the Red Banner of Labor twice. He was also the subject of *Direktor,* a volume of memoirs of ZiL workers, ITR, and managers, and of the biography by Tamara Leont'eva. By the end of the First FYP, Likhachev and Stepanov were the two most well known directors in Moscow. Like Stepanov, Likhachev only was able to establish his authority at AMO after a difficult struggle in the late 1920s, when he succeeded in placing his own young managers and engineers into crucial positions on the managerial and technical staffs. The memoirs collected in the volume *Direktor* might be read as the homage of Likhachev's new management team to the boss-patron.

The first memoir, by A. V. Kuznetsov, noted that Likhachev quickly brought in his own people: V. G. Lapin as technical director; D. V. Golaiev as production boss; and F. S. Demianiuk and M. A. Shestakov, who became the most important engineers in the plant. In 1928, Likhachev took Demianiuk and Kuznetsov to the Mercedes plant in Germany to observe production methods. Returning to Moscow, he established a new Bureau of Methods at AMO to emulate aspects of the German plant. The bureau was headed by Demianiuk and Kuznetsov.[42]

Kuznetsov was among those who worked his way up from *master* to a top managerial position with long tenure in the plant. Mikhail Abramovich Fil'tser was another. A mechanic who graduated from the AMO FZU, during his forty-three-year career he became a shop boss. So did Fedor Mikhailovich Khironnikov, who began as an unskilled worker at AMO in 1926 and ended as the deputy of the shop boss. Andrei Petrovich Churaev began in 1925 as an instructor in the FZU and ended as the boss of the ZiS laboratory.[43] In retirement, he chaired the commission on the history of the factory. These two were perfect examples of *vydvizhentsy*, individuals promoted from the bench to top management positions in a factory. They were, however, the exceptions in Likhachev's management team, which like Stepanov was pieced together almost exclusively with graduates from technical colleges who had never seen a factory work bench before they were hired at ZiS.

Covering some of the same ground as Kuznetsov's memoir, the official factory *History* gives brief biographical sketches of many of these men who comprised the Likhachev management team. They included N. A. Bakulov, S. D. Chaikov, A. D. Assonov, A. M. Vel'tishchev, Churaev, V. N. Lialin, V. A. Chernyshevich, Fil'tser, A. A. Gul', and D. V. Goliaev, all of whom went to Germany, England, or the United States to observe the leading auto plants. With the exception of Fil'tser and Churaev, they all came to AMO as soon as they graduated from the institutes of higher education, without any prior shop-floor experience. The brief biographical sketches provided in the *History* do not always give complete information, but seem to indicate that they were engineers from the day they arrived.[44]

Three examples of young and highly educated appointees appointed directly from the institute to to positions on the shop floor were Lialin, Demianiuk, and Barsukov. Lialin began in 1924 as the chief mechanic, then became chief constructor, then chief engineer before retiring in 1944. Goliaev began as shop boss during the First FYP and then became chief engineer before 1936. Later he worked in aviation, then in the Moscow Aviation Institute where he became a professor. Demianiuk became a doctor of technology in the Academy of Sciences and a professor after 1952. Barsukov was also placed in a highly responsible position at AMO, and he was credited with playing a key role in the reconstruction in the early 1930s.[45]

Most of these men were already chief shop engineers or bosses during the First FYP and the first reconstruction of the factory. That would include Lialin, Goliaev, Chernyshevich, and also Gorbunov, Evseev, Tsipulin, Lapin, Kabalevskii, Bogdanov, Chaikov, and Smirnov. The official history chose Demianiuk as the best representative of this cohort. He graduated from a higher institute of learning, the MVTU, and came to AMO as an engineer at the same time as Likhachev, in 1926. He became the boss of the mechanical tool shop and the chief expert on the technology of the factory.[46]

These men formed the core of Likhachev's management team. Like Stepanov, he appointed mostly young men, graduates of the VUZs or technical colleges, without production experience. Likhachev relied on them from the outset, even more than Stepanov, because he did not seem to have had any figures of the stature of Gaidul' or Filatov in his *partkom* to mobilize support within the party apparatus for his plans for reconstructing the factory. Likhachev, more than Stepanov, was firmly in control at the outset of reconstruction.

Kuznetsov's memoir provides the best biographical sketch of Likhachev's management team and his methods of appointment. He described Likhachev as having "a remarkable memory and a fine knowledge of men" that "helped him to always find the candidate who fit." He would consult with his shop and shift bosses concerning appointments, and according to Kuznetsov, was a "good psychologist, with an excellent understanding of his shop and department bosses."[47] Describing other shop and shift bosses that Likhachev appointed, he mentioned Chernushevich, Gorbunov, Smetanin, Ivanov, Petrov, Lottershtein, and Zakharov.

Of these, only Zakharov was a *vydvizhenets* from the bench. The only boss who was a specialist from the old school under Likhachev was A. A. Evseev, superintendent of the forge shop. Apparently he used his experience in France to design bus and car chassis.[48] Kuznetsov himself, as I noted above, was a *vydvizhenets*. He was a *master* in the gear-cutting shop at ZiS. Then, when Likhachev became commissar of mid-level machine construction, he appointed Kuznetsov to become Red Director of the new KIM auto plant, (Communist Youth International) built adjacent to the ZiS plant.

Thus, neither old specialists nor worker promotees played much of a role in the consolidation of Likhachev's new management team. With the exceptions of Kuznetsov, Khironnikov, and Zakharov, who were promotees, and of Evseev, an Old Regime specialist, the rest of the management team consisted of highly educated engineers, technicians, and managers with little or no workplace experience when Likhachev recruited them. They served him well in the struggle with the Americans from the Brandt firm and with Sorokin from Avtotrest over the design of the first reconstruction of the factory. They would serve him well again, during the second reconstruction, 1934–1937. Perhaps even more than Stepanov, Likhachev had already put together his management team and he did not need to rely on any rising young Stalinist stalwarts in the plant party committee, like Filatov or Gaidul', to push through the first or second reconstruction projects.

The Shift in Managerial Production Politics

The politics of reconstructing SiM and AMO-ZiS reflected, in microcosm, the politics of reconstruction of the PR, of Moscow, and of the entire USSR. It was a process of acute social conflict, called "class struggle" by the Stalinists. Out of this conflict there emerged the outlines of what is now called the Stalinist administrative-command socioeconomic system. As R. W. Davies has shown, following along the lines of Granick's interpretation of flexibility in management decision making, the managers and administrators were not as subject to the rigid control of the plan and of administrative hierarchy as it would have seemed.[49]

My findings are consistent with this interpretation, but emphasize the room for maneuver or autonomy of the Red Directors in two important respects, which has not been considered heretofore. First, they were making the shift from "class struggle" to "social contract" even before they had won the battles over the reconstruction of SiM and AMO in 1929 and 1930. As organization men, once their factory's future was secure and their management team was in place, they had little use for the class struggle. Their desire to remove Old Regime specialists seemed to have been limited to powerfully placed opponents of their reconstruction projects with whom they had direct conflict of interest. They were not anxious to "expose wreckers," nor did they encourage specialist-baiting, or *spetseedstvo*. Second, in their attitude toward factory workers, particularly newcomers, they shifted from blaming the newcomers to training them. That was essential, since the politics of the class struggle had been such a total failure in integrating new workers by threat and intimidation.

In this respect, the Red Directors were crucial in bridging the gap between the workers and the regime. They seemed to understand key aspects of the two social processes that I have described in terms of the factory as melting pot and community organizer, and they had a very significant influence over how the regime's social policy was applied. They shifted from class struggle to social contract, and this provides some explanation for how ideas percolated upward and where the "Six Conditions" strategy came from, as well as how the new policies descended from on high. It should be obvious that the Red Directors' switch in managerial strategy was, in no small measure, a response to and an articulation of the interests and needs of the Soviet workers, both established and newcomers.

At SiM, by 1935, Stepanov's managerial team consisted of the chief engineer, L. V. Marmorshtein; the technical director, N. B. Rodzevich; the boss of the rolling mill shop, D. I. Tarlinskii; chief engineer in the same shop, Sagaidak; the boss of the open hearth shop, M. N. Korolev; his chief engineer, A. G. Pogonchenkov; and boss of the sheet metal shop, N. P. Gromov.[50] Many of them were already in leading positions during the First FYP. Virtually none of them were workers from the bench at SiM. Ordzhonikidze praised Stepanov for putting together a successful management team by combining new and old specialists. Indeed, the key word here was "specialists," since almost all of them were new.

What was important, as I have suggested, was not whether these specialists had come from working-class families and been admitted into the VUZs as part of a proletarianization campaign. Many probably had. Rather, what was significant about them was the attitudes that they brought to the shop floor with their college education. With the exception of those few workers at the bench who went through *rabfaki* and then were appointed to managerial and technical positions, the other new appointees lacked industrial experience. That, it seems clear, was what Stepanov and Likhachev wanted. They wanted young men who knew science and technology, but who were also dependent on the director for finding their way inside the plant.

The impact of the Great Terror was to disrupt the social contract by shaking up the managerial teams put in place by Stepanov and Likhachev. Part of the purpose was obviously to undermine Ordzhonikidze. Likewise, removing Stepanov meant removing his entire managerial team, his clientele network. Likhachev's fate was completely different, even though his ties to Ordzhonikidze by 1937 would seem to have been no different than Stepanov's. His team was broken apart, however, and so when he returned to the plant in 1940 and then after the Second World War, he had to reassemble a management team. Il'in at SiM, a Stakhanovite smelter promoted from the bench to become the new Red Director in 1938, did the same. Despite the tremendous disruption of 1937–38, nothing was fundamentally changed by the terror in terms of the system of management, industrial relations, and labor relations. The patterns were intact in 1939 and 1940, as new faces filled the slots vacated in one of the greatest zigzags in Soviet history. The main impact, beyond removing an entire generation, was to promote the curse of turnover from the top down as the confusion and chaos generated in the terror caused workers to resume the First FYP custom of constantly searching for other jobs, which blended into the massive disruptions caused by turnover among production workers with increased drafting after 1939.

Still, one might argue that the Red Directors' willingness in 1929 and 1930 to unleash the class struggle rhetoric against select Old Regime specialists who blocked their projects for reconstructing SiM and AMO both in the factories and in the upper levels of Soviet administration, came back to haunt them in 1937, when others, far more unscrupulous, would use the same methods to discredit Stepanov and the management teams that he and Likhachev had assembled. Of course, some workers in every factory had serious conflicts with foremen or bosses and were happy to see the factory administration in jeopadary in 1937. Social contract or not, the Soviet factory like capitalist enterprises, was never conflict-free. While, some disgruntled workers were no doubt happy to see these organization men fall in the terror, it seems evident that, to the extent that workers had won the social contract through compromises together with the Red Directors, they must have been disgusted with the regime's terror, which was an attempt to tear up that contract. The result was a new round of labor turnover.

This new round of turnover, as we have seen, provoked new draconian labor laws from 1938 to 1940 that recalled the first wave of 1930–32. The social contract seemed again to have been discarded in favor of Stalinist class struggle policy and ideology. However, the Great Terror saw no resurgence of the class struggle ideology; "wreckers" were castigated strictly in the jargon of Soviet patriotism. Nor did it destroy the industrial relations system, which I suggest was a social contract, that had evolved between the Red Director and his manangement team, and the foremen and workers on the shop floor. It destroyed the men who had built that system, replacing them with new men.

The result was a stable system, so stable that it proved to be sclerotic, as the failure of the Khrushchev, Kosygin, and Gorbachev reforms would demonstrate. I suggest that it was built in the same way the party-state was built under Stalin, on the personalized foundations of patron-client networks. That network could vary from factory to factory, but generally speaking, the Red Director played a crucial role, establishing a form of *edinonachalie* that was based on a new management team. Red Directors like Stepanov and Likhachev surged to prominence, in part, by gaining the respect and trust of leaders like Ordzhonikidze, and in part because of their success in putting together a new and loyal management team in the factory. These patron-client networks were powerful and allowed the Red Director to manage effectively. The shop-floor bargain over production norms and wages also proved to be stabilizing, as under capitalism, but probably even more stabilizing under Soviet conditions. That was because it was based on a status revolution that had suddenly integrated peasants, women, and youth with established workers in a social melting pot and because workers and managers turned the factory into a community organizer. The Great Terror very seriously disrupted the social contract and this industrial relations system; it did not destroy either.

During the Stalin era, the regime's slogan "he who does not work shall not eat" was a crude social Darwinism that expressed the regime's understanding of its new social contract. This slogan never seemed to catch on among workers, who were not sure, after the famine of 1932–33 and the terror of 1937–38, that the regime intended to fulfill its part of the bargain at all, let alone build the shining future. Still, for the most part, despite famine and terror, people worked hard in those years, a fact which this study has attempted to explain in terms other than fear or enthusiasm. By the time of Brezhnev, workers who mouthed the counter-slogan and counter–social contract, "they pretend to pay us and we pretend to work," captured the realities of a stable but sclerotic industrial relations system quite accurately. While that sclerosis was significantly due to management's total refusal to innovate in production and failure to introduce technologies long since available, its origins were in the social contract and industrial system established on the shop floor by Stepanov at SiM and by Likhachev at AMO-ZiS. This sclerosis was hidden, for many decades, by the extremely dynamic era of social transformation, the era of working-class formation, which began in 1930.

10

THE MAKING OF THE NEW SOVIET WORKING CLASS

s Marx assumed, implied, or stated on virtually every page of *Capital,* the factory was the dominant and formative institution of capitalist society by the mid-nineteenth century. With the coming of the second industrial revolution, from roughly 1880 to 1914, the Marxist approach seemed to have been fully vindicated, as giant new factory complexes such as the Krupp Works, sprawling industrial cities, like Bochum, and new industrial regions, such as the Ruhr, came to dominate the social and physical landscape of north-central Europe.[1] Even the periphery of Europe, including Italy, Spain, the Austro-Hungarian Empire, the Ottoman Empire, and especially the Russian Empire, as I have argued, showed signs of this industrial transformation in certain zones and cities, although they were more scattered in a still largely agrarian hinterland.

Marx had already concluded during the 1840s that the two modern classes of capitalist society, bourgeoisie and proletariat, would inevitably confront one another in a decisive class struggle. This also seemed to be coming true in the late nineteenth century, as evidenced by the growing frequency and violence of strikes and the new wave of union organizing that established the British Trades Union Council, the French Confédération Générale du Travail, the German "Free Unions," and the American Federation of Labor. These labor movements, the AFL excepted, were all closely connected to the rise of socialist parties and to the Second International. Furthermore, the rising frequency and the growing intensity of shop-floor conflicts and strikes concerning deskilling, workers' control, wage rates and work norms, seemed to verify Marx's argument that under capitalism, the skilled worker would be reduced to the lowest common denominator of what he called "simple labor," while many unskilled workers would also be rendered redundant by investment in machinery.[2]

Despite the evidence of rising labor and political turbulence, however, fin-de-siècle social scientists challenged Marx's assumptions about social structure, classes, and class struggle. First, Emile Durkheim predicted a future of a stable "modern industrial society" in *The Division of Labor in Society*, and then Max Weber proposed a triadic theory of "class, status, and party" in his essay by that title in *Economy and Society*. Each rejected Marx's assumptions on the centrality of the class struggle and his conclusions on where class struggle would lead in capitalist society.

Durkheim began with Marx's premise on the pivotal importance of the factory and of the labor process, but he drew diametrically opposite conclusions. With the concentration of workers in modern industry, he argued, the specialization of the labor process and of management would assume new forms. He foresaw the rise of a new type of "organic solidarity" replacing what he called the primitive "mechanical solidarity" of preindustrial and of early industrial development. He attributed the social and political tensions of the late nineteenth century, and the increasing labor unrest, to the process of "modernization," which he defined as the transition in solidarities. With the transition from "mechanical" to "organic" solidarity would come consensus and social equilibrium, a theory which I believe is uniquely relevant to the USSR in the 1930s.

Durkheim also anticipated a parallel shift in juridical practice, from an emphasis on "punitive" or "penal law" to an emphasis on civil law, commercial law, procedural law, and also on administrative and constitutional law, which he lumped together under the rubric "restitutive" law, that would foster this social equilibrium and consensus.[3] This legal aspect of Durkheim's theory, while it might have some relevance to legal Soviet legal theory during NEP, and in particular to Pashukanis commodity-exchange theory of the law, clearly does not apply to Soviet developments during the 1930s, as the law under Stalinism was not an arena for restitution or conflict resolution. The second edition of *The Division of Labor in Society*, published in 1902, offered a theory of "corporatism" in which the unions, enterprises, and the state would resolve conflicts and establish equilibrium. This, I believe, is highly suggestive for developments during the 1920s in Western Europe, and perhaps would apply to Soviet NEP in some ways. Once again, however, this does not apply to Soviet developments during the 1930s.[4] Rather, it is Durkheim's emphasis on the impact of the intensified division of labor which is applicable.

Durkheim's theory of a shift from mechanical to organic solidarity in the labor process is uniquely relevant to the Soviet experience in the 1930s and subsequent decades because of the peculiarities of Russian history, especially its bifurcated, dual labor market and the lingering impact of peasant work culture on working-class formation. With the shift during the 1930s from the seasonal and migratory labor patterns long prevalent among the peasant subaltern workers to permanent urban factory work, and with the shift to a unified labor market, something very much like the transition from mechanical to organic that Durkheim had envisioned was underway in the Soviet industrialization drive.

Max Weber, contrary to Marx and Durkheim, rejected the premise that two classes and their conflict or cooperation would dominate modern society and its political landscape. He also rejected the premise that the factory was the dominant institution shaping patterns of conflict or solidarity in modern society. Instead, he defined "economic classes" more amorphously than either Marx or Durkheim and in the nondichotomous terms of differing "market situations," or what we might call "market capacities." This was a decided advance over Marx or Durkheim in that it opened up a discussion of labor markets. Whereas Marx saw all workers being reduced to the status of "simple labor," Durkheim posited universally rising skill levels with specialization and the new division of labor, and thus "organic solidarity" in modern industry. Both were grossly oversimplified assumptions about labor markets and worker deskilling or skilling. On the other hand, Weber's "market situations" could absorb the increasingly important role of education.

Weber's approach to "market situations" in his seminal essay "Class, Status, and Party" suggested that individuals would bring their "capacities" into the labor market and that these included more than the dichotomy between "capital" and "labor." It included skill and knowledge or what now would be called "human capital" as a critical variable. He also suggested that labor markets would always be "imperfect" because in any society, factors such as "castes" (estates), religion, slavery (racism), and status groups determined who could obtain certain jobs or qualify for specific occupations. Such imperfections, we now know, exist in every labor market, since none functions as a perfect neoclassical grid of supply and demand, in which marginal product and marginal labor cost are equalized. Neither Marx nor Durkheim were theoretically as well situated as Weber to account for these inevitable labor market imperfections.

In other words, Weber had anticipated labor economics as the field has evolved since the 1960s, wherein human capital (education and skill) and dual or segmented labor markets (a theory of a labor market governed by its imperfections) have constituted the two most important new theoretical insights. The significance of the dual labor market in the Russian and early Soviet context has been a central theme in this study. Another has been the significance of education and vocational training during the 1930s. Education and training were crucially important in the USSR, not so much in distinguishing the human capital of individuals in a tight labor market, which was Weber's presumption and one which was quite valid in most capitalist societies, but rather in transforming the attitudes, values, and skills of an entire generation, and thus in helping to dissolve the dual labor market and to establish a relatively homogeneous labor market. The new Soviet labor market was uniquely "inverted," and thus was also remarkably unified, which explains why Durkheim's theory of specialization of labor generating a new "organic" solidarity applies so well to the Soviet 1930s.

Weber also situated class more broadly than Marx or Durkheim, arguing that status groups and party affiliation might reinforce or contradict class distinctions. Weber's multivariant approach to class, social identities, and social solidarities proved to be more relevant for Western Europe during the first half of the twentieth century, and especially during the second half of the century, than either Marx or Durkheim. Even prior to the Second World War, the class struggle that Marx anticipated did not supersede other social identities, such as nationalism, while the "corporatism" that Durkheim foresaw in 1902 as the solution to the class struggle in the factory and in the polity had limited success in both arenas until the 1920s and would never result in the type of stability that he anticipated, even in the most quiescent 1950s.[5] Weber's analysis, more than Marx's or Durkheim's, better accounts for the wide variety of conflicts that shook the industrialized states of Europe to their very foundations in the first half of the twentieth century and the ways in which they were resolved. With one exception that is: Imperial Russia and then Soviet Russia and the USSR.

In the Russian and Soviet context, the theories outlined by Marx and Durkheim proved to be more relevant than Weber's. Prior to 1917, Marxism provides the best explanation, and after 1929, Durkheim's theory does. Their shared premises, namely that the factory would shape either bourgeois or modern and industrial society and that the resolution of class conflict would be the decisive issue in modern history, proved to be an apt characterization of the unique aspects of the Russian and Soviet experience. The peculiarities of Russia's pattern of "combined development," which made Marxism especially relevant prior to 1917 when the revolutionary impulse swept over virtually all of the society, also made Durkheim particularly relevant to the Soviet scene during the 1930s.

The configuration of the dual labor market prior to 1917 in Russia was destabilizing in the extreme, while the obliteration of the dual labor market and the developing homogeneous labor market during the 1930s was highly stabilizing. The construction of fifteen hundred factories during the First FYP brought with it a final flourish of peasant-migrant labor. The entire Union became a "foundation pit," and construction of new factories, roads, apartments, and entire cities, saw very minimal if any labor specialization or mechanization in construction labor. The foundations were dug by hand, with shovels, picks, and axes, based on a very primitive type of gang labor that was typical of peasant work patterns. This, it turned out was the final flourish of gang labor.

Gang labor was undifferentiated labor in which the work was almost all done by hand, and the workers were literally expendable, as became brutally clear when *gulag* and other forms of compulsory labor replaced shock-work enthusiasts and voluntary peasant-migrants in undertaking and completing many of the construction projects during the First FYP and increasingly thereafter. The single most characteristic feature of gang labor was transience and, with it, lack of job specialization, so that substituting one worker for another made no difference. Labor turnover, a typical phenomenon of any labor market which was exacerbated under Soviet inverted labor market conditions, was not the same as this type of gang labor transience. The Stalin regime mistakenly lumped the two together, as have historians since that time.

A type of gang labor in sowing and harvesting had prevailed in the peasant commune for centuries, and despite the inroads of market forces in the village, this was still characteristic of village work during the late imperial era and Soviet NEP.[6] The peasant-migrants had applied and adapted these same work traditions to out-migration for wage labor in agriculture, construction, forestry, mining, and also to manufacture and industry. With the *artel'* and *zemliachestvo* networks, peasants on *otkhod* from a single village or region went to a factory via existing networks and found work in teams with fellow villagers.

Under the *artel'*, work gangs were organized by an elder in the village, and then they were transplanted as a group to a construction site or a factory, where they labored as a sort of subcontracting unit. Under *zemliachestvo*, individual villagers migrated to the city and sought out the village acquaintance, the *zemliak,* when they arrived at a factory or city and joined a work team that way. In this case, the *zemliak* might himself be a *master,* that is highly skilled worker who trained apprentices and functioned as a protoforeman, or he might direct the peasant-migrant to work under any other *master* with whom he was connected. That was how the peasant-recruits came to work under lifelong urban factory worker-foremen, who treated them as if they were gang labor.

Either way, work styles adopted in industry resembled that familiar on the land for the peasant-migrants. In a steel plant like Guzhon, the peasant gangs were given the heaviest, most dangerous, and hottest jobs at the open hearth furnaces or rolling mills, which required no skill and which they performed year after year, without any possibility of promotion. That was because they were seasonal and interchangeable; they considered themselves to be transients on the urban scene and were treated as such by the managers and foremen. They compensated for such difficult, tedious, unskilled work in three ways. They used work-gang rhythms, familiar on the land, to adapt to and to survive heavy and hot physical work. It was a type of preindustrial "tracking," typified by the song of the Volga boatmen or the exclamation *"vzyali,"* which translates something like "got it."[7] They worked seasonally, and if a job became too intolerable would not hesitate to leave and set out for a different job or return to the village. Finally, they would endure the hot and heavy work because it was temporary and it paid more, and they envisioned factory labor as only a temporary expedient in which they wanted to earn as much as possible in as short a stint as was possible, to bring their earnings back to their family in the village. Thus, they were "birds of passage," but since they did not have to cross an ocean or move from one country to another, we can link Piore's metaphor with Stalin's slogan and call them "birds of passage within one country."

Given the lack of excavation and other building equipment for construction on the scale undertaken during the First FYP, it is hard to envision how anything other than the gang labor traditions could have been used to construct the new factories and cities. By any criterion of efficiency, however, gang labor was hopelessly backward, and for machine-based industry and for modern assembly-line manufacturing it was totally inapplicable. Gang labor meant interchangeable personnel, it meant little or no occupational specialization, it meant working the laborer until he or she was burned out, and it meant transience. Gang labor during the First FYP, when construction crews were pulled together and then dissolved overnight, might not even have fostered much of the type of mechanical solidarity that Durkheim found typical of premodern capitalism.

Soviet patterns of labor recruiting during the First FYP, with peasant mi-

grants and urban youth in work gangs, seemed to have replicated older imperial patterns. However, that was only superficially true, and true but for a
brief moment, since gang labor very quickly yielded to specialized labor
brigades and to new forms of specialized labor. The shift was made with the
transition from construction work to production work. That is why the *pusk,*
the starting-up of the factory or putting a conveyer on-line, was so symboli-
cally significant and ritualized. When Likhachev celebrated "sewing the coat
around the button," he was also celebrating a shift from construction to production and from gang labor to specialized labor. It was also the end of the
dual labor market and the beginning of the formation of a new Soviet working class.

The transition from construction to manufacturing work in industry for
most peasants (and many urban youth) in the first years of Stalinist industrialization went via "conveyers" from "field to factory." The most important
conveyer, in the First FYP, as in tsarist times, was construction work, while logging, mining, and extraction work, and in transportation, loading and unloading work, were also important. In these conveyer jobs, mechanization
was minimal and gang labor methods and labor transience prevailed, despite
the efforts of the regime to transform them along the model of manufacturing work, that is, to mechanize them and make the work force permanent in
construction and all of these industries.

In manufacturing, permanent jobs were available for the taking, and
work brigades as well as job differentiation were evolving to cope with the
specialization of production. The long-term significance of gang labor in Soviet society was limited to mining and forestry and construction in the *gulag,*
and agriculture on the *kolkhoz,* with bad results in all of them. Gang labor is
what constructed factories in record time, but they were often in need of repair even before they were finished and then required frequent capital reconstruction during the Second and Third FYPs. Gang labor in the camps of
the *gulag* was a terrible waste of human resources. On the *kolkhoz,* many aspects of the age-old peasant work traditions were replicated on the large collective fields, where if anything the work was even less differentiated than in
the precollectivization village. Furthermore, labor differentiation within
each peasant household was sharply reduced by collectivization, at least until
a tiny household plot was legalized once again. Such gang labor, especially
among peasant women, persisted alongside the tractors and harvesters into
the 1980s. This was the major factor retarding Soviet agriculture, and an indication of its backwardness. In industry, however, gang labor died out during the 1930s when seasonal labor migration ended. In fact, gang labor
mostly disappeared in the First FYP.

The conveyers did not, by themselves, guarantee permanent peasant out-migration, and *orgnabor* campaigns to hire peasants from the *kolkhoz* initially relied on seasonal migrants. That is why the *otkhod* and the *orgnabor* figures are so hopelessly confused for 1930–32. Seasonal migrants and permanent migrants were both included under the generic heading of *orgnabor* recruits, and seasonal migrants may well have been double- or triple-counted (see chap. 3 above). The confusion was resolved by the shift from seasonal to permanent migration. *Otkhod* was yielding to permanent one-way migration, still called *otkhod*. The "bird of passage" was settling in the city.

The end of the "bird of passage" outlook meant not only that the peasant-migrant himself (traditionally, most out-migrants were men) was moving permanently to the city, but also that he was going to settle his wife and children in the city. It also meant that unmarried peasant women and men came to the city in record numbers, married there, and had children there. Either way, the split family, and the symbiotic pattern of migration between village and city, agriculture and industry, was thus finally and decisively severed.[8]

Two factors explain this. First the collectivization of agriculture made seasonal migration patterns and the split family both economically impossible and undesirable, as the *kolkhoz* was rightly seen by the peasant-migrant as offering no advantages worth preserving. Without household land to farm, there was no point to maintaining a household in the village, since the land was collectivized and remuneration (in kind) soon corresponded entirely to the household's accumulated workdays. Second, the inversion of the labor market and the shift to permanent, year-round production in factories meant that full-time urban jobs were finally available for peasant migrants and that bosses would, for the first time, frown on seasonal migration and prefer to hire permanent workers. Draconian labor laws were basically unnecessary, because transient and seasonal labor patterns were giving way to permanent factory work during the 1930s, due to the changing outlook of both the migrants and of the factory managers and foremen.

The inversion of the labor market by the First FYP opened the factory gates to virtually all social groups. The subaltern workers, many coming via these conveyers, settled in at the workbench in record numbers. Instead of mass unemployment or rather, the underemployment, typical of imperial and NEP labor patterns, the industrializing economy was now characterized by acute labor shortages. The social impact was dramatic. An entirely new type of industrial work force emerged as the dual labor market dissolved, from which a new Soviet working class emerged. This working class would not define itself in opposition to any managerial equivalent of a bourgeoisie, nor would it primarily define itself in opposition to the party-state, in sharp contrast to both the Thompsonian world of nineteenth-century England and late imperial Russia.

This was a working class "in formation" in many respects. First, it absorbed workers from the subaltern social groups, meaning that this working class fundamentally redefined itself, so that inclusivity replaced exclusivity as its defining characteristic. Second, the dual labor market disappeared and with it the bifurcated workplace, as workers took on specialized new occupations in newly organized work brigades, establishing a deep social homogenization. Third, the urban protocommunity, or the outlines of a new urban factory-community were becoming visible, as workers, ITR, and factory management began to conceptualize the factory as the institution that could resolve pressing material problems of housing, food, and transportation. Finally, the new working class was formed by defining its own interests in terms of what it wanted from the party-state and what it was willing to offer the party-state on the shop floor. Thus, they were looking for an ersatz social contract, and not a class struggle.

The regime's line of class struggle against the alien classes who allegedly were worming their way into the Soviet factory, was a logic that would have pitted most established workers against most of the newcomers, that is roughly half the workers against the other half by the end of the First FYP. Such a logic would have further disrupted production relations, already in chaos, and it was rejected by the working class. Instead, all workers, newcomers and established, found themselves improvising industrial relations vis-à-vis factory administrators and managers on the shop floor, and vis-à-vis the party-state. I do not mean to suggest that the working class adopted struggle against the regime ("us" versus "them") or against the managers-technicians. Instead, it found itself in the position of negotiating its class interests with them in the suddenly favorable, inverted labor market, that is, of redefining its class interests vis-à-vis the regime and factory management. That was more than individualized resistance by "voting with their feet," or the apathy of "working to rule," or a striving for upward mobility, or striving to emulate Stakhanovites. It was working with hands and brains to create a new industrial relations system and melting pot on the shop floor, and a new factory community. Yet, this definition of class interest did not envision the party-state as its "class enemy."

Durkheim's conception of working-class organic solidarity, leading to a type of social stability (or perhaps a "positive" or "parallel" integration), much like Marx's discussion of the inevitability of class struggle, can only make sense in historical context, that is, in relation to other classes, social groups, and types of state regimes. E. P. Thompson showed how the British working class defined itself in the process of its formation, through a class struggle that was led by artisans and their friendly associations (which Marx had all but ignored and which Eric Hobsbawm discovered almost a century later) and who defined themselves in strident opposition to the laissez-faire ideology of the Whig regime.[9] This revolutionized the study of labor and labor organization. It is Thompson's method, and not the content of his study and the particularly crucial role of artisans and of the "moral economy" of displaced artisans and peasant-farmers, that takes us a long way toward clarifying the Soviet experience.

Thompson's method suggests the possibility of alternative paths of working-class formation and of alternative class consciousness to that of the early nineteenth-century British workers or early twentieth-century Russian workers, which was based on a dichotomous ideology and reality of class struggle. In fact, his very method requires such alternatives, since with the Reform Bill of 1832, the circumstances and politics of working-class formation in England shifted decisively. To understand the Soviet working class in the 1930s, we must abandon the early nineteenth-century Thompsonian world of dispossessed artisans and farmers, of those who were defending "moral economy" and imparting oppositional values and culture through their friendly societies and associations.

Instead, the new Soviet working-class consciousness came into being as the established production workers and the newcomers were both abandoning notions of "moral economy," not crystallizing them. The established workers, disgruntled by "regime of economy" and "rationalization of production" schemes in the late NEP years, were forced to abandon much of their notion of "moral economy," which consisted of apprenticeship-style training and skill- and wage-based hierarchies, as the impact of the industrialization drive was felt in the rise of semiskilled work in modern work brigades. They adjusted primarily by becoming foremen or leading technical workers or heading new production brigades in new factories. Newcomers to Soviet industry—above all peasants, women, and youth, but also some craftsmen and white-collar employees who were driven into the factories by state policy—instead of fighting for a "moral economy" that they may have brought with them from the peasant *mir* or the craft-based manufacturing called *kustar* and *remeslo*, were initially preoccupied with a sharp social struggle against the established workers, which ranged from job definition and work process to urban living space. Ironically, they were also confronted with the state's class struggle ideology, which was penalizing them for their non-working-class social origins. They seized the chance to gain a semiskilled position or occupation in the new work brigade through vocational training and remedial education. The state gradually alleviated their predicament by abandoning its class struggle ideology and legitimizing the newcomers as full-fledged members of the new working class.

Peasants, artisans, students, and houswives coming into the factories during the First FYP without any prior industrial experience were anxious to abandon their old identities and status as subaltern groups or semiproletariat and were equally anxious to gain the status of members of the working class.[10] No doubt part of the reason was their desire to discard the petty-bourgeois class label under the repressive class struggle ideology. But that was only part of the story. The more important part were their own motivations for adapting.

Whereas the Mensheviks explained the lack of a working-class opposition to Stalinism in terms of the "peasantization" of the labor force in the 1930s and the decline of class consciousness, my explanation has focused on the unique pattern of working-class formation and consciousness during the 1930s, and above all on the integration of peasants, women, and youth into the factory work force, destroying the long-term legacy of the dual labor market. In this respect, I suggest that we adopt Thompson's historical method, while inverting his findings, much as the Soviet labor market itself was inverted. There was a "making" and a "self-making" of the Soviet working class, as surely as the English, although the contrast in how that occurred could not be sharper or clearer.

Class consciousness took shape in the Soviet context in the 1930s by the very process of overcoming the chaos in production and the attendant social conflict of the First FYP, chaos and social conflict that the regime had unleashed with the industrialization drive and then had fanned through its class struggle ideology with collectivization, the Shakhty affair, and industrial policy aimed at punishing class aliens. In this narrow sense of a defensive resistance to Stalinist ideology, newcomers were in opposition to the regime. However, such opposition was short-lived. In the new factories, the newcomers were becoming semiskilled machine operatives and assembly-line workers, often in a matter of months, but in any case, within a few years. The introduction of impersonal methods of vocational training, remedial education, and new technologies meant a decline in conflict with the established workers over job definition and assignment. Labor brigades were forming in which the workers had a specialized function or, for the first time, an occupation. The brigades themselves were increasingly differentiated one from the other. All this meant integration of the newcomers. Established workers were promoted or were themselves adapting to new job specialization. Now it was a matter of convincing the regime to drop the "class enemies" laws, rhetoric, and ideology.

Starting with Stalin's "Six Conditions" speech of 23 June 1931, when he proposed an ersatz social contract that strictly delimited the workers' obligations to the state and then vaguely outlined the state's obligations to the worker, the regime began to accept the reality of a new Soviet working class and to deemphasize its attack on the class aliens in the factory. The same tendency was evident in the regime's shift in emphasis from shock-work brigades as heroic leaders in the class struggle, to shock-work brigades as cost-accounting brigades. While the shift was marked by frequent zigzags in policy and ideology, most notably in the use the regime made of Stakhanovism in 1935 and 1936 and the purge-terror of 1937–38, the shift from class struggle ideology to class inclusive ideology was permanent. It was officially consecrated in the Stalin Constitution. In the end, the interests of the newcomers, who needed an inclusive definition of working class, and the desire of all workers for steady work routines, specialized occupations, and stable work brigades, would prevail. The shift in regime ideology and policy occurred, in large measure, because of the workers' support of managers and ITR and the articulation of Red Directors, who wanted and needed the same things. The very real social conflicts of the First FYP, artificially exacerbated by the regime, quickly gave way to a striking degree of cooperation between established workers and newcomers and between all of them and Red Directors and their staffs.[11]

Durkheim's theory, activated by Thompson's method of understanding class formation as a process, offers an alternative to individualism, alienation, fragmentation, and even contingent solidarities. It suggests how class formation and class consciousness were emerging. I suggest that we abandon the commonly held notions that rampant labor turnover, on the one hand, and widening wage differentiation and social stratification, on the other, meant that there was only severely limited solidarity among workers in Soviet society and no possibility of a working-class consciousness. The assumption that Soviet workers were predominantly engaging in peasant-type resistance by dissimulation, or by "voting with their feet," or by "working to rule," also should be discarded. The assumption that regime policy of wage differentiation effectively promoted worker individualism and the desire for upward mobility should be revised. Such arguments miss the more important social trends of the 1930s and beyond, namely, the rise of a new type of working class with new solidarities.

Clearly there was historically unprecedented social mobility in the 1930s in the USSR, and the forms of mobility included urbanization, geographic population shifts, occupational and status shifts, and to be sure, some *vydvizhenie*. What was remarkable, however, was how easy it was for people on the move to fit in when they arrived at a new factory, city, or job. That was because, at least in part, despite the very high rates of labor turnover, a sense of a stable work collective and community life was taking shape. And it looked pretty much the same, whether one was settling in Magnitogorsk, where peasant-migrants and leading cadre came from far away, or in Moscow itself, where the peasant-migrants came from the immediately surrounding provinces with their *zemliachestvo* and *artel'* networks firmly intact. In the midst of all this mobility, a stable urban and factory-based socioeconomic order and society was solidifying. It saw the unified urban family rather than the split family of the peasant-proletarian symbiosis. It saw the small proletarian family with low fertility rather than the large peasant family with high fertility. It saw entirely new gender relations, which I have not even begun to explore in this study, but which cries out for a serious new historical investigation.

This new working class looked pretty much the same throughout the USSR, with the possible important exception of ethnic or national minority regions. Even here, the migration of Russians, and perhaps also Ukrainians, should be seen as part of a wide geographic pattern of Sovietization on much of the periphery of the USSR. Or, at least, a Sovietization of its "inner" periphery.[12] The process of social integration may have been most rapid for peasants on the industrial periphery, say at Magnitogorsk, and most rapid for women in the industrial northwest surrounding Leningrad, or in the CIR surrounding Moscow. It was very rapid for youth in all three industrial zones, and this factor would prove to be decisive in the homogenization of the workers in the various geographical zones of the USSR, so that the old distinctions between geographical regions and patterns of industrial working-class formation lost most of their meaning during the 1930s. Geographic homogeneity prevailed, as did factory workplace homogeneity and factory community homogeneity.

Soviet workers were not voting with their feet so much as they were voting with their hands and brains on the shop floor and in the community. A new culture of class was created on the shop floor and in the urban proto-community, inclusive and "democratic" in its openness to all, regardless of class origins. The appropriate metaphors for the factory community emerging during the First FYP were not a "Bolshevik fortress" or "forge of the new Soviet man," nor the opposite metaphors of a "revolving door," or "entry courtyard," or "sieve." The U.S. metaphor, from a very different historical context, of a social "melting pot" where the factory became a type of "community organizer," is more appropriate.

The only outsiders in Soviet urban society, given an inclusive working-class and factory community that had no fundamental quarrel with factory managers, engineers, technicians, and the clerks and personnel of the state institutions in the city, could be "traitors" or "enemies of the people," which explains the striking absence of class discourse during the show trials and the terror.[13] Perhaps this degree of urban social solidarity also accounts, at least in part, for the passive outlook of many persons concerning these events and also for the active participation of a substantial layer of the population in making denunciations. Manichaean values, it would appear, were preserved even as more and more social groups became insiders in the factory and urban community. I would not push this explanation too far, as fear of death might be the better explanation for the actions or inactions of most of the urban population during the terror.

The second factor usually cited as negating any possible working-class formation and consciousness, was differentiation. Again, Stalin's "Six Conditions" speech, with its emphasis on wage incentive systems and wage differentiation, and with its system of unequal distribution of housing, food, and consumer goods, is seen as the end of working-class egalitarianism. The regime did establish both a thin layer of highly privileged worker heroes and a much broader layer of privileged workers, first calling them shock workers and then Stakhanovites. Ironically, this merely accelerated the homogenizing impact of the industrialization drive on labor markets, helping to overcome the legacies of social origins. The new forms of wage differentiation, except for the thin layer of the highly privileged, were relatively superficial.

This irony could be attributed, first, to the fact that such redifferentiation contributed to the process of breaking down the iron grip of "class origins," since one's work was evaluated in terms of output regardless of parents' occupation, place of birth, length of industrial work tenure, or any other factors of "origin" that had previously determined who was assigned particular jobs. Second, the widening differentials in the pay scales were largely negated by the simultaneously narrowing skill differentials, a consequence of the "middling" of worker occupations in the semiskilled categories. Furthermore, since the pay differentials were based on current levels of output and these fluctuated dramatically from one month to the next, rather than hardening into a well-defined social stratum, such as a labor aristocracy, there was fluidity of labor between pay brackets.

The regime would constantly complain about the fluidity of pay, almost as much as about the fluidity of labor due to turnover. It would try to tighten loopholes, curb supplemental pay and bonuses, and improve the work of norming and job description, just as it would try to "attach" workers at the bench. Each was a losing battle, not only because of changes in technology and work organization, but also because the regime's own crazy use of piece-rate pay systems, "progressive" piece-rate systems, and premiums made stable pay categories irrelevant in determining the worker's wages. The impact of this fluidity in pay was to *prevent* any hardening of defined strata within the working class, that is, to promote a new type of working-class homogenization.

This is strikingly clear if we consider the mass of shock workers or

Stakhanovites. Far from forming any kind of defined or hardened social strata, these categories fluctuated weekly. As Stakhanovite shops, decades, and entire factories were proclaimed, masses of shock workers and shock-work brigades were entirely forgotten, a fact which Ordzhonikidze lamented in the summer of 1936.[14] The same thing happened to masses of Stakhanovites during and after 1937 when, with the regime's failure to transform Stakhanovism into a mass movement, it declined almost as rapidly as it had appeared. Siegelbaum was right to distinguish the shifting mass of Stakhanovites from a very thin layer of outstanding Stakhanovites, who "numbered no more than a few hundred"[15] and were the next installment of what I have called the exceptional shock-worker heroes of the First FYP. The regime certainly intended to make them models for worker emulation, but it seems doubtful that such a tiny number could be considered to have constituted anything like a labor aristocracy. Rather, the outstanding shock workers and then Stakhanovites had a Horatio Alger, myth-making function regarding interclass mobility. Whether the politics of encouraging emulation worked or not is a theme for further research, and is connected to the issue of a new middle class.

The differentiation that was developing within the working class was a shallow new redifferentiation, while the main trend was social homogenization. Social homogenization was structural; it was the rooting out of long-term and historically formed social class distinctions between artisans and factory workers, or between peasants and factory workers, or between housewives and male factory workers or between apprenticing youth and older skilled *mastery*. These deep structural divisions were obviously reflected in the culture and/or culturally constructed. Whatever their origins, structural or cultural, these divisions were dissolved into the factory melting pot. The dominant trend during the 1930s was the rise of the subaltern workers into the mainstream or middling ranks of the working class, in what I have called a social status revolution. Youth were the wedge for peasants and women.

This integration of the subaltern newcomers was the foundation for an homogenizing tendency in every geographic region of the USSR, which took root regardless of upward mobility, geographic mobility, or labor turnover mobility. Homogenization was the social glue that held urban society together, and it continued to do so in the later 1930s and early 1940s, despite Stalinist terror and Nazi invasion.

With time, however, new functionally differentiating factors of the type emphasized by Shkaratan, those relating to the transformation of industry and of industrial employment patterns that came with the postwar scientific-technological revolution, deepened their impact on an increasingly diversified urban society. Perhaps this diversity acquired social-class features through the intergenerational conveyence of "social-class" expectations.[16] Perhaps the new social identity of white-collar workers, technicians, engineers, and others are better understood as occupational strata rather than as a middle class. In any case, this did not rapidly supplant the solidarities of the working class that derived from its formation process during the 1930s and that remained a powerful social force even through the Brezhnev years.

There was, of course, one stratum, class, or elite, which was becoming ever more distant and differentiated from society during the 1930s, and that was the party-state. Why that was tolerated by the working class has been a central theme in this study. Workers were defining their class interests, I have argued, vis-à-vis the objectives of a regime hell-bent on industrialization, and they reached a sort of accommodation with the regime as it began shifting from class struggle to ersatz social contract. The state's objectives, industrialization in particular, were compatible with those class interests, but the terms of exchange between labor power and wage compensation had to be worked out in practice, as did the system of industrial relations, that is labor-management relations. The regime, largely thanks to the efforts of the Red Directors, recognized that fact. It shifted its ideology to conform with the emerging system of industrial relations and the new inclusive working-class consciousness, and the result was a striking degree of working-class quiescence. Workers might well grumble, and did, at the lack of food or consumer goods, but the principle of fair compensation and the promise of improved compensation for work was as embedded in official ideology as it was in workers' expectations for the *svetloe budushchee,* the "bright future," which meant something during the 1930s and 1940s before it because such a source of ridicule during the Brezhnev years.

The integration of newcomers into the working class, that is, the process of formation of a new working class, was the decisive factor in Soviet history in the 1930s and 1940s, and it defined the social landscape of Stalinism. No other factor or factors, not fear, not enthusiasm, not selfish material interest, not upward mobility, not rampant labor turnover and dissimulation, not "voting with feet," was so important. The "parallel" or "social" integration of the new working class was critical in stabilizing the Stalinist regime. E. P. Thompson was right, above all, to emphasize the historical process of working-class formation. It was historically decisive for an entire Soviet generation.

GLOSSARY AND ACRONYMS

NOTES

BIBLIOGRAPHICAL ESSAY

BIBLIOGRAPHY

INDEX

GLOSSARY AND ACRONYMS

General Terminology

artel' – peasant wage-labor team, usually recruited in the village by an elder or *starosta*

birzh truda – labor exchange, official employment office

bronia – quota

buntarstvo – spontaneous militancy, usually referring to peasants or workers, something like uprising

elektrichka – commuter electric train

gorkom – city party committee

kadre, kadrovye – cadre workers, also used to mean skilled workers, hereditary workers, highly skilled and technical staff, and also qualified or competent workers

kolkhoz – collective farm in which peasant households received payment in kind, after state procurements were collected

kombinat – like an enterprise-factory, a complex of several factories in close proximity and under a single management team

kommandirovka – temporary job assignment in another city, business trip

kommunal'ka – communal apartment building in which families typically occupied a small room while sharing kitchen and bath with an entire floor of families

kotlovan – foundation pit

kvalifitsirovanyi rabochii – skilled worker

kustar – artisan manufacture, often rural (see *remeslo*)

letuny – "rolling stones," a pejorative term for workers who moved from job to job

meshchanstvo – lower-middle classes, with petty bourgeois values, often pejorative

meshchane – Third Estate, urban residents with property, prior to 1917

metallisty – metalworkers

mir – the peasant commune, traditionally practicing periodic land repartitioning and cooperative labor; legally replaced by the *kolkhoz* in 1930

mnogotirazhka – multicirculation paper published by a factory

muzhik – peasant male, usually meaning head of household

nachal'nik – shop or shift superintendant

nizy – the lower classes

obezlichka – lack of personal responsibility

oblast' – province

obkom – the province party committee

orgnabor – organized recruitment of labor from the villages for the factories

otkhod – out-migration of peasants from the village, typically seasonal, but after the 1930s this was usually permanent relocation to the city

otkhodniki – peasant-migrants

partprosloika – the party layer or element in a factory or organization

praktik – a person appointed as technician or engineer without higher education, usually a skilled machinist with long work tenure

pribezhiki – (pejorative) labor deserters, workers who moved from job to job

prikhlebatel' – (pejorative) a freeloader who illegally used factory stories or lived in factory apartments

proekt – design for a factory, or building

rabkory – worker-correspondents

raion – district

raikom – the *raion* party committee

raisoviet – the district soviet or elected council; local legislative body

remeslo – artisan manufacture or cooperative manufacture, usually urban

rvachi – (pejorative) self-seekers; could include *prikhlebatel' pribezhik*

sheftsvo – temporary inspection of an institution, or one institution taking temporary control of improving the work of another

smychka – worker-peasant alliance or coalition

sovkhoz – state farm, theoretically different from collective farm of *kolkhoz* in that employees were paid wages and according to workday units

spetseedstvo—specialist baiting; denouncing specialists (ITR or management) for alleged "bourgeois" class origins or foreign orgins or connections

starosta – village elder

stazherovka – an extended assignment to another factory

stengazeta – a wall-newspaper in a factory

tekstil'shchiki – textile workers, half male (skilled machinists), half female (semiskilled and unskilled machine operatives)

tekuchest' – labor turnover

tolkach – pusher, or procurer; a semilegal practice, involving barter or trade, usually to get scarce materials, equipment, or to recruit workers under the *orgnabor* system

upolnomochie – plenipotentiary

uravnilovka – "petty bourgeois egalitarianism," leveling in a pejorative sense

vydvizhenie – upward mobility, promotion, leapfrogging (*vydvizhentsy*, the promotees)

zagotovki – state grain procurements, technically purchased by state organs from the *kolkhoz*, in reality taken from them at low fixed prices *zemliachestvo* – the practice of seeking a fellow villager (*zemliak*), when a peasant-migrant arrived in a city on *otkhod)*

zhenorg – the women's organizer in a factory; perhaps sometimes a committee

Moscow Terminology

Moskva metallicheskaia – metal Moscow

Moskva sitsevaia – calico Moscow

Moscow Rings – Boulevard Ring, Garden Ring, Kamer-Kollezheskii Val, Circular Railroad, and the MKAD (auto beltway), five cocentric rings, from the inside out, that define the historical growth of the city

PR – Proletarskii Raion (Proletarian District), formerly the Rogozhskii and Simonvskii Districts in the southeast quadrant of Moscow (not used in Soviet sources)

Krasno-Presnenskii Raion – the Red Presnia District, chief textile district, on the opposite side of Moscow from the PR, with the oldest large factories in the city

Baumanskii Raion – formerly Basmanyi District, adjacent to the PR, to its northwest

Zamoskvoretskii Raion – the district of the city across the river from the PR to its west

Stalinskii Raion – a new district of Moscow in 1930, to the north and east of the PR

Factories

PR Factories

Aviamotornyi Zavod – airplane motor plant

Bauman Institute – also MVTU, the Moscow Higher Technical Institute

Dinamo – electro-machine construction plant built in 1899; known as the Westinghouse plant in the first decade of the twentieth century and was nationalized during the First World War

Elektroprovod – electric cable

Elektrozavod – electrical products, transformers, generators, located in Stalinskii District

Frezer – metal cutting plant located in the Sokolniki District, then Stalinskii District

GPZ-1 – Kaganovich First State Ballbearing plant

Kalibr – metal calibrating plant located in Liubertsy

KIM – Komsomol auto plant, manufacturer of the "Moskvich" car; founded in 1930

Kompressor – produced over 1,000 compressors in 1935

Moskabel – electric cable

Parostroi – vertical and horizontal beams for construction

SiM – Serp i Molot (Hammer and Sickle), steel plant founded in 1883; known as the Guzhon plant until 1917 and the MMZ or Moscow metallurgy plant until 1922 (the acronym was not used in Soviet sources; it is my creation)

Velozavod – bicycle plant

Voitovich – repaired train wagons

ZiS – AMO-ZiS, the Stalin auto plant, the first Soviet auto and light truck plant, founded in 1916 by the Riabushinskii clan and known as AMO, the Moscow Auto Combine, until 1931 when it was renamed ZiS; in 1956 it was renamed ZiL, or the Likhachev plant

Other Moscow Factories

Bromlei (later Krasnyi Proletarii) – machine construction

Danilovskaia Manufaktura – textiles

List – machine construction

Mikhelson – machine construction

Prokhorovskaia Trekhgornaia Manufaktura – textiles

Related Factories in Other Cities

GAZ – the Gor'kii auto plant, originally the Nizhni Novgorod auto plant, renamed in 1936 when the city was renamed for Gor'kii

MMK – Magnitogorsk Metallurgical Kombinat, the Magnitogorsk steel plant

Magnitostroi – construction site for the MMK

Dneprostroi – construction site for the Dnepr Dam and Hydroelectric power complex

Kuznetskstroi – construction site for the Kuznetsk steel plant in Western Siberia

Putilov Plant – also Red Putilov, Kirov plant, the largest factory in the world in 1900, and a giant still during the 1930s; located in Leningrad; produced iron and steel and manufactured tractors, machines, and some light trucks

Factory Terminology

brak – defective output, which must be scrapped and remanufactured

brigada – work crew or unit, usually several on each shift for an *uchastka*

chernorabochii – unskilled worker, laborer

detsad – kindergarten, day-care center for children

doplaty – additional pay

fabrika – factory, generally for light industry, in particular textiles

fabzavkom – factory trade union committee (also called *zavkom*)

iasli – crèche, day-care center for infants

kadrovyi rabochii – highly skilled or competent worker

lichnaia kartochka – worker's personnel card issued in all plants by 1928–29, giving place of birth, social origins, previous employment, occupation, skill level, and wages

MOP – *mladshii obsluzhivaiushchii personnel,* nonproduction auxiliary workers, service workers, including janitors, cafeteria workers, clinic personnel, and others

ORS – *otdel rabochii snabzhenie,* department of workers' supply

otdel – departments or subdivisions

otdel kadrov – personnel department legally responsible for all hiring; conducted most hiring by interviewing and processing applicants who simply showed up at the factory gate

partkom – the party committee in a factory, consisting of cells in shops and on shifts

predpriatia – an enterprise, a legal entity with a director, a factory or plant

promfinplan – the factory's plan output targets, the industrial-financial plan

propusk – housing pass

prostoi – idleness due to equipment or machinery breakdown, failure, or absence, or due to lack or raw materials or semifinished products to manufacture

pusk – putting a newly constructed factory on-line

rabochee mesto – work post, the space an individual worker occupied (on one or several machines)

ratsenki – piece rates

razriady – ranks on a wage scale

sluzhashchie – white-collar personnel

smena – shift

stalevar – steel smelter in the open hearth shop

stanka – the work bench

stazh – work tenure

tarifnyi razriad – wage ranking

tarifnaia setka – wage scale

tarifnyaia stavka – the base piece-rate for the first rank on the wage scale

tekhminimum – an exam establishing a minimal technical standard for all occupations

tekuchest' – labor turnover

trudovaia kniga – worker's workbook, issued after the December 1938 law, incorporating information of the personnel card and recording disciplinary infractions, firings, or reasons for prior severance

tsekh – shop or department, basic production subdivisions of factory

uchastok – shop section

val'tsovshchik – rolling mill operator

work collective – the entire work force, including wage and salaried employees, production workers, auxiliary workers, and white-collar personnel

zavkom – the trade-union committee in a factory

zavod – plant, generally for heavy industry such as metallurgy and metalworking

zavodskii kollektiv – plant work collective, including the entire work force (wage and salaried employees), production workers, auxiliary workers (MOP), engineers and technicians (ITR), white-collar staff, and management

zdravpunkt – first-aid station

ZRK – *zakritii rabochii kooperativ,* closed workers' cooperative

Factory Management

brigadir – work crew boss, the foreman for the work brigade; used with increasing frequency after 1930 until it became universal *edinonachalie* – "one man management"; the plant administration, under the leadership of the Red Director, became legally responsible for the plant's economic performance in September 1929

glavnyi enzhinir tsekha – shop chief engineer

instruktor – training instructor

ITR – engineering and technical workers

master – the foreman prior to 1930; after that often the head of an *uchastka* encompassing several work brigades; also an instructor for apprentices

nachal'niki tsekha – shop superintendents

nachal'niki smena – shift superintendents

PPO – Production-Planning Department

praktiki – technicians who had learned on-the-job, without formal training

Red Director – Krasnyi Direktor, the "boss" of the factory after September 1929

Shock Work and Stakhanovism

buksirnaia brigada – a shock-work brigade that helps another; tugboating brigade

khozraschetnaia brigada – the final form of shock-work brigade, based on cost accounting

otlichniki – outstanding workers, precursors to Stakhanovites

skorostniki – speedsters, successors to Stakhanovites

skvoznaia brigada – a shock-work brigade involved in troubleshooting or overcoming bottlenecks in production

sotssorevnovanie – socialist competitions between brigades, shops, and factories

Stakhanovites – a mass movement named for Aleksei Stakhanov, a Donbass coal miner who set a record on 1 September 1935 by mining 102 tons of coal, while the shift norm was 6.5 tons; superseded shock work in late 1935–36

udarnaia brigada – shock-work brigade

udarnichestvo – shock work; a movement striving to overfullfill production plans

udarniki – shock workers; workers who overfulfilled production plans and were rewarded with bonus payments

Shops (*Tsekha*) of a Typical Soviet Steel Plant

Metiznye Tsekha – metal processing shops, also known as cold shops

staleprovolochnyi tsekh – wire manufacturing shop

pressovyi tsekh – metal pressing shop

fasonno-liteinyi tsekh – form casting shop or foundry

kanatnyi tsekh – cable manufacturing shop

Metallurgicheskie Tsekha – iron- or steel-producing shops, also known as hot shops

domnyi tsekh – blast furnaces manufacturing pig iron

martenovskii tsekh – open hearth shop, manufacturing steel from pig iron and coke

prokatnyi tsekh – rolling steel shop

listoprokatnyi tsekh – sheet rolling shop

Soviet Terms and Acronyms

CIR – Central Industrial Region consisting of eight provinces: Moscow, Tver, Iarsolavl, Vladimir, Riazin, Tula, Kaluga, and Smolensk – commissar – head of a commissariat

commissariat – basic state organs; in January 1932, VSNKh was split into three economic commissariats, NKTP, NKLP, and NKPS; in the later 1930s they were subdivided further into more then ten economic commissariats, and after World War II they were named ministries, of which there were over thirty by 1952

Donbass – coal and steel basin in eastern Ukraine, Donetsk

FYP – Five-Year Plan: First, 1928–32; Second, 1933–37; Third, 1938–41

Gipromez – State Institute for Design of Metallurgy Plants

glavk – highest subdvision of a commissariat (later a ministry), roughly corresponding to a branch or subbranch of industry

Glavmetal – the *glavk* for metalworking and metallurgical industries during the 1920s

Gosplan – State Planning Agency, formed in 1924

GUMP – The *glavka* for all metallurgy industry

Kuzbass – Siberian coal and steel basin, Kuznetsk

Mashtrest – Machine Construction Trust

MK – Moscow Party Committee

MKK – Moscow Control Commission

MOPR – international organization to provide aid to workers

NEP – New Economic Policy, 1921–28

NKLP – Commissariat of Light Industry

NKPS – Commissariat of Transportation and Communications

NKT – Narkomtrud, Commissariat of Labor

NKTP – Narkomtiazhprom, Commissariat of Heavy Industry; headed by Ordzhonikidze until his death in February 1937

OKS – Division of Capital Construction

Politburo – Political Bureau of the Central Committee of the Communist Party

RABKRIN – Workers' and Peasants' Inspectorate, headed by a commissar, initially Stalin and later Ordzhonikidze

RKK – state committee to adjudicate conflicts over piece rates, output norms, and wages

RZhSKT – Workers' Housing Construction Cooperative Trust

SNK – Sovnarkom Council of Peoples' Commissars, the cabinet

Sovnarkom – Council of Peoples' Commissars (equivalent to a cabinet)

Spetstal' – Special Steels Trust

TsK – Central Committee of the Communist Party

TsKK – Central Control Commission

VATO – All-Union Auto and Tractor Combine

VKK – Temporary Control Commission, often in a factory

VKP(b) – All-Union Communist Party (Bolshevik)

VSNKh – All-Union Council of the National Economy (Commissariat of Economics); headed by Kuibyshev until November 1930, then by Ordzhonikidze; divided in 1932 into three commissariats: NKTP, NKLP, NKPS

VTsSPS – All-Union Central Council of Trade Unions; headed by Tomsky until December 1928 and by M. N. Shvernik after 1930

Vocational Training and Education

DRO – Dopolnitel'noe Rabochee Obrazovanie, Supplemental Workers' Education

FZO – successor to the FZU, established in 1940

FZTK – Factory Technical Courses

FZS – factory-based seven-year school

FZU – factory vocational school, enrolling youth aged 16–18, typically a two-year program

KRO – Kombinatov Rabochego Obrazovaniia, Combine for Workers' Education

PPK – Proizvodstvenno-Politekhnicheskie Kursy, Production-Polytechnical Courses

PTK – Proizvodstvenno-Tekhnicheskie Kursy, Production-Technical Courses, successor to PPK in 1933

PTU – Occupational Technical School, successor to FZU and FZO in the 1950s

Rabfak – workers' faculty, special schools for a crash program of higher learning, usually technical education, for selected workers; in 1929–31 became the central institutions in selecting and training the new elite, the *vydvizhentsy;* they were redundant once the VUZ and VTUZ colleges were restored in 1932

RTSh – Workers' Technical School

tekhnikum – school for training technicians, a high school with some higher education

VRSh – Evening Workers' School

VTUZ – higher technical institute (college)

VUZ – higher institute of education (college)

NOTES

Introduction

1. See, e.g., Schorske, Fin-de-Siècle Vienna; Engelstein, *The Keys to Happiness.*

2. In this respect, I am consciously applying E. P. Thompson's methodology from *The Making of the English Working Class* to Russia and the Soviet Union a full century later. I find deep resonance in Thompson's method even as I reject the entire content of his artisan-based analysis for the Soviet experience in the 1930s (see chapter 10 below).

3. Henri Bergson, *Matière et Mémoire,* developed what he saw as a new and dualistic theory of consciousness. Bergson was attempting to resolve the dichotomy between idealism and materialism in ways that were different from Kantean categories. He focused on memory, which was fundamentally shaped by language. There are, by now, a wide variety of schools of thought within the linguistic turn, which tend to revolve around focus on the text, the author, or the audience. One such school, the "new historicism," has been pioneered by Stephen J. Greenblatt and Carlo Ginzburg.

4. See, e.g., the studies of French labor history by Sewell, *Work and Revolution in France,* and by Rancière, *The Nights of Labor;* the studies of British labor history by Jones, *Languages of Class,* and Joyce, *Visions of the People;* and more recently, and from a gendered and discourse perspective, the studies by Rose, *Limited Livelihoods,* and Canning, *Languages of Labor and Gender.* These studies mark important advances in conceptualizing and describing class in the historical "process" by considering multiple identities, but almost all of them, with the possible exception of Jones's work, look to "deconstruct" class. Likewise, Suny's studies, mostly on the periphery of the Russian and Soviet Empire, deconstructs and reconstructs class from the angle of nationality.

5. The work of Furet has profoundly influenced (and been influenced by) Roger Chartier, Keith Michael Baker, Mona Ozouf, Colin Lucas, and Lynn Hunt, to mention but a few.

6. Recent books by Richard Pipes, *The Russian Revolution* and his *Russia Under the Bolshevik Regime,* mark an attempt to shift toward political history, but without any new analysis of ideology or culture comparable to that undertaken by the Furet school.

7. Lewin, "Who Was the Soviet Kulak?"

8. Carr, *Bolshevik Revolution,* vol. 2, p. 196. Shliapnikov leveled his taunt at Lenin on behalf of the Workers' Opposition in the first round of the trade-union debate at the Ninth Party Congress in 1920. See Carr, p. 225.

9. See, e.g., Fitzpatrick, "The Bolsheviks' Dilemma."

10. Excellent discussions of this literature can be found in Tucker, *Stalinism,* and Boffa, *The Stalin Phenomenon.* The most influential texts were Trotsky, *The Revolution Betrayed,* and Djilas, *The New Class.* A much later attempt, influenced by Maoism, was Bettelheim, *Class Struggles in the USSR.*

11. See Fainsod, *How Russia Is Ruled*, and *Smolensk Under Soviet Rule;* and Schapiro, *The Communist Party;* Rigby, *Communist Party Membership in the USSR*, "Stalinism and the Mono-Organizational Society," and *Lenin's Government*.

12. While the dual term *party-state* has been widely used in the literature, its meaning has often been confused, since both the most powerful governing officials and white-collar personnel who were mere clerks were part of the state. Even enterprise employees and workers (most of urban society!) were also technically part of the "state," since they were on its payroll. By party-state, I mean the regime, that is, the top personnel who governed Soviet society. Their numbers have been variously estimated, but we would not go far wrong if we adopted Stalin's militarized formulations. In a Plenum speech in 1937, in the midst of the terror, Stalin noted: "In our party, if we have in mind its leading strata, there are about 3,000 to 4,000 first rank leaders whom I would call our party's corps of generals. Then there are about 30,000 to 40,000 middle rank leaders who are our party's corps of officers. Then there are about 100,000 to 150,000 lower rank party command staff who are, so to speak, our Party's non-commissioned officers" (Fainsod, *How Russia Is Ruled*, p. 178). The party, at the time comprised roughly 2 million persons.

On the state side, using a published document from the Central State Economic Archives (TsGANKh), Lewin has estimated that of more than half a million leading cadre in industry, 175,000 worked in "factory-administration" and the rest on the shop floor. Lewin calls the 75,000 personnel listed at the "plant-management level" (presumably including the 13,530 Red Directors), as the top of the command structure; 43,888 shop superintendents *(nachal'niki tsekha)* and their deputies and chief shop engineers as the "middle ranks"; and he classifies the 138,363 foremen at the bottom, as NCOs (*The Making of the Soviet System*, pp. 243–44). Of course, these figures do not pertain to Soviet officials serving in a noneconomic administrative capacity on local, city, province, republic, or all-union (supreme) soviets. The roughly parallel sizes of the party and state apparatuses reflects a duality of functions and of structures between party and state and was present at almost every level of the administration under Stalinism (see Kotkin, *Magnetic Mountain*, chap. 7). Perhaps the relations of party to soviet resembled church-state relations, as Kotkin suggests (p. 286), but the *nomenklatura* for both the party and the state organs originated within the secretariat of the Central Committee of the VKP(b). Carr and Rigby argued that the party controlled the Soviet and that there was "interlocking" of the two, a point that various oppositions noted well before Trotsky denounced this tendency in *The New Course* late in 1923. Still, Kotkin is right to emphasize the importance of parallelism, particularly during the terror of 1937, when suddenly, state organs, especially the NKVD, decimated the party. My thanks to Jonathan Harris for urging me to clarify what I mean by *party-state*.

13. Bottomore, *Elites and Society*, p. 42, suggests that the Soviet regime might be the classic example of such a power elite, because the society has no class structure. I agree with his premise concerning the state, but disagree concerning society.

14. Mills, *The Power Elite*.

15. Following the studies by Schapiro, Fainsod, and Rigby cited above, the most important and corroborating works were Fitzpatrick, "Stalin and the Making of a New Elite," and Bialer, *Stalin's Successors*.

16. Fitzpatrick, "Stalin and the Making of a New Elite," pp. 399–402.

17. Schapiro, *The Communist Party*, chaps. 22, 23.

18. Party-state relations remained in flux through the late Stalin years, until Khrushchev restored the primacy of the party in his rise to power after 1953.

19. Rieber, "Editor's Introduction," pp. xxi–xlii, to Presniakov, *The Formation of the Great Russian State.*

20. As Engelstein has convincingly argued in "Combined Underdevelopment," pp. 338–54, the law would deteriorate under Soviet power until it was a mere tool for furthering the purposes of the regime. Kotkin, *Magnetic Mountain,* chap. 5, discusses the power of the language of the regime.

21. See Giddens, *Class Structure,* chap. 13, and Bottomore, *Elites and Society.*

22. I am borrowing a formulation from Skocpol, "Bringing the State Back In," but instead of granting "relative autonomy" to the state, I am granting it to Soviet society.

23. The idea of negative integration was suggested by Roth in *The Social Democrats of Imperial Germany.* It was derived, in part, from Max Weber's discussion of the SPD and German Free Unions as creating a "socialist ghetto," and in part from the functionalist paradigms popular in sociology at the time. Kotkin has suggested a positive integration under Stalinist civilization, in which, quoting Hobsbawm, he finds that individuals negotiated their way within the parameters of that civilization to their "minimum disadvantage" by learning to "speak Bolshevik." By parallel integration, I mean to suggest that the integration was a trend in Soviet society itself, among urban industrial workers, and that the process of negotiation was between this new urban industrial society (its classes, its social groups, its family groups) and the regime.

24. As Kotkin suggested, in reading this book in manuscript form, the regime succeeded in recruiting a new labor force to staff its factories *despite* its policies.

25. While this will no doubt recall, for many readers, Ira Katznelson's four "levels" of class formation, I would shy away from his approach in favor of E. P. Thompson's, whose discussion of "class consciousness," I think, links structure and agency, or material and cultural worlds in a less teleological or hierarchical ordering. See the introduction by Katznelson in *Working-Class Formation,* p. 14.

26. The terms *melting pot* and *community organizer* are adopted from the American context, where they mean something else. Rieber suggested the term *protocommunity* to me.

Chapter 1. From Revolutionary Russian Proletariat to Quiescent Soviet Working Class

1. There were, of course, strikes in the early 1930s, and reports of strikes in the 1960s and 1970s filtered out of Novocherkask, Togliatti, and other cities. Since the official press would not report on them, and since they were repressed in one way or another, only word of mouth and publication abroad in the emigre press or later in broadcasts or news analysis by RFE/RL disseminated such information.

2. Trotsky, *The Revolution Betrayed,* and *Biulleten' Oppozitsii,* published from July 1929 to August 1941. The theory of permanent revolution was first presented in *Itogi i Perspektivy* (1906), and elaborated in *Nasha Revoliutsiia* (1907). The "law of combined development" was proposed in the first chapter of *History of the Russian Revolution,* p. 9.

3. Haimson, "Dual Polarization in Urban Russia, 1905–1917." By *nizy* Haimson meant all the lower classes, or the non-property-owning, noncensus urban society and the peasants. He did not use the word "contain," but his article showed that the alienation of the *nizy* was so fundamental that it could explode into spontaneous militant or revolutionary action.

4. Haimson, "The Problem of Social Identities"; Haimson and Tilly, *Strikes, War, and Revolution;* and Koenker and Rosenberg, *Strikes and Revolution in Russia, 1917.*

5. On soviets, see Anweiler, *The Soviets,* and Koenker, *Moscow Workers.* On the trade unions, see Bonnell, *Roots of Rebellion.* On factory committees in Petrograd, see Smith, *Red Petrograd,* Mandel, *The Petrograd Workers and the Fall of the Old Regime* and *Petrograd Workers and the Soviet Seizure of Power;* and in the CIR, Husband, *Revolution in the Factory,* and Koenker, *Moscow Workers.* On labor-management relations see Hogan, *Forging Revolution.* On the Red Guards, see Wade, *The Red Guards.* On the Bolsheviks, see Rabinowitch, *Prelude to Revolution* and *The Bolsheviks Come to Power.*

6. See Wynn, *Workers, Strikes, and Pogroms,* and Neuberger, *Hooliganism.*

7. See Suny, "Toward a Social History of the October Revolution," and his updating of this article in "Revising the Old Story."

8. Dual labor market theory evolved from the American context. Dunlop, in *Industrial Relations Systems,* traced the impact of unions and collective bargaining on wages and productivity and showed that there were "internal" and "external" labor markets that had to be distinguished, primarily based on the impact of collective bargaining and the collective contract in certain key industries. Kerr, *Labor Markets and Wage Determination,* extended this insight, distinguishing "ports of entry" that are controlled in different ways by craft and industrial unions. The distinction between internal and external labor markets was then systematized and broadened in Doeringer and Piore, *Internal Labor Markets,* to take into account labor market "distortions" caused by new technologies, on the one hand, and discrimination, on the other. Dual labor market theories tended to focus on race and gender, while segmented market theories continued along these lines, incorporating technological change and its impact on labor relations. The findings of this school were summarized in Gordon, Edwards, and Reich, *Segmented Work, Divided Workers.*

I am suggesting that the dual labor market model works especially well for the Russian pattern of industrialization. In particular, Piore's image *(Birds of Passage)* could be applied literally to the Russian peasant-proletarian, who was just as much a "bird of passage" in Moscow or St. Petersburg in 1900 as were Italians, Poles, or Jews working in Pennsylvania or the Lower East Side of New York.

9. See Hobsbawm, *Workers,* chaps. 12–14, on the debate between income-based concepts of a "labor aristocracy" and culturally based concepts. Ranajit Guha developed the concept of the "subaltern" workers. For a discussion of this concept in various national contexts, see the articles by Gyan Prakash, Florencia Mallon, and Frederick Cooper in the forum of the *American Historical Review* 99 (1994): 1475–1516.

10. See Rashin, *Formirovanie Promyshlennogo Proletariata,* pt. 4. My account of the term *hereditary workers* is based, in particular, on Zelnik, *Labor and Society in Tsarist Russia.* See also his "Russian Bebels."

11. Sonin, *Vosproizvodstvo Rabochei Sily.* See chapter 7 below.

12. Perhaps a fourth subgroup consisting of non-Russian nationalities or ethnic groups should be added, at least for many regions of the Russian Empire. My study abstracts from the "national question" and considers working-class formation in terms of its ethnic Slavic core rather than the non-Slavic periphery. The presence of some Tatar workers at the Hammer and Sickle plant was reflected in the attempt to publish occasional issues of the factory newspaper in Turkic. The sources indicate, however, that the overwhelming majority of workers in the Moscow factories were Russian, with Belorussian and Ukrainian the next largest contingents.

13. My ideas about residential patterns and hereditary workers are derived from Johnson, *Peasant and Proletarian;* Bradley, *Muzhik and Muscovite;* and Engel, *Between the Fields and the City.* On the status of women in the work force, see Glickman, *Russian Factory Women.*

On the position of youth in industrial apprenticeships, see Bonnell, *Roots of Rebellion,* pp. 47–52.

14. The assumption of passivity was widespread among the Social Democrats, who believed that peasant-migrants would simply leave the city and factory and return to the village during a strike action. See Zelnik, *A Radical Worker.* However, Wynn shows plenty of *buntarstvo* among the peasant-workers in the Donbass mines and mill towns, as does Neuberger for Petersburg youth. On gender and militancy among female workers, see Smith, "Class and Gender." My thanks to Jennifer Evans for calling this article to my attention.

15. The idea of symbiosis was suggested by Johnson in *Peasant and Proletarian* and has been widely adopted. See also Bradley, *Muzhik and Muscovite,* and Engel, *Between the Fields and the City.* On injustice and alternative visions see, in particular, Moore, *Injustice,* and Stites, *Revolutionary Dreams.*

16. See notes 4 and 5 above.

17. Often, the path from field to factory went via the army, as Wildman, *The End of the Imperial Russian Army* showed for the imperial era and Von Hagen, *Soldiers in the Proletarian Dictatorship* show for the early Soviet era. In the Imperial army, Wildman shows that peasant-soldiers faced gentry-officers, and a replication of the hierarchy of social inferiority that they felt in the village. Likewise, women faced patriarchy in the peasant household and village, in urban society, and, in particular, on the shop floor (see Glickman, *Russian Factory Women*). Youth faced a difficult paternalism in all spheres of life: village, army, school, and factory. My point is that the replication of similar and oppressive hierarchies in all spheres of life in imperial Russia, a combination of oppressive patriarchy, paternalism, the legal hierarchy of estates, and class status, might be said to have "overdetermined" the revolutionary response in Althusser's sense of this term (see *For Marx,* p. 106).

18. See Lel'chuk, *Sostialisticheskaia Industrializatsiia SSSR,* and Gladkov, *Istoriia Sotsialisticheskoi Ekonomiki SSSR.* "Restoration" was defined as 1921–25, while the new construction that began in 1926 was called "reconstruction" or "socialist reconstruction" of the economy. The dividing mark, as Lel'chuk shows, came to be seen as the Fourteenth Party Congress, the so-called Congress of Industrialization in December 1925. This Soviet periodization became standard during and after the Stalin years, and it mistakenly restricted the objective of NEP to "restoration of the economy" to its 1913 level, and thus ended NEP in 1925. The subsequent and final two years of NEP (1926–1928) were falsely amalgamated to the era of Stalinist planned economy and to the First FYP under the term "reconstruction of the economy." The best source on employment data in industry during NEP is still Adolf G. Rashin, *Sostav Fabrichno-Zavodskogo Proletariata SSSR,* which dates the shift in NEP to 1925. Before that, industry was primarily rehiring workers with prior industrial experience who had left the workforce during the years of war and revolution, while afterward industry was primarily hiring new workers without any prior industrial work experience.

19. See Deutscher, *Soviet Trade Unions,* and Dewar, *Labour Policy in the USSR.* NKT established the labor exchanges and ran them in cooperation or conflict with VTsSPS.

20. As suggested by Johnson, "Family Life in Moscow During NEP."

21. See Vas'kina, *Rabochii Klass SSSR,* p. 93, on the skill breakdown of the labor force, and pp. 167–68 on the calculation of unemployment.

22. Danilov, *Rural Russia Under the New Regime,* pp. 264–65, notes the highly speculative nature of calculations of surplus rural population. Gosplan relied heavily on estimates of the State Land Colonization Institute and on L. E. Mintz's estimates. The institute estimated rural overpopulation at between 24.5 and 32.5 million people of working age,

whereas Mintz's estimate was much lower at 8.5 million. See *International Labor Review* 27 (March 1933): 352–53.

23. On restricting the registration of unemployed, see Carr, *Socialism in One Country*, p. 389–90, and Carr and Davies, *Foundations of a Planned Economy*, p. 955.

24. I suggest that the *smychka* offered an alternative to "dictatorship of the proletariat" as a theory of the role of the state in socialist construction. Under the *smychka*, the state could play the role of "coordinator" between urban and rural society, mediating the interests of peasants and workers while charting a program of economic development for both and appealing to both for political support. The regime, in this way under NEP, would have offered a genuine "social contract" with society, in contrast to the "ersatz social contract" proposed by Stalin in June 1931 (see chapter 4).

25. Historians of the Communist Party, including Fainsod, Schapiro, and Rigby, have all emphasized the problem of weak party saturation of rural areas during NEP, and of the tendency of the local party organ, instead, to be "absorbed" by the well-to-do in the villages. Lewin, *Russian Peasants and Soviet Power,* noted the same problem of weak party "saturation" in the countryside but placed it into the broader perspective of a wide cultural gap between rural and urban society.

26. These issues are discussed in Chase, *Workers, Society, and the Soviet State,* and Ward, *Russia's Cotton Workers.* On Left and Right Opposition during NEP, see Lewin, *Political Undercurrents,* chaps. 2–5.

27. It is likely that the German Democratic Republic and Czechoslovakia experienced a similar inversion in the labor market, especially from 1948 to 1953. However, there and in Hungary, the labor shortage was a short-lived phenomenon, confined to the years of the Stalinist investment drive in heavy industry. Certainly, Poland and the Balkan socialist states never experienced this type of chronic labor deficit, given their large peasant population. Nor did China, Korea, Vietnam, or even India, to consider a different type of socialism, obviously for the same reason.

28. Stalin, "God Velikogo Pereloma," *Sochineniia,* vol. 12.

29. The "revolution from above" should be first on the list of Stalin's oxymorons. See Goldman, *Women, the State, and Revolution,* conclusion. The idea of "revolution from below" was linked to "Cultural Revolution" in many essays in Fitzpatrick, *Cultural Revolution in Russia.*

30. For the best statements of the opposing positions on the "continuity question," see Cohen, *Rethinking the Soviet Experience,* and Fitzpatrick, *The Russian Revolution.* The historiographical debate as it impinges on this issue is well recounted and analyzed in Siegelbaum, *Soviet State and Society.*

31. Lewin, *Russian Peasants and Soviet Power.* The first to emphasize this point were Erlich, *The Soviet Industrialization Debate,* and Jasny, *Soviet Industrialization.* See also Zaleskii, *Planning for Economic Growth,* and Hunter and Szyrmer, *Faulty Foundations.*

32. Davies, *Collectivization of Soviet Agriculture* and *The Soviet Collective Farm,* and Fitzpatrick, *Stalin's Peasants,* confirm Lewin's findings on the origins of forced collectivization.

33. On the seven-hour shift and continuous production, see Carr and Davies, *Foundations of a Planned Economy,* pp. 496–500. See also, Ward, *Russia's Cotton Workers,* chap. 13, and Chase, *Workers, Society, and the Soviet State,* chap. 6, on how the regime's production campaigns disrupted industrial relations in 1927 and 1928. On the disruption caused by the Ural-Siberian methods in agriculture, see Lewin, *Russian Peasants,* pp. 386–88.

34. See Rassweiler, *The Generation of Power,* on Dneprostroi, and Kotkin, *Magnetic Mountain,* on Magnitogorsk.

35. See Carr and Davies, *Foundations of a Planned Economy*, pp. 436–50. Whereas, in 1927 VSNKh listed 391 new factories and targeted 891 million rubles investment for them (ibid., p. 434), 1,500 new factories were built or started during the First FYP. See *Industrializatsiia SSSR*, p. 9.

36. In addition to the studies by Rassweiler and Kotkin, see also Hoffmann, *Peasant Metropolis*.

37. For "quicksand society," see Lewin, *The Making of the Soviet System*, p. 221.

38. Fainsod, *Smolensk Under Soviet Rule*, and Inkeles and Bauer, *The Soviet Citizen*.

39. See Fitzpatrick, *Cultural Revolution in Russia* and *Education and Social Mobility*.

40. Fainsod, *Smolensk Under Soviet Rule*, is the classic statement of the totalitarian thesis. Getty, *Origins of the Great Purges; the Soviet Communist Party Reconsidered* (Cambridge, 1985), revised it based on the same Smolensk archives. The debate should be reconsidered in light of Theda Skocpol's idea of "admininstrative capacities" in *Bringing the State Back In* and *Protecting Soldiers and Mothers*. This was attempted in Fairbanks and Thornton, "Soviet Decision Making and Bureaucratic Representation."

41. Thurston, *Life and Terror in Stalin's Russia* also reaches some of the same conclusions.

42. See Fitzpatrick's contribution to the debate in *Russian Review* 45 (1986): 357–74.

43. Schwarz, *Labour in the Soviet Union*. Schwarz was not aware of the contradictory assumption, embedded in his subsequent study of Menshevism and Bolshevism and the workers' movement in the 1905 Revolution, that peasant influence among the workers accounted for their revolutionary militancy, which Schwarz, like Martov, saw as "spontaneity" rather than "consciousness." Why, then, in the 1930s, would peasant influence among workers yield quiescence? See Schwarz, *The Russian Revolution of 1905*.

44. Filtzer, *Soviet Workers and Stalinist Industrialization*.

45. Kuromiya, *Stalin's Industrial Revolution;* Andrle, *Workers in Stalin's Russia;* and Siegelbaum, *Stakhanovism*.

46. The seminal Soviet works are Sonin, *Vosproivodstvo;* Shkaratan, *Problemy Sotsial'noi Struktury;* and Vdovin and Drobizhev, *Rost Rabochego Klassa*. I also consider John Barber's articles, in which he argues that a new working class was in formation, anticipating my own approach.

47. Dissertations by Clayton Black, "Krasnyi Putilovets, 1923–32: A Case Study of Soviet Industry in Transition" (Indiana University), and William Wolf, "Building the Socialist Future: The Construction of the Moscow Subway" (Ohio State University), will add to the list of microstudies.

48. Lewin, *The Making of the Soviet System*, p. 227.

49. Lewin (ibid., pp. 221–22) suggested that disciplinary laws and also a new ideology of state conservatism, which Timasheff called the "Great Retreat," helped bring stability to the "quicksand society"and make workers more productive. However, the new studies find little evidence for effectiveness of the draconian labor laws, while the Great Retreat, which Lewin calls "a set of classical measures of social conservatism, law and order strategies complete with a nationalist revival, and efforts to instill values of discipline, patriotism, conformism, authority, and orderly careerism," only took shape during the course of the decade and initially could have had very minimal impact on workers and their outlook. In general, the findings of the microstudies emphasize neither disciplinary laws and repression nor this socially conservative Stalinist ideology, but rather, focus on new social solidarities that might explain why a type of nationalist-conservative Stalinist ideology could become influential, or why law and order policies could become effective.

50. Rassweiler, *The Generation of Power,* pp. 143–50.

51. Kotkin, *Magnetic Mountain,* pp. 235–36.

52. Ibid., pp. 236–37.

53. Ibid., p. 202.

54. Lewin, *The Making of the Soviet System,* pp. 222–25.

55. See Kotkin, *Magnetic Mountain,* p. 390, n. 78, citing B. I. Nikolskii, who observed in the 21 December 1936 issue of *Magnitogorskii Rabochii* that Moscow's Shosse Entuziastov (a new boulevard with new factories all along it radiating out through the PR) resembled Magnitogorsk, but that Kuznetskii Most, in central Moscow, did not.

56. Trotsky, *The Revolution Betrayed;* Berdyaev, *The Origin of Russian Communism;* and Timasheff, *The Great Retreat.* Lewin and Fitzpatrick both advanced similar arguments in 1978, in Fitzpatrick, *Cultural Revolution in Russia.* So did Tucker in *The Soviet Political Mind,* and then more forcefully in *Stalin in Power,* which suggests that Stalin would literally apply the "lessons" of the reigns of Ivan the Terrible and Peter the Great to Soviet society.

Chapter 2. Moscow's Proletarian District and Hammer and Sickle Steel Plant

1. See Engelstein, *Moscow 1905,* pp. 40–50, and Koenker, *Moscow Workers,* pp. 12–21, for detailed descriptions of Moscow's districts as they evolved in the first decades of the twentieth century. Moscow is a city that grew up in concentric rings. By 1917 the Garden Ring separated "inner Moscow" and "outer Moscow," but the separation was based on distinctions of wealth and property. The idea of an "architecture of power" comes from my reading of Kotkin's discussion of architecture in Magnitogorsk in *Magnetic Mountain,* p. 289, and Colton's discussion of an architecture of "monumentalism" in *Moscow,* pp. 326–29.

2. The first outlines for a plan were adopted by the Central Committee Plenum resolutions of 11–15 June 1931 that called for rapid expansion of housing construction, canteens and bakeries, electrical and energy network, city transport (including trams, buses, subway, and railroad), and water supply. See *KPSS v Rezoliutsiiakh,* vol. 5, pp. 315–22. The 1935 plan was published as *Moskva v Novykh Raionakh,* a document drafted by the Moscow City Planning Commission and the Moscow City Economic Administration, appointed by the Moscow Soviet. See Colton, *Moscow,* pp. 272–80.

3. See Tarkhanov and Kavtaradze, *Architecture of the Stalin Era,* p. 132; and Colton, *Moscow,* pp. 329–31.

4. See Ruble, "Moscow's Revolutionary Architecture," pp. 121–24.

5. On the origins of these giant factories, see Hogan, *Forging Revolution,* pp. 5–8. In 1902, St. Petersburg factories employed 70,032 metalworkers and 36,036 textile workers, while Moscow factories employed 18,002 metalworkers and 51,932 textile workers. See Bonnell, *Roots of Rebellion,* pp. 32–33.

6. See Zelnik, *Labor and Society;* Hogan, *Forging Revolution;* Surh, *1905 in St. Petersburg;* McKean, *St. Petersburg Between the Revolutions;* Smith, *Red Petrograd;* Mandel, *The Petrograd Workers;* and Koenker and Rosenberg *Strikes and Revolution.*

7. However, as Rashin's analysis of the 1929 trade-union census of metalworkers and textile workers showed, the predominantly "male cadre" metalworkers had stronger "ties" to the land than the "female" textile workers, confounding Bolshevik and Menshevik assumptions. See Rashin, *Sostav Fabrichno-Zavodskogo Proletariata,* p. xii of the introduction by Evreinov.

8. See McKean, *St. Petersburg Between the Revolutions,* p. 19, for population statistics. For comparable Moscow figures, see Bradley, *Muzhik and Muscovite,* p. 34.

9. See Friedgut, *Iuzovka and Revolution.*

10. Wynn, *Workers, Strikes, and Pogroms,* pp. 38–39.

11. See Bradley, *Muzhik and Muscovite,* p. 12. The surrounding provinces were Smolensk, Kaluga, Tula, Riazan, Vladimir, Iaroslavl', and Tver.

12. Bonnell, *Roots of Rebellion,* pp. 32–33.

13. Trotsky, *1905,* pp. 19–23.

14. Koenker, *Moscow Workers,* p. 24.

15. *Istoriia Rabochikh Moskvy,* pp. 166–67. The slogan was apparently coined at the Sixteenth Gubernia Party Conference, 20–28 November 1927.

16. See Hogan, *Forging Revolution,* pp. 35–38, and Koenker, *Moscow Workers,* p. 21.

17. Another useful map of the major factories in 1917 can be found in *Istoriia Moskvy,* vol. 6, pp. 104–05. I thank William Husband for this reference. See also Engelstein, *Moscow 1905,* p. 48, for a map of 1905, and Koenker, *Moscow Workers,* pp. 30–36, for a list of key plants in 1917.

18. See *Svet nad Zastavoi* for a detailed although poorly argued account of the history of the SiM plant from its founding. Two interesting articles are Meller, "Iz Istorii Zavoda 'Serp i Molot,'" and Pankratova, "Rabochie Zavoda 'Serp I Molota v 1905 g."

19. A three-volume history of the Westinghouse or Dinamo plant was published in the 1960s, as was a history of the AMO, or Likhachev plant. See the bibliographical essay for a discussion of these factory histories.

20. Bradley, *Muzhik and Muscovite,* p. 231.

21. See Johnson, "Family Life in Moscow During NEP," p. 119, on the effects of *otkhod.* *Istoriia Moskvy,* vol. 6, bk. 2, pp. 7–10, indicates that a third of the housing stock was destroyed by 1920, by 1923 it had been restored, and in 1924–25, 265 new buildings were constructed. Electrification of the city dwellings was universal by the end of 1925.

22. Compare the figures in Koenker, *Moscow Workers,* p. 37, and Chase, *Workers, Society, and the Soviet State,* p. 106. Chase's data show a 30 percent decline in employees in small factories (1–100 workers) between 1917 and 1925. His appendices 5 and 6, pp. 311–12, show a precipitous decline of proprietors with wage laborers and proprietors with family or *artel'* members' labor, between 1912 and 1926.

23. *Istoriia Rabochikh Moskvy,* p. 180.

24. *Moskva v Tsifrakh* (1934), pp. 16–17. Among women, the ratio shifted from one-third to almost one-half. MOP in the factories included sanitation workers, cafeteria workers, and other "labor hygiene" *(okhrana truda)* personnel.

25. *Istoriia Moskvy,* pp. 19, 11.

26. See *Istoriia Moskovskogo Avtozavoda,* p. 169.

27. *Moskva v Tsifrakh* (1934), pp. 42–43.

28. Ibid., pp. 40–41.

29. Manganese, chrome-molybdenum, and other types of alloy sheets for the manufacture of machinery, automobiles, and aircraft were to be produced there. M. G. Clark, *The Economics of Soviet Steel,* p. 311.

30. *Istoriia Moskovskogo Avtozavoda,* pp. 189, 248.

31. Martov, "Rekonstruktsiia Zavoda 'Serp i Molot,'" p. 195.

32. *Moskva v Tsifrakh* (1934), p. 60.

33. GARF f. 7952, op. 3, d. 331, l. 1.

34. Ibid., l. 2.

35. Martov, "Rekonstruktsiia Zavoda "Serp i Molot,'" p. 200.

36. *Istoriia Rabochikh Moskvy,* pp. 220–21.

37. *Moskva v Tsifrakh* (1934), p. 56.

38. See *Moskva v Novykh Raionakh*, pp. 500–600.

39. Ibid., pp. 502–03; *Moskva Entsiklopediia*, p. 99.

40. Liubertsy seems to have become a spin-off from the PR, with other new plants such as the Liuberetskii agricultural machine plant also closely interwoven to the PR factories. Cadre were moved from the established plants to these newer ones.

41. *Istoriia Moskovskogo Avtozavoda*, p. 223.

42. *Moskva v Tsifrakh* (1934), pp. 56–57, 62.

43. The institutional history of planning the reconstruction of Moscow and converting it into a "socialist" city is described in *Istoriia Mosvky*, vol. 6, bk. 2, pp. 19–21, 42–45.

44. Ibid., p. 43.

45. *KPSS v Rezoliutsiiakh*, vol. 6, p. 242.

46. Ibid., p. 243.

47. The debacle of Le Corbusier's plans for Moscow rivaled the debacle of Ernst May's plans for Magnitogorsk. See Kotkin, *Magnetic Mountain*, pp. 108–20.

48. See, for the American case, Chandler, *The Visible Hand.*

49. The contrast between vertical integration in the PR and the famous Vyborg and Nevskii districts of St. Petersburg, in which both textile plants and metalworking plants were haphazardly thrown together without any integration between them, is striking. See Hogan, *Forging Revolution*, chap. 1.

50. "To Be or Not to Be a Factory?" was the title for a chapter of what was to have been a history of the factory. The chapter is stored in GARF f. 7952, op. 3, d. 331.

51. Bailes, *Technology and Society*, chaps. 3–5. See esp. chap. 3 on the Shakhty Affair.

52. GARF f. 7952, op. 3, d. 326, ll. 5–10. Mashtrest was the trust directly above SiM in the hierarchy of economic administration, and in the NEP period, funded the plant. Above the trust was the *glavka*, which in this case was Glavmetal. Above the *glavka* was VSNKh, the All-Union Council of the National Economy, with powers of a commissariat.

53. Ibid., l. 9.

54. Ibid., l. 11.

55. GARF f. 7952, op. 3, d. 326, l. 6. On the changing composition of the Moscow Party Committee and its connection to the Right Opposition, see Cohen, *Bukharin,* pp. 234–35. See also Conquest, *The Great Terror,* pp. 18–21, 30–31, 114, 143–44.

56. GARF f. 7952, op. 3, d. 326, l. 11.

57. GARF f. 7952, op. 3, d. 326, l. 12, and GARF f. 7952, op. 3, d. 331, ll. 3–4.

58. See Alim Kuchushev, "Magnitka na Sadovom," *Priroda i Chelovek,* no. 7 (1989): 3–5. My thanks to William Freeman for bringing this article to my attention.

59. Erlich, *The Soviet Industrialization Debate,* chap. 3.

60. GARF f. 7952, op. 3, d. 331, ll. 4–5.

61. Ibid., ll. 5–6.

62. The Kalinin Line, which opened in 1979, finally linked the factory to its workers' housing at Novogireevo, Perovo, and Shosse Entuziastov, and also to the city center at the next stop after Ploshchad' Il'icha, the Marksistskaia-Taganskaia station with connections to the Circle and the Zhdanovsko-Krasnopresnenskaia Lines. *Moskva Entsiklopediia*, pp. 401, 506.

63. GARF f. 7952, op. 3, d. 331. These events are also described in GARF f. 7952, op. 3, d. 326, l. 15, in a document entitled "Chapter 13, The Party in the Struggle to Reconstruct the Plant." Evidently, this document was supposed to have been the thirteenth chapter of the Gor'kii Project volume on SiM.

64. GARF f. 7952, op. 3, d. 326, l. 16.

65. GARF f. 7952, op. 3, d. 331, ll. 8–9. P. N. Miliukov's famous "treason or stupidity" speech was given when the Fourth State Duma was reconvened on 1 November 1916, and accused the tsarist government of undermining the Entente. See Burdzhalov, *Russia's Second Revolution*, p. 57.

66. GARF f. 7952, op. 3, d. 331, l. 9.

67. Ibid., l. 10.

68. GARF f. 7952, op. 3, d. 330, ll. 10–12. It was also published in *Rabochaia Gazeta.*

69. Ibid., ll. 14–15.

70. Ibid., ll. 15–16.

71. Ibid., l. 18.

72. Ibid., l. 19.

73. Ibid., l. 21.

74. According to the document "To Be or Not to Be a Factory?" Sattel' and List told workers at SiM that they would be sent to work at other plants when SiM was shut down. See GARF f. 7952, op. 3, d. 331, l. 7.

75. I am assuming that inflation roughly halved the value of the ruble during the First FYP, following Nove, *An Economic History of the USSR*, p. 208, citing Malafeyev, *Istoriia Tsenoobrazovaniia v SSSR* (Moscow, 1964), p. 174. The conflicting figures on First FYP investment at SiM reflect differences between plan and reality.

76. Filatov, *Partrabota*, p. 14. My thanks to David Hoffmann for pointing out this source to me.

77. Ibid., pp. 15–16. The eight projects were: (1) building two new open hearth furnaces, each with a 60-ton capacity; (2) mechanization of the rolling steel shop and installing a blooming mill; (3) expansion of the sheet metal shop; (4) construction of a new model-forge shop, with 30–40,000-ton capacity; (5) construction of a new calibrating shop, with a capacity of 25–30,000 tons of calibrated metal; (6) construction of a new forge shop with the capacity to produce 10–15,000 tons of forging; (7) construction of a new mechanical shop; (8) construction of a new model shop.

78. GARF f. 7952, op. 3, d. 331, l. 25.

79. Ibid., l. 26.

80. Ibid., l. 27.

81. Ibid.

82. Ibid., l. 28.

83. See Martov, "Rekonstruktsiia Zavoda 'Serp I Molot,'" p. 198. Martov states that in 1930–31 every shop was undergoing reconstruction simultaneously, and nothing was being accomplished since the resources were spread too thin. In 1931, still lacking a general plan, the plant management decided to give first priority to completing the calibrating shop. See pp. 199–200.

84. This was Likhachev's use of a Russian metaphor to describe the massive reconstruction of the AMO plant, on 1 October 1931, at a celebration of putting the new shops on-line. See *Istoriia Moskovskogo Avtozavoda*, p. 180.

85. Ibid., p. 149.

86. *Direktor*, p. 13. My thanks to Moshe Lewin for calling this work to my attention.

87. *Istoriia Moskovskogo Avtozavoda*, p. 150.

88. *Direktor*, pp. 13–15. A. V. Kuznetsov's essay, "Talant Organizatora," is the first in this excellent collection of memoirs dedicated to Likhachev.

89. Ibid., p. 219. Likhachev was testifying before a commission handling the party purge at ZiS from September through November 1933.

90. *Direktor*, p. 51. This is taken from S. S. Ignatov's memoir, "Difficulties of Growth."

Ignatov was a party organizer in the plant. Of Sorokin, he writes: "Sorokin simply did not want to tell the government that the factory would cost not 12 but 50 million rubles. He was afraid to admit his mistake, and preferred to deceive the state" (p. 47).

91. Ibid., p. 51.

92. *Istoriia Moskovskogo Avtozavoda,* pp. 154, 157. Obviously, neither Likhachev nor the Politburo was willing to dispense with Sorokin's expertise.

93. Ibid., p. 155.

94. *Direktor,* p. 15.

95. *Istoriia Moskovskogo Avtozavoda,* p. 156.

96. Reuther, *The Brothers Reuther,* chap. 9, "Tooling at Gorky." In a personal interview with Mr. Reuther in Washington, D.C., in 1988, he described his experiences at the Gorky plant in 1933 and 1934, emphasizing the new workers' (particulary the peasants') lack of skills, of industrial work culture, and of a sense of factory time, particularly among the peasant newcomers.

97. Ibid., quoting Sorenson, p. 91.

98. Sutton, *Western Technology,* pp. 248–49.

99. See Wheatcroft, Davies, and Cooper, "Soviet Industrialization Reconsidered, p. 279: "Most new models were copies of foreign designs, but the copying and innovation were almost entirely undertaken by Soviet engineers and workers, as was the construction of the machine-tool factories."

100. Whether the Red Directors were "organization men" or "cogs in the machine" or militant "Stalinist industrializers" has been debated, notably by Granick, Azrael, and Berliner. See Vladimir Andrle, *Managerial Power in the Soviet Union,* p. 4. Chapter 9 presents a new interpretation by drawing a distinction in their behavior and function between the First and Second FYPs.

101. *Istoriia Moskovskogo Avtozavoda,* p. 624, notes that they converted from the AMO-3 model to the ZiS-5 in 1933. See also *Direktor,* pp. 19–20, where Kuznetsov states that they completed reconstruction for the AMO-3 and then made this conversion to the ZiS-5 without halting production.

102. *Direktor,* pp. 13, 19.

103. *Istoriia Moskovskogo Avtozavoda,* p. 210.

104. *KPSS v Rezoliutsiiakh,* vol. 5, pp. 276–84.

105. Ibid., p. 281.

106. The acronyms stand for the All-Union Council of the National Economy, two construction trusts, and the Commissariat of Roads and Communications.

107. *KPSS v Rezoliutsiiakh,* p. 278.

108. *Istoriia Moskovskogo Avtozavoda,* pp. 262, 625, 632–38.

109. See, e.g., Kuznetsov's memoir in *Direktor,* pp. 28–30, where he tells of going as a "pusher" (facilitator) to the Tula military factory, on behalf of Likhachev, to get some workbenches that were badly needed for overcoming a "bottleneck" at ZiS. Likhachev phoned the Tula plant director, Vannikov, and Kuznetsov went on *kommandirovka*. In other cases, according to Kuznetsov, they improvised and built their own workbenches at ZiS, or in one instance, after the war, "attached" a Korean factory and "subcontracted" some parts.

Chapter 3. Recruiting Workers

1. See Rogachevskaia, *Likvidatsiia Bezrabotitsy;* see also Suvorov, *Istoricheskii Opyt.*

2. *Martenovka,* 15 May 1930, p. 2.

3. *Martenovka,* 23 December 1939, p. 2. On 6 October 1930, Gaidul', the secretary of the SiM *partkom,* was promoted to secretary of the *raikom.*

4. Ibid.

5. Ibid.

6. *Martenovka,* 12 October 1930, p. 3. The Special Quarter ran from 1 October to 31 December 1930. After 1 January 1931, the economic year coincided with the calendar year.

7. *Martenovka,* 23 December 1930, p. 2.

8. *Martenovka,* 24 December 1930, p. 2.

9. *Martenovka,* 28 December 1930, p. 3.

10. Veselov, *Professional'no-Tekhnicheskoe Obrazovanie,* p. 274.

11. *Sostav Novykh Millionov,* pp. 10, 13.

12. *Profsoiuznaia Perepis',* pp. 15, 74, 14.

13. Kornakovskii, "Zavod 'Serp i Molot,'" p. 199.

14. Filatov, *Partrabota,* p. 112.

15. GARF f. 5469, op. 10, d. 222, l. 107.

16. I quote the contract as published in *Martenovka,* 6 February 1931, p. 2.

17. GARF f. 5515, op. 15, d. 204, l. 1.

18. *Za Industrializatsiiu,* 10 April 1931, and also GARF f. 5469, op. 14, d. 313, l. 45. He proposed setting up a new VSNKh fund for the FZU, rapid construction of new schools, and a special recruitment "decade" from 20 April through 1 May 1931. He noted that 330,000 youth were already in training in the FZUs at the beginning of 1931, and that 360,000 more had to be recruited during 1931.

19. *Trud,* 6 August 1931, p. 4. Shvernik's article was entitled "The Unions Must Fight for Enterprise Schools Just as the Komsomol Fight for the FZU."

20. GARF f. 7952, op. 3, d. 283, ll. 156–57.

21. Veselov, *Professional'no-Tekhnicheskoe Obrazovanie,* pp. 289, 302.

22. Cf. Sonin, *Vosproizvodstvo Rabochei Sily,* p. 284. He argues that the State Labor Reserves trained 11 million qualified workers from 1940 to 1959, and that it was a success in recruitment and distribution. However, Sonin's discussion of the rise of the PTU would suggest otherwise (see pp. 301–03).

23. *Profsoiuznaia Perepis',* p. 19.

24. Vdovin and Drobizhev, *Rost Rabochego Klassa,* p. 132.

25. *Itogy Vsesoiuznoi Perepisi,* p. 167.

26. See Slavko and Kornakovskii, *"Metodika,"* p. 105.

27. *Profsoiuznaia Perepis',* p. 20. *Sostav Novykh Millionov,* p. 7, reaches the same conclusion.

28. Kornakovskii, "Zavod 'Serp i Molot,'" pp. 196–97.

29. *Profsoiuznaia Perepis',* pp. 74, 82, 94, 118.

30. Lel'chuk, *Industrial'noe Razvitie,* p. 434.

31. *Martenovka,* 10 February 1932, p. 3. Another article on this same page, "One Thousand One Hundred and Eighty Female Shock Workers, the Result of Bolshevik Work," discusses a number of occupations in which women were still poorly represented although they could easily do the work. It set the goal of bringing the number of women in the semiskilled job categories up from 7 percent to 21 percent, primarily by mechanizing and rationalizing production.

32. *Rabochaia Gazeta,* 8 March 1931, p. 4.

33. Ibid.

34. A point noted by Goldman, *Women, the State, and Revolution,* p. 316.

35. This is the finding of Barbara Anderson for all cohorts of Soviet women, including those who were coming of age during the 1930s. See "The Life Course of Soviet Women," p. 235.

36. *Itogy Vypolneniia Pervogo Piatiletnego Plana,* p. 174. Vdovin and Drobizhev, *Rost Rabochego Klassa,* p. 116, state that peasants constituted 68 percent of new recruits for the First FYP and 54 percent for the Second FYP. An August 1940 Gosplan document, reprinted in *Industrializatsiia SSSR,* vol. 4, pp. 248–51, indicates that of new recruits in industry during the Second FYP, FZU graduates accounted for 1.4 million, urban housewives and other urban "reserves" about 1 million, and peasants for 2.5 million.

37. *Profsoiuznaia Perepis',* p. 26.

38. Ibid., p. 94.

39. Sonin, *Vosproizvodstvo Rabochei Sily,* pp. 182–83.

40. Panfilova, *Formirovanie Rabochego Klassa,* pp. 84–86.

41. Arutiunian, "Kollektivizatsiia Sel'skogo Khoziaistva," *pp. 100–16.*

42. *Panfilova, Formirovanie Rabochego Klassa,* pp. 68–71, 97.

43. RGAE f. 4086, op. 2, d. 4896, l.121. This instance of *zemliachestvo* was at the Petrovskii metallurgy plant in Dnepropetrovsk.

44. Sonin, *Vosproizvodstvo Rabochei Sily,* p. 182.

45. Panfilova, *Formirovanie Rabochego Klassa,* p. 84.

46. *Industrializatsiia SSSR,* vol. 3, pp. 493–94.

47. Hoffmann, *Peasant Metropolis,* pp. 60–63, describes these city-to-village information networks.

48. GARF f. 7952, op. 3, d. 283, l.183.

49. For every Naum Sirota, probably two or three peasant-migrants without a bed in the barracks came and left SiM. Sirota's case is described in GARF f. 7952. op.3, d. 289, l. 59.

50. Hoffmann, *Peasant Metropolis,* pp. 60–63, 89.

51. Kornakovskii, "Zavod 'Serp i Molot,'" pp. 203–09. On p. 209, Kornakovskii concludes that urban recruits were channeled into the *metiznye* shops because they were more educated and thus better able to handle the new technology. He argues on p. 243, however, that the older metallurgical shops were staffed by workers with higher skills and longer tenure. This contradiction is unresolved, since he believes that urban workers had higher skill levels, on average, and longer tenure.

52. *Istoriia Moskovskogo Avtozavoda,* pp. 189, 240, 264.

53. One source, GARF f. 7952, op. 3, d. 283, l. 160, mentions a total of 14,800 trade unionists at SiM in 1932, accounting for 98 percent of the total work force.

54. RGAE f. 4086, op. 2, d. 260, l. 1–11 gives a shop-by-shop breakdown of the needs of the Krivorozhskii metallurgy plant and shows how planned recruitment would, in theory, account for all of the new workers. TsGAOR g. Moskvy, f. R-415, op. 7, d. 19, l. 1, shows that in 1940 at the AMO-ZiS plant, out of a total of 3,940 workers needed at the fourth and fifth *razriadi,* the plant expected to promote 2,000 from the lower *razriadi,* train 500 in the *tekhnikumy* and FZU, and recruit another 2,410.

55. *Martenovka,* 4 March 1936, pp. 2–3.

56. GARF f. 5469, op. 14, d. 24, l. 51.

57. Ibid., l. 80.

58. *KPSS v Resoliutsiia,* vol. 6, pp. 17–21.

59. The issues were debated in the policy journals of NKT, *Voprosy Truda,* and of VtsSPS, *Professional'nye Soiuzy.* These debates on wage irregularities anticipated Stalin's argument in his "Six Conditions" speech of 23 June 1931, in which he spoke against "petty bourgeois wage egalitarianism" (see Straus, "The Transformation of the Soviet Working Class," pp. 568–85).

60. The most complete monograph representing the Soviet view is Rogachevskaia, *Likvidatsiia Bezrabotitsy*. See also Suvorov, *Istoricheskii opyt*. These monographs argue forcefully that eliminating unemployment was an important objective of Soviet policy and that it was accomplished by a series of planned policies under the program of socialist industrialization. For a non-Soviet interpretation, see R. W. Davies, "The Ending of Mass Unemployment in the USSR," in David Lane, ed., *Labour and Employment in the USSR* (New York, 1986), pp. 19–35. Granick, *Job Rights in the Soviet Union*, argues that full employment was maintained by a conscious decision to sacrifice some degree of economic efficiency. Davies's argument may have more merit for the 1930s and 1940s, whereas Granick's may account better for the 1960s and 1970s.

61. The term is from Kornai, *Economics of Shortage.*

62. See Davies, "The Management of Soviet Industry," pp. 114–15.

63. Zaleski, *Stalinist Planning*, p. 258. Based on his reconstruction of Soviet data, he estimates that national income grew by 6.6 percent in 1933, but that investment declined by 19.3 percent, as compared with 1932 levels.

64. Kornai, *Resource-Constrained Versus Demand-Constrained Systems*, p. 34. My thanks to Nellie Ohr for pointing out this source to me.

65. Stalin, "Novaia Obstanovka," *Sochineniia*, vol. 13, p. 53.

66. Arutiunian, "Kollektivizatsiia Sel'skogo Khoziaistva," pp. 103, 112.

67. *International and Labor Information* 45 (6 Feb. 1933): 199: "The reserve labour supply in Russian agriculture is estimated at from 8 to 20 million workers, according to the method of calculation and the criteria adopted." *International Labour Review* 27 (March 1933): 352–53, explains that Gosplan relied heavily on estimates by the State Land Colonization Institute and by L. Mintz. The institute estimated rural overpopulation at between 24.5 and 32.5 million persons of working age. Mintz's estimate was 8.5 million at the beginning of the First FYP. Danilov, *Rural Russia Under the New Regime*, pp. 264–65, argues that the calculation of surplus rural population in the 1920s was highly speculative, producing figures ranging from 5 to 30 million.

68. *Sostav Novykh Millionov*, p. 10.

Chapter 4. Attaching Workers

1. As Stephen Kotkin pointed out to me, the Russian root *krep*, in the verb "to attach," is also the root in the word for serfdom, *krepostnoe pravo*.

2. Schwarz, *Labour in the Soviet Union*, pp. 90–98.

3. Ibid., p. 98.

4. Ibid.

5. Ibid., p. 22, citing *Izvestiia*, 31 January 1933; and *Sotsialisticheskoe Stroiltel'stvo*, p. 508.

6. Ibid., pp. 22, 23.

7. Ibid., pp. 100–06.

8. Ibid., p. 107.

9. Ibid., pp. 77–78. However, Schwarz also notes that the plans for conscripting juvenile labor in this way were limited to between 800,000 and 1 million annual recruits and was voluntary, unless this level of recruitment was not achieved.

10. Khlevniuk, "26 Iunia 1940 Goda," pp. 86–96. See also Kotkin, *Magnetic Mountain*, p. 21, citing Pierre Bourdieu, *Outline of a Theory of Praxis* (Cambridge, 1977), pp. 72–87.

11. Filtzer, *Soviet Workers and Stalinist Industrialization*, pp. 82–86, 112, 115.

12. Ibid., pp. 135, 136.

13. Ibid., p. 136, n. 41.

14. Ibid., p. 136.

15. Filtzer, *Soviet Workers and Stalinist Industrialization,* pp. 52, 141. See p. 28 for data on the years 1923–28. By the first half of 1939, turnover had reached an annual rate of 96 percent.

16. Ibid., p. 135.

17. Kornakovskii, "Zavod 'Serp i Molot,'" pp. 223, 231.

18. GARF f. 7952, op. 3, d. 283, l. 80; GARF f. 7952, op. 3, d. 326, l. 57.

19. *Martenovka,* 18 November 1932, p. 1.

20. Gaidul', "Problema Snizheniia Raskhodov," p. 7.

21. *Martenovka,* 3 February 1935, p. 3.

22. Ibid., p. 2.

23. Ibid.

24. Ibid.

25. *Martenovka,* 26 May 1937, p. 3.

26. *Martenovka,* 4 April 1938, p. 1, 17 May 1939, p. 3, and 24 May 1939, p. 1, "Put a Halt to Turnover of Labor Power at the Plant." This article indicated that in the first quarter of 1939, 953 workers had been hired and 888 had left.

27. Filtzer, *Soviet Workers and Stalinist Industrialization,* p. 115.

28. Ibid., pp. 127–28. Citing A. V. Mitrofanova, *Rabochii Klass SSSR v Gody Velikoi Otechestvennoi Voiny* (Moscow, 1971), who noted that the Red Army expanded from 1.4 million in 1937 to 4.2 million in 1941.

29. John Barber suggested a similar point in "The Development of Soviet Employment and Labour Policy."

30. Stalin, "Novaia Obstanovka," *Sochineniia,* vol. 13, p. 55.

31. The contrast between competing objectives of equality and efficiency was observed for a much later period by Ed Hewett in his *Reforming the Soviet Economy; Equality versus Efficiency* (Washington DC: Brookings Institute, 1988). I discuss the history of Soviet wage policy, 1917–28, in my dissertation, pp. 545–85.

32. Ibid., p. 59. This passage defined fundamental obligations of the worker to the state (output), and fundamental obligations of the state to the worker (food, housing, leisure activity). It replaced the old NEP ideal of the state as mediating between the interests of workers and peasants, and as guide over the development of the economy on behalf of society as a whole. That NEP vision was a role of the state not so unlike Durkheim's vision of "corporatism," a type of modernized social contract. Stalin's ersatz social contract, however, pitted the interests of workers and more broadly of "society" on one side, and the interests of the state on the other side. Both the NEP corporatist tendencies and Stalin's ersatz social contract were incompatible with the Bolshevik theory of a "dictatorship of the proletariat," which was a theoretical flaw in Leninism-Bolshevism. Stalin would exploit that flaw with his new doctrine of the state "strengthening" rather than "withering" under socialism.

33. Ibid., pp. 60–76.

34. The emphasis in *Voprosy Truda,* organ of the Commissariat of Labor (Narkomtrud) and of the newspaper *Za Industrializatsiiu,* organ of VSNKh, was on wage irregularity or irrationality, *pestrota.* Stalin substituted an attack on wage egalitarianism for an attack on wage irregularity. See my dissertation, pp. 568–85.

35. Ivanov, "V Novykh Usloviiakh—po Novomy Rabotat'" (Under New Conditions—Work in a New Way), published in the 23 June 1932 edition of *Za Industrializatsiiu,* the daily paper of VSNKh, touched off a year-long debate over how to best organize the exchange and distribution of supplies between Soviet enterprises. Davies analyzed this de-

bate in "The Socialist Market." He claims that Ivanov was really Birbraer, a maverick who may have had Ordzhonikidze's support, and who would propose market principles for setting industrial prices (p. 206).

36. Ivanov, "V Novykh Usloviiakh—po Novomy Rabotat'," pp. 2–3.

37. Ibid.

38. Ibid.

39. According to Rabkina and Rimashevskaia, "Raspredelitel'nye Otnosheniia," p. 20, wage differentials of the top decile to the bottom decile declined from 3.33:1 in 1930 to 3.16:1 in 1934, after which they rose very rapidly, to 4:1 in 1941, and to 5.43:1 in 1946. The gap was not narrowed until the Khrushchev labor reforms of 1956.

40. *Martenovka,* 30 October 1932, p. 4.

41. Economically, I suggest, the turning point between "early" and "mature" Stalinism was 1933. However, in the political arena, the turning point came in 1939, when the purges were concluded, as Bialer argues in *Stalin's Successors,* pp. 9–14.

42. *Martenovka* used the term *prokhodnyi dvor* or "entry courtyard." In English, "revolving door" is closer to the meaning intended.

43. The hiring freeze was, in practice, to be guaranteed by the Passport Act, which was designed to keep starving peasants out of the cities and to prevent peasant-migrants from arriving at the factory gates and personnel department. In fact, not only was hiring frozen, but there was significant downsizing in 1933, as 3–5 percent labor force reductions were typical. At SiM, the decline was much more precipitous, as perhaps as many as one-third, or 5,000 workers and salaried employees were laid off.

44. *KPSS v Rezoliutsiiakh,* vol. 6, pp. 17–18.

45. See Vdovin and Drobizhev, *Rost Rabochego Klassa,* pp. 109–13, esp. the chart on p. 113 tracing the changing annual composition of the work force from 1927 through 1940 by work tenure in years, and showing a 9–10 percent annual increment from 1934 to 1940. I consider this to be their most important, and their most neglected, finding. It formed the basis for my rethinking of the Soviet labor market in this chapter.

46. Sonin, *Vosproizvodstvo Rabochei Sily,* p. 185.

47. Jasny, *Soviet Industrialization,* was the first economist to call attention to the phenomenon of "business cycles" in Stalinist industrialization that did not correspond well, or at all, to the parameters of the FYPs. Without meaning to lend credence to the notion of "planned economy" under Stalinism, we could characterize the First FYP and World War II as "phase 1" and the 2–3 and 4–5 FYPs as "phase 2."

48. In both periods, improvisation virtually replaced planning, and this improvisation was disguised by superannuated administrative direction. This is contrary to Voznesenskii's account of wartime planned economy in *Voennaia Ekonomika SSSR,* but is in agreement with Harrison, *Soviet Planning in Peace and War,* p. 101, who emphasizes improvisation during 1941. And yet, there was a type of improvised planning, since the "pilot-satellite" model, improvised during the First FYP, provided some guidelines for the evacuation of factories in 1941.

49. The distinction between new construction and the relocation of factories in the Second World War was not so great. Relocation was frequently equivalent to new construction, as existing machinery was transported and then placed in a new shell of a factory.

50. See Harrison, *Soviet Planning in Peace and War,* p. 78.

51. "Population reserves" and "mobilization" were the regime's terms in both eras. The military jargon of the First FYP, such as "storming fortresses" and "battle plans," building "Bolshevik fortresses," and "catching up and surpassing," is well known.

52. *Itogy Vypolneniia Pervogo Piatiletnego Plana,* p. 267.

53. Mitrofanova, *Rabochii Klass SSSR,* p. 437.

54. On the rehiring of veterans, see Seniavskii and Tel'pukhovskii, *Rabochii Klass SSSR,* pp. 139–43. The hiring of school graduates virtually ceased (p. 151), and the hiring of FZO graduates seemed to have resumed in 1947 (p. 166). They note that women peaked at 55 percent of the labor force in 1945, and then the figures declined (p. 113). The issue of demobilization has hardly been studied.

55. Schwarz, *Labour in the Soviet Union,* p. 29, notes that the projected increase was 6 million whereas the actual increase was 10 million. The increase of 3 million in 1946 disguises the displacement of children, pensioners, and some women by veterans.

56. One notable exception is Andrle, "How Backward Workers Became Soviet," and *Workers in Stalin's Russia,* which develops the theme of how workers began acquiring industrial work-time discipline during the Second FYP. The economic historians Jasny and Zaleski had, earlier on, pointed out the stabilization of the economy during those same years, which Jasny called "Three Good Years."

57. For Thermidor, see Trotsky, *The Revolution Betrayed,* and Timasheff, *The Great Retreat.*

58. Filtzer, *Soviet Workers and Stalinist Industrialization,* pp. 152–54.

59. See Siegelbaum, "Masters of the Shop Floor," p. 174. Citing a Soviet source from 1935, Siegelbaum suggests that 75 percent of Soviet foremen in November 1933 had been workers and that 54 percent had been promoted during the First FYP.

60. Hoffmann, in *Peasant Metropolis,* emphasizes this type of conflict.

61. *Trud,* 10 September 1931, p. 1.

62. Schwartz, *Labour in the Soviet Union,* p. 88, citing Z. Mokhov, "Increase in Labor Turnover, 1929/30," *Voprosy Truda,* June 1930, p. 22.

63. Filtzer, *Soviet Workers and Stalinist Industrialization,* pp. 136, 139.

64. Ibid., p. 28, presents data showing annual fluctuation from 89.1 percent to 103.3 percent from 1923 to 1928.

Chapter 5. Training Workers

1. Fitzpatrick, *The Commissariat of Enlightenment,* and *Education and Social Mobility;* Holmes, *The Kremlin and the Schoolhouse.*

2. See Fitzpatrick, *Education and Social Mobility,* pp. 218–20, on the restoration of higher education, and pp. 221–23, on traditional elementary and secondary schooling. See also Timasheff, *The Great Retreat,* pp. 218–19.

3. Fitzpatrick, "Cultural Revolution as Class War," in Fitzpatrick, *Cultural Revolution in Russia.*

4. Fitzpatrick, *The Cultural Front,* p. 160.

5. Fitzpatrick, *The Russian Revolution,* pp. 104–06, 144–45.

6. Ibid., pp. 160–61. Fitzpatrick notes that Brezhnev, Kosygin, Ustinov, Malyshev, Patolichev, and Chuianov all began as *vydvizhentsy,* with almost identical higher education profiles in engineering. Fitzpatrick also noted that 20 of 138 full and candidate Central Committee members elected at the Eighteenth Party Congress in 1939 were *vydvizhentsy* and that this cohort reached 36 percent of the Central Committee elected at the Nineteenth Party Congress in 1952 (pp. 178–79). See "Stalin and the Making of a New Elite, 1928–1939," *Slavic Review* 38 (September 1979): 377–402.

7. Nicolaevsky, *Power and the Soviet Elite.* For the prospographical approach to the Stalin leadership and the terror see Fainsod, *How Russia Is Ruled;* Hough and Fainsod, *How the Soviet Union Is Governed;* and Bialer, *Stalin's Successors.*

8. In particular, it should be linked to the mind-set of the "commanders of industry" and leading industrialist-specialists, figures such as Tevosian, Zaveniagin, Vannikov, Shakhurin, etc. See Davies, "The Management of Soviet Industry," p. 115.

9. See Inkeles and Bauer, *The Soviet Citizen*, pp. 76–77, 131. Similar findings are reported, some forty years later, in Millar, *Politics, Work, and Daily Life in the USSR*, esp. Michael Swafford, "Perceptions of Social Status in the USSR."

10. See Inkeles and Bauer, *The Soviet Citizen*, pp. 282, 337.

11. See Siegelbaum, *Stakhanovism*, p. 179, and chapter 6.

12. Fitzpatrick, *Education and Social Mobility*, p. 203, suggested that the FZU was becoming a path to higher education: a survey of FZU graduates at SiM (reported in *Za Promyshlennye Kadry*, 1933, nos. 8–9, p. 276) showed that only 210 out of 900 FZU graduates in 1933 ended up working at SiM upon graduation; the FZU became "in effect general secondary schools" (p. 205). That may have been true briefly, during and after the Cultural Revolution, but not after 1933. Fitzpatrick herself noted that in the summer of 1933 the FZU were once again designated as a strictly vocational school (pp. 225–26). Enrollment data also shows that, after 1933, the path to the VUZ (college) was the ten-year school, as enrollment in the FZU declined sharply that year, and never recovered.

13. Veselov, *Professional'no-Tekhnicheskoe Obrazovanie*, p. 208.

14. GARF f. 5469, op. 10, d. 222, l. 12.

15. Ibid., l. 83.

16. Veselov, *Professional'no-Tekhnicheskoe Obrazovanie*, p. 208.

17. We have to assume, without better data, that FZU trainees were the sons and nephews of skilled male workers. However, in industries where female labor was substantial, women might have placed their sons or daughters in the FZU. The data for the PR metalworking factories from 1926, however, indicate that male workers rarely placed daughters in these schools.

18. Filatov, *Partrabota*, p. 112. The idea of the factory as "forge" or "smithy" of persons became a widespread metaphor during the First FYP (see chapter 8).

19. Ibid., pp. 110–12.

20. GARF f. 5469, op. 14, d. 24, l. 24.

21. Ibid. This was stated in provision no. 85.

22. GARF f. 5515, op. 17, d. 204, l. 1.

23. Fitzpatrick, *Education and Social Mobility*, pp. 47–48, 147–48, 148–49, 151.

24. GARF f. 5469, op. 14, d. 313, l. 45.

25. Filatov, *Partrabota*, pp. 112, 113.

26. Veselov, *Professional'no-Tekhnicheskoe Obrazovanie*, p. 285.

27. Ibid.

28. For the numbers who graduated from the FZU, see *Industrializatsiia SSSR*, vol. 3, p. 424. For the numbers enrolled in the FZU, see Veselov, *Professional'no-Tekhnicheskoe Obrazovanie*, p. 279.

29. See the figures in ibid., p. 289.

30. Kiselev and Malkin, *Sbornik*, p. 111–12.

31. RGAE f. 4086, op. 2, d. 2283, l. 140.

32. *Industrializatsiia SSSR, 1938–41*, vol. 4, p. 250.

33. Filatov, *Partrabota*, pp. 114–15.

34. Ibid., p. 116.

35. GARF f. 7952, op. 3, d. 340, l. 33. This is from a document, "Put' Kul'turnoi Revoliutsii," which from its contents can be dated to 1931 or 1932.

36. The figures are from Filatov, *Partrabota*, p. 117.

37. TsGAOR g. Moskvy, f. 100, op. 1, d. 11, l. 1.

38. Veselov, *Professional'no-Tekhnicheskoe Obrazovanie*, pp. 295–96.

39. Filatov, *Partrabota*, p. 119.

40. Veselov, *Professional'no-Tekhnicheskoe Obrazovanie*, pp. 185, 279.

41. See Lapidus, "Educational Strategies and Cultural Revolution," in Fitzpatrick, *Cultural Revolution in Russia*, p. 96, and Fitzpatrick, *Education and Social Mobility*, pp. 148–49.

42. Filatov, *Partrabota*, p. 122.

43. See Fitzpatrick, *The Commissariat of Enlightenment.*

44. That was the only distinction that Filatov could make clear and comprehensible (*Partrabota*, p. 123).

45. Ibid., pp. 123–24.

46. GARF f. 5469, op. 14, d. 316, l. 51.

47. GARF f. 7952, op. 3, d. 283, ll. 186–87.

48. GARF f. 5469, op. 14, d. 316, ll. 52–53.

49. See, for example, Dewey's well-known claims about the need to integrate manual and mental labor in *Democracy and Education*, pp. 315–16.

50. GARF f. 5469, op. 14, d. 316, l. 54.

51. Ibid., l. 68.

52. Ibid., l. 55–56.

53. See Bailes, "Alexei Gastev and the Controversy Over Taylorism," and Siegelbaum, "Soviet Norm Determination," for the popularity and then discrediting of the so-called functionalism (Taylorism) in management. As Siegelbaum argues in "Masters of the Shop Floor," the decline of Taylorism in 1933 was the beginning of the second rise of the foreman (p. 183).

54. GARF f. 5469, op. 14, d. 316, l. 58.

55. Ibid., ll. 75–78.

56. See Fitzpatrick, *Cultural Revolution*, and *The Cultural Front.*

57. *Martenovka*, 1 January 1933, p. 1. In this speech, Molotov announced the objective of a hiring cap of 2 percent for 1933, with the plan for GNP to expand by 16.5 percent.

58. Ibid.

59. Fitzpatrick, *Education and Social Mobility*, pp. 224–25.

60. Veselov, *Professional'no-Tekhnicheskoe Obrazovanie*, p. 302.

61. Ibid.

62. See esp. *A Radical Worker in Tsarist Russia.*

63. Veselov, *Professional'no-Tekhnicheskoe Obrazovanie*, p. 298.

64. Ibid., pp. 298–99.

65. Ibid., pp. 299–300.

66. Ibid., p. 300.

67. Ibid., pp. 300–01.

68. Ibid., p. 303.

69. Sonin, *Vosproizvodstvo Rabochei Sily*, pp. 182–83, and Veselov, *Professional'no-Tekhnicheskoe Obrazovanie*, p. 279.

70. TsGAOR g. Moskvy, f. 415, op. 7, d. 22, l.1. The document was signed by the head of the Division of Technical Education, Guraev; the head of the Planning Division, Genkin; and the head of the Cadre Division, Buianov.

71. Ibid., l. 2. The acronym OTO might have stood for Division of Technical Training.

72. Ibid., l. 2.

73. TsGAOR g. Moskvy, f. 415, op. 7, d. 19, ll. 1–2. The document was signed by the

head of the Division of Technical Training, Churaev, and by the head of the Planning Bureau, Boguslavskii.

74. Ibid.

75. TsGAOR g. Moskvy, f. R-415, op. 7, d. 11, l. 1. The occupational breakdown on l. 2 showed that in 1938 at AMO-ZIS, 5,988 trainees enrolled, and that 5,281 of these passed the GTE, of which 1,541 passed with a mark of "excellent."

76. TsGAOR g. Moskvy, f. R-415, op. 7, d. 24, l. 1.

77. Ibid., l. 1.

78. Veselov, *Professional'no-Tekhnicheskoe Obrazovanie*, pp. 279, 303. In 1937, the industrial and construction branches of the economy had 1,790,643 graduates and 988,336 still enrolled in uninterrupted courses. In 1938, these figures fell slightly to 1,654,267 graduates and 869,814 still enrolled.

79. Stalin, "O Zadachakh Khoziaistvennikov," *Sochineniia*, vol. 13, p. 41. He actually said, "technology [or technique] in the reconstruction period determines everything." Stalin also said that unless the USSR achieved West European production levels within ten years, the USSR would be crushed militarily, as Russia had so often been beaten by its more technologically advanced enemies.

80. Ibid., vol. 14, pp. 63–64.

Chapter 6. R-r-r-r-Revolutionary Shock Work and Socialist Competition

1. "R-r-r-revolutionary" was Stalin's derisive formula in his "Dizzy with Success" article published in *Pravda* on 2 March 1930, castigating the rank and file for removing church bells in the villages during the collectivization drive and, more widely, for using compulsion to force peasant families into the kolkhoz (*Sochineniia*, vol. 12, p. 198). By thus attributing disastrous policies that came from himself and the center to the excessive zeal or political amateurishness of the party rank and file, he found a formula for deflecting blame and popular discontent that he would use time and again through the 1930s, most notably during the purge-terror. See Tucker, *Stalin in Power*, p. 464.

2. The most significant studies include Rogachevskaia, *Sotsialisticheskoe Sorevnovanie;* Lebedeva and Shkaratan, *Ocherki Istorii Sotsialisticheskogo Sorevnovaniia;* Lebedeva, *Partiinoe Rukovodstvo Sotsialisticheskim Sorevnovaniem;* Dadykin, *Nachalo Massovogo Sotsialisticheskogo Sorevnovaniia;* and the collection of documents *Sotsialisticheskoe Sorevnovanie.* For the standard Soviet perspective, summarizing the findings of the studies listed above on the origins of shock work, see *Istoriia Sovetskogo Rabochego Klassa*, vol. 2, pp. 252–259.

3. On the origins of shock work, see Siegelbaum, "Shock Workers," pp. 23–27. Following Siegelbaum, I see the first shock-work brigades arising after the middle 1920s, building on earlier tendencies during the Civil War and early NEP years and responding to regime imperatives and stimuli among certain groups of rank-and-file party members, Komsomol, and production workers. A similar combination of regime stimulus and lower-level initiative, it would appear, best explains the origins of Stakhanovism in 1935. See Siegelbaum, *Stakhanovism*, chap. 1.

4. *Istoriia Kirovskogo Zavoda*, p. 291. For the response at SiM, see *Svet nad Zastavoi*, p. 169. On the wide impact of "How to Organize Competition," written by Lenin in December 1917, see *Istoriia Sovetskogo Rabochego Klassa*, vol. 2, p. 259. The staunch egalitarianism of his famous article "A Great Beginning," which offered a very different approach to promoting worker initiative and enthusiasm, published in June 1919, obviously was not suited to the needs of the regime in January 1929. Nor was Lenin's famous definition of class and discussion of how class differences would be gradually reduced under socialism in "A Great Beginning" of any use to the Stalin regime in 1929.

5. *Svet nad Zastavoi,* p. 169, and Kornakovskii, "Zavod 'Serp i Molot,'" p. 316.

6. Kornakovskii, "Zavod 'Serp i Molot,'" p. 319.

7. See Kornakovskii, "I. M. Romanov," p. 38.

8. Kornakovskii, "Zavod 'Serp i Molot,'" p. 319. It is not clear if this included the Vyborzhetsy sheet metal workers, or if theirs was a plantwide challenge.

9. *Istoriia Sovetskogo Rabochego Klassa,* vol. 2, p. 259.

10. *KPSS v Rezoliutsiiakh,* vol. 4, p. 509.

11. Kornakovskii, "Zavod 'Serp i Molot,'" p. 319.

12. Ibid., p. 321.

13. Ibid., p. 318.

14. *Svet nad Zastavoi,* p. 170.

15. Mikhailov, *The Fight for Steel,* pp. 3–4.

16. GARF f. 7952, op. 3, d. 282, l. 92. Podrubaev was later credited with founding the first "cost-accounting brigade" in March 1931 at SiM. See ibid., l. 53.

17. See *Nas Vyrastil Stalin,* p. 5; *Pervoprokhodtsy,* pp. 165–80.

18. Filatov, *Partrabota,* p. 11; Kornakovskii, "Zavod 'Serp i Molot,'" p. 310.

19. Abramov and Bil'dziukevich, *Peredovik Sovetskoi Metallurgii,* p. 15.

20. Ibid., p. 18.

21. Ibid., p. 19.

22. *Istoriia Moskovskogo Avtozavoda,* pp. 157–58, 159–160. See also the biographical sketch of Aleksandr Petrovich Salov coauthored by Ostapenko and Rogahevskaia in *Novatory,* pp. 22–43.

23. Ibid.

24. Vdovin and Drobizhev, *Rost Rabochego Klassa,* p. 162.

25. Ibid., p. 163.

26. *Industrializatsiia SSSR,* vol. 2, pp. 503, 557.

27. *Istoriia Sovetskogo Rabochego Klassa,* vol. 2, p. 266.

28. Filatov, *Partrabota,* pp. 58–59; *Martenovka,* 10 May 1930, p. 1.

29. GARF f. 5469, op. 14, d. 193, l. 11

30. Ibid., l. 12.

31. Ibid., l. 321.

32. Ibid., l. 36.

33. Ibid.

34. Ibid., ll. 40–41.

35. *Industrializatsiia SSSR,* vol. 3, pp. 548–54.

36. GARF f. 5469, op. 14, d. 242, l. 40.

37. *Istoriia Sovetskogo Rabochego Klassa,* vol. 2, pp. 261–62.

38. GARF f. 5469, op. 14, d. 242, l. 39. It was partly this problem that led to the decision to reconstruct SiM at its existing site, so as to provide high quality steel for AMO-ZiS.

39. Tolkachi is usually translated as "pushers" or "expediters." They were "professionals" on the directors' staff, as Berliner showed in *Factory and Manager,* chap. 12. Apparently, in the shock-work movement, workers attempted to supplement or supplant them by taking their own initiative to procure raw materials, supplies, machines, and equipment, so as to reduce idle time.

40. GARF f. 5469, op. 14, d. 242, l. 39. *Buksir* brigades were sent by AMO-ZiS to the Brake Factory and to Elektrostal', both important suppliers for AMO-ZiS that were always running late with their deliveries.

41. Ibid., l. 40.

42. Siegelbaum, *Stakhanovism,* p. 46.

43. GARF f. 5469, op. 14, d. 374, ll. 82–83. In the typical shock brigade and in the productive collectives and communes, work would be organized according to single work "card," which assigned them a group task with a group deadline and a lump sum payment. Pay was then distributed within the shock brigade to each worker strictly in accordance with their skill ranking *(tarifnyi razriad)* and output. In the collective, however, pay would be given to workers in skill groups, which lumped together three of the *tarifnye razriady*. Pay would still vary for individuals depending on the hours worked and time or piece rates. In the communes, pay apparently varied not according to skill groups but only according to the number of dependents or "eaters" in the family of each worker.

44. GARF f. 5469, op. 14, d. 193, l. 132.

45. GARF f. 7952, op. 3, d. 341, l. 42.

46. GARF f. 7952, op. 3, d. 290, l. 35.

47. Ibid., ll. 36–37.

48. See, for example, the discussion of the collective contract for 1930 at Dinamo in GARF f. 5469, op. 14, d. 24, ll. 20–25.

49. GARF f. 7952, op. 3, d. 282, ll. 36–37. L'vov's "Cost Accounting—A Method of Management of Enterprises" was included in the document "Essays and Articles on SiM, 1928–1932." This was part of the Gor'kii Project, "History of Soviet Factories."

50. *Dognat' i Peregnat'*, 1932, no. 24, p. 3.

51. Ibid., p. 3.

52. Excerpted from "Biulletin Finansogo i Khoziaistvennogo Zakonodatelstva," 1934, no. 43, in *Sbornik Vazhneishikh Postanovlenii po Trudu*, compiled by Ia. L. Kiselev and S. E. Malkin (Moscow, 1936), pp. 18–21.

53. Ibid., p. 21.

54. Ibid., p. 18. The only restriction was that the brigades had to facilitate the reduction of costs. But this was still very hard to measure under Soviet conditions!

55. GARF f. 7952, op. 3, d. 282, l. 62.

56. Ibid.

57. See Lebedeva and Shkaratan, *Ocherki Istorii Sotsialisticheskogo Sorevnovaniia*, p. 111; and *Sotsialisticheskoe Sorevnovanie*, p. 476.

58. GARF, f. 5469, op. 14, d. 193, ll. 1–2.

59. Shapiro, *The Communist Party*, argues that at the Seventeenth Party Congress (January–February 1934), "signs of compromise between Stalin and the more 'moderate' members of the Politburo became most evident" (p. 396). Conquest argued that, by 1932, leading party moderates functioned as a bloc to prevent the execution of the oppositionist Riutin, which Stalin was demanding (*The Great Terror*, p. 29). Bailes argues that a moderate view, pushed by Ordzhonikidze, Kirov, and Kuibyshev, had won out within the Politburo as early as the spring of 1931 (*Technology and Society*, p. 175). Fitzpatrick, while emphasizing the same trend toward moderation in 1932, disagrees, arguing that Stalin and Molotov were in the forefront of the new policy (*Education and Social Mobility*, p. 211).

60. Stalin, "The Results of the First Five-Year Plan," *Sochineniia*, vol. 13, p. 186.

61. *Martenovka*, 6 October 1930, p. 3.

62. Kornakovskii, "Zavod 'Serp i Molot,'" p. 319.

63. To put this in perspective, the leading brigade at SiM in the sheet metal shop in the summer of 1959 was Viktor Diuzhev's "shock brigade of Communist labor," which averaged 420–500 sheets per shift, one and one-half times the shift norm. Thus the norm was approximately 330 sheets per shift. See the biographical sketch of Diuzhev by B. Kazantsev in *Pervoprokhodtsy*, p. 173.

This norm, however, pertained to newly mechanized mills installed at SiM in July

1959. Furthermore, there probably had been many other technical changes in the interim (1930–59), so it is difficult to compare data. But it is interesting that the Khrushchev version of shock brigades and socialist competitions began in the same shop at SiM where its prototype, Gladyshev's shock brigade, first formed exactly thirty years before. It was as if, after nearly three decades of promoting shock worker-heroes, the regime had rediscovered that the brigade as a whole was the important unit in calculating productivity. Regime strategies had come full circle, back to the second stage of shock work of 1929.

64. *Svet Nad Zastavoi,* p. 177.

65. GARF f. 7952, op. 3, d. 326, ll. 136–38, 191.

66. Ibid., l. 92.

67. Ibid., l. 53.

68. Kornakovskii, "Zavod 'Serp i Molot,'" p. 318.

69. *Martenovka,* 6 October 1930, p. 3.

70. See Kornakovskii, "I. M. Romanov," pp. 34–35. This biographical sketch was published in Moscow in 1983 in a volume of biographical essays, *Nastavniki.*

71. Mikhailov, *The Fight for Steel,* pp. 35–38. A similar change in Monger's outlook is described in Shipilin's collection of essays on the factory, *Krepche Stali,* pp. 93–95. How realistic these accounts were is impossible to verify. Both have substantial descriptions of Monger and his interactions with other workers. Iakov Zakharovich Shvedov's novel *Poiski Otechestva* is a fictionalized account of Monger's life, centering on the question of why this transplanted Englishman stayed in Moscow after 1917 and, like the pamphlet by Besborodov, *Thomas Monger,* is mainly concerned with linking "proletarian internationalism" with the idea of Soviet patriotism.

72. Abramov and Bil'dziukevich, *Peredovik Sovetskoi Metallurgii,* p. 59.

73. At a meeting of 250 men from the sheet metal rolling shop, Monger attempted to answer the charges that he ran the shop like a dictator and played favorites, especially that he had helped Gladyshev establish a new record, but he was unable to speak because his emotions got the better of him and he was weeping. Gaidul' stood up and defended Monger for spending up to sixteen hours daily at work, for his experience and knowledge from his earlier work at a case-hardening plant, and for helping to collect signatures for the Third Industrial Loan. He denounced the anonymous letter, as "Trotskyism." See Besborodov, *Thomas Monger,* pp. 22–3, and Mikhailov, *The Fight for Steel,* p. 14.

74. Kornakovskii, "Zavod 'Serp i Molot,'" p. 322, suggests that he left in the mid-1930s. His name is mentioned in the British Public Records Office Documents several times during the 1920s and 1930s, but there is no evidence of when he left the USSR, of how he was repatriated, and if he was "debriefed" in London.

75. *Nastavniki,* p. 33.

76. Ibid., p. 35.

77. Ibid., pp. 38–39.

78. *Svet Nad Zastavoi,* p. 190.

79. *Nastavniki,* p. 36.

80. *Pervoprokhodtsy,* pp. 165–80.

81. Kornakovskii, "Zavod 'Serp i Molot,'" p. 322.

82. On Nikita Izotov, a coal miner known as the "human cutting machine" and a precursor to Aleksei Stakhanov, see Siegelbaum, *Stakhanovism,* pp. 54–56.

83. Markevich and Urnis, *U Zastavy Il'icha,* pp. 17, 34–35.

84. Abramov and Bil'dziukevich, *Peredovik Sovetskoi Metallurgii,* p. 78.

85. *Svet Nad Zastavoi,* p. 249.

86. Grudkov, *Peredovoi Opyt-Vsem Stalevaram,* pp. 13–15.

87. *Moskvichi*, pp. 96, 97–98. The essay on Chesnokov, "Moscow Metallurgist," was written by S. Martich.

88. Ibid., pp. 108–18.

89. Rikhter, *Stal Frontu*, p. 6.

90. Siegelbaum, *Stakhanovism*, pp. 76–77.

91. See Gershberg, *Stakhanov i Stakhanovtsy*, p. 35 for a biographical sketch of Stakhanov, and p. 56 for Busygin. For Ivan Gudov, see his autobiography *Sud'ba Rabochego*, pp. 5–7. The economist O. A. Ermanski noted, "The ovewhelming majority [of the Stakhanovitess] were . . . young, from 20–25 and rarely thirty years old; . . . they had not come to the factory so long ago. The majority came during the heroic years of the First FYP, mainly from the countrside" (*Stakhanovskoe Dvizhenie*, p. 283).

92. *Profsoiuznaia Perepis'*, p. 74. More than 46 percent of SiM workers were twenty-three years old or less according to this trade-union census. At AMO-ZiS, out of 12,671 surveyed workers, 49.4 percent were twenty-three years old or less and 55 percent had three years or less production tenure (p. 82).

93. See Kuromiya, *Stalin's Industrial Revolution,* chap. 4.

94. A fine example of the regime's model for family life and consumption patterns was provided by Zosim Ivanovich Chernyshev's account of his attempt to raise his children in *Martenovka*, 11 March 1935, p. 2. See my dissertation, pp. 671–89, for a discussion of Chernyshev's family life.

95. By "industrial relations system" I mean what John Dunlop, Clark Kerr, and Daniel Bell had in mind in the 1950s in the United States: a stable system of production relations in which shop-floor bargaining over norms and pay rates was a daily phenomenon. However, the American system of shop-floor bargaining was linked to a nationwide bargaining system between the corporations and the AFL-CIO, with occasional arbitration and regulatory intervention by the federal government. The latter, obviously, had no counterpart in the Soviet system. However, the Red Directors and their staff, shop-floor party officials *(partkom)* and shop-floor union officials *(zavkom),* mediated between party-state interests, on the one hand, and the workers' interests, on the other. Thus, a distinctly Soviet industrial relations system emerged, one that resembled the systems evolving in Western Europe and in the United States. See Dunlop, *Industrial Relations Systems,* and Dunlop et al., *Industrialism and Industrial Man.* On how it worked in practice in the United States, see Dubofsky, *The State and Labor in Modern America,* chap. 8.

96. Siegelbaum, *Stakhanovism*, chaps. 1–2.

Chapter 7. The Factory as "Social Melting Pot"

1. Kuromiya, *Stalin's Industrial Revolution;* Andrle, *Workers in Stalin's Russia;* and Siegelbaum, *Stakhanovism.*

2. See Davies, "Management of Soviet Industry," p. 114. The "pathos" of First FYP construction, also called the "deviation" of construction, was the terminology adopted in the Plenum resolutions from January 1933. See *KPSS v Resoliutsiiakh,* vol. 6., p. 17.

3. Andrle, *Workers in Stalin's Russia,* citing D. Roy, p. 119.

4. Ibid., p. 195.

5. Ibid., pp. 114–15. Andrle was applying E. P. Thompson's seminal ideas on time orientation and task orientation. See Thompson, "Time, Work Discipline and Industrial Capitalism," pp. 56–97.

6. *Siegelbaum, Stakhanovism,* pp. 49–50.

7. Ibid., pp. 2–4, 12.

8. Ibid., pp. 222, 281.

9. Ibid., pp. 179, 186–90.

10. Ibid., pp. 190–204.

11. Ibid., p. 143.

12. Ibid., pp. 160–61.

13. See chapter 1, n. 45, above. See Barber, "The Standard of Living of Soviet Industrial Workers, 1928–1941," "The Development of Soviet Employment and Labor Policy, 1930–1941," and "The Composition of the Soviet Working Class, 1928–1941," CREES Discussion Paper, SIPS Series No.16, Birmingham, 1978 (unpublished), cited with permission.

14. For a review of the Soviet literature on the working class during the 1920s and the 1930s, see Shkaratan, *Problemy Sotsial'noi Struktury,* and Vdovin and Drobizhev, *Rost Rabochego Klassa.* The most detailed historiographical surveys are Vorozheikin, *Ocherk Istoriografii Rabochego Klassa,* and Vorozheikin and Seniavskii, *Rabochii Klass.* I have also relied on works by Rogachevskaia, Panfilova, Mitrofanova, and Sokolov. Sonin, like Strumilin and Rashin, was able to publish important work in the Khrushchev years on the Soviet working class in the 1920s and 1930s using data collected but unpublishable during the Stalin years.

15. Sonin, *Vosproizvodstvo Rabochei Sily,* pp. 182–85, 188–89, 192–93.

16. Shkaratan, *Problemy Sotsial'noi Struktury,* p. 132. Stalin's categories were presented at the Seventh Plenum of the IKKI in December 1926; see "Eshcho Raz o Sotsial'—Demokraticheskom Uklone v Nashei Partii," *Sochineniia,* vol. 9, pp. 10–11.

17. See Shkaratan, *Problemy Sotsial'noi Struktury,* pp. 4, 44–45, 100–04, on the technical intelligentsia and white-collar workers as part of a "broadened" working class under socialism.

18. Ibid., pp. 59–61; Inkeles and Bauer, *The Soviet Citizen,* p. 75. They emphasized "convergence," that the Soviet social structure resembled that of any industrial society.

19. Shkaratan emphasized that social differentiation based on education, skill, or culture was not class differentiation and that the Soviet working class was becoming broader and broader as it increasingly incorporated "mental" workers, at the upper end, and agrarian workers at the lower end. However, the fact that social differentiation was not necessarily economic class differentiation, and that social conflict could reflect status differences and differences in political power, was precisely Weber's point. See Weber, "Class, Status, Party."

20. Vdovin and Drobizhev, *Rost Rabochego Klassa,* p. 113. Their data was for the entire wage-earning and salaried work force *(rabochie i sluzhashchie)* and was organized in terms of years of work tenure.

21. Ibid., chap. 4.

22. Barber, "The Composition." Stalin used the phrase *new Soviet working class* in the 1936 constitution to signify the supposed absence of exploitation. Barber and I use the phrase not in Stalin's sense, but empirically, in ways similar to Shkaratan's analysis. Stalin's usage, at one level, might strike us as absurd. At another level, however, we might note that it was highly influential and significant not because of the reality of the end of exploitation, but because it meant the end of the regime's "class struggle" approach against "class aliens" and thus the acceptance of subaltern workers as part of the Soviet working class.

23. Barber, "The Standard of Living," pp. 118–19. See also his "The Development of Soviet Employment and Labour Policy," p. 63, where he argues that a labor market functioned throughout the 1930s.

24. See, in particular, Cohen, *Making a New Deal.*

25. See , e.g., the Kommunist Academy census at SiM in April 1931. GARF f. 7952, op. 3, d. 341, l. 32.

26. Rabkina and Rimashevskaia, "Raspredelitel'nye Otnosheniia," p. 20; Bergson, *The Structure of Soviet Wages.*

27. The factors of overtime pay, bonuses, and premium pay, not to mention the impact of piece rates and progressive piece rate pay systems, widely used after 1931, meant that decile ratios were at best a rough approximation of actual wage differentiation.

28. Matthews, *Class and Society in Soviet Russia,* and *Poverty in the Soviet Union;* Yanowitch, *Social and Economic Inequality,* and other studies.

29. These studies were broadly consistent with the findings of Alex Inkeles and others in the Harvard Refugee Interview Project in the 1940s, and of James Millar and others in the Soviet Interview Project in the 1980s, in that education rather than parents' occupation was a good indicator of career choice. This reflected, in my view, the fact that social integration had been achieved in the 1930s and 1940s.

30. McAuley, *Women's Work and Wages,* pp. 49–52. The Second World War no doubt favored womens' participation in previously segregated professions and industrial occupations, but McAuley's findings indicate that after 1939 there was a tendency toward segregation. One cause was that formerly prestigious professions, such as medicine, not integrated until 1917, after 1939 became more than 75 percent female, and thus, according to McAuley's category, "predominantly segregated." With this there came a declining status for doctors after 1939.

31. Kornakovskii's 1979 manuscript (never published) is in INION, the Social Science Library of the Academy of Sciences, MS no. 10062.

32. Kornakovskii and Slavko, "Metodika," pp. 76–113.

33. Kornakovskii, "Zavod 'Serp i Molot,'" pp. 237–38.

34. Ibid. Kornakovskii was citing *Trud v SSSR: Ezhegodnik* (Moscow, 1935), pp. 270–71.

35. Boltianskii, *Voprosy Sotsialisticheskoi Organizatsii Truda,* p. 95.

36. Manevich, *Zarabotnaia Plata,* pp. 109–12.

37. Kornakovskii and Slavko, "Metodika," p. 105.

38. Vdovin and Drobizhev, *Rost Rabochego Klassa,* p. 244. This argument was anticipated in Shkaratan, *Problemy Sotsial'noi Struktury,* p. 395, where he suggested that the greatest increase in earnings for Leningrad workers in 1965 were for those with 3–5 years' work tenure.

39. Vdovin and Drobizhev, *Rost Rabochego Klassa,* p. 116. In the First FYP, they claim that 68 percent of recruits were peasants.

40. *Industrializatsiia SSSR,* vol. 4, pp. 248–51. The discrepancy between these figures is probably accounted for by retirements, deaths, etc.

41. Ibid., pp. 249–51.

42. See Hoffmann, *Peasant Metropolis.*

43. Kuromiya, "The Crisis of Proletarian Identity," pp. 280–97, and *Stalin's Industrial Revolution,* chap. 4 and appendix, pp. 319–24. Rather than a "crisis of proletarian identity," this may be better described as a crisis in regime categories.

44. While the rate of recruiting in the first years of reconstruction, 1925/26–1927/28 was nowhere near the First FYP levels, still it marked a departure. Rashin argues that until 1925 workers with previous industrial experience were being rehired, whereas after that date new workers without experience were being hired. But his data also show that it was mainly urban male youth who were being newly hired, and as I have suggested, they were primarily sons and nephews of cadre workers. The new recruits only began to change in social origin during the First FYP. See Rashin, *Sostav Fabrichno-Zavodskogo Proletariata,* p. 22.

Chapter 8. The Factory as Community Organizer

1. *KPSS v Resoliutsiiakh,* vol. 5, pp. 317–18.
2. *Moskva v Tsifrakh* (1934), pp. 183, 13.
3. Ibid., p. 183.
4. *KPSS v Resoliutsiiakh,* vol. 5, p. 317.
5. Ibid., pp. 317–26.
6. *Istoriia Moskvy,* vol. 6, bk. 2, pp. 44, 87.
7. *Moskva v Tsifrakh* (1934), p. 106.
8. Ibid., p. 107.
9. Poletaev, "Zhilishchnoe Stroitel'stvo," p. 4.
10. Lapitskaia, "Zhilishchnoe Stroitel'stvo," pp. 220–21; Poletaev, "Zhilishchnoe Stroitel'stvo," p. 10.
11. See *Moskva Entsiklopediia,* pp. 229–30, 252. Dangauerovka was an old workers' settlement from the second half of the nineteenth century, when the Dangauer and Kaiser factories were built there.
12. See the photo of the Dangauerovka settlement, prominentely featuring the new school, in *Istoriia Moskvy,* vol. 6, bk. 2, p. 15. The same photo also appeared several times in *Martenovka* during the 1930s.
13. GARF f. 7952, op. 3, d. 340, ll. 54–55 describes the conditions facing the 1,500 peasant-recruits; GARF f. 7952, op. 3, d. 283, l. 80, discusses the construction of six new barracks.
14. Report issued by the SiM "Lenin Committee of the Union of Workers of Heavy Metallurgy of the Center" (*Martenovka,* 24 May 1939, pp. 2–3).
15. *Martenovka,* 26 February 1932, p. 4.
16. Ibid.
17. *Istoriia Moskovskogo Avtozavoda,* p. 271.
18. *Direktor,* p. 20. The second reconstruction envisioned an increase in annual output from 20,000 vehicles in 1933 to 80,000 by 1938.
19. *Martenovka,* 28 November 1934, p. 1. Crimes of this type were infrequently discussed in *Martenovka;* Soviet media generally did not report crimes unless they could link the prosecution of the criminals to a political point.
20. Ibid.
21. *Martenovka,* 14 January 1935, p. 2; May 14, 1935, p. 1; 26 August 1939, p. 2.
22. *Martenovka,* 30 March 1932, p. 4.
23. *Martenovka,* 10 January 1934, pp. 2–3.
24. *Svet nad Zastavoi,* pp. 95–96.
25. *Istoriia Moskovskogo Avtozavoda,* p. 34.
26. *Moskva Entsiklopediia,* p. 435.
27. On the new bridges built in 1938, see ibid., p. 435, and on the two Ustinskii bridges, see photo, p. 615, and description, p. 621.
28. *KPSS v Resoliutsiiakh,* vol. 5, p. 320.
29. *Moskva Entsiklopediia,* pp. 97, 506.
30. *KPSS v Resoliutsiiakh,* vol. 5, p. 320.
31. Andrei Platonov's evocative title *Kotlovan,* or *Foundation Pit,* translated by Thomas Whitney (Ann Arbor: Ardis Publishers, 1973) presented a nightmarish dystopia of the Soviet urban scene, in which the anomie of the antihero defies sociological analysis. It was finally published serially in the Soviet Union in *Novyi Mir* (1987). It was written at the height of the collectivization drive, between December 1929 and April 1930. (Thanks to Michael

Gelb for providing me with the Ardis edition.) A glorified image of the new socialist city under construction was presented in socialist realist art, for example in T.V . Riannel's painting, 1973, titled *Kotlovan,* depicting the construction of the Saiano-Shushenskii Electric Station, or in Iu. I. Pimenov's 1962 painting titled *Wedding on Tommorrow's Streets,* portraying the newlyweds heading, presumably to their apartment, in a new district of Moscow still under construction. See *Iskusstvo i Rabochii Klass* (Leningrad, 1983), plates 172, 123.

32. See *"Dinamo" na Putiakh k Oktiabriu,* p. 9; *Istoriia Moskovskogo Avtozavoda,* p. 11.

33. On the tsarist passport system, see Robinson, *Rural Russia Under the Old Regime,* pp. 78–79, 108. By the 1897 census, 5 million of these passport holders lived in cities. On the Stalin passport, see Fitzpatrick, *Stalin's Peasants,* pp. 95–96, who notes that, except for 1933, the passport system did not hinder peasant rural-urban migration and thus does not include it in discussing the "second serfdom" in her fifth chapter.

34. Cited in Dewar, *Labour Policy in the USSR,* p. 148. See also Piore, *Birds of Passage.*

35. See chapter 2, n. 84.

36. GARF f. 7952, op. 3, d. 326, l. 131; GARF f. 7952, op. 3, d. 283, l. 182.

37. GARF f. 7952, op. 3, d. 326, l. 132; GARF f. 7952, op. 3, d. 283, ll. 1–2.

38. GARF f. 7952, op. 3, d. 283, ll. 1–2.

39. *KPSS v Resoliutsiiakh,* vol. 5, pp. 151–53. For the resolutions adopted by the Congress, see pp. 178–80. These resolutions address rising income, rising living standards, and then, in No. 4, note "The Congress considers that the trade unions, in the past period, have devoted completely inadequate attention to the questions of workers supply, to the struggle to lower costs, and to improve the work of the cooperatives. . . . The trade unions must achieve a faster development of the network of factory-kitchens, and improve their quality while reducing the price of 'social meals' *[obshchestvennoe pitanie].*"

40. *Martenovka,* 20 June 1932, p. 4; 12 January 1934, p. 3; 14 January 1934, p. 3.

41. Workers could often purchase food at the buffets to take home to their families. They functioned as a kind of internal food distribution network.

42. *Istoriia Moskovskogo Avtozavoda,* pp. 272–73.

43. GARF f. 7952, op. 3, d. 326, l. 132, emphasis added.

44. Most of this "help" actually involved bringing the party line on collectivization to the countryside. See Filatov, *Partrabota,* pp. 131–37.

45. Ibid., p. 130. A pood *(pud)* was the equivalent of 16.38 kilograms or 36 pounds.

46. *Istoriia Moskovskogo Avtozavoda,* p. 272.

47. GARF f. 7952, op. 3, d. 326, l. 133.

48. Salov, *Organizatsiia,* p. 10.

49. See Lewin, "Taking Grain."

50. Salov, *Organizatsiia,* pp. 3, 8.

51. Ibid., p. 8.

52. *Istoriia Moskovskogo Avtozavoda,* p. 272.

53. GARF f. 7952, op. 3, d. 283, ll. 2, 6.

54. *Martenovka,* 23 December 1930, p. 1.

55. *Martenovka,* 6 December 1932, pp. 2–3.

56. Ibid. Prosecution would occur under article 58, paragraph 7, and article 105 of the Criminal Law Code of the RSFSR.

57. The original law was dated 20 May 1932, but it was amended, as Lewin notes in "Taking Grain . . ." (p. 298), so that first the *zagotovki* had to be sold to the state at fixed low prices, and then the surplus could be marketed in the city's *bazaar* or *rynok,* legalized urban markets, which quickly became the most abundant source of food in the city, al-

though few could afford their prices.

58. *Svet nad Zastavoi*, p. 368. A *fel'dsher* was a doctor's assistant, without formal degree in medicine.

59. See *Trud i Zdorov'e*. Thanks to Susan Gross Solomon for pointing out this source.

60. *Martenovka*, 29 November 1934, p. 1.

61. Ibid.

62. *Svet nad Zastavoi*, p. 368.

63. *Istoriia Moskovskogo Avtozavoda*, p. 272.

64. *Martenovka*, 20 June 1932, p. 4. The graduated payments for day care, which were egalitarian in orientation, contradicted the Stalin line after 23 June 1931.

65. *Martenovka*, 4 June 1936, p. 1.

66. *Istoriia Moskovskogo Avtozavoda*, p. 273.

67. This factory-organized social welfare system, built on traditions of European trade unionism, paralleled the rise of the modern corporation in Japan and anticipated the British welfare state, in which state-run and private corporations provided similar services.

68. I thank Alfred Rieber, who suggested the idea of a "protocommunity" emerging during the 1930s.

69. *Svet nad Zastavoi*, pp. 198–99.

70. Ikonnikov, *Arkhitektura Moskvy*, p. 62, and Khan-Magomedov, *Alexandr Vesnin*, pp. 172–76. It is not clear why the building was ever completed, long after constructivism had been rejected as ideologically retrograde.

71. *Istoriia Moskovskogo Avtozavoda*, pp. 199, 202.

72. GARF f. 7952, op. 3, d. 347, ll. 1–11 for a list of authors and titles. See also the bibliographical essay.

73. *Istoriia Moskovskogo Avtozavoda*, pp. 144, 623–24, 638.

74. *Novatory*, pp. 38–40.

75. *Istoriia Moskovskogo Avtozavoda*, p. 204.

76. Ibid., p. 274.

77. Stites, *Russian Popular Culture*, pp. 64–67; Clark, *The Soviet Novel*, pp. 131–33. My idea of a middle-brow culture comes mainly from Stites's discussion of film.

78. *Martenovka*, 24 May 1939, p. 3.

79. See Edelman, *Serious Fun*.

80. Leont'eva, *Likhachev*, pp. 128, 148–49, and photographs following p. 192.

81. *Istoriia Moskovskogo Avtozavoda*, pp. 180, 273.

82. *Martenovka*, 1 February 1934, p. 1; 5 March 1934, pp. 2–3; 3 February 1935, p. 3; 4 February 1935, p. 1.

83. *Martenovka*, 6 October 1930, p. 3; 12 December 1934, p. 1. The factory had even more representation on the local *raisoviet*.

84. *Martenovka*, 30 December 1934, p. 1.

85. This included limiting their fertility. *Moskva v Tsifrakh* (1939), p. 49, shows that the birth rate in 1938 in Moscow was 28.5 per thousand (total births were 117,200), a much higher rate than Berlin, London, Paris, and New York. This rate was far below the all-union 39 per thousand in 1938, however, not to mention the 1926 rate of 45.6 per thousand. The 1926 figure is reliable, as it comes from the accurate All-Union Census of that year, while the 1938 figure is an estimate based on fragmentary evidence from the inaccurate 1937 and 1939 censuses. See *Naselenie Sovetskogo Soiuza*, p. 120. An appalling lack of basic data confronts the historian interested in changes in birth rates. These data are vital to our understanding of how peasant-migrants, coming from a high fertility culture in the countryside, were making the "demographic transition" to limited fertility in one generation. The

role of women in this transition and changes in patterns of family life are important questions yet to be explored.

86. Ostrovskii's novel was published serially, 1930–1934. Katerina Clark, *The Soviet Novel*, pp. 131–33, discusses the novel's contribution to the Stalinist myth of the "great family" and hero worship.

87. Zinoviev's book was published in Lausanne in Russian in 1981, as were his fictional dystopias *Ziiaushchie Vysoty* (1976) and *Svetloe Budushchee* (1978), translated as *The Yawning Heights* and *The Bright Future.*

88. For discussion of prerevolutionary "factory patriotism" see Bonnell, *Roots of Rebellion,* pp. 62, 145–47, and elsewhere. For the revolutionary period, see Pankratova, *Fabzavkomy Rossii,* and *Fabzavkomy i Profsoiuzy;* Avrich, "The Bolshevik Revolution," pp. 47–63; Sirianni, *Workers' Control;* Smith, *Red Petrograd;* Koenker, *Moscow Workers;* and Husband, *Revolution in the Factory.*

89. Foucault, *Discipline and Punish,* p. 202.

90. See, in particular, Siegelbaum, "Soviet Norm Determination," 45–68, and *Stakhanovism,* pp. 156–63. The attempt to shift from "observational" norms to "technical" norms in no respect signified a diminution in observing, timing, and attempting to rationalize the work process. See also Andrle, *Workers in Stalin's Russia,* chap. 4.

91. Foucault, *Discipline and Punish,* p. 203.

92. I see a parallel in the application of penal labor to Engelstein's discussion of the function of the law more broadly in Russian and especially Soviet society. The law was much more bluntly formulated and applied as a mechanism of social control than the subtle mechanisms which Foucault had described, and so too was the prescriptive example of the penal laborers. See "Combined Underdevelopment," pp. 338–54.

93. Filatov, *Partrabota,* p. 85. My thanks to Stephen Kotkin for his discussion of this issue and his interpretation of the significance of this passage.

94. *Martenovka,* 24 February 1934, pp. 1–3.

95. Peasant studies emphasize the adaptability of the *mir* and its "modernizing" tendencies in crop rotation and agronomy, but I do not believe that this fundamentally altered the long-established undifferentiated patterns of labor in agriculture. Out-migration was the one significant new dimension in peasant labor practice, which became especially significant after the Emancipation. For a perspective that emphasizes *mir* adaptability and modernization of communal agriculture in terms of field and crop rotation, see Kingston-Mann, "Peasant Communes and Economic Innovation."

96. Buroway, *Manufacturing Consent.*

97. The idea of negative integration was developed by Roth, *The Social Democrats of Imperial Germany,* building on Max Weber's observations about the SPD and a "socialist ghetto," in which the SPD and the Free Unions organized a counter-society, separate and unequal, from the dominant Wilhelmite society and culture. The idea of positive integration is Kotkin's, in *Magnetic Mountain,* pp. 235–37.

Chapter 9. The Red Directors Transform Soviet Industrial Relations

1. GARF f. 7952, op. 3, d. 341, l. 21.

2. GARF f. 7952, op. 3, d. 258, ll. 1–2.

3. Ibid., ll. 3–6. Burdachev was promoted into the trust responsible at the time for steel and other metalworking industries, Mashtrest, and he seems to have lost all ties to SiM after that.

4. GARF f. 7952, op. 3, d. 258, ll. 3, 7–8.

5. GARF f. 7952, op. 3, d. 341, ll. 7–8.

6. Ibid., l. 23.

7. See Kuromiya, "Edinonachalie and the Soviet Industrial Manager."

8. GARF f. 7952, op. 3, d. 341, ll. 19–20.

9. Ibid., ll. 23–24.

10. Moscow Party Archives (MPA, now MGAOD), f. 429, op. 1, d. 191, "Stenogram of a Meeting of the SiM Factory Triangle and the Shop Triangles on Fulfilling the November Plan," 20 November 1936. Thus, Korolev was still boss of the open hearth shop, and Tarlinskii was boss of the rolling steel shop. Boliubskii, who was boss of the steel-pipe shop, must have been appointed shortly after 1932, while others who spoke at that 20 November 1936 Meeting included Andreev, Minervin, Pogonchenkov, Tin'kov, and Gorshkov.

11. See *Martenovka*, 15 April 1937, 11 May 1937, 28 May 1937. Only on 26 July 1938 did Martenovka mention in passing that a smelter, G. M. Il'in, had replaced Stepanov as plant director, while A. G. Pogonchenkov was named temporarily as technical director.

12. Personal communication from I. L. Kornakovskii, spring 1987.

13. Their names appeared frequently in *Martenovka* and the Gor'kii Project archives in f. 7952. These documents provide no biographical information, however. From the context of the paper and archival sources, they were obviousy the team that Stepanov relied on and the most important decision makers in the plant.

14. Of course, the Red Directors themselves were "promotees," but their lack of interest in promoting workers from the bench is more significant. If SiM was typical, and the same pattern is clear at ZiS, then the promotion of proletarians into management was something of a regime myth in the First FYP factory. The Red Directors were the symbols of the myth in the mid-1920s, much like the Stakhanovites a decade later.

15. Two articles on Soviet foremen and their revived significance in management after 1933 are provided by Siegelbaum and Kuromiya in *Social Dimensions of Soviet Industrialization.*

16. As Andrle suggested to me, a skilled worker would have had to try hard to *avoid* promotion to the lower ranks of management during the First FYP.

17. GARF f. 7952, op. 3, d. 341, ll. 24–26.

18. GARF f. 7952, op. 3, d. 258, l. 12.

19. GARF f. 7952, op. 3, d. 337, l. 31; GARF f. 7952, op. 3, d. 338, l. 17.

20. Ibid., ll. 17, 19, 24–27.

21. *Martenovka*, 12 October 1930, p. 3.

22. GARF f. 7952, op. 3, d. 326, ll. 6, 24–27.

23. *Martenovka*, 25 June 1930, p. 2; 7 July 1930, p. 1; 12 October 1930, p. 3; 18 October 1933, pp. 2–3. See also GARF f. 7952, op. 3, d. 338, l. 45, and GARF f. 7952, op. 3, d. 283, l. 219.

24. *Martenovka*, 12 October 1930, p. 3.

25. GARF f. 7952, op. 3, d. 341, ll. 26–27.

26. *Martenovka*, 12 October 1930, p. 3.

27. Ibid.

28. GARF f. 7952, op. 3, d. 341, ll. 26–28.

29. *Martenovka*, 12 October 1930, p. 3.

30. I could trace him only in the Moscow Party Archive. See MGAOD f. 429, op. 1, d. 125, l. 1. This *opis* shows his successor as fully cooperating with Stepanov's team and rarely taking any initiative in discussion that shaped or implemented shop-floor policy.

31. GARF f. 7952, op. 3, d. 258, ll. 13–14.

32. Venediktov, *Organizatsiia Gosudarstvennoi Promyshlennosti*, vol. 2, p. 582, covers the

breakup of VSNKh. See also Fitzpatrick, "Ordzhonikidze's Takeover of Vesenkha."

33. According to R. W. Davies, *Soviet History in the Gorbachev Revolution*, p. 88, Tevosian was the model for the hero of Aleksandr Bek's novel, *Novoe Naznachenie.*

34. This interpretation is closer to David Granick's perspective than to that of Joseph Berliner and Jeremy Azrael. In *Management of the Industrial Firm* and in *The Red Executive*, Granick argued that the Red Directors were flexible decision makers, problem solvers, and conflict resolvers, indeed organization men much like top managers in U.S. enterprises. Berliner and Azrael argued that they were much less autonomous than managers under capitalism, indeed, that they were more like cogs of a machine than organization men. Vladimir Andrle provides a good summary of the debate in *Managerial Power in the Soviet Union*, p. 4.

35. Leont'eva, *Likhachev*, p. 5.

36. *Direktor*, p. 4.

37. *Istoriia Moskovskogo Avtozavoda*, p. 627. As far as I know, it was the only Soviet factory ever named for its director.

38. Granick, *Management of the Industrial Firm in the USSR*, pp. 48–49.

39. *Direktor*, p. 9.

40. See Granick, *Management of the Industrial Firm in the USSR*, pp. 35–39, for sketches of eight directors of three major steel plants.

41. *Direktor*, p. 26. As Kuznetsov explained in his memoir, "In 1937 the factory experienced great difficulties with the leadership cadre. Staffs of the shop superintendents were almost entirely removed, and the plant administration saw its chief engineer and his deputies, and production superintendents all removed."

42. Ibid., pp. 10–12.

43. Ibid., pp. 275–76.

44. *Istoriia Moskovskogo Avtozavoda*, pp. 155–56, 635.

45. Ibid., p. 635.

46. Ibid., p. 156.

47. *Direktor*, p. 32.

48. Ibid., p. 34.

49. The concept "administrative-command system" is criticized by Davies in "The Management of Soviet Industry."

50. *Martenovka*, 22 February 1935, pp. 2–3.

Chapter 10. The Making of the New Soviet Working Class

1. Crew, *Town on the Ruhr.*

2. Marx, *Capital*, vol. 1, esp. chaps. 15, 25.

3. Durkheim, *The Division of Labor in Society*, p. 69.

4. See esp. Maier's discussion of "corporatism" in his introduction to *Recasting Bourgeois Europe.*

5. This is not to deny the broad significance of class struggle in the factory and in the polity. See Haimson and Tilly, *Strikes, War, and Revolution.* Nor is it to deny the importance of "corporatism," particularly in fascist Italy, Republican France, and Weimar Germany during the 1920s, as analyzed by Maier in *Recasting Bourgeois Europe.* Or for Soviet NEP. By the 1930s, however, such corporatist tendencies had proved to be too subtle and complex for containing social conflicts and cultural tensions, at least in Italy, Germany, and the Soviet Union. In all three cases, during the 1930s, *étatisme* replaced corporatist trends, as in Franco's Spain and Pétain's France following the Popular Fronts, which were more far-

reaching attempts at a corporatist system than Weimar Germany. Franco, Pétain, neofascist dictatorships in Eastern Europe, fascist Italy, and Nazi Germany, during the 1930s, all used corporatist slogans as myth and ideology during the 1930s. Something like "corporatism" had its greatest success, I suggest, in the United States under the New Deal. Stalinist *etatisme* was so far removed from corporatism, that Soviet management seems more often than not to have shielded labor from the demands of the state.

6. The argument here is not that the *mir* itself was primitive and traditional and hence incapable of adapting to markets or of adopting new agricultural techniques. Rather, the argument is that labor specialization in the village was limited to division of labor within the household *(dvor)* itself and that when the village worked as a team in the fields, everyone was performing the same task or similar tasks of sowing or harvesting at the peak season. These same patterns persisted in wage labor among peasant-migrants in the *artel'*.

7. Lewin, *The Making of the Soviet System*, p. 37.

8. The one exception was that some villagers commuted daily by commuter rail, the *elektrichka*, from the village to the city. The entire family continued to live in the village, and some family members may have worked on the *kolkhoz*. There is no data on how widespread this was.

9. See Hobsbawm, *Labouring Men*, pp. 183–84, 275, and *The Age of Revolution*, p. 253.

10. Kotkin, *Magnetic Mountain*, p. 223, describes this as a process of "Bolshevization," akin to "Americanization." Perhaps "Sovietization" would be more accurate, since the party had little to do with it, whereas becoming a member of the working class meant becoming a full Soviet citizen.

11. Francesco Benvenuti suggested to me that I might be describing a rise of "civic consciousness" rather than "working-class consciousness," that is, Weber rather than Marx or Durkheim. I find that suggestion provocative, but I wonder which Weber is more relevant: Max or Eugen? "Peasants into Soviet citizens" conveys some aspects of what I think was happening, too. In any case, the "inclusive" class consciousness that I am describing was very close to a new type of "civic consciousness" and a "Soviet consciousness," since it made real, for millions of urban citizens, something like the socialist ideal, in which the working class was "becoming all." If that is what Kotkin meant by "positive integration," namely the belief among the workers and urban population that they were building socialism during the 1930s, then I agree.

12. Magnitogorsk and the Kuzbass, which would be populated by a majority of Slavic settlers, were the "inner" periphery. The "outer" periphery, as it might be called, would include much of Central Asia and the Caucasus (e.g., Baku), where non-Russians were probably more significant than Russians among the factory work force during the 1930s.

13. See Fitzpatrick, *The Russian Revolution*, p. 169.

14. *Martenovka*, 10 July 1936, p. 1; *Pravda*, 27 June 1936.

15. Siegelbaum, *Stakhanovism*, pp. 146–47, 179.

16. This is the finding of Inkeles and Bauer in *The Soviet Citizen*, with their six-class model of Soviet society, and supported by Michael Swafford's article in *Politics, Work, and Daily Life in the USSR*, ed. Millar, who argues on p. 279 that, as Bowles and Gintis found in America, class expectations are conveyed from parents to children, exerting an important influence on their educational performance.

BIBLIOGRAPHICAL ESSAY

The Factory Newspaper and the Gor'kii Files

There are two fundamentally useful sources for writing the social history of the Soviet Union and particularly for Soviet labor history, that have only recently been explored. These are local and factory newspapers, and the memoirs of workers, ITR, and managers collected in the archives in what I call the Gor'kii Files. The newspapers have only recently seen systematic use by non-Soviet scholars as access has opened, and the Gor'kii Files, which in theory were open for decades, have also until recently remained unexplored. For Soviet scholars, the use of such sources was limited by ideological strictures, while, with a few exceptions, post-Soviet Russian historians seem to have little interest in them.[1]

Local newspapers and especially the factory newspaper, the *mnogotirazhka*, or multicirculation newspaper, are invaluable sources. My most important source was *Martenovka*, the factory newspaper of SiM, because it was one of the outstanding examples of the genre. It is a major reason that my study focused on SiM rather than ZiS or Dinamo. The ZiS *mnogotirazhka*, first called *Amovets* and then renamed *Dognat' i Peregnat'*, is useful, but the quality is not as high as that of *Martenovka*. The quality of both was much higher than that of the Dinamo paper, *Motor*. For all of them, quality deteriorated after 1935 and especially in 1937. Differences in quality reflected, in the first instance, differences on the editorial collectives.

The Gor'kii Files are collections of memoirs of workers, ITR, and managers, that were catalogued in 1955 in the Central State Archive of the October Revolution, or TsGAOR (since 1991 renamed State Archive of the Russian Federation, or GARF).[2] The Gor'kii Files consist of 2,862 files (*dela*) covering thirty-four enterprises in Moscow Province, sixteen in Leningrad Province, eighteen in Ukraine, and seventeen in the Urals.[3] They are stored in archival *fond* 7952, with each region assigned its own *opis* or index, which were then subdivided into *dela*. (Each *delo* was subdivided and designated by the Russian word *list* or page; thus l. = p. and ll. = pp.) SiM, for example was *fond* 7952, *opis* 3, and had 175 *dela*. The AMO-ZiS plant was *fond* 7952, *opis* 3, with only 2 *dela*, but some of its material was also stored in *fondy* 94, 374, 3429, 1562, 472, 326, 353, and 1508. This material was collected by teams of writers, worker-correspondents or *rabkory*, and journalists, who were mobilized and organized by Maksim Gor'kii for a project called the History of Plants and Factories. This was my second most important source.

The local and factory newspapers are invaluable because they provide the type of day-by-day coverage of events in a city or in a factory that is impossible to reconstruct through the central press, obsessed as it was with the party-state and its policy, and that cannot be traced chronologically through archival sources, no matter how rich these are. The memoirs are invaluable, because they provide the feel of the times as well as the opinions of all major personalities and participants in a particular factory. These are unavailable in any other form. Published memoirs, in many cases, were much more extensive; the archival materials are merely fragments from the recollections of each individual. But the published memoirs are not concentrated in the same way around a single institution, and when the fragmentary recollections of dozens of persons from a single factory are combined, one gets a picture not of their personalities, but of the institution. Published memoirs also suffered from a greater degree of censorship.[4]

The central press, starting with *Pravda* and *Izvestiia,* and including *Trud* (the central trade-union organ), *Za Industrializatsiiu,* later called *Industriia* (organ of the Commissariat of Heavy Industry), *Komsomolskaia Pravda, Krasnaia Zvezda,* and *Literaturnaia Gazeta,* to list only those with the largest circulation during the 1930s, all provide what could be called a daily chronicle of events as initiated and interpreted by the party-state. The press in Moscow from the 1930s, including *Vechernaia Moskva, Rabochaia Moskva,* and *Moskovskaia Pravda,* is highly useful for understanding Moscow, but was still closely modeled after the central press, and might also be called a chronicle of events as seen by the party-state.[5]

What was exceptional about the factory newspaper was the degree to which it revealed detail about the everyday life of the workers, both on the shop floor and in the community. The *mnogotirazhka* was, I would argue, written from the standpoint of management. It focused on the implementation of party-state policy, and it exposed various problems in the implementation of that policy. Through that, it revealed a great deal about the fallacies of state policy and also about ideological fallacies of the regime. I have traced these in detail, especially the class struggle ideology. More important, it revealed more about working life than any other source.

To be sure, the *mnogotirazhka* devoted considerable ink to announcing and explaining party-state policy, as did the central press, but what was different was how much ink it devoted to explaining how that policy was or was not being implemented on the shop floor. That exceptional quality, I believe, can be traced to two factors; first, the determination of factory management to get at the root of serious production problems by shedding light on the situation (*glasnost'*); and second, the unique role of the *rabkory* in the factory newspaper. It was a management paper with a strong worker voice.

The *rabkory* were amateur journalists who remained full-time workers-at-the-bench, and their proximity to the point of production and the frank discussion of problems in production, community life, and in implementation of state policy makes for sobering reading. In some instances where the regime wanted to expose an egregious or scandalous problem in many factories or cities, articles in the factory or local papers were reprinted in the central press, but this was the exception. More important were the hundreds of instances where such criticisms were not reprinted. Where did such a degree of *glasnost'* come from and why was it tolerated during the 1930s?

I would argue that the openness of criticism came from the needs of the factory managers. This reflected the origins of the *mnogotirazhka* from the *stengazeta* or wall-paper of the 1920s. These wall-papers, with their praise of some workers and work units and opprobrium for others, were management devices. They were also a means of conveying information to the worker directly from the Red Director, the shop or shift boss, and even from foremen. The *stengazeta* was a single sheet, or sometimes two pages, that was tacked onto the bulletin board in the different shops of the factory. At AMO, the first wall-paper, *Vagranka,* was put up in 1921. At SiM, the first wall-paper was *Martenovka,* put up in 1922.[6] In 1930, there were seventeen different wall-papers at SiM, mostly corresponding to the different shops, and *Martenovka* had become the factory multicirculation newspaper. By Press Day, 6 May 1930, *Martenovka* was published once weekly with a circulation of 6,000, and plans were announced to publish it every third working day starting on 15 May 1930 (p. 2). Then, starting on 1 September 1930, publication was stepped up to every other day. At the same time, the cost of a subscription was lowered from 25 to 15 kopeks monthly (p. 2).

In 1930, and throughout the decade, the format of *Martenovka* remained at four pages. On the first page one found coverage of important party-state decisions affecting all heavy metallurgy and the SiM factory, along with data on the monthly, quarterly, and yearly battle for plan fulfillment at SiM or in the metallurgy industry as a whole. There was also some basic coverage of important national and international news. On pages 2 and 3 one usually found more detailed discussions of successes and problems in the various SiM shops and in the factory as a whole. Technology and labor organization issues, "breakthroughs" and production records, pictures of leading shock workers or Stakhanovites were typical layouts. Page 4 was generally reserved for sports, cultural events, and club events in the factory, the local community, and in Moscow. Circulation, in the first instance, was among workers and their families. A 4 July 1930 article indicated that 3,819 subscriptions were taken by factory workers (p. 4), while by 28 December, 8,000 copies were in circulation (p. 4).

The editorial collective of *Martenovka* consisted of professional journalists, worker-writers, and worker-journalists. Sergei Tanatov, an editor of *Martenovka,* and L. L. Shipilin, who became its chief editor, were both worker-journalists who became professionals.[7] Both wrote and published nonfictional accounts of the factory as well.[8] Worker-correspondents provided a flow of information that the editors and professional journalists could not possibly have uncovered. At SiM, in 1932, according to one document, there were 1,600 *rabkory.*[9] On Press Day in 1932, *Martenovka* claimed that it had a staff of 5,000 worker-correspondents.[10] That would seem to have been an exaggeration, but the role of these *rabkory* in the factory newspaper was fundamental. In many instances, in *Martenovka,* they wrote to expose serious problems, and often they wrote on behalf of groups of disgruntled workers.

There were no letters to the editor in the factory newspaper. Instead, the articles by the *rabkory* provided reporting of problems and grievances that was similar to letters to the editor, but much better. Their articles were much more in-depth than letters in the central press, in many cases exposing serious problems in the plant's work. Full-time workers, these nonprofessionals understood and reflected the discontents of groups of workers in their articles. But the reason that worker-correspondents' articles are more useful than the letters to the editor in the central press is that they were less likely to have been initiated or proliferated by orchestration from above.

The tone of the *mnogotirazhka*, like the *stengazeta* before it, rather than expressing the views of trade unions or workers, reflected the perspective of the factory management and particularly of the Red Director. It also reflected the tone of the party-state, and hence, the *mnogotirazhka* could hardly be called a voice of the rank and file. The fact is, however, that management, and *partkom* and *zavkom* representatives who became increasingly subordinate to management, could not begin to resolve the problems of production without some participation of the workers. Their nearly constant attempts to solicit workers' suggestions through the suggestion box and factory-wide production meetings may have introduced improvements; but these meetings were soon routinized, much like the shock work from which they stemmed, and became formalistic and resented. The worker-correspondent offered a unique opportunity to tap into the creative energy of workers and to expose the serious, gnawing dissatisfactions of many workers, both with production routine and community life.

It was in the interests of management to expose those defects and dissatisfactions in order to begin to correct them. Without this degree of *glasnost'*, management's tasks were made much more difficult. Articles exposing defects and problems, however, went beyond the shop floor in their implications and showed that party-state policy was generally only ineffectively implemented, if it was implemented at all. That could suggest conscious or unconscious opposition by factory management (or workers), or it could suggest the irrelevance or even the counterproductive nature of regime policy. Again, the question arises, why did Glavlit, the censorship organ that proofread all factory newspapers, tolerate this degree of *glasnost'*?

It was tolerated, I would argue, because management needed it and because the regime could regulate the degree and tone of criticism within tolerable boundaries through its censorship. Criticism of top officials, official policies, or even top plant officials was off-limits. Whenever there was such criticism in the press, as was especially common in 1937, it was clearly evidence that the center was directing the purge-terror against the individual in question and did not reflect *glasnost'* whatsoever. Such stylized criticism was orchestrated from above.

The permissible critical tone of factory newspaper articles was to adopt the stance that party-state policy was not being implemented, rather than that it was wrong. The Stalin regime could conveniently blame such problems on Red Directors, or bosses, or foremen, rather than on Stalin, Molotov, or Kaganovich, that is, rather than on the policymakers. By putatively sticking to problems of implementation, however, the *mnogotirazhka* could uncover serious problems, not only of implementation, but of policy itself. These problems might then be discussed in the central press as well, where they could be vaguely attributed to problems in Soviet society, or less vaguely blamed on lower-level party cadre or officials, in the way Stalin had in his r-r-r-revolutionary formula in "Dizzy with Success." Sometimes, such airing of problems led Stalin or his Politburo to initiate a shift in policy and even ideology, as with the attack on *uravnilovka*.

The problem of wage irregularities was an important topic in the central economic press (*Voprosy Truda, Za Industrializatsiiu*) in 1930 or 1931, and anticipated Stalin's "Six Conditions" speech. Stalin politicized the problem as a matter of "petty bourgeois egalitarian," and in this case he would falsely attribute the blame to Mikhail Tomskii and to the All-Union Central Council of Trade Unions, which he headed. Tomskii, in 1927, had indeed called for much greater egalitarianism. In the intervening years, however, there was no significant trend toward wage egalitarianism. Instead, the piece-rate pay system was almost universalized, and this trend was accelerated by shock work. This system was, in fact, antithetical to egalitarianism, which was why Stalin emphasized them even more in his speech. Shock work and the use of progressive piece rates, that is, policies pushed by Stalin and not Tomskii, were the cause of wage irregularities. Hence, by tracing the issue through the press, we can see the real problems that managers and administrators were discussing in the newspapers and journals, and how Stalin responded to their concerns.

It is on the basis of the exposure of poor implementation in the *mnogotirazhka*, in which policy often poorly corresponded to shop-floor or community realities, that I have attempted to reconstruct the social history of the Soviet factory and urban community. It is a type of history from below, but one in which the "from below" is still very closely dictated by censorship and control "from above." The same holds true of the worker memoirs stored in the factory archives in the Gor'kii Files.

It was logical that the editorial collective of *Martenovka* and of *Dognat' i Peregnat'*, and those involved in the writers' circles Valtsovka or Vagranka, would play a leading role at SiM and ZiS in organizing the committees to write the history of these factories. The same was true in all large Soviet factories. Gor'kii had been personally active in encouraging the formation of these writers' circles and the editorial boards of the *mnogotirazhka*, and he encouraged both young professional journalists and young authors to help factory workers develop as competent worker-correspondents and to join the writers' circles and write novels and nonfictional accounts based on factory work and life.

Among those who became famous authors, he directed and encouraged A. Bek, A. Tolstoi, K. Paustovskii, F. Gladkov, V. Kataev, I. Ehrenburg, and V. Grossman to go out to the factories and describe what they saw. They gained all-union fame from the novels they wrote at the construction sites and factories.[11] Valentin Kataev's *Vremia Vpered* (Time Forward) (Moscow, 1932), based on what he observed at Magnitostroi, was arguably the most famous fictional account of this genre.

Gor'kii was active in encouraging such projects upon returning to the Soviet Union in 1928, and even when abroad, as I have noted with his meeting with Salov in Capri. On 3 September 1931, in a speech before the Russian Association of Proletarian Writers, he suggested that workers and authors write a multivolume History of Plants and Factories. On 7 September 1931, the central press published the speech in an edited version.[12] The Gor'kii Project then gained the endorsement of the Central Committee, which on 10 October 1931 established a central editorial board that included the leading political figures Postyshev, Andreyev, and Shvernik, and the historian A. M. Pankratova, as well as Gor'kii.[13] Other leading political figures who were also involved with the project included Kirov, Ordzhonikidze, and Krupskaia. Kalinin spoke on the subject at a meeting of workers at SiM.[14]

Among the first products of this work were chapters on the history of ZiS, published by the factory press; *Byli Gory Vysokoi,* based on memoirs of Magnitostroi workers; and F. N. Samoilov, ed., *Krasnyi Perekop.* Articles about how to write the history of factories by Gor'kii, Pankratova, Ia. N. Il'in, and N. P. Paialin appeared in two new journals, *Istoriia Zavodov* and *Bor'ba Klassov,* the first of which was established to help organize the work on the factory histories. Gor'kii edited manuscripts by N. Shushkanov on the history of the Zlatoustovskii and *Byli Gory Vysokoi.*[15] He also edited, together with Averbakh and Firin, the now notorious and infamous account of the construction of the Belomor Canal.[16]

Among the first published volumes in the Gor'kii Project were the history of the Putilov, the Red Triangle, and the Izhorskii plants, all key factories in the 1917 Revolution in Petrograd.[17] Averbakh edited a volume with articles on SiM by V. Meller, on ZiS by S. Ginzburg and N. Atfel'dt, and by S. Lapitskaia on the Moscow textile plant, Trekhgornaia Manufaktura.[18] A list of the editorial collectives to write histories for the Gor'kii Project at thirty factories were given in *Istoriia Zavodov.*[19]

At SiM, two volumes were projected, the first historical and the second fictional. The editorial collective for the first volume included the historians Pankratova, Meller, Gaisinovich, Sokolovskaia, Martov, and Spanovskii. For the second volume, the editorial collective included worker-writers and professional authors, Shvedov, Krutianskii, Mikhailov, Pandul, Shipilin, Tanatov, Velichko, Iacheistov, Bebchuk, and Sobol'chikov.[20] Most of these men were members of the Val'tsovka writers' circle. Before the collective at SiM could publish anything, the regime suppressed the entire project.

While neither volume was ever produced, a number of short stories, novels, and nonfictional accounts were published. Among the historians, Pankratova published an interesting article on the Guzhon plant in the 1905 Revolution, and Poselianina published a fine article on labor and remuneration at SiM during War Communism and into NEP.[21] This was, however, only the tip of the iceberg of what had been collected in workers' memoirs at SiM. The rest was stored away in the archives for the duration of the 1930s, 1940s, and until 1955, when it was placed in TsGAOR f. 7952, and opened for research in 1956.

Gor'kii noted that on 1 June 1932, collectives had been established at thirty factories, and work on their history, based on workers' memoirs was ongoing. He also noted that he had already sent out a letter to twenty-six plants, telling them that their work on the history had to be completed in 1932.[22] In point of fact, however, only those listed above, a fraction of the total, were published before Gor'kii died in 1936, and the project was dissolved, or the plant editorial committees were dissolved, sometime in 1934 or 1935, without any announcement or explanation. Only with the opening of archival access after 1955 was the Gor'kii Project resumed.

Gor'kii, obviously, was attempting two things simultaneously. He was attempting to lay the foundations for socialist realism, on the one hand, and on the other hand for the journalism that could produce the factory *mnogotirazhky* and the historical publications. The problem, for the historian, is not only that he was consciously combining fact and fiction in socialist realism, but that, as we know, Soviet journalism and historical publications during the 1930s also often mixed the two, creating a Stalinist history and journalism built on falsifications. Skeptics will say that studies based on such foundations are of limited value. I'll return to this issue below.

The memoir material from the History of Factories and Plants was stored in the archives, in the Gor'kii Files, where, after Stalin died, it found use once again when a number of Soviet historians and also factory collectives began work on the project. In all, according to the three Soviet historians evaluating the work from the vantage point of 1980, 30 volumes were published during the 1930s, 250 during the decade 1956–65, and 30–40 were published annually during the decade 1966–75.[23] In my opinion, the work published after 1955 is of low quality, and only work published after 1965 has material which is of use for the historian. Even this post-1965 output, however, is limited by ideological strictures.

The publications on SiM and ZiS indicate the weaknesses and strengths of this historical literature. Typical of the material published during the Khrushchev years was the volume *Svet nad Zastavoi* (Light Above the Gateway), a title derived from the light cast by steel production on the Rogozhskaia Gateway where the Guzhon plant was located. The volume was put together by a collective of journalists and retired workers, headed by the editor N. Gudkova and including G. P. Aleksandrov, F. Ia. Babun, P. P. Baibarin, Ts. Z. Vainshtein, and many others. The volume has little to recommend it. Composed in a popular, nonacademic style, it gives a simplistic party-line narrative that glosses over or ignores all thorny historical issues.

For example, *Svet nad Zastavoi* never asked why the Zubatov unions had more support at the Guzhon plant than the Social Democratic unions prior to 1905, or why Iulii Guzhon's paternalism succeeded in diverting many workers from the class struggle.[24] Nor does the volume examine why the Guzhon workers failed to strike on 7 October 1905, when virtually all workers in the Rogozhskii District and most workers in every district of Moscow were on strike. Or why they remained at work until 7 November, when they finally went on strike.[25] Or why the Socialist Revolutionaries (SRs) had more support than the Social Democrats at Guzhon in February 1917.[26]

The answer, suggested in the articles that described these events, was that the steel plant workers were mostly peasant-workers, whose class consciousness was not well developed, and who were easily divided (labor aristocracy), bought off (through benefits awarded by Guzhon, the paternalist), and fooled (by Zubatov unions). Tying all this together was the rural origins of most Guzhon workers. In other words, the answers of Soviet historians come back to a central theme in this study, the issue of the subaltern workers, and particularly those from a rural background.

That issue was never adequately addressed by Soviet historians, not only for SiM but for all Soviet workers. However, the manuscript by I. L. Kornakovskii, "Zavod 'Serp i Molot' 1883–1932: Opyt Istoriko-Sotsiologicheskogo Issledovaniia" (Moscow,

1979), deposited in the Library of the Social Sciences (INION) as no. 10062, posed and did not shy away from the problems of the preponderance of first- and second-generation peasant-migrants at SiM throughout the first fifty years of the plant's existence. Kornakovskii uncovered a number of facts at SiM that clearly contradicted Soviet and particularly Stalinist ideological strictures. For example, in those shops where the workers had the highest average skill level, they also had below average education and literacy levels. Furthermore, the shops with the highest average skill levels also had the greatest number of first- and second-generation peasant-workers. Kornakovskii argued that this was due to the concentration of older workers with longer tenure and higher skill, and also peasant-migrants, in the metallurgical shops, and of younger and urban-born workers, with higher levels of education and literacy, in the metal processing shops.[27] That may be so, but it fails to explain how the Soviet categories of advanced and backward workers corresponded to sociological realities.

In fact, this very dilemma of the Soviet categories was already posed in 1930 in A. G. Rashin's pioneering analysis of the 1929 trade-union census. Rashin forthrightly suggested that workers whose production tenure dated to pre-1917 had stronger ties to the land than workers hired since 1925, that skill and connections to the land were positively correlated, and that metalworkers had greater ties to the land than textile workers.[28] That, of course, made shambles of the 1929 Stalinist categories of labor "cadre" or "vanguard" or "shock workers." It is consistent, however, with my findings on subaltern and hereditary workers.[29]

Kornakovskii's was an exceptional study in a number of ways, but it remained confined within Soviet categories. Likewise, the volume produced on ZiS in 1966, *Istoriia Moskovskogo Avtozavoda imeni I. A. Likhacheva,* was an exceptional attempt to achieve Gor'kii's ideal, based as it was on the work of historians, professional journalists, and retired factory workers, but it also remained confined within Soviet sociological categories, which explain very little about the formation of the new working class. Particularly disappointing in this volume is the lack of information about the rank-and-file women, who made up 40 percent of the work force by 1941. Still, this volume and the new history of the Putilov plant, published in 1966 in Moscow as *Istoriia Kirovskogo Zavoda, 1917–1945,* arguably are the two most comprehensive and useful of the Soviet histories of factories, precisely because they made excellent use of the *mnogotirazhka* and the Gor'kii Files for these factories.

Returning, in conclusion, to the primary sources, in the Gor'kii Files as with *Martenovka* and other *mnogotirazhky,* I have tried to sort out the party-state "general line" from more genuine expressions of thoughts, ideas, and attitudes of workers, managers, and ITR. It is, of course, not always possible to do so. My argument is not that the Gor'kii File memoirs or the factory newspaper reveal the truth, whereas the central press and published material only reflects the party line. Rather, the point is to attempt to discern the valid and insightful observations of the participants, or at least their actual opinions, regardless of the party line. This can, and must be done, both for published sources, and in the archives. The *mnogotirazhky* and the Gor'kii Files offer the historian the best opportunity to do so. They are the richest sources available on urban and work life, notwithstanding the recent flood of material coming out of the former Central Party Archive (now the RtsKhIDNI) and the Presidential Files.[30]

While today in Russia, as in America, many historians and the critical reading public would criticize any study of Stalinism based on newspapers (factory, local, or central) or memoirs that were collected in the archives under official guidelines or that were published, I suggest that they are invaluable for study of Soviet industrialization, labor and industrial relations, and urban society and the working class. That they have a built-in bias in favor of the Stalin regime goes without saying. Like other published and unpublished archival material from that era, they often distorted or fabricated data, memoir accounts, and historical events. Nonetheless, these factory newspapers and archival memoirs are invaluable precisely because they were designed with the idea of convincing the Soviet public, in this case the workers and managers in the factory themselves, of the underlying validity of the state strategy of superindustrialization, and they could only do this by exposing real problems. Furthermore, they were propagating information and the managerial ideas of the Red Director and his staff for improving productivity and labor relations.

To serve effectively as propaganda in these respects required the presentation of valid information, not fabrications and obfuscation. It required a degree of *glasnost'* that could expose the ubiquitous and serious problems of labor organization and industrial relations so as to propose realistic and convincing solutions. It required coming to terms with the needs of workers, which included safer and much better working conditions, more housing space, food, consumer goods, and a cultural or community life. It is for this reason that the *mnogotirazhky* and the Gor'kii Files provide so much information about daily life in the community and factory. I will let the readers of this study reach their own conclusions on the plausibility of my argument in interpreting these documents, and in sorting out what was real from what was fabricated in them.

Notes

1. Among non-Soviet scholars who have made use of local and factory newspapers are Rassweiler, Hoffmann, Kotkin, and Fitzpatrick. Soviet studies that make extensive use of the Gor'kii Files and of factory newspaper include *Istoriia Moskovskogo Avtozavoda* and *Istoriia Kirovskogo Zavoda*.

2. See the "guidebook" to the Gor'kii Files, *A.M. Gor'kii i Sozdanie Istorii Fabrik i Zavodov*, p. 255.

3. Ibid., p. 256.

4. For a very thorough collection of published memoir materials, see V. Z. Drobizhev, ed., *Sovetskoe Obshchestvo v Vospominaniiakh i Dnevnikakh*, vol. 1 (vol. 2 was edited by A. A. Liberman.) See also Fitzpatrick and Viola, *A Researcher's Guide*.

5. For a good summary, see Fitzpatrick, "Newspapers and Journals," in Fitzpatrick and Viola *A Researcher's Guide*. For a comprehensive listing of all Soviet periodical literature see *Periodicheskaia Pechat' SSSR 1917–1949*.

6. Slanskaia, "K Istorii Vozniknoveniia Mnogotirazhnykh Gazet," p. 22.

7. GARF f. 7952, op. 3, d. 320, l. 1; GARF f. 7952, op. 3, d. 338, l. 51.

8. See GARF f. 7952, op. 3, d. 347, ll.1–11, for a list of the Val'tsovka writers and their published and unpublished works.

9. GARF f. 7952, op. 3, d. 283, l.156.

10. *Martenovka,* 5 May 1932, p. 1.

11. See *A. M. Gor'kii i Sozdanie Istorii Fabrik,* p. 8.

12. Ibid., p. 3.

13. See Mitrofanova, Ostapenko, and Rogachevskaia, "Itogy i Perspektivye," p. 365.

14. *A. M. Gor'kii i Sozdanie Istorii Fabrik,* pp. 8–9.

15. Ibid., pp. 7–8, 9, 11.

16. This was allegedly written by reformed prisoners, the "zeks," who had worked on this project under the *gulag.* Over one hundred thousand worked there and many perished. Solzhenitsyn, *The Gulag Archipelago,* vol. 2, pp. 80–81.

17. *A. M. Gor'kii i Sozdanie Istorii Fabrik,* p. 11.

18. Averbakh, *Shestnadtsat' Zavodov.*

19. *Istoriia Zavodov,* vypusk 3 (1932): 6, listed a collective for the ZiS plant of Ruben (chief editor), Bogushevskii, Agapov, M. Koltsov, Zel'tser, and N. Popov, and for SiM of A. M. Pankratova (chief editor), Sokolovskaia, Viasberg, Bakhmetev, and Rzhanov. On p. 5, it reprinted a *protokol* issued by the "political editorial collective" for the project dated August 16, 1932, which lists, as attending the meeting, Gor'kii, Kaganovich, Enukidze, Stetskii, Irivov, Pisarev, Tsikhon, Bogushevskii, Ivanov, Kriuchkov, Shushkanov, and Tikhonov. A political editorial board consisting of Gor'kii, Kaganovich, Postyshev, Stetskii, and Enukidze was established.

20. *Istoriia Zavodov* 2 (1932): 112–13.

21. See Pankratova, "Rabochie Zavoda 'Serp i Molot' v 1905 g"; Poselianina, "Bor'ba za Sotsialisticheskuiu Organizatsiiu Truda," pp. 178–95.

22. *Istoriia Zavodov* 2 (1932): 5, 9.

23. Mitrofanova, Ostapenko, and Rogachevskaia, "Itogy i Perspektivye," pp. 366–68.

24. This issue was posed, although not satisfactorily answered, in the articles by Koniaev, "Guzhon," and Pankratova, "Rabochie Zavoda 'Serp i Molot' v 1905 g."

25. Gaisinovich, "Oktiabr-Dekabr 1905 g. na Zavode," poses this question and describes the conflict between strikebreakers at Guzhon and striking workers on 12 October.

26. See Meller, "Na Putiakh k Oktiabriu."

27. Kornakovskii, "Zavod 'Serp i Molot,'" pp. 243–44, 223–29.

28. Rashin, *Sostav Fabrichno-Zavodskogo Proletariata.* The editor, N. Evreinov, summarizes these findings on p. xii.

29. That is because "subalterns" included not only peasant-migrants but also urban youth and women (housewives) in my analysis and because permanent urban workers with ties to the land are not in the same category as peasant-migrants. The studies by Rashin and Kornakovskii suggest that before 1929 many long-term skilled factory workers had extended family still living in the village and thus were not so unambiguously "hereditary" urban factory workers as I have assumed. Although Rashin's findings were mostly ignored, Shkaratan noted the value of his analysis of the 1929 census in *Problemy Sotsial'noi Struktury,* pp. 171–73.

30. If material from OGPU-NKVD archives became available, it might offer a very important new dimension on workers' attitudes and discontents. Such a dimension might also be addressed through published procuracy and court records.

BIBLIOGRAPHY

Russian-Language Sources
Archives
GARF: State Archives of the Russian Federation (formerly TsGAOR, the Central State Archive of the Russian Revolution)
> Fond 7952: History of Factories and Plants (Gor'kii Archive)
> Fond 5469: All-Soviet Union of Metalworkers (VSRM)
> Fond 5515: Narkomtrud (NKT)

RGAE: Russian State Archive of the Economy (formerly TsGANKh, or Central State Archive of the National Economy)
> Fond 4086: GUMP (Glavk for Metallurgy Industry)

MGAOD: Moscow State Archive of Social Movements (formerly MPA, or Moscow Party Archive)
> Fond 429: "Serp i Molot"

TsGAOR g. Moskvy (now under the Unified Moscow City Archives)
> Fond R414: AMO-ZiS
> Fond F 100: Dinamo

Newspapers and Journals
Bor'ba Klassov
Dognat' i Peregnat'
EKO
Istoriia Proletariata SSSR
Istoriia Zavodov
Istoricheskie Zapiski
Martenovka
Mashinostroenie
Professional'nye Soiuzy
Rabochaia Gazeta
Sovetskaia Metallurgia
Trud
Vestnik Moskovskogo Universiteta
Voprosy Truda
Za Industrializatsiiu

Laws, Censuses, and Published Archival Documents
Biulletin Finansogo i Khoziaistvennogo Zakonodatelstva.

Industrializatsiia SSSR. Vol. 2 (1929–32). Moscow, 1970. Vol. 3 (1933–37). Moscow, 1971. Vol. 4 (1938–41. Moscow, 1973.

Itogy Vsesoiuznoi Perepisi Naseleniia 1959 goda SSSR (Svodnyi Tom). Moscow, 1962.

Itogy Vypolneniia Pervogo Piatiletnego Plana Razvitiia Narodnogo Khoziaistva SSSR. Moscow, 1933.

Kiselev, Ia. L., and Malkin, S. E. *Sbornik Vazhneishikh Postanovlenii po Trudu.* Moscow, 1938.

KPSS v Rezoliutsiiakh i Resheniiakh S'ezdov, Konferentsii i Plenumov TsK. Vol. 4 (1926–29). Moscow, 1984. Vol. 5 (1929–32). Moscow, 1984. Vol. 6 (1933–37). Moscow, 1985.

Lel'chuk, V. S., ed. *Industrial'noe Razvitie Tsentral'nogo Promyshlennogo Raiona, 1926–1932.* Moscow, 1969.

Leningrad v Tsifrakh. Leningrad, 1935.

Moskva v Novykh Raionakh. Moscow, 1936.

Moskva v Tsifrakh. Moscow, 1934.

Moskva v Tsifrakh. Moscow, 1939.

Naselenie Sovetskogo Soiuza, 1922–1991. Moscow, 1993.

Periodicheskaia Pechat' SSSR, 1917–1949: Bibliograficheskii Ukazatel'. 9 vols. Moscow, 1955–63.

Profsoiuznaia Perepis' 1932–33 gg. Moscow, 1934.

Sostav Novykh Millionov Chlenov Profsoiuzov. Moscow, 1933.

Sotsialisticheskoe Sorevnovanie v SSSR, 1918–1964: Dokumenty i Materialy Profsoiuzov. Moscow, 1965.

Books and Articles

Abramov, I., and Bil'dziukevich, A. *Peredovik Sovetskoi Metallurgii, "Serp i Molot".* Moscow-Leningrad-Sverdlovsk, 1935.

A. M. Gor'kii i Sozdanie Istorii Fabrik i Zavodov. Moscow, 1959.

Arutiunian, Iu. V. "Kollektivizatsiia Sel'skogo Khoziaistva i Vysvobozhdenie Rabochei Sily Dlia Promyshlennosti." In *Formirovanie i Razvitie Sovetskogo Rabochego Klassa, 1917–1961 gg.* Moscow, 1964.

Averbakh, L. L. *Shestnadtsat' Zavodov: Glavy iz Istorii.* Moscow, 1935.

Boltianskii, A. *Voprosy Sotsialisticheskoi Organizatsii Truda i Zarabotnoi Platy v Potochnom Proizvodstve.* Moscow, 1953.

Dadykin, R. P. *Nachalo Massovogo Sotsialisticheskogo Sorevnovanie v SSSR.* Moscow, 1954.

"Dinamo" na Putiakh k Oktiabriu. Moscow, 1961.

Direktor: I. A. Likhachev v Vospominaniiakh Sovremennikov. Moscow, 1971.

Drobizhev, V. Z., ed. *Sovetskoe Obshchestvo v Vospominaniiakh i Dnevnikakh, 1917–1941.* vol. 1. Moscow, 1987.

Ermanski, O. A. *Stakhanovskoe Dvizhenie i Stakhanovskie Metody.* Moscow, 1940.

Filatov, S. *Partrabota na Zavode "Serp i Molot."* Moscow-Leningrad, 1931.

Gaidul', E. I. "Problema Snizheniia Raskhodov po Trudy v Chernoi Metallurgii." *Sovetskaia Metallurgia* 1 (1936).

Gaisinovich, A. "Oktiabr-Dekabr 1905 g. na Zavode." *Istoriia Zavodov* 3 (1932): 77–85.

Gershberg, Semen. *Stakhanov i Stakhanovtsy.* Moscow, 1985. Reiussued from the 1930s.

Gladkov, I. A., ed. *Istoriia Sotsialisticheskoi Ekonomiki SSSR.* Vol. 3. Moscow, 1977.

Grudkov, V. *Peredovoi Opyt-Vsem Stalevaram.* Moscow, 1958.

Gudov, Ivan. *Sud'ba Rabochego.* Moscow, 1974.

Ikonnikov, A. V. *Arkhitektura Moskvy XX Vek.* Moscow, 1984.

Ivanov, I. "V Novykh Usloviiakh—po Novomy Rabotat'." *Za Industrializatsiiu,* 23 June 1932, pp. 2–3.

Iskusstvo i Rabochii Klass. Leningrad, 1983.

Istoriia Kirovskogo Zavoda, 1917–1945. Moscow, 1966.

Istoriia Moskovskogo Avtozavoda imeni I. A. Likhacheva. Moscow, 1966.

Istoriia Moskvy. Vol. 6, bk. 2. Moscow, 1959.

Istoriia Rabochikh Moskvy: 1917–1945. Moscow, 1983.

Istoriia Sovetskogo Rabochego Klassa, 1921–1937. Vol. 2. Moscow, 1984.

Khlevniuk, Oleg. "26 Iunia 1940 Goda: Iliuzii i Real'nosti Administrirovaniia." *Kommunist* 9 (June 1983): 86–96.

Kislev, Ia. L., and S. E. Malkin, *Sbornik Vazhneishikh Postanovlenii p. Trodu.* Moscow, 1938.

Koniaev, A. "Guzhon." *Istoriia Zavodov* 3 (1932): 68–76.

Kornakovskii, I. L. "I. M. Romanov." In *Nastavniki.* Moscow, 1983.

——. "Zavod 'Serp i Molot,' 1883–1932: Opyt Istoriko-Sotsiologicheskogo Issle-dovaniia." Moscow, 1979. MS deposited in the Library of the Social Sciences, INION no. 10062.

Kornakovskii, I. L., and T. I. Slavko. "Metodika Razrabotki Uchetnykh Kartochek Rabochikh i Sluzhashchikh Promyshlennykh Predpriatii na Primera Zavoda 'Serp i Molot.'" *Istochnikovedenie Istorii Sovetskogo Obshchestva*, vyp. 3, 1978.

Lapitskaia, S. *Byt Rabochikh Trekhgornoi Manufaktury.* Moscow, 1935.

——. "Zhilishnoe Stroitel'stvo Novoi Moskvy." *Bor'ba Klassov* (1934), no. 7–8.

Lebedeva, N. B., and O. I. Shkaratan. *Ocherki Istorii Sotsialisticheskogo Sorevnovaniia.* Leningrad, 1966.

——. *Partiinoe Rukovodstvo Sotsialisticheskim Sorevnovaniem: Istoriia i Sovremennost.* Leningrad, 1979.

Lel'chuk, Vitalii Semenovich. *Sotsialisticheskaia Industrializatsiia SSSR i Ee Osveshchenie v Sovetskoi Istoriografii.* Moscow, 1975.

Lenin, V. I. *Polnoe Sobranie Sochinenii.* Vols. 35, 39. Moscow, 1969, 1970.

Leont'eva, Tamara. *Likhachev.* Moscow, 1987.

Manevich, E. L. *Zarabotnaia Plata i Ee Formy v Promyshlennosti SSSR.* Moscow, 1951.

Markevich, N., and S. Urnis. *U Zastavy Il'icha: Metallurgicheskii Zavod "Serp i Molot".* Moscow, 1937.

Martov, B. "Rekonstruktsiia Zavoda 'Serp i Molot.'" *Bor'ba Klassov* (1934), no. 7–8.

Matiugin, A. A. *Rabochii Klass SSSR v Gody Vosstanovleniia Narodnogo Khoziaistva, 1921–1925.* Moscow, 1962.

Meller, V. "Iz Istorii Zavoda 'Serp i Molot.'" *Bor'ba Klassov* (1931), no. 6–7.

——. "Na Putiakh k Oktiabriu (Zavod 'Serp i Molot,' byvsh. 'Guzhon'). In Averbakh, *Shestnadtsat' Zavodov: Glavy iz Istorii.* Moscow, 1935.

Mikhailov, N. *Bor'ba za Stal'.* Moscow, 1931. (Translated as *The Fight for Steel*).

Mitrofanova, A. V. *Rabochii Klass SSSR v Gody Velikoi Otechestvennoi Voiny, 1941–45.* Moscow, 1971.

Mitrofanova, A. V., I. P. Ostapenko, and L. S. Rogachevskaia. "Itogy i Perspektivye Izucheniia Istorii Predpriatii SSSR." In *Rabochii Klass Strany Sovietov.* Minsk, 1980.

Moskva Entsiklopediia. Moscow, 1980.

Moskvichi. Moscow, 1950.

Nastavniki. Moscow, 1983.

Nas Vyrastil' Stalin: Rasskazy Laureatov Stalinskikh Premii. Moscow, 1951.

Novatory. Moscow, 1972.

Ostrovskii, Nikolai. *Kak Zakalalas' Stal'.* Moscow, 1934.

Pankratova, A. *Fabzavkomy i Profsoiuzy v Revoliutsii 1917 Goda.* Moscow-Leningrad, 1927.

————. *Fabzavkomy Rossii v Bor'be za Sotsialisticheskuiu Fabriku.* Moscow, 1923.

————. "Rabochie Zavoda 'Serp i Molot' v 1905 g.: K Postanovke Opyta Izucheniia Avto-biografii Starykh Rabochikh." In A. M. Pankratova, *Rabochii Klass Rossii: Izbrannye Trudy.* Moscow, 1983.

Panfilova, A. M. *Formirovanie Rabochego Klassa SSSR v Gody Pervoi Piatiletkh.* Moscow, 1964.

Pervoprokhodtsy. Moscow, 1980.

Platonov, Andrei Platonovich. "Kotlovan." Serialized in *Novyi Mir* in 1987 and then published in *Gosudarstvennyi Zhitel',* pp. 108–97. Moscow, 1988.

Poletaev, V. E. "Zhilishchnoe Stroitel'stvo v Moskve v 1931–1934 gg." *Istoricheskie Zapiski* 66 (1960).

Poselianina, A. "Bor'ba za Sotsialisticheskuiu Organizatsiiu Truda." *Istoriia Proletariata* 3 (1934):178–95.

————. "Vostanovlenie Zavoda 'Serp i Molot'" *Bor'ba Klassov* (1934), no. 7–8.

Rabkina, N. E., and Rimashevskaia, N. M. "Raspredelitel'nye Otnosheniia i Sotsial'noe Razvitie" *EKO* (1978), no. 5.

Rashin, Adolf G. *Formirovanie Promyshlennogo Proletariata v Rossii: Statistiko-Ekonomicheskie Ocherki.* Moscow, 1940.

————. *Sostav Fabrichno-Zavodskogo Proletariata SSSR: Predvaritel'nye Itogi Perepisi Metallistov, Gornorabochikh i Tekstil'shchikov v 1929 g.* Moscow, 1930.

Rikhter, Zinaida. *Stal Frontu.* Moscow, 1943.

Rogachevskaia, L. S. *Likvidatsiia Bezrabotitsy v SSSR, 1917–1930 gg.* Moscow, 1973.

————. *Rabochii Klass SSSR, 1926–1929.* Moscow, 1960.

————. *Sotsialisticheskoe Sorevnovanie v SSSR: Istoricheskie Ocherki, 1917–1970 gg.* Moscow, 1977.

Salov, A. *Organizatsiia Rabochego Snabzheniia.* Moscow, 1933.

Seniavskii, S. L., and Tel'pukhovskii, V. B. *Rabochii Klass SSSR, 1938–1965.* Moscow, 1971.

Shestnadsat' Zavodov: Glavy iz Istorii. Moscow, 1935.

Shipilin, L. *Krepche Stali: Ocherki o Zaovde "Serp i Molot".* Moscow-Leningrad, 1931.

Shkaratan, O. I. *Problemy Sotsial'noi Struktury Rabochego Klassa SSSR.* Moscow, 1970.

Shvedov, Iakov, *Poiski Otechestva: Povest'.* Moscow, 1933.

Slanskaia, M. D. "K Istorii Vozniknoveniia Mnogotirazhnykh Gazet na Zavodov i Stroikakh Sovetskoi Strany, 1922–1932 gg." *Vestnik Moskovskogo Universiteta* (1971), no. 5.

Sokolov, Andrei K. *Rabochii Klass—Vedushchaia Sila Sovetskogo Obshchestva: Voprosy Metodologii i Istoriografii.* Moscow, 1987.

Sonin, M. Ia. *Vosproizvodstvo Rabochei Sily v SSSR i Balans Truda.* Moscow, 1959.

Sotsialisticheskoe Stroitel'stvo. Moscow, 1936.

Stalin, I. V. *Sochineniia.* t. 9, 1926 (Moscow, 1952), t. 12, 1929–1930 (Moscow, 1949), t. 13, 1930–1934 (Moscow, 1951), and t. 14, 1934–1940 . Stanford: Hoover Institution, 1967.

Suvorov, K. I. *Istoricheskii Opyt KPSS po Likvidatsii Bezrabotitsy.* Moscow, 1968.

Svet nad Zastavoi. Moscow, 1959.

Trud i Zdorov'e Rabochikh v Staleliteinykh i Prokatnykh Tsekhakh 'Serp i Molot'. Moscow, 1926.

Vas'kina, Lidia I. *Rabochii Klass SSSR Nakanune Sotsialisticheskoi Industrializatsii: Chislennost', Sostav, Razmeshchenie.* Moscow, 1981.

Vdovin, A. I., and V. Z. Drobizhev. *Rost Rabochego Klassa SSSR, 1917–1940.* Moscow, 1976.

Venediktov, A. V. *Organizatsiia Gosudarstvennoi Promyshlennosti v SSSR.* Vol. 2. Leningrad, 1961.

Veselov, A. N. *Professional'no-Tekhnicheskoe Obrazovanie v SSSR: Ocherki po Istorii Srednego i Nis-chego Proftekhobrazovaniia.* Moscow, 1961.

Vorozheikin, I. E. *Ocherk Istoriografii Rabochego Klassa SSSR.* Moscow, 1975.

Vorozheikin, I. E., and Siniavskii, S. L. *Rabochii Klass—Vedushchaia Sila Sovetskogo Obshch-estva: Voprosy Metodologii i Istoriografii.* Moscow, 1977.

Voznesenskii, N. A. *Voennaia Ekonomika SSSR v Period Otechestvennoi Voiny.* Moscow, 1947.

Zinoviev, Aleksandr. *Kommunizm kak Real'nost'.* Lausanne, L'Age d'Homme, 1981.

——. *Ziiaushchie Vysoty.* Lausanne: L'Age d'Homme, 1976.

——. *Svetloe Budushchee.* Lausanne: L'Age d'Homme, 1978.

English-Language Sources

Journals
American Historical Review
International and Labor Information
International Labour Review
Soviet Studies
Slavic Review

Books and Articles

Adams, Mark. "Science, Ideology, and Structure: The Kol'tsov Institute, 1900–1970." In L. Lubrano and S. Solomon, eds., *The Social Context of Soviet Science.* Boulder, Colo.: Westview, 1980.

Althusser, Louis. *For Marx.* Translated by Ben Brewster. London: Verso, 1979.

Anderson, Barbara. "The Life Course of Soviet Women Born 1905–1960." In James Millar, ed., *Politics, Work, and Daily Life in the USSR: A Survey of Former Soviet Citizens,* pp. 203–40. Cambridge: Cambridge University Press, 1987.

Andrle, Vladimir. "How Backward Workers Became Soviet: Industrialization of Labor and the Politics of Efficiency Under the Second Five Year Plan, 1933–1937." *Social History* 10, no. 2 (May 1985): 147–69.

——. *Managerial Power in the Soviet Union.* Lexington, Mass.: Lexington Books, 1976.

——. *Workers in Stalin's Russia: Industrialization and Social Change in a Planned Economy.* New York: St. Martin's Press, 1988.

Anweiler, Oskar. *The Soviets: The Russian Workers, Peasants, and Soldiers Councils, 1905–1921.* Translated by Ruth Hein. New York: Pantheon, 1974.

Avrich, Paul. "The Bolshevik Revolution and Workers' Control in Russian Industry." *Slavic Review* 1 (1963): 47–63.

Azrael, Jeremy. *Managerial Power and Soviet Politics.* Cambridge: Harvard University Press, 1966.

Bailes, Kendall. "Alexei Gastev and the Controversy Over Taylorism, 1918–1924." *Soviet Studies* 29 (July 1977): 373–94.

——. *Technology and Society Under Lenin and Stalin: Origins of the Soviet Technical Intelli-gentsia, 1917–1941.* Princeton: Princeton University Press, 1978.

Barber, John. "The Composition of the Soviet Working Class, 1928–1941." University of Birmingham, CREES Discussion Paper, SIPS Series 16, 1978.

——. "The Development of Soviet Employment and Labour Policy, 1930–1941." In David Lane, ed., *Labour and Employment in the USSR.* New York, 1986.

——. "The Standard of Living of Soviet Industrial Workers, 1928–1941." In Charles Bet-telheim, ed., *L'Industrialisation de l'URSS dans les années trente.* Paris, 1982.

Berdyaev, Nicholas. *The Origin of Russian Communism.* New York: Geoffrey Bles, 1937.

Bergson, Abram. *The Structure of Soviet Wages: A Study in Socialist Economics.* Cambridge: Harvard University Press, 1944.

Berliner, Joseph. *Factory and Manager in the USSR.* Cambridge: Harvard University Press, 1956.

Besborodov, S. *Thomas Monger and Johann Liebhardt: Heroes of Socialist Construction.* Moscow: Cooperative Publishing Society of Foreign Workers, 1932.

Bettelheim, Charles. *Class Struggles in the USSR.* 2 vols. New York: Monthly Review Press, 1976, 1978.

Bettelheim, Charles, ed. *L'Industrialisation de l'URSS dans les années trente.* Paris: Éditions de l'École des Hautes Etudes en Sciences Sociales, 1982.

Bialer, Seweryn. *Stalin's Successors: Leadership, Stability, and Change in the Soviet Union.* Cambridge: Cambridge University Press, 1988.

Boffa, Guiseppa. *The Stalin Phenomenon.* Ithaca: Cornell University Press, 1992.

Bonnell, Victoria. *Roots of Rebellion: Workers' Politics and Organizations in St. Petersburg and Moscow, 1900–1914.* Berkeley and Los Angeles: University of California Press, 1983.

Bottomore, T. B. *Elites and Society.* London: Penguin, 1964.

Bradley, Joseph. *Muzhik and Muscovite: Urbanization in Late Imperial Russia.* Berkeley and Los Angeles: University of California Press, 1985.

Brumfield, William C., ed. *Reshaping Russian Architecture: Western Technology Utopian Dreams.* Washington, D.C.: Woodrow Wilson Center, 1990.

Burdzhalov, E. N. *Russia's Second Revolution: The February 1917 Uprising in Petrograd.* Translated and edited by Donald J. Raleigh. Bloomington: Indiana University Press, 1987.

Buroway, Michael. *Manufacturing Consent: Changes in the Labor Process Under Monopoly Capitalism.* Chicago: University of Chicago Press, 1979.

Canning, Kathleen. *Languages of Labor and Gender: Female Factory Work in Germany, 1850–1914.* Ithaca: Cornell University Press, 1996.

Carr, E. H. *The Bolshevik Revolution.* Vol. 2. London: Macmillan, 1952.

———. *Socialism in One Country.* Vol. 1. London: Macmillan, 1958.

Carr, E. H., and R. W. Davies. *Foundations of a Planned Economy, 1926–1929.* Vol. 1, pt. 2. London: Macmillan, 1969.

Chandler, Alfred D., Jr. *The Visible Hand: The Managerial Revolution in American Business.* Cambridge: Harvard University Press, 1977.

Chase, William. *Workers, Society, and the Soviet State: Labor and Life in Moscow, 1928–1929.* Champaign-Urbana: University of Illinois Press, 1987.

Clark, Katerina. *The Soviet Novel: History as Ritual.* Chicago: University of Chicago Press, 1981.

Clark, M. Gardner. *The Economics of Soviet Steel.* Cambridge: Harvard University Press, 1956.

Cohen, Lizabeth. *Making a New Deal: Industrial Workers in Chicago, 1919–1939.* Cambridge: Cambridge University Press, 1990.

Cohen, Stephen. *Bukharin and the Bolshevik Revolution: A Political Biography, 1888–1938.* Oxford: Oxford University Press, 1971.

———. *Rethinking the Soviet Experience: Politics and History Since 1917.* Oxford: Oxford University Press, 1986.

Colton, Timothy. *Moscow: Governing the Socialist Metropolis.* Cambridge: Harvard University Press, 1995.

Conquest, Robert. *The Great Terror: Stalin's Purge of the Thirties.* London: Macmillan, 1968.

Crew, David. *Town on the Ruhr: A Social History of Bochum, 1860–1914.* New York: Columbia University Press, 1979.

Danilov, V. P. *Rural Russia Under the New Regime.* Translated by O. Figes. Bloomington: Indiana University Press, 1988.

Davies, R. W. *Collectivization of Soviet Agriculture.* Cambridge: Harvard University Press, 1980.

———. "The Ending of Mass Unemployment in the USSR." In David Lane, ed. *Labour and Employment in the USSR,* pp. 19–49.

———. "The Management of Soviet Industry, 1928–41." In William Rosenberg and Lewis Siegelbaum, eds., *Social Dimensions of Soviet Industrialization.*

———. "The Socialist Market: A Debate in Soviet Industry, 1932–33." *Slavic Review* 42 (summer 1984): 201–23.

———. *The Soviet Collective Farm.* Cambridge: Harvard University Press, 1980.

———. *Soviet History in the Gorbachev Revolution.* Bloomington: Indiana University Press, 1989.

Deutscher, Isaac. *Soviet Trade Unions: Their Place in Soviet Labor Policy.* London: Royal Institute of International Affairs, 1950.

Dewar, Margaret. *Labour Policy in the USSR, 1917–1928.* Oxford, 1956. London: Royal Institute of International Affairs, 1956.

Dewey, John. *Democracy and Education.* New York: Free Press, 1916. Rpt. 1966.

Djilas, Milovan. *The New Class: An Analysis of the Communist System.* New York: Praeger, 1957.

Doeringer, Peter B., and Michael J. Piore. *Internal Labor Markets and Manpower Analysis.* Lexington, Mass: Heath, 1971.

Dubofsky, Melvyn. *The State and Labor in Modern America.* Chapel Hill: University of North Carolina Press, 1994.

Dunlop, John. *Industrial Relations Systems.* New York: Holt, 1958.

Dunlop, John, Frederick Harbison, Clark Kerr, and Charles Myers. *Industrialism and Industrial Man.* Cambridge: Harvard University Press, 1960.

Durkheim, Emile. *The Division of Labor in Society.* New York: Free Press, 1964.

Edelman, Robert. *Serious Fun: A History of Spectator Sports in the USSR.* New York: Oxford University Press, 1993.

Engel, Barbara. *Between the Fields and the City: Women, Work, and Family in Russia, 1861–1914.* Cambridge: Cambridge University Press, 1994.

Engelstein, Laura. "Combined Underdevelopment: Discipline and the Law in Imperial and Soviet Russia." *American Historical Review* 98 (April 1993): 338–54.

———. *The Keys to Happiness: Sex and the Search for Modernity in Fin-de-Siècle Russia.* Ithaca: Cornell University Press, 1992.

———. *Moscow 1905: Working-Class Organization and Political Conflict.* Stanford: Stanford University Press, 1982.

Erlich, Alexander. *The Soviet Industrializtion Debate.* Cambridge: Harvard University Press, 1960.

Fainsod, Merle. *How Russia Is Ruled.* Cambridge: Harvard University Press, 1959.

———. *Smolensk Under Soviet Rule.* Cambridge: Harvard University Press, 1958.

Fairbanks, Charles H., Jr., and Susan A. Thornton. "Soviet Decision-Making and Bureaucratic Representation: Evidence from the Smolensk Archive and an American Comparison." *Soviet Studies* 42 (1990): 627–54.

Filtzer, Donald. *Soviet Workers and De-Stalinization: The Consolidation of the Modern System of Soviet Production Relations, 1953–1964.* Cambridge: Cambridge University Press, 1992.

———. *Soviet Workers and Stalinist Industrialization: The Formation of Modern Soviet Production Relations.* Armonk, N.Y.: M. E. Sharpe, 1986.

Fitzpatrick, Sheila. "The Bolsheviks' Dilemma: Class, Culture, and Politics." *Slavic Review* 47 (winter 1988): 599–613.

———. *The Commissariat of Enlightenment: Soviet Organization of Education and the Arts Under Lunacharsky.* Cambridge: Cambridge University Press, 1979.

———. *The Cultural Front: Power and Culture in Revolutionary Russia.* Ithaca: Cornell University Press, 1992.

———. *Education and Social Mobility in the Soviet Union, 1921-1934.* Cambridge: Cambridge University Press, 1979.

———. "Ordzhonikidze's Takeover of VESENKha." *Soviet Studies* 37 (April 1985): 153–72.

———. *The Russian Revolution.* 2d ed. Oxford: Oxford University Press, 1994.

———. "Stalin and the Making of a New Elite, 1928–1939." *Slavic Review* 38 (September 1979): 377–402.

———. *Stalin's Peasants: Resistance and Survival in the Russian Village After Collectivization.* Oxford: Oxford University Press, 1994.

Fitzpatrick, Sheila, ed. *Cultural Revolution in Russia, 1928–1931.* Bloomington: Indiana University Press, 1978.

Fitzpatrick, Sheila, Alexander Rabinowitch, and Richard Stites, eds. *Russia in the Era of NEP: Explorations in Soviet Society and Culture.* Bloomington: Indiana University Press, 1991.

Fitzpatrick, Sheila, and Lynne Viola, eds. *A Researcher's Guide to Sources on Soviet Social History in the 1930s.* Armonk, N.Y.: M. E. Sharpe, 1990.

Foucault, Michel. *Discipline and Punish: The Birth of the Prison.* Translated by Alan Sheridan. New York: Vintage, 1979.

Friedgut, Theodore. *Iuzovka and Revolution.* Princeton: Princeton University Press, 1989.

Furet, François. *Interpreting the French Revolution.* Cambridge: Cambridge University Press, 1981.

———. *Marx and the French Revolution.* Chicago: University of Chicago Press, 1988.

———. *Revolutionary France, 1770–1880.* Oxford: Blackwell, 1992.

Furet, François, and Mona Ozouf, eds. *Critical Dictionary of the French Revolution.* Cambridge: Harvard University Press, 1989.

Getty, J. Arch. *Origins of the Great Purges: The Soviet Communist Party Reconsidered.* Cambridge: Cambridge University Press, 1985.

Giddens, Anthony. *The Class Structure of the Advanced Societies.* New York: Harper and Row, 1975.

Glickman, Rose. *Russian Factory Women: Workplace and Society, 1880–1914.* Berkeley and Los Angeles: University of California Press, 1984.

Goldman, Wendy. *Women, the State, and Revolution: Soviet Family Policy and Social Life, 1917–1936.* Cambridge: Cambridge University Press, 1993.

Gordon, David, Richard Edwards, and Michael Reich. *Segmented Work, Divided Workers: The Historical Transformation of Labor in the United States.* Cambridge: Cambridge University Press, 1982.

Granick, David. *Job Rights in the Soviet Union: Their Consequences.* Cambridge: Cambridge University Press, 1987.

———. *Management of the Industrial Firm in the USSR.* New York: Columbia University Press, 1954.

———. *The Red Executive: A Study of the Organization Man in Russian Industry.* New York, 1960.

Haimson, Leopold. "Dual Polarization in Urban Russia." *Slavic Review* 23 (December 1964): 619–42; ibid., 24 (March 1965): 1–22.

————. "The Problem of Social Identities in Early Twentieth Century Russia." *Slavic Review* 47 (spring 1988): 1–20.

Haimson, Leopold, and Charles Tilly, eds. *Strikes, War, and Revolution: Comparative Studies and Quantative Analysis of Strike Waves in Six Major Industrial Countries in the Late Nineteenth and Early Twentieth Centuries.* Cambridge: Cambridge University Press, 1989.

Harrison, Mark. *Soviet Planning in Peace and War, 1938–1945.* Cambridge: Cambridge University Press, 1985.

Hewett, Ed. *Reforming the Soviet Economy: Equality versus Efficiency.* Washington, D.C.: Brookings, 1988.

Hobsbawm, Eric. *The Age of Revolution.* New York: Mentor, 1962.

————. *Labouring Men: Studies in the History of Labour.* London: Basic Books, 1964.

————. *Workers: Worlds of Labor.* New York: Pantheon, 1984.

Hoffmann, David. *Peasant Metropolis: Social Identities in Moscow, 1929–1941.* Ithaca: Cornell University Press, 1994.

Hogan, Heather. *Forging Revolution: Metalworkers, Managers, and the State in St. Petersburg, 1890–1914.* Bloomington: Indiana University Press, 1993.

Holmes, Larry. *The Kremlin and the Schoolhouse.* Bloomington: Indiana University Press, 1991.

Hough, Jerry, and Merle Fainsod. *How the Soviet Union Is Governed.* Cambridge: Harvard University Press, 1979.

Huizinga, Johan. *The Waning of the Middle Ages: A Study of the Forms of Life, Thought, and Art in France and the Netherlands in the Dawn of the Renaissance.* New York: Doubleday, 1954.

Hunter, Holland, and Janus Szyrmer. *Faulty Foundations: Soviet Economic Policies, 1928–1940.* Princeton: Princeton University Press, 1992.

Husband, William. *Revolution in the Factory: The Birth of the Soviet Textile Industry, 1917–1920.* Oxford: Oxford University Press, 1990.

Inkeles, Alex, and Raymond Bauer. *The Soviet Citizen: Daily Life in a Totalitarian Society.* Cambridge: Harvard University Press, 1959.

Jasny, Naum. *Soviet Industrialization, 1928–1952.* Chicago: University of Chicago Press, 1961.

Johnson, Robert E. "Family Life in Moscow During NEP." In Sheila Fitzpatrick, Alexander Rabinowitch, and Richard Stites, eds. *Russia in the Era of NEP: Explorations in Soviet Society and Culture.* Bloomington: Indiana University Press, 1991.

————. *Peasant and Proletarian: The Working Class of Moscow in the Late Nineteenth Century.* New Brunswick, N.J.: Rutgers University Press, 1979.

Jones, Gareth Stedman. *Languages of Class: Studies in English Working Class History, 1832–1982.* Cambridge: Cambridge University Press, 1983.

Joyce, Patrick. *Visions of the People: Industrial England and the Question of Class, 1848–1914.* Cambridge: Cambridge University Press, 1991.

Kabakov, Ilya. "Ten Characters." Exhibition catalog, Hirshhorn Museum, Smithsonian Institution, Washington D.C., March–June 1990.

Kaiser, Daniel. *The Workers' Revolution in Russia: The View from Below.* Cambridge: Cambridge University Press, 1987.

Katznelson, Ira, and Aristide Zolberg, eds. *Working-Class Formation: Nineteenth-Century Patterns in Western Europe and the United States.* Princeton: Princeton University Press, 1986.

Kavtaradze, Sergei, and Alexei Tarkhanov. *Architecture of the Stalin Era.* New York: Rizzolli, 1992.

Kerr, Clark. *Labor Markets and Wage Determination: The Balkanization of Labor Markets and Other Essays*. Berkeley and Los Angeles: University of California Press, 1977.

Khan-Magomedov, Selim Omarovich. *Alexandr Vesnin and Russian Constructivism*. New York: Rizzoli, 1986.

Kingston-Mann, Esther. "Peasant Communes and Economic Innovation: A Preliminary Inquiry." In Esther Kingston-Mann and Timothy Mixter, eds., *Peasant Economy, Culture, and Politics of European Russia, 1800–1921*. Princeton: Princeton University Press, 1991.

Kingston-Mann, Esther, and Timothy Mixter, eds. *Peasant Economy, Culture, and Politics of European Russia, 1800–1921*. Princeton: Princeton University Press, 1991.

Koenker, Diane. *Moscow Workers and the 1917 Revolution*. Princeton: Princeton University Press, 1981.

Koenker, Diane, and William Rosenberg. *Strikes and Revolution in Russia, 1917*. Princeton: Princeton University Press, 1989.

Kotkin, Stephen. *Magnetic Mountain: Stalinism as a Civilization*. Berkeley and Los Angeles: University of California Press, 1995.

Kornai, Janos. *Economics of Shortage*. 2 vols. New York: North-Holland, 1980.

——. *Resource-Constrained Versus Demand-Constrained Systems*. Institute for International Economic Studies, University of Stockholm, 1978.

——. *Shortage and Efficiency: A Macrodynamic Model of the Socialist Economy*. Oxford: Basil Blackwell, 1982.

Kuromiya, Hiroaki. "The Commander and the Rank and File: Managing the Soviet Coal-Mining Industry, 1928–1933." In Rosenberg and Siegelbaum, eds., *Social Dimensions of Soviet Industrialization*.

——. "The Crisis of Proletarian Identity in the Soviet Factory, 1928–1929." *Slavic Review* 44 (summer 1985) 280–97.

——. "*Edinonachalie* and the Soviet Industrial Manager, 1928–1937." *Soviet Studies* 36 (April 1984): 185–204.

——. *Stalin's Industrial Revolution: Politics and Workers, 1928–1932*. Cambridge: Cambridge University Press, 1988.

Lane, David, ed. *Labour and Employment in the USSR*. Brighton, Sussex: Wheatsheaf, 1986.

Lewin, Moshe. *The Making of the Soviet System*. New York, 1985.

——. *Political Undercurrents in Soviet Economic Debates: From Bukharin to the Modern Reformers*. Princeton: Princeton University Press, 1974.

——. *Russian Peasants and Soviet Power: A Study in Collectivization*. New York: Norton, 1968.

——. "Taking Grain: Soviet Policies of Agricultural Procurements Before the War." In C. Abramsky, ed., *Essays in Honour of E. H. Carr*. London: Macmillan, 1974.

——. "Who Was the Soviet Kulak?" *Soviet Studies* 18 (1966): 189–212.

Maier, Charles. *Recasting Bourgeois Europe: Stabilization in France, Germany, and Italy in the Decade After World War I*. Princeton: Princeton University Press, 1975.

Mandel, David. *The Petrograd Workers and the Fall of the Old Regime*. London: Macmillan, 1983.

——. *Petrograd Workers and the Soviet Seizure of Power*. London: Macmillan, 1984.

Matthews, Mervyn. *Class and Society in Soviet Russia*. New York, 1972.

——. *Poverty in the Soviet Union: The Life-Styles of the Underprivileged in Recent Years*. Cambridge: Cambridge University Press, 1986.

Marx, Karl. *Capital*. Vol. 1. New York: New World, 1967.

McAuley, Alistair. *Women's Work and Wages in the Soviet Union.* London: Allen and Unwin, 1981.

McKean, Robert. *St. Petersburg Between the Revolutions: Workers and Revolutionaries, June 1907–February 1917.* New Haven: Yale University Press, 1990.

Medvedev, Zhores. *The Rise and Fall of T. D. Lysenko.* New York: Doubleday, 1971.

Mikhailov, N. *The Fight for Steel.* Moscow, 1931. Translation of *Bor'ba za Stal'*.

Millar, James, ed. *Politics, Work, and Daily Life in the USSR: A Survey of Former Soviet Citizens.* Cambridge: Cambridge University Press, 1987.

Mills, C. Wright. *The Power Elite.* New York: Oxford University Press, 1956.

Moore, Barrington, Jr. *Injustice: The Social Bases of Obedience and Revolt.* Armonk, N.Y.: M. E. Sharpe, 1978.

Neuberger, Joan. *Hooliganism: Crime, Culture and Power in St. Petersburg, 1900–1914.* Berkeley and Los Angeles: University of California Press, 1993.

Nicolaevsky, Boris. *Power and the Soviet Elite: The Letter of an Old Bolshevik and Other Essays.* Edited by Janet Zagoria. Ann Arbor: University of Michigan Press, 1965.

Nove, Alec. *An Economic History of the USSR, 1917–1991.* 3rd ed. London: Penguin, 1992.

Pethybridge, Roger. *One Step Backwards, Two Steps Forward: Soviet Society and Politics in the New Economic Policy.* Oxford: Oxford University Press, 1990.

Piore, Michael J. *Birds of Passage: Migrant Labor and Industrial Societies.* Cambridge: Cambridge University Press, 1979.

Pipes, Richard. *The Russian Revolution.* New York: Knopf, 1990.

——. *Russia Under the Bolshevik Regime.* New York: Knopf, 1993.

Presniakov, A. E. *The Formation of the Great Russian State.* Translated by A. E. Moorhouse. Chicago: Quadrangle, 1970.

Rabinowitch, Alexander. *The Bolsheviks Come to Power: The Revolution of 1917 in Petrograd.* New York: Norton, 1976.

——. *Prelude to Revolution: The Petrograd Bolsheviks and the July 1917 Uprising.* Bloomington: Indiana University Press, 1968.

Rancière, Jacques. *The Nights of Labor: The Workers' Dream in Nineteenth-Century France.* Philadelphia: Temple University Press, 1989.

Rassweiler, Anne. *The Generation of Power: The History of Dneprostroi.* New York: Oxford University Press, 1988.

Reuther, Victor. *The Brothers Reuther and the Story of the UAW.* Boston: Houghton Mifflin, 1976.

Rieber, Alfred. Introduction to A. E. Presniakov, *The Formation of the Great Russian State.* Chicago: Quadrangle, 1970.

Rigby, T. H. *Communist Party Membership in the USSR.* Princeton: Princeton University Press, 1968.

——. *Lenin's Government: Sovnarkom, 1917–1922.* Cambridge: Cambridge University Press, 1979.

——. "The Mono-Organizational Society." In Robert Tucker, ed., *Stalinism: Essays in Historical Interpretation.*

Robinson, G. T. *Rural Russia Under the Old Regime.* Berkeley: University of California Press, 1932.

Rose, Sonya. *Limited Livelihoods: Gender and Class in Nineteenth-Century England.* Berkeley and Los Angeles: University of California Press, 1992.

Rosenberg, William, and Lewis Siegelbaum, eds. *Social Dimensions of Soviet Industrialization.* Bloomington: Indiana University Press, 1993.

Roth, Gunther. *The Social Democrats of Imperial Germany: Working Class Isolation and National Integration.* Totowa, N.J.: Bedminster Press, 1963.

Ruble, Blair. "Moscow's Revolutionary Architecture and Its Aftermath: A Critical Guide." In William C. Brumfield, ed., *Reshaping Russian Architecture: Western Technology, Utopian Dreams.* Washington, D.C.: Woodrow Wilson Center, 1990.

Schapiro, Leonard. *The Communist Party of the Soviet Union.* New York: Vintage, 1960.

Schwarz, Solomon. *Labour in the Soviet Union.* New York: Praeger, 1952.

———. *The Russian Revolution of 1905: The Workers' Movement and the Formation of Menshevism and Bolshivism.* Chicago: University of Chicago Press, 1967.

Sewell, William. *Work and Revolution in France: The Language of Labor from the Old Regime to 1948.* Cambridge: Cambridge University Press, 1980.

Shorske, Carl E. *Fin-de-Siècle Vienna: Politics and Culture.* New York: Vintage, 1980.

Siegelbaum, Lewis. "Masters of the Shop Floor: Foremen and Soviet Industrialization." In William Rosenberg and Lewis Siegelbaum, eds., *Social Dimensions of Soviet Industrialization.*

———. "Shock Workers." In *The Modern Encyclopedia of Russian and Soviet History*, 34:23–27. Gulf Breeze, Fla.: Academic International Press, 1983.

———. "Soviet Norm Determination in Theory and Practice." *Soviet Studies* 36 (1984): 45–68.

———. *Soviet State and Society Between Revolutions, 1918–1929.* Cambridge: Cambridge University Press, 1992.

———. *Stakhanovism and the Politics of Productivity in the USSR, 1935–1941.* Cambridge: Cambridge University Press, 1988.

Siriani, Carmen. *Workers' Control and Social Democracy: The Soviet Experience.* London: New Left Books, 1982.

Skocpol, Theda. "Bringing the State Back In." In Peter Evans, Dietrich Rueschmeyer, and Theda Skocpol, eds., *Bringing the State Back In.* Cambridge: Cambridge University Press, 1985.

———. *Protecting Soldiers and Mothers: The Political Origins of Social Policy in the United States.* Cambridge: Harvard University Press, 1992.

Smith, Steve. "Class and Gender: Women's Strikes in St. Petersburg, 1895–1917 and in Shanghai 1895–1927." *Social History* 19 (May 1994): 141–68.

———. *Red Petrograd: Revolution in the Factories.* Cambridge: Cambridge University Press, 1983.

Solzhenitsyn, Aleksandr. *The Gulag Archipelago.* Vol. 2. New York: Harper and Row, 1975.

Stites, Richard. *Revolutionary Dreams: Utopian Vision and Experimental Life in the Russian Revolution.* New York: Oxford University Press, 1989.

———. *Russian Popular Culture: Entertainment and Popular Culture.* Cambridge: Cambridge University Press, 1992.

Straus, Kenneth. "The Transformation of the Soviet Working Class, 1929–1935: The Regime in Search of a New Social Stability." Ph.D. diss., University of Pennsylvania, 1990.

Suny, Ronald G. *The Baku Commune, 1917–1918: Class and Nationality in the Russian Revolution.* Princeton: Princeton University Press, 1972.

———. *Looking Toward Ararat: Armenia in Modern History.* Bloomington: Indiana University Press, 1993.

———. *The Making of the Georgian Nation.* Bloomington: Indiana University Press, 1988.

———. *Revenge of the Past.* Stanford: Stanford University Press, 1993.

———. "Revising the Old Story: The 1917 Revolution in Light of New Sources." In Daniel H. Kaiser, ed., *The Workers' Revolution in Russia, 1917: The View from Below*. Cambridge: Cambridge University Press, 1987.

———. "Toward a Social History of the October Revolution." *American Historical Review* 88 (1983): 32–52.

Surh, Gerald. *1905 in St. Petersburg: Labor, Society, and Revolution*. Stanford, Calif.: Stanford University Press, 1989.

Sutton, Anthony C. *Western Technology and Soviet Economic Development, 1917 to 1930*. Stanford: Hoover Institute, 1968.

Swafford, Michael. "Perceptions of Social Status in the USSR." In Millar, ed., *Politics, Work, and Daily Life in the USSR*, pp. 279–300.

Thompson, E. P. *The Making of the English Working Class*. New York: Vintage, 1963.

———. "Time, Work Discipline, and Industrial Capitalism." *Past and Present* 38 (December 1967): 56–97.

Thurston, Robert. *Life and Terror in Stalin's Russia, 1934–1941*. New Haven: Yale University Press, 1996.

Timasheff, Nicholas. *The Great Retreat: The Growth and Decline of Communism in Russia*. New York: E. P. Dutton, 1946.

Trotsky, Leon. *History of the Russian Revolution*. Ann Arbor: University of Michigan Press, 1932.

———. *1905*. New York: Vintage, 1971.

———. *The Revolution Betrayed: What Is the Soviet Union and Where Is It Going?*. New York: Pathfinder, 1937.

Tucker, Robert. *The Soviet Political Mind: Stalinism and Post-Stalin Change*. New York: Norton, 1971.

———. *Stalin in Power: The Revolution from Above, 1928–1941*. New York: Norton, 1990.

Tucker, Robert, ed. *Stalinism: Essays in Historical Interpretation*. New York: Norton, 1977.

Viola, Lynne. *The Best Sons of the Fatherland: Workers in the Vanguard of Soviet Collectivization*. Oxford: Oxford University Press, 1987.

Von Hagen, Mark. *Soldiers in the Proletarian Dictatorship: The Red Army and the Soviet Socialist State, 1917–1930*. Ithaca: Cornell University Press, 1990.

Wade, Rex. *The Red Guard and Workers' Militias in the Russian Revolution*. Stanford: Stanford University Press, 1984.

Ward, Chris. *Russia's Cotton Workers and the New Economic Policy: Shop-Floor Culture and State Policy, 1921–1929*. Cambridge: Cambridge University Press, 1990.

Weber, Max. "Class, Status and Party." In H. H. Gerth and C. Wright Mills, eds., *From Max Weber: Essays in Sociology*. New York: Oxford University Press, 1946.

Wildman, Alan. *The End of the Imperial Russian Army*. Princeton: Princeton University Press, 1980.

Wheatcroft, S. G., R. W. Davies, and J. M. Cooper. "Soviet Industrialization Reconsidered: Some Preliminary Conclusions About Economic Development Between 1926 and 1941." *Economic History Review* 39 (May 1986): 264–94.

Wynn, Charters. *Workers, Strikes, and Pogroms: The Donbass-Dnepr Bend in Late Imperial Russia, 1870–1905*. Princeton: Princeton University Press, 1992.

Yanowitch, Murray. *Social and Economic Inequality in the Soviet Union: Six Studies*. Armonk, N.Y.: M. E. Sharpe, 1977.

Zaslavsky, Victor. *Neo-Stalinist State: Class, Ethnicity, and Consensus in Soviet Society*. Armonk, N.Y.: M. E. Sharpe, 1982.

Zaleski, Eugene. *Planning for Economic Growth in the Soviet Union, 1918–1932.* Chapel Hill: University of North Carolina Press, 1971.

———. *Stalinist Planning for Economic Growth, 1933–1952.* Chapel Hill: University of North Carolina Press, 1980.

Zelnik, Reginald. *Labor and Society in Tsarist Russia: The Factory Workers of St. Petersburg, 1855–1870.* Stanford: Stanford University Press, 1971.

———. "Russian Bebels: An Introduction to the Memoirs of Semen Kanatchikov and Matvei Fisher" *Russian Review* 35 (July 1976): 249–89; ibid., 4 (October 1976): 417–47.

Zelnik, Reginald, ed. and trans. *A Radical Worker in Tsarist Russia: The Autobiography of Semen Ivanovich Kanatchikov.* Stanford, Calif.: Stanford University Press, 1986.

INDEX